The
SOCIAL BOND

An Introduction to
the Study of Society

Consulting Editor: CHARLES PAGE, *University of Massachusetts*

The
SOCIAL BOND

An Introduction to
the Study of Society

ROBERT A. NISBET

University of California, Riverside

ALFRED · A · KNOPF   *New York*

Preface

I have tried in this book to distill from the rich grain of modern sociological research those central concepts and perspectives that give sociology its distinctive place among the sciences of man. No one who has ever tried to encapsulate in a single volume the diversity of a discipline as far flung and specialized as contemporary sociology will suppose the task to be an easy one or, when done, beyond easy criticism. I have no illusions about the matter. The task is a vital one for the discipline and an immensely challenging one for the writer.

My book is addressed to the beginning student and also to the general reader. The relative brevity of this book is evident enough, even to those unacquainted with the extent and specialized diversity of sociology. I do not apologize. No single book, of whatever bulk, could possibly be adequate if the criterion of excellence were faithful representation of all currently going on in a discipline as lively in research as sociology is today.

There is an old architectural adage that has bearing on the predicament facing any writer of an introductory book: if the space is too small and cannot be made larger, make it smaller. The meaning is clear. By making the space smaller, the function of the space is changed. So with any introductory book today in the sciences. If even a very large book remains too small for the objective of representation of all activities in the field, make it as small as possible—as small, that is, as is permitted by the conceptual structure of the field concerned.

The objective of this book, then, is neither representation nor coverage. I wish to set forth as succinctly as possible the fundamental concepts, the orienting perspectives, and withal the *method* of sociology, taking the last in the full and rich sense which is inseparable from sociology's root ideas and their application to human behavior. All else has been made subordinate to this objective.

There is a great advantage, it seems to me, in the smaller book. It allows the reader the precious option of deepening his command of one or another aspect of the discipline through direct and simultaneous reading drawn from the sociological classics. By "classic" I mean a book or an article that remains fresh and stimulating to the sociological imagination no matter when it was written—a hundred years ago or day before yesterday. *Ancient Law* by Sir Henry Maine, *Suicide* by Emile Durkheim, *The Secret Society* by Georg Simmel, *Politics as Vocation* by Max Weber, *Folkways* by William Graham Sumner, *Social Organization* by Charles H. Cooley, *Middletown* by Robert and Helen Lynd, *Community* by Robert M. McIver—each of these, though written many years ago, is as vital to readers today as when it was written. Similarly, *The Lonely Crowd* by David Riesman, *Encounters* by Erving Goffman, *Street Corner Society* by William F. Whyte, *Philadelphia Gentleman* by Digby Baltzell, *The Sociological Imagination* by C. Wright Mills— each of these, though written recently, has the indubitable mark of the classic: each clarifies some single area of experience but in the process widens it.

Why should we, as teachers, run the risk of boring or alienating the eager reader by depending uniformly upon mechanical and extended summary when the excitement of the original work is so often, through the wonders of paperback distribution, right at hand? There must of course be comprehensiveness; otherwise sight of the discipline is lost. But with comprehensiveness there must also be opportunity for direct contact with some original work, however small in bulk and specialized in nature it may be.

A science is made up of more than data, principles, and method. It is composed, most significantly and lastingly, of seminal teachers and of books, monographs, and articles in which the authors' own thrill of discovery is a very part of the contents. Only through great teachers and original works that are directly encountered can any science hope to deepen its roots and to make possible the reaching out of one generation to the next.

Great teaching is not, of course, subject to instant call. But original and evocative sociological writing is. I can only sympathize with the student whose introduction to sociology is altogether devoid of acquaintance with books and articles in which the creative impulse and the passion for discovery or explanation are made immediate and real. In each such work, however small or specialized it may be, data, method, and conclusion are all indissolubly joined. The *why* and the *how* are set firmly in the *what*.

The essential and continuing subject of this book is the nature of the social bond. In the same way that modern chemistry investigates the nature of the chemical bond, the forces which hold atoms together in molecules and substances, so does sociology investigate the forces which hold individual human beings together in the groups and institutions in which we actually encounter them in experience. Except only for the two introductory chapters in which I deal with, first, the nature of science as a form of knowledge and, second, the historical roots of the sociological imagination, the entire book is concerned with the elements, structures, and processes of change which are yielded by analysis of the social bond.

My approach throughout is conceptual. I stress this. The conceptual approach is today much to be preferred, it seems to me, to the more common "institutional" approach in an introductory work. In the latter, all too often, the reader is merely taken on a kind of tour of such institutions in society as family, school, community, church, industry, political government, and social class, among others. Sociological insights pertinent to each are noted in passing. The varied problems associated with each are duly described. I do not deny that much useful information about society is garnered in this fashion. The trouble is that the nature and unity of the discipline of sociology are lost. After all, social institutions are the common interest of *all* the social sciences. What is wanted, I believe, in an introductory book is understanding of those concepts and perspectives which are distinctive to the science in question. What we want to know is what unique or special light is thrown upon the common body of data *by the particular science of sociology*.

Every genuine science is known by its basic concepts, not by the general areas of subject matter to which it makes its way. We learn chemistry through such concepts as atomic theory, bonding, electronic interaction, and entropy. We do *not* learn chemistry through a mere listing or description of the organic and inorganic compounds which are, so to speak, chemistry's point of departure.

More than thirty years ago, well before the present wave of institutionally oriented books had commenced, Robert M. MacIver wrote:

> *Every science has certain ultimate concepts on which the whole system is built, not of course deductively, but in the sense that the unity and the nexus of its subject-matter are discovered to depend on these ultimates. In other words a science is the logic of reality or rather of what our observation and experiment lead us to impute to reality. Unless there are certain fundamental concepts which integrate a subject-matter, there is no science but only a series of detached formulations, conventionally bound together. And the revolutionary changes in a science are those which modify or overthrow its fundamental concepts. When that happens, the whole science has to be rebuilt, as has happened in biology and recently in physics.*[1]

Professor MacIver's words have proved to be as prescient for the the social sciences as they were correctly descriptive of what was then happening in biology and physics. The really decisive changes that have taken place during the past three decades in all the social sciences have been those associated with concepts and perspectives. Sociology is no exception to this.

What are the distinctive concepts of sociology today? The following would appear to be fundamental: (1) *social interaction*, including such basic, specific processes of interaction as *exchange, coercion, conformity, cooperation*, and *conflict*; (2) *social aggregates*, under which we consider the types, structures, and functions of the several forms of human association; (3) *social authority*, which includes the codes, conventions, and mores, as well as laws through which the inner order of social aggregates is maintained; (4) *social roles*, which are the functional positions human beings occupy in the social order; (5) *social status*, the concept through which we account for the universal facts of hierarchy and stratification in society; (6) *social norms*, the ends or objectives, socially transmitted, which supply purpose both to social groups and to human personality; (7) *social entropy*, a single concept covering three distinguishable but related negative processes of behavior: *alienation, anomie*, and *deviance*; (8) *social change*, a master concept within which we deal with the variations and mutations over time that all forms of social behavior are subject to.

[1] Robert MacIver's words are from an unpublished manuscript. I am indebted to Charles Page for their highly pertinent use here.

These, briefly stated, are the central concepts of sociology today. Through them the sociologist explores the complexities of social behavior. No one of them is a fixed quantity, the same in statement today as it was a decade ago, or will be a decade hence. It is the mark of a science that formulations of its concepts and principles change from time to time. The idea of immutable laws or principles lying in nature or society, awaiting discovery for all time, is in very large part myth. What has been called "the endless frontier of science" is a frontier of concepts as well as of facts.

Throughout this book I have stressed the *social* nature of the social bond. If this seems obvious at first sight, I can only call the reader's attention to the considerable number of books currently popular in which the *biological* nature of the social bond and of dislocations of the social bond is stressed. I refer to such works as those written by Konrad Lorenz, Robert Ardrey, and Desmond Morris, whose contentions regarding the ineradicability of the instincts of aggression and "territoriality" seem, at first sight, both novel and persuasive. A little thought and learning remind us, however, that they are very old and very widespread in human consciousness. They are also, in their common statement, very naive.

That man is a biological being equipped with many of the same, genetically transmitted drives and mechanisms we find in lower orders of life permits no doubt whatever. Man is, after all, a product of the evolutionary process in the organic world. But out of this same evolution has come a set of capacities which man does *not* share with other animals—capacities which serve profoundly to modify the operation of instincts and drives. I refer to man's capacities for speech, for abstract thought, for symbolic communication, and for interaction around values which are socially, not biologically, transmitted in time. To overlook this immensely important sphere of human personality, and of human association, is to overlook not merely what is distinctive in man but generally decisive in his behavior.

As sociologists, we do not deal with man alone. We deal with *man-in-society*. The difference between these two envisagements of the matter is profound. Failure to know, or to remember, the difference is the chief reason, I think, for the abundance of facile theories around us today in which biological explanations are given to the tensions of urban behavior, to social status, to the varied types of conflict in the social order, and even to the social bond itself.

But if we say that our subject is man-in-society, it is equally important, and not at all inconsistent, to say that in sociology we deal with *society-in-man*. Society is not something abstract and external, something "out there"; society, as the sociologist understands the word, is inseparable from the social behavior of human beings, from their actions, motivations, normative aspirations, and interactions with one another. What Durkheim wrote many years ago on this point is still valid and as illuminating today as when he wrote it:

> *If we should withdraw from men their language, sciences, arts, and moral beliefs, they would drop to the level of animals. The characteristic attributes of human nature come from society.* But on the other hand, society exists and lives only in and through individuals. *If the idea of society were extinguished in the individual mind, and the beliefs, traditions, and aspirations of the group were no longer felt and shared by individuals, society would die.*[2]

Actually, at bottom, it is neither "individual" nor "society" that we study in sociology and the other social sciences. It is rather social behavior: the behavior of human beings as this behavior has been socially acquired and socially internalized, and as it remains socially oriented and reinforced throughout the human being's entire life. Does such a statement imply denial of the biological roots of human action? It does not. No more than it implies denial of the existence of the chemical compounds, molecules, and atoms of which we are composed. Man is indeed a biological being. So too is man, depending upon the perspective, a chemical and physical being.

But man is also social. And it is the distinctive character of man that his ways of behavior are inseparable from causal forces which cannot be reduced to the biological or the chemical. I refer to such forces as symbolic communication, normative action, and the whole set of codes, traditions, and roles and statuses which are inherited socially, not biologically. To ignore these forces of social causation when we are concerned with, say, urban violence, ethnic conflict, or the nature of family and community, and to take easy refuge in asserted biological drives and compulsions is to ignore the very nature of what we are in fact given in experience: that is, *man-in-society* and *society-in-man*.

I have given a great deal of attention in this book to the types, processes, and mechanisms of *social change*. One of the unfortunate by-products of sociology's concern with "social systems" and "structural-functional" analysis during the past two or three decades has been the general waning of a sociological interest in change, which was at

---

[2] Emile Durkheim, *The Elementary Forms of Religious Life*. London: Allen and Uniwn, 1915. Emphasis added.

one time paramount in the discipline. Just as the rich concreteness of human behavior has so often been lost in these "social systems" approaches, so has the dynamic element that we call change. It is not easy—I would go farther and say it is impossible—to reckon with and to account for social change when such matters as social roles, social statuses, and social norms are dealt with as fixed points in an organismically conceived *system*, rather than as modes of social behavior which are subject to countless influences from the world outside the individual's particular social circle, group, or system.

Too often in contemporary sociological writing, especially that which is found in introductory books and treatises in sociological theory, social change is either ignored or else it is simply assumed, as one might assume growth in a plant or an organism. Change, it is commonly said, is a fixed part of all social behavior; everything social is in constant process of change; and this change arises, moreover, out of the same elements in social behavior that give order and consensus to a group or society.

But this kind of treatment—dismissal is perhaps the better word for it—of change will never do. Not if what we are after is insight into the mechanisms and processes of social change, and usable knowledge of the specific ways by which social institutions have changed in the past and, when need arises, can be changed in the present. We shall never acquire this vital knowledge as long as we content ourselves with *assuming* change, or with likening it in society to the normal and ordered processes of growth in the biological sphere. Even if social change were like organic growth, we should still wish to know, just as the physiologist wishes to know, what the crucial factors are that are involved in change or growth.

The more important fact here, however, is the fundamental error that lies in all analogies of social change to organic growth. I want to be emphatic on this. It is no more possible to derive change deductively from social structure and its elements than it is possible to derive these latter deductively from the biological nature of the individual. Only by abandoning theoretical models of static systems and only by dealing with social behavior and its several manifestations as we find these in the real world of *events*, *conflicts*, and *crises* of all kinds can we hope to understand social change.

Social change is much too important—even vital—a need of the world we live in for it to be left to analogies, metaphors, and easy assumptions of its normality and inevitability. Change in society is *not* normal and inevitable—however much we might wish it were. The

unhappy conclusion we are forced to accept, as we look around us and
see the sheer volume of entrenched interests, survivals of the outmoded
past, and institutionalized resistances to change, is that social and cultural change, far from being a regular and built-in feature of the social
bond, is in fact one of the rarest and most difficult of objectives to
achieve. One need only reflect on the infrequency of genuine innovation
and reform. Everything that goes into the whole socialization process,
the ordinary mechanisms of social interaction, the nature of social
authority, roles, statuses, and norms, goes also into making, not change,
but persistence and fixity all too manifest in the troubled society this
generation lives in.

Hence the amount of attention I have chosen to give in this book
to the problem of change, its conditions, processes, mechanisms, and
major types. I would be the last to declare finality for the concepts
I have dealt with in Part III of the book: such concepts as *crisis*, *discontinuity*, *intrusion*, and *event*. But, as I think I have established reasonably well, these concepts are highly pertinent to the subject. And if
the concepts I have elaborated have the slightest effect in stimulating in
the reader additional, and perhaps wiser, conclusions about the problem
and nature of change, I shall be content.

One further aspect of the book requires note here. I refer to the
comparative-historical character of the treatment throughout. As I
have tried to make plain, it is impossible to deal with the processes and
the larger reality of social change except in terms of comparative history.
But the comparative-historical framework seems to me equally necessary
even for discussion of the structural elements of the social bond—social
interaction, authority, roles, statuses, and norms—as well as those
embedded processes of social entropy which I deal with under the
headings of alienation, anomie, and deviance.

It is one of the signal deficiencies of so many introductory books in
American sociology—and the social sciences generally in this country—
that so much stress is placed upon American materials alone. Of
course we are interested—those of us, at least, who live in the United
States—primarily in American problems, processes, and structures.
But the crucial point is that we cannot hope to understand, really understand, these unless we see them in comparative perspective—that is, in
terms of cognate problems, processes, and structures in other societies
and other periods of history.

By "history," I should explain immediately, I do not mean mere
chronological narrative. Narrative is only one of the ways by which
the historical past is illuminated and made relevant to the interests of

the present.   In its larger and lasting sense, historical observation is simply *comparison of things in time*.[3]   It is therefore closely related to the kind of comparison that involves, not time, but *space*.   In most sections of this book I have utilized the comparative-historical perspective wherever it seemed to me to illuminate the social structure or process under consideration.   When I have had to choose between comparison-in-time and comparison-in-space, I have generally chosen the former. After all, the past is rich in recorded, verifiable social experiences, and it allows us the advantage of a detachment that is more difficult to attain for experiences in the present.   I would like to stress, however, that it is the *present* that forms my point of departure and point of return throughout the book.

Finally, in writing this book, I have made every effort to be as lucid and direct as possible.   But clarity has never been achieved, to the best of my knowledge, through simplification of *subject matter*.   Clarity achieved in this manner is not clarity; it is distortion.   The only firm assurance I can give readers of the book in advance is that, whatever its faults, calculated simplification is not one of them.   All things may be forgiven an author except the crime of premeditated condescension. There is none of that in this book.

[3] I would like to thank Arthur Strimling for this felicitous and pithy characterization of historical observation.

ACKNOWLEDGMENTS

I have deliberately held notes and references in this book to a minimum. Even so, I think my larger intellectual obligations have been expressed in the text or the bibliographical appendix. There are, however, four signal exceptions: Herbert Blumer, Kingsley Davis, Robert Merton, and Charles Page. To each of them I owe much more than could be indicated by either footnote or reference. I am indebted to their distinguished writings and their other contributions to American sociology, but mostly I am indebted for the personal stimulus and benefaction of a friendship with each that goes back many years.

To Charles Page I am additionally indebted for the generous care with which he has read the manuscript of this book. There is not a page in it that has not had the benefit of commentary or suggestion drawn from his large fund of social learning and insight. Whatever defects remain in the book, their number would be greater had it not been for the kindness and vigilance of Professor Page's reading of the manuscript. Naturally, only the author can be held responsible for whatever defects remain.

It is a pleasure to thank my friends Theodore Caris, Arthur Strimling, and Muriel Smith, all of Random House-Knopf, for intellectual interest and contribution to the book that have gone well beyond the call of professional duty. I have learned much from them in the course of this book.

Finally, in place of a dedication, I want to thank the students I have been privileged to teach and learn from during the past thirty years at Berkeley, Columbia, Bologna, and Riverside.

R. N.

Riverside, California

Contents

PART III SOCIAL CHANGE

I
BACKGROUNDS

1

Sociology as a Science

THE OBJECTIVES OF SOCIOLOGY

The fundamental objectives of sociology are the same as those of science generally—discovery and explanation. To *discover* the essential data of social behavior and the connections among the data is the first objective of sociology. To *explain* the data and the connections is the second and larger objective. Science makes its advances in terms of both of these objectives. Sometimes it is the discovery of a new element or set of elements that marks a major breakthrough in the history of a scientific discipline. Closely related to such discovery is the discovery of relationships of data that had never been noted before. All of this is, as we know, of immense importance in science. But the drama of discovery, in this sense, can sometimes lead us to overlook the greater importance of explanation of what is revealed by the data. Sometimes decades, even centuries, pass before known connections and relationships are actually explained. Discovery and explanation are the two great interpenetrating, interacting realms of science.

The order of reality that interests the scientist is the *empirical* order, that is, the order of data and phenomena revealed to us through observation or experience. To be precise or explicit about what is, and is not, revealed by observation is not always easy, to be sure. And often it is necessary for our natural powers of observation to be supplemented by the most intricate of mechanical aids for a given object to become "empirical" in the sense just used. That the electron is not as immediately visible as is the mountain range does not mean, obviously, that it is any less empirical. That social behavior does not lend itself to as quick and accurate description as, say, chemical behavior of gases and compounds does not mean that social roles, statuses, and attitudes are any less empirical than molecules and tissues. What is empirical and observable today may have been nonexistent in scientific consciousness a decade ago. Moreover, the empirical is often data *inferred* from direct observation. All of this is clear enough, and we should make no pretense that there are not often shadow areas between the empirical and the nonempirical. Nevertheless, the first point to make about any science, physical or social, is that its world of data is the empirical world. A very large amount of scientific energy goes merely into the work of expanding the frontiers, through discovery, of the known, observable, empirical world.

From observation or discovery we move to *explanation*. The explanation sought by the scientist is, of course, not at all like the explanation sought by the theologian or metaphysician. The scientist is not interested—not, that is, in his role of scientist—in ultimate, transcendental, or divine causes of what he sets himself to explain. He is interested in explanations that are as empirical as the data themselves. If it is the high incidence of crime in a certain part of a large city that requires explanation, the scientist is obliged to offer his explanation in terms of factors which are as empirically real as the phenomenon of crime itself. He does not explain the problem, for example, in terms of references to the will of God, demons, or original sin. A satisfactory explanation is one that is not only empirical, however, but one that can be stated in the terms of a *causal proposition*. Description is an indispensable point of beginning, but description is not explanation. It is well to stress this point, for there are all too many scientists, or would-be scientists, who are primarily concerned with data gathering, data counting, and data describing, and who seem to forget that such operations, however useful, are but the first step. Until we have accounted for the problem at hand, explained it causally by referring the data to some principle or generalization already established, or to some new principle or generalization, we have not explained anything.

An example of the foregoing, and one highly relevant to sociology, is provided by the study of suicide. What, it is asked, causes certain persons to take their own lives? No doubt every person has his own explanation, one based upon what he believes to have been operative perhaps in some friend or acquaintance who killed himself. A "common sense" approach might be to shrug when the question is asked and say that there is no accounting, that insight into the motive dies with the individual himself, or that the suicide was the will of God, which is beyond human detection.

But scientific *discovery* has made it very clear that the incidence of suicide varies in the human race from people to people, nation to nation, and, within a given people or nation, from one ethnic, professional, or residential group to another. We find, for instance, that suicide is much higher in incidence in the United States than in certain other countries (Mexico, for instance) and that within the United States it is virtually absent among some ethnic or occupational groups and extremely high in incidence among others. All of this, be it noted, is not explanation. It is discovery. But discovery is the beginning of science, and with respect to the study of suicide it is quite plain that until the variable incidence of suicide was discovered among human beings, any possibly sound explanation would have been impossible. Plainly, explanations that do not rest on all the data, or at least all relevant data, are of only the most limited value. So, discovery of data is by no means to be depreciated. Some, though not all, of the greatest episodes in the history of science have been inaugurated by discovery of data—of processes, events, connections, substances, and so forth—which had not previously been known. Going back to suicide, no mean step was taken when someone in the nineteenth century first became aware, through studies of official registers, of the highly variable incidence of suicide in populations.

Still, the next step is the more notable, the step we call explanation. How do we explain the fact that year after year, decade after decade, middle-class, white, professional men are more likely to commit suicide than individuals in other sectors of the population, and that this likelihood becomes even greater if they are unmarried or, if married, childless and cut off from the ties of religion or a similar community of ethical purpose? Bear in mind that we are not saying that each and every individual answering to the description just given will commit suicide or that he probably will. To think sociologically is to be able to think in terms of aggregates of people, of rates of incidence or frequency among these aggregates. Our sociological question is, How do we explain the manifest rate of suicide among certain individuals in the population? What are the causal relations? What are the operating processes that link suicide with human behavior generally and with the norms and structures which form the cultural environment of human beings who commit suicide? We can dispense with explanations drawn from biology, for there is no evidence—not yet at least—that suicides are differently constituted than nonsuicides.   Psychological explanations, while potentially more helpful or relevant, are rendered suspect by the patterns we have discovered of the incidence of suicide: the patterns are social and economic, not biological or psychological.

Emile Durkheim, one of the greatest of modern sociologists, working in the 1890s on precisely this problem—the variable incidence of suicide in the population—offered an explanation that in its larger outlines can be taken as a very model of what a scientific explanation should be in sociology.[1]   The rates of suicide, Durkheim declared, vary inversely with the degree of social and moral cohesion of the groups of which individuals are parts.   In those parts of the population where social ties and moral values tend to be close and authoritative in the life of the individual, suicide is rare or nonexistent.   But in those sectors of society, such as in contemporary middle-class, industrial or professional sectors, where opposite conditions prevail, the incidence of suicide is much higher.   And this holds true irrespective of race, nationality, or geography.

In short, through the variable factors of social cohesion and normative rigor Durkheim explained those patterns of connection among the data of suicide incidence that others had long been aware of but had failed to explain crucially.   But his explanation did not stop simply with a demonstration of the unvarying correlation between high incidence of suicide and social and moral disorganization.   For, although this *is* explanation, in that it throws light upon the original problem (that is, the incidence of suicide in its variable manifestations in a society), it is what we would have to call a low order of explanation.   After all, the subject of sociology is man himself and, more particularly, man's social behavior.   Until we have been able to relate what we find in the data to man himself—his personality, social needs, drives, and psychosocial processes generally—we have failed in attaining the order of explanation that any scientist desires.

It was not enough, then, for Durkheim simply to note the high correlation between greater or lesser intensities of the social bond and greater or smaller numbers of suicides.   What he attempted to do was relate this association to that wider area of scientific knowledge concerned with the nature of social behavior generally.   We thus find in Durkheim's great study an effort to explain, through still higher or more general levels of knowledge about man and his behavior, what his studies had revealed with respect to suicide and social cohesion.   Unhappily this aspect of Durkheim's work is not as successful as the former.   By the standards of contemporary principles in the study of social behavior, Durkheim's theory of social order and personality is not wholly adequate in its effort to explain.

This, however, is of no importance to our point. What is important is the type of data, the type of question asked, the discovery of crucial variables, and, finally, the efforts, in ascending degrees of generality, to *explain* the data and the connections of the data which earlier discovery had made manifest. And all of this is made as vivid in Durkheim's study of suicide as it could be through any example chosen from chemistry or physics.

THE FRAMEWORK OF SCIENCE

We must now turn to the method, or as I prefer to put it, the *framework* within which the objectives of discovery and explanation are characteristically to be found in any science. After all, discovery and explanation by themselves are inalienable attributes of all intellectual behavior, whether at the ordinary behavioral level, or in scholarship, philosophy, art, and religion. And indeed we should remind ourselves that there is a lasting affinity between science and other types of intellectual activity, especially art. The sources of the creativity that finds expression in the discoveries and explanations of science are, in strictly psychological terms, much the same for the scientist and the artist. Nothing in the way of mere technique or procedure can ever take the place of imagination, insight, sustained vision, and sheer intellectual comprehension. These are intellectual qualities as vital to the artist and scholar as they are to the scientist.

Nevertheless, science is different from these other activities, at least in its mode of expression, which I have called its framework. And it is to the differences that I now turn.

First and foremost in the scientific framework is the *question* that it asked by the scientist. At bottom, leaving out all niceties and rhetorical flourishes, this question is a simple one: *How does it operate?* Whatever the sphere of empirical reality at hand, the stellar universe, the chromosomal composition of the human body, the family, or a criminal conspiracy, what the scientist wants to know is, first of all, what the crucial component elements are, what the key processes of action or behavior are, and what the fundamental relationships, internal and external, are. In short, he wants to know how it operates. The whole of science, physical, biological, or social, may be regarded as a vast collection of questions of this sort, made specific and relevant to the data at hand, of the means involved in seeking the answers to the questions, and, ultimately, of the answers themselves. Naturally, our standards of what constitutes an acceptable answer, that is, a valid explanation, become ever more exacting and precise. But the fundamental question itself of how things work, operate, or behave in time and space remains the lasting point of departure of the scientist's work.

But for the scientist this question calls for a certain type of answer. Scientific answers or explanations must be capable of empirical verification by others, proceeding in the same way toward the same end. The answers cannot derive from some special *mystique* or from the peculiar and unique character of the scientist's own set of faculties and dispositions, or from his religion, his patriotism, his commitment to a given social-action cause, or from any factor that he alone possesses. Science is by its nature universal, and the unity of science comes from the fact that the same question directed to the same body of data can produce the same answer to all, assuming they follow the procedures dictated by the character of the problem. This is what we mean by the objectivity and universality of science. In science an answer or conclusion is valid irrespective of one's personal, political, or religious likes and dislikes.

In this respect science differs from certain other forms of what many would call "knowledge." No one would argue that the "truth" of the artist's or religious mystic's work depends upon others being able to reach precisely the same result with the same expenditure of effort, system, and materials. How often have we looked at some painting or listened to a piece of music or read a poem that illuminated experience in a way that it had never been illuminated before? Who, looking at Picasso's Spanish Civil War paintings, could say that some special form of understanding was not transmitted? Or perhaps listening to a Beethoven or Ravel quartet, reading a poem by Blake or Randall Jarrell, or walking through the Sistine Chapel or a Frank Lloyd Wright building? From all of these experiences we derive, in one degree or another, some form of illumination, some deepening of understanding that we are prone to say "adds to my knowledge." And so it does, taking the word "knowledge" in its largest sense. But no one would ever suppose that any amount of sheer preparation, sheer perfecting of method and technique, or sheer hard work would enable him to duplicate what is distinctive in a great painting, poem, or musical composition. Nor would anyone, however advantaged he might feel in the way of knowledge from one or another of these artistic experiences, suppose that it either could be or should be "verified."

But verification, or possibility of verification, is the very essence of science. Science, in short, is concerned with answers, conclusions, and principles which are, as we commonly say, testable. If I were to declare suicide a consequence of mankind's imperishable urge to destroy itself, this might be true in some ultimate religious or metaphysical sense. But the conclusion would not be verifiable or testable. If, on the other hand, I declare that frequency of suicides in the population is determined by the weather, this answer is verifiable; which is to say that it can be determined to be right or wrong. So also with respect to war, crime, violence, poverty. We may choose to declare each a manifestation of God's will, and in the ultimate reach of imagination this may well be true. But there is, obviously, no way of testing or verifying it. Thus a scientific answer to the question of the causes of war, poverty, violence, ethnic discrimination, or of any other part of the social order must limit itself to those conditions and factors which, in the form of some hypothesis that is itself a *tentative* answer, can be verified.

What I am saying here does not, of course, rule out the strong possibility that our hypotheses, our postulates, even our ways of seeing the data before us, may be conditioned and shaped by nonscientific, nonrational factors. No one is completely a scientist or a rationalist. No one is immune to the operation of influences that may be governed by self-interest, ideology, or political or religious faith. And there is the further fact that however rational and logical a given scientific formulation may be in the presentation, its actual psychological roots may lie anywhere—in fantasy, in reverie, in sheer unstructured imagination. But irrespective of source or conditioning influence, what gives identity to the scientific statement in the long run is its verifiability by others.

This conclusion leads us to a frequently misunderstood aspect of science: *prediction*. The test of a science, it is commonly said, is its power to predict. There is a sense in which this is true, but the sense has nothing whatsoever to do with the revelation of "things to come," with ability to read the future in the fashion of the fortuneteller. Scientific prediction is not in any way concerned with the forecasting of unprecedented or unique events in history. Prediction in any scientific sense is no more than a statement of the high probability of the occurrence, or recurrence, of some form of behavior, physical or social, *that is inseparable from a previously discovered regularity in nature*. When the astronomer "predicts" an eclipse of the sun for some hour and day in the future, he is not really extracting from the future, as we commonly think of the future. He is merely noting that among the great regularities of relation of earth, moon, and sun is that which periodically manifests itself by obscuration of the light of the sun by the intervention of the moon for a very brief period between the sun and a point of the earth. That it is possible for the astronomer to give this a precise date in the future—the "future," that is, within our own arbitrary, man-made, system of reckoning time—is but incidental to the vital point, which is that the eclipse is simply a point on a great, endlessly recurrent cycle of motions in the relation of earth, moon, and sun. Predicting an eclipse is not one bit different from predicting that the sun will rise tomorrow morning.

So with all scientific prediction. When the epidemiologist predicts that an influenza epidemic of a certain type is highly probable he is doing nothing more than drawing from what is known of a previously discovered causal relationship. Repeated experiences have made clear that the outbreak of influenza epidemics is closely related to the presence of certain crucial, functionally related conditions having to do with increased incidence of virus strains, foreseeable congestion of people in, say, the Christmas holiday period of the year, normal incidence of mild respiratory ailments, and so on. Predicting an influenza epidemic is not very different from predicting that the individual who allows himself to be exposed to certain types of disease will in all probability fall victim to the disease.

Do we predict in the social sciences? Of course we do. Not, to be sure, with the same degree of success or accuracy that is to be found in astronomy with respect to eclipses, for the materials that the social scientist works with do not fall within regularities as fixed as those which confront the astronomer. Making allowance for the possibility of an accuracy in the social sciences in the future that we have not yet achieved, the unbanishable element of *choice* in human behavior will doubtless forever make fixed laws and also accurate prediction unlikely. Social science predicts, nonetheless, and, all things considered, with quite a high degree of success. But such success is contingent upon the social scientist's ability to rigorously avoid temptations to match wits with the card-reader or haruspex and his determination to stay within the framework of science.

We may go back once again to the study of suicide in society. On the basis of careful studies of the conditions or causes of high incidence of suicide, it is possible to predict that rates of suicide will go up in a given population as the result of certain changes of social structure already apparent. Or that rates will go down as the result of opposite types of change. Such prediction, to the degree that it is successful, is no more than a reaping of the rewards of sound studies of social causation in suicide. It is emphatically not a foretelling of the future as we popularly understand this. Repeated studies of urban violence have shown clearly that the prelude to massive outbreaks of violence is a certain set of conditions: poverty coupled with strong feelings of resentment, the presence of potential leaders of such violence, ineffective police protection, climatic conditions favoring large assemblies, and so on. It is, then, possible to predict violence on the basis of the known existence of these conditions.

Where prediction is successful in science we can be sure that prior studies have revealed certain fixed, or largely fixed, regularities of relationship. We can be certain, in sum, that we have managed to find out "how things work," which, as I have said, is the fundamental question of all science. What is important really is not prediction but the causal or functional relationships we have managed to discover and to explain. Insofar as our discoveries have been relevant and our explanations sound, prediction—in the scientific sense—will also be sound. But again warning must be voiced: in the social sciences such causal relationships and such predictions will always be more uncertain and precarious than in the physical sciences. The subject of the social sciences is man himself, and a rather highly developed cerebrum allows him, if not what used to be called free will, at least a range and diversity of possible responses unknown to atoms and viruses. Still, as we shall have ample opportunity to see in the chapters ahead, man's plasticity of response notwithstanding, his behavior in society does fall within institutionalized regularities that permit scientific statements analogous to those of the physical sciences.

Something must be said at this point about scientific statements, or propositions, as we more commonly call them. There are many references in the literature of and about science to "hypotheses," "laws," and "principles." All of these, let it be stressed, are *statements about natural or social behavior.* Each, in varying degree of probability or certainty, is an explanatory statement about the patterns of behavior which the scientist has studied. Some statements have so high a degree of validity and reliability that we call them "laws." The law of gravitation in physics is the classic example. Others, dealing with more complex and uncertain phenomena, or proceeding from still-imperfect understanding, are less likely to be referred to as laws. But they are nonetheless scientific statements in as full a sense as the other. A "hypothesis" is also a statement about observed phenomena, but of so tentative and unverified a character that we refrain from calling it a law or principle. It is a statement whose validity remains hypothetical or speculative until an investigator can test it, verify it, or otherwise reinforce the statement through its exposure to the crucial data.

The important point here, however, is that neither laws nor principles in the world of science are enacted or decreed as are the laws that govern us in civilized society. Social laws do not lie out in nature waiting to be discovered, as so much popular conception of science would have it. Alexander Pope's famous couplets on Newton and the physical world exemplify an attitude nearly as rife today as then: "Nature and nature's laws lay hid in night; God said, Let Newton be, and all was light." But laws lie nowhere save in the scientist's consciousness. They may be of absolute and unvarying validity, but they are still propositions or statements that serve to explain phenomena and connections among phenomena.

There is today, in certain quarters of the social sciences, a rather deep conviction that before one can study society scientifically he must know "methodology." What this commonly turns out to be is statistics, supplemented perhaps by analysis of case study or survey techniques. Today, the gathering of statistics is highly important, even indispensable, for the social scientist. It is indeed a mode of literacy, for how else than through knowledge of the real significance of averages, means, medians, and the like, can one hope to read and understand contemporary population, crime, divorce, marriage, education, and other reports on populations? We have no way of discovering the all-important connections among data and classes of data, when these are vast or complex, except through statistical techniques that arrange our data for proper explanation. Survey techniques, case-study techniques, and other modes of disciplining or refining observation are also important. No science can do without its techniques, and techniques vary from discipline to discipline.

But this said, we must nevertheless constantly bear in mind that the *method* of science is none of these. It is not statistics, not case study, not survey, not mathematics, not experiment. All of these are techniques that serve, in their different ways, the scientist's efforts to discover and to explain. In certain areas of sociology mathematics is fundamental to any approach whatsoever to the subject matter; in other areas experiment has the same role of importance. But both mathematics and experiment remain techniques nonetheless. They are not, in themselves, the method of sociology. The method of sociology is inseparable from the disciplined imagination of the scientist when he is making discoveries or seeking explanations. He does so with respect to the question of how things operate and casts his results in the form of statements that are understandable and, potentially at least, verifiable.

It is well to make use here of an old and very sound distinction between the *logic of discovery* and the *logic of demonstration*. The latter can be stated simply enough. It is no more than the propositions themselves but set forth in a sequential and ordered fashion, with hypothesis, arrangements of data, techniques, and ultimate conclusions all articulated in such a way as to be understood easily by others. The logic of discovery, however, is frequently as random and disordered as the human imagination itself. When we talk about the logic of discovery we are talking about the ways by which the scientist has in fact reached his conclusion; we are often in the presence of modes of intuition and insight which are anything but ordered and sequential. The conclusion may come in a single, sudden flash of inspiration after months of seemingly hopeless effort. It is this aspect of the matter that has led so many of the really great scientists to deny that anything resembling the orderly processes of a "method" was involved in their work.

In fact, there *is* a method, and I would not wish to seem to imply the contrary. But this method—I am referring to the method or logic of *discovery*—is bound up with the kind of question that is asked and the kind of conclusion that is reached in science in contrast to art, metaphysics, or religion. The method is emphatically *not* something that can be reduced to simple and sequential steps derived from a manual. Least of all is method in the social sciences identical with any one or another of the numerous techniques by which observation, discovery, and explanation are aided.

There is, finally, one other important element in what I have called the framework of sociology. This is the set of concepts that gives distinctiveness and identity to the discipline. Every science is known by the signal ideas or concepts through which reality is approached in the terms of that discipline. It would be impossible either to describe or to work within physics, for example, except in the terms of the fundamental concepts of energy, mass, quantum, and the like. The same is true of each of the other sciences. I am not suggesting that such concepts are hard and fast within any science. The opposite is true. Nothing is more evident in the present period of scientific efflorescence than the breakdown of what were once thought to be fixed and eternal boundaries among the sciences. Today, more or less despairingly, we are prone to say that chemistry is what chemists do and physics is what goes on in the physics building on the campus. Also, the concepts of one science extend dramatically into the work of another. Within the last generation biology has been revolutionized by what it has drawn from, first, chemistry, then physics, in its studies of the elements of life. Nowhere has the phenomenon of extension of concept been more vivid than among the social sciences. One need only compare introductory textbooks in each of the social sciences written a half-century ago with those of the present day to be made aware of the breaking of boundaries, the borrowing and lending of concepts here as in the physical sciences.

So much is true. But equally true is the fact that at any given moment each science is a complex of concepts that give it identity—no matter how rapidly some of the concepts may seem to come and go or be otherwise changed. And in the largest sense the "method" of any science is the application of these concepts to the world of things and processes that does not itself know any disciplinary boundaries but, as experience has shown, can best be approached from the large number of specialized viewpoints to be found in the different sciences.

The method of sociology is in *general* the method of each of the other sciences. But the distinctive and *specific* method of sociology derives directly from the fundamental concepts of sociology and their use in offering explanation of the myriad ways of human behavior. Concepts such as *social role, status, norm, group*, and *function* are not merely descriptive counters to be arranged and rearranged for reassurance of what we already know. They are windows to the outside world; they are the operating means of shedding light upon the same residual subject matter that all of the social sciences take for their province. I repeat, there is no such thing as a strictly sociological subject matter in the living world of reality; no more is there a strictly economic or political or anthropological subject matter. The common concern of all the social sciences is the behavior of human beings in culture and society. But it has been made clear beyond further doubt that in the interpretation of social behavior—in both discovery and explanation, in both prediction and control of social behavior—the concepts I have mentioned, along with others, provide indispensable means. The distinctive method of sociology is, in sum, inseparable from the fundamental concepts that give it content.

We shall have much more to say about these concepts and, hence, method in later chapters. But before leaving the subject I would like to utter a word of warning against obsessive concern with concepts. We cannot too often remind ourselves that the subject matter of sociology is not, ultimately, concepts or social systems, social wholes, or abstract forms of rhetoric misconceived as social theory. *The subject matter of sociology is social behavior*—the behavior of individual human beings as we find them. This, in the present context, may seem a mere platitude. But no one can read very far in the modern literature of sociology without becoming aware of how preoccupation with concepts sometimes actually replaces concern with the empirical stuff of social behavior. We find some sociologists declaring in effect that until we have refined and polished our concepts, made them epistemologically pure and logically faultless, we cannot proceed with our real mission, which is the study of social behavior.

To this misconception I can reply only with the gist of what the great scientist Wolfgang Köhler had to say on the subject. Had Galileo and Newton and the other pioneering figures in modern physics been too much preoccupied with the epistemological purity of their concepts of gravitation and energy instead of going ahead in a pragmatically naïve and happily undisturbed way, physics would never have become a science. To which may be added the statement that zoology, botany, and geology did not start out as sciences with correct and adequate definitions of plants and animals. The real work in the science of sociology has only just begun; there is immense need at the present time for new data to be discovered and for new explanations which are more in accord with the data we have.

THE PROBLEMS OF SOCIOLOGY

A science is also known by its problems. Someone has said that the great men of science are not those who solved the problems but those who discovered them. Herbert Butterfield, distinguished historian of science, has told us that some of the most revolutionary changes in modern science have taken place *not* as the results of new observations or additional evidence but by transpositions taking place in the minds of the scientists themselves. Fundamentally these transpositions had to do with ways in which problems were envisaged. Too often a "problem" in a discipline can hang on and on through inertia even when its very statement is predicated on circularities or known misconceptions.

Of all forms of intellectual activity one of the most difficult is that of confronting or handling the same data as before but, as Professor Butterfield notes, *placing them in a new system of relations with one another by giving them a different framework.* Or, in other words, by stating the question or problem differently. Michael Polanyi, distinguished physical scientist and notable philosopher, writes:

It is a commonplace that all research must start from a problem.
Research can be successful only if the problem is good; it can be
original only if the problem is original. But how can one see a
problem, any problem, let alone a good and original problem? For
to see a problem is to see something that is hidden. It is to have an
intimation of the coherence of hitherto not comprehended particulars.[2]

Polanyi tells us that this applies to even the most radically novel discoveries. In sheer brilliance and lasting importance nothing exceeds
the quantum theory in physics set forth by the remarkable Max Planck
in 1900. But Polanyi notes that all the material on which Planck
founded his theory was open to inspection by other physicists. Polanyi
writes, "He alone saw inscribed in it a new order transforming the outlook of man." What Max Planck did, most fundamentally, was find a
completely new way of posing the problem. This example demonstrates
the absolute importance, whatever may be the necessary restraints of
method and technique in science, of preserving at all costs unobstructed
perceptions and uncluttered imagination.

What are the fundamental problems of sociology? Proper answer
obviously must await the chapters that follow. It will suffice to say at
this point that the problems of sociology are those of *the nature of the*
social bond: the patterns of social interaction, the social aggregates, the
systems of authority, the social roles, statuses, and norms which form the
social bond. The problems are also, of course, the processes by which
these patterns and elements are changed. Earlier, I described this book
as one concerned with the essential concepts of sociology. But there is
always a close and mutually determining relation between the concepts
and the problems of any science. Science, which has been well described
as a never ending quest, draws its concepts from its attacks upon problems and its problems from its consideration of existing concepts.

Here a very important distinction is in order between the *problems*
of sociology and what we commonly call *social problems*. Few things
have led to more misconception of the nature of sociology as a science
than the failure to make this distinction. When we refer to social problems we have in mind such matters as crime, racial tensions, juvenile
delinquency, mental disorders, family breakdown, and international war.
Plainly, all of these reflect disruptions of the social bond. Equally
plainly, all of them deserve our best efforts to correct them. They are
and should be subjects of social policy at all levels of government and
society.

But not one of them is *as such* a constitutive problem of sociology.

That sociology can and does throw much light upon these and other social problems is not to be denied. But so does each of the other social sciences. The essential point here is that social problems are common property of *all* the social sciences. Consider crime alone. It is indeed a problem to which sociology, with its primary interests in social behavior, can contribute significant insight. But crime is also an economic matter; it cannot be divorced from the economic system—from matters of property and wealth. In addition, crime is a phenomenon with psychological aspects: there are students of the subject who have made personality deficiencies or abnormalities the point of departure for understanding criminal behavior. Crime is also a subject for the political scientist, for we have discovered repeatedly that methods of framing, administering, and interpreting laws have much to do with the incidence and types of criminal behavior in a society. What is true of crime is true as well of each of the other great social problems in our time. Without exception they are subjects for all the social sciences.

There is another aspect of the matter that should be stressed. When we think of social problems we are dealing with matters which are inseparable from *policy*, that is, public policy, the policy that is ultimately decided by citizens, elected officials, and the administrators of a society. Science is an invaluable aid to the formation of public policy; but it cannot be, by itself, the formulator of policy for a people. Moral, legal, and other considerations, including those of personal freedom, are bound to influence judgment when policy is being formed. Consider the use of tobacco, for example. Ample research has by now made it clear that tobacco, especially in the form of cigarettes, is harmful to human health. Few persons, however, would wish to judge the matter of public policy on tobacco—that is, political legislation designed to prevent or lessen smoking—solely in the terms presented by scientists. Most of us would consider extreme legislation along this line, however beneficently intended, as a violation of our freedom. Policy on tobacco is obviously subject to more than scientific considerations. The same is true with respect to other matters that enter public consciousness as problems: urban violence, crime, drugs, sexual deviance, mental illness, and so on. Each embodies behavior that is or should be within the province of the scientist in his search for causes, conditions, and effects. Wise public policy on any of these matters deserves and needs the advice of scientists qualified to provide it. Such advice should be influential and often followed meticulously. But it should never be controlling as such, for public policy in a free society must also draw from considerations that are outside the province of science.

In sum, the problems of the science of sociology, like the problems of any science, are specialized, limited to the sphere formed by the kind of data and concepts sociology works with, and addressed to the universal question of all science: *How does it operate?* Inherently, there is no more reason to assume that social problems such as crime and family disorganization are the problems of the discipline of sociology than to assume that public health problems such as tuberculosis and venereal diseases are the problems of physiology. Obviously physiology as a basic science can contribute to what eventually becomes control of these diseases. But control will be established only after the results of physiology have been fused with those of other disciplines and transferred from the realm of basic science to that of applied science.

Sociology is one of the basic sciences, and as such its progress involves ever greater specialization, just as is so manifestly the case in physics, biology, and the other sciences. It is in the applied disciplines —medicine for the biological sciences, public administration and social work among the social sciences—that the specialized and necessarily limited results of the several basic sciences are brought together and then focused on specific practical or social problems.

The true problems of sociology, then, are but specialized refinements of the underlying question of how social behavior operates. They are simply the problems of the nature of social behavior and its changes in time.

Notes

1. Emile Durkheim, *Suicide: A Study in Sociology.* Published in 1897, Durkheim's book is justly regarded as a classic in the social sciences. Whatever its deficiencies—inevitable in any truly original or pioneering work—the larger conclusions are as valid today as they were in Durkheim's time.
2. Michael Polanyi, *The Tacit Dimension* (New York: Doubleday, 1966), p. 21.

2

Some Sources of the Sociological Imagination

INTELLECTUAL BACKGROUNDS

Having presented some of the more distinctive properties of sociology as one of the modern sciences, we shall now examine a few of the major sources of modern scientific sociology. The late C. Wright Mills wrote a profound and exciting book several years ago called *The Sociological Imagination*. It should be read by all who are interested in the true sources of sociology and in the shaping contexts of those individuals who have, by their philosophical and scientific works, contributed the most to the discipline of sociology. Although the approach and content in this chapter will be very different from that of Mills, is common interest in the sociological mind.

I shall deal with two main subjects. The first will cover the principal *intellectual movements* or *sources* from which modern sociology has sprung. Here the emphasis will be on ideas and idea systems. The second subject will entail a brief look into the work of each of the *major sociologists* whose research and writings in the late nineteenth and early twentieth centuries may be seen today as the immediate ancestry of contemporary sociology. We shall begin, appropriately, with the sources.

There are four major intellectual sources of the sociological imagination, all of them vital parts of Western culture. They are *critical rationalism, humanitarianism, positivism*, and *ideology*. No one of

21

them should be confused with sociology or with the sociological imagination. Taken together, however, they provide necessary background
for an understanding of sociology.

Critical Rationalism

This term refers to a temper of thought that first made its appearance in modern Western society during the great Enlightenment in the
latter part of the eighteenth century. The essence of critical rationalism
is its insistence upon seeing the condition and problems of mankind
not in the ancient terms of passive acceptance but rather in the terms of,
first, critical scrutiny and, second, control or reform. The critical rationalists—men such as Voltaire, Diderot, Rousseau, Adam Smith, Jeremy
Bentham, and many others—were not, of course, the first in Western
thought to deal with institutions through the categories of good and
evil. They were, however, the first (at least since classical Greek
and Roman philosophers) to add to moral appraisal of traditional
groups and institutions the profound conviction that through human
reason evils could be corrected or banished from society—that such evils
were not necessarily a timeless aspect of human nature.

In the seventeenth century the great English philosopher Francis
Bacon had suggested that the test of genuine knowledge is its direct
relation to, and capacity to control, the physical world around us. It
was this pragmatic emphasis on control that passed in the eighteenth
century to social philosophers, most notably in France, where it became
an essential part of their view of the surrounding social order. This
order was an amalgam of social and religious traditions inherited from
feudalism and of political and economic structures reflective of the groups
in France just coming to power. To the critical rationalists, or *philosophes* as they are frequently called, the task was a clear one: root out
those institutions that have lost their viability and destroy those structures
that, through corruption of original purpose, have become tyrannous
and oppressive.

It was not to God, or tradition, or simple goodness that the critical
rationalists appealed in their writings. Instead, they appealed to *reason*.
The only good order is a rational order. So declared the *philosophes*
in a great variety of contexts—political, economic, religous, and social.
Some, such as Quesnay and Adam Smith, constructed the outlines of a
rational economic order, one which would be in conformity to the true
nature of man and society. Others, such as Rousseau and Bentham,

wrote what were in effect blueprints of the rational political order. Still others, such as Hume and Diderot, directed their attention to a rational religion, one freed of all the purely superstitious and ritualistic attributes of revealed religion. Almost without exception the critical rationalists opposed or were skeptical of Christianity as well as the feudal social system.

Out of the critical and secular rationalist philosophy of the eighteenth century emerged a habit of mind that has become steadily more pervasive in Western society. This habit of mind, summarized briefly, is that of critical assessment of the social and moral order in terms of human reason with the object of correcting the evils and inadequacies through rational social action. Sociology could never have made its appearance in the nineteenth century had there not already been present in Western Europe the more and more widely accepted view that human reason is as qualified to *control* as it is to understand and criticize social processes.

Humanitarianism

The second of the great sources of the sociological imagination is related to the first in practice but is, nonetheless, distinguishable. Humanitarianism is based upon compassion, which is a universal and timeless sentiment. We may define humanitarianism as the *institutionalization* of compassion, as the conversion of a timeless human sentiment to a more systematic effort that would involve the resources of the whole of society. Compassion is to be found in all societies and all ages of man. But until recently its scope has tended to be limited to very small circles of association—families, clans, small communities, and churches. What lay within one of these circles might be fit subject for pity, charity, compassion. But what lay outside could as properly be a matter of indifference, as though the suffering belonged to a different order of reality.

In the late eighteenth and early nineteenth centuries we find, almost for the first time in human history, the conviction spreading in Western Europe that human suffering of whatever source or type represents a claim upon the attention of the more privileged and, above all, of the social order itself. This is what we mean by humanitarianism. It is one of the most notable intellectual tendencies of modern Western history; and, as Alexis de Tocqueville pointed out more than a century ago, humanitarianism is inseparable from the modern history of social *equality*. For, as Tocqueville shrewdly noted, it was only when the spreading

sentiment of equality made all men feel related in some degree and, more
importantly, made of the same fundamental clay that it was really possible for the sufferings of some to enter the consciousness and the conscience of others.   It is not necessary to emphasize the fact that
humanitarianism has only very slowly come to include literally all human
beings in society. For a long time, because of ethnocentric prejudices
or those of race, humanitarian institutions tended to by-pass many minorities in society.   As Tocqueville observed, the humanitarianism of his
day had come to encompass all white persons in American society, but
it had not come to include the blacks, whose torments under slavery
were invisible to large numbers of whites.   But humanitarianism, once
begun, once rooted in the thoughtways of the West, grew and spread
steadily.   The idea that the resources of human thought and wealth
should promote the moral and social betterment of man became just as
deeply rooted in the West as the idea that human institutions are subject to rational understanding and control.   There has been in fact a
close tie between critical rationalism and humanitarianism from the very
beginning of each in the eighteenth century.   Sociology's roots are as deep
in one as in the other.

Positivism

This term refers to one of the most distinctive and far-reaching
intellectual tendencies in the modern world: the systematic effort to put
the study of man and society on the same scientific foundations that also
underlay the investigation of the physical and biological worlds.   The
rational study of man and society is, of course, as old as early Greek
thought.   There is a long philosophical tradition extending from the
Greeks to the present in which such matters as human nature, law, the
state, and civil society are central.   Before the nineteenth century, however, there is nothing in Western thought that can properly be called
the *science* of society.   Admittedly, many of the premises, hypotheses,
and principles of the science of society were drawn, in one form or another, from preceding philosophical theories.   And to the present moment there is a close relation between social philosophy and social science.

Nevertheless, something very new made its appearance in the nineteenth-century approach to an understanding of man and society.   This
was the attempt, on a very wide scale, to apply to social behavior the
same fundamental method and many of the same techniques that had
come so resplendently into being a century or two earlier in connection
with study of the physical and biological worlds.   Positivism is a ge-

neric term covering the investigations from which the contemporary social and behavioral sciences have come. Such men as Auguste Comte, David Ricardo, Karl Marx, Herbert Spencer, Henry T. Buckle, and Edward Tylor were concerned with achieving an understanding of man and his institutions that would be as empirical, systematic, and *positive* as anything to be found among the physical sciences. To deal with human behavior, property, religion, kinship, law, and even forms of literature and philosophy in the same positive and exact way in which atoms, molecules, and organic tissues were dealt with was the great objective of these men and of scores of others in the nineteenth century. In their minds was the conscious and explicit desire to remove the *science* of social behavior as far from historic social philosophy and the humanistic tradition as chemists, physicists, and biologists were removing their own spheres of work from historic physical philosophy.

It is easy today to see behind the façades of the works of the earliest social scientists ideas and conclusions which were far from scientific by present-day standards. Presuppositions and values entered directly from philosophy into the assertedly scientific work of Comte, Marx, Spencer, and others. Also, each of these men sought to construct by his own efforts what would prove to be *the* science of mankind without much reference to the ideas and principles of others, either of their own time or those who might come later. Of all this there is no question. But nothing noted in retrospect can take away from this important group of thinkers the signal achievement of having made the *idea* of a science of society—or of culture, institutions, or social behavior—a powerful one. The idea of a *science* of anything, physical or social, is very modern. It reflects the hope of making the study of the external world, or even of man's own mind, dispassionate, objective, and free of the special interests or values which throughout most of human history have been the motivations of study as well as action.

Even today there are more than a few who resist the idea that man and his works can be studied as objectively as the physical world. That there may be regularities of thought and behavior among human beings, that these may become the material of scientific laws as valid in their way as physical laws, is opposed by individuals today—from religious, moral, or humanistic positions—just as it was opposed, far more widely, in the nineteenth century. But positivism, in the sense in which I have used the word here, argued then as now that there is, or can be, a science of human behavior in the full sense of the word "science." The roots of sociology lie deep in this whole current of thought.

Ideology

This aspect of modern intellectual history is, in a sense, the very opposite of positivism. I said that sociology is a manifestation of positivist or scientific currents in the nineteenth century. But sociology is also deeply involved in nineteenth-century currents of thought that were anything but positivist. Those currents of thought are reflected in the great movements of ideas which we call liberalism, radicalism, and conservatism today. These too, in the form in which we now know them, are products of the last century. Even if we grant that the makers of modern social science were men sworn, so to speak, to the objective of pure science, it is impossible to overlook the further fact that one and all they were touched by one or more of the three great ideologies of the century—ideologies which, of course, have come down to our own day.

Ideology is one of the consequences of the two revolutions, industrial and democratic, which ushered in the nineteenth century. The shattering impact of the revolutions upon traditional institutions such as the political state, religion, social class, and property, made it inevitable that human beings would vary greatly in their assessments of the changes taking place. They would vary above all in their convictions of what constituted a good society. We may say all that we wish about the positivist or scientific objectives of Comte, Marx, and Spencer; we can hardly overlook the fact that each of these men also reflected the powerful currents of ideological thought in nineteenth-century society. Comte was, to a very large degree, *conservative* in his thinking about such matters as religion, property, social class, family, and community. Not that there was any manifest desire on Comte's part to preserve the existing order; this he regarded as a scene of intolerable confusion and uncertainty. Nor did he express the desire to restore the old and by then defunct social order of feudalism. Belief in progress was very strong in Comte. But if we examine carefully the ideal conceptions of social institutions and groups that he provides us in his writings, it is clear beyond question that these have a profoundly traditionalist cast. By the standards of all the major consequences or values of the French Revolution, Comte was a conservative. So was Frederick Le Play.

Marx, on the other hand, was a radical by any standard. He was no less devoted to the dream of an objective social science than Comte. But when we look at the content of his various envisagements of the good society, he is at the opposite extreme from Comte. He repudiated any thought of private property, of religion, of social class, or of the traditional family as far as the future under socialism was concerned. His overriding objective was the destruction of the capitalist social order, a destruction that he thought would come primarily from developmental forces—from the conflicts and contradictions which had been accumulating for centuries. However, this annihilation of capitalist society would require revolutionary action on the part of workers to accomplish it fully and to bring into existence the socialist society that would be free of all that now seemed to oppress and alienate man.

Herbert Spencer had scarcely more use for inherited traditions than Marx had. Spencer thought the existing institutions of his day, private property alone excepted, were archaic, or on their way to becoming archaic. Those institutions included the church, aristocracy, guilds, parishes, village communities, and even the universities. He envisioned a future in which human beings would be adapted to their environment in direct proportion to their abilities and without the artificial props furnished by inherited rank, title, and membership. But Spencer did not advocate revolutionary action as did the radicals of his day. He opposed even the programs and laws which form the substance of humanitarianism. His attitude toward social reform was categorically negative. Spencer was, by the criteria of that day, a liberal; this meant that for him the ultimate aim was a society in which maximum freedom of the individual existed—economic, political, and intellectual. And such freedom could only come, Spencer thought, through the natural play of evolutionary forces and processes, the very same forces and processes through which man and society had reached their present condition. All efforts to hasten, to adapt, to transform these forces and processes would end, Spencer believed, in an actual disruption of the progress taking place slowly and naturally. Hence Spencer's zealous devotion to a social scene as individualistic as possible, one in which the natural forces of competition and conflict would in the long run reduce the number of the ill-fitted individuals to zero and thus make possible a beneficent social order that would spring directly from natural abilities.

These, briefly stated, are the three great ideologies of the nineteenth century. From them came political parties, social movements, and individual philosophies throughout Western society. How one reacted to industrialism, profits, religion, labor, workers' organizations, socialism, war, and all the other issues presented by the modern age was dependent in large part upon one's ideology—if we use the word to refer to the larger pattern of values, beliefs, and objectives as this pattern was

related to one or another of the dominant social interests created by the
two revolutions, industrial and democratic, at the end of the eighteenth
century.

Given the power of these ideologies and their permeative character
in nineteenth-century thought, it was inevitable that the social sciences
would be affected by them. For, clearly, the social sciences dealt with
the same basic subjects in society around which ideologies were formed.
And what was true of the social sciences generally was true specifically
of sociology. Even when we pass from the ranks of the earliest sociologists such as Comte, Marx, and Tocqueville to the men—Durkheim,
Weber, Simmel, Spencer, and Sumner, among others—who by common
assent are the systematic builders of modern sociology, it is still plain
that sociology has never been very far from the currents of political and
social ideology. How could it be? After all, as we have seen, many of
the selfsame problems in the social order which are, so to speak, the
crude ore of sociological problems, are the central issues around which
political ideology is formed.

True, the social sciences are not the only ones in this position. When
one thinks of nuclear energy, the entire chemistry of explosives and
gases, the immense problems of air, water, and sound pollution in our
society, and many other similar problems, it is clear that the physical
sciences also deal with matters that can become central issues of ideological debate. Who, a mere generation ago, would ever have thought
that the remote atom of physicists' theory and experiment would become,
after World War II, a subject of national policy and debate? Whether
it is nuclear energy, poverty, the protection of rivers and air from industrial pollution, or that greatest of all problems, modern international
war, it is clear that science and ideology are never far from each other
in modern society.

THE MAKERS OF
MODERN SOCIOLOGY

It would be unfortunate if so-
ciology or any other science were allowed to seem only a composite of
problems, theories, concepts, and data. Every science is also a *community of scientists*: a community that extends from past to present to
future. Apart from the creative inspiration, the ingenious discoveries,
and the often brilliant explanations provided by extraordinary individuals, there would be no physical, no social, science.

In the century and a half since Auguste Comte founded sociology as a single, distinct, and systematic discipline, giving it its name in the process, there have been many thousands of sociologists, all engaged in the objectives of the discipline, all involved in the work of discovery of data, formulation of problems, and explanation of social behavior. No doubt all of them are responsible in some degree for the character of sociology as we find it today. But, as is always the case in the history of a science, certain individuals can be seen to have a commanding position denied to most of the rest of us. They are the ones who have set up the most distinctive problems, who have reached the most luminous visions of reality, who have made the most fruitful discoveries, who have formulated the most successful unifying theories and concepts. Throughout this book we shall have occasion to consider some of these figures, those living as well as those dead. At this point, however, I shall sketch briefly those who have done most to give sociology its present identity as one of the social sciences.

Auguste Comte (1798–1857)

It was Comte who coined the word "sociology," having first used the phrase "social physics" to cover the science of social phenomena that he believed to be emerging in his own time. Although Comte is best known for his *law of three stages*—by which all ideas and societies are declared to pass in time through the three stages of the religious, the metaphysical, and the positive or scientific—he is in fact most important for his delineation of the major areas of sociological investigation. These are *social statics* and *social dynamics*. The volumes of Comte's two major works, *The Positive Philosophy* (published through the years 1830–1842) and *The Positive Polity* (published 1851–1854) set forth the essential concepts, principles, and types of data in sociology as he envisaged this new science. The two books also point out techniques for the study of data. Unfortunately Comte infused his later work with convictions of his own messianic role in the new science. Therefore, it is sometimes difficult to avoid seeing his new science as more nearly religious in function than scientific. Nevertheless, it was Comte who set forth the basic theoretical divisions and perspectives of modern sociology, and many of his specific analyses of the statics and dynamics of social behavior could take their place with contemporary treatments.

Alexis de Tocqueville (1805–1859)

Although Tocqueville did not describe himself as a sociologist (for several decades in the nineteenth century the word "sociology" was used almost entirely by direct followers of Comte), his great *Democracy in America*, which was published in two volumes (Vol. 1 in 1835 and Vol. 2 in 1840), must be regarded as sociological to the very core. It is perhaps the first systematic sociological study of a specific society—the United States—in terms of its systems of power, stratification, and culture, and also of its detailed patterns of kinship, religion, voluntary associations, local community, military, and other forms of institutional behavior. The guiding aim of the work is to show the impact of revolutionary democracy upon the institutions of traditional society. The genius with which Tocqueville proceeded in his analysis of Americans was such that his book is regarded even today as the best study of American culture ever made, one that is as contemporary in its most fundamental insights as it was when he wrote it. Tocqueville, in this work and also in his *The Old Regime and the Revolution* (1856), presented a macroscopic view of the social order in the West, one which he saw dominated in large degree by political centralization, social fragmentation, mass culture, and a kind of endemic alienation of the human spirit. Although profoundly liberal in political sympathies, his mind was nevertheless deeply influenced by the conservative's apprehensions of radical democracy.

Karl Marx (1818–1883)

Although for many years Marx's major contributions were thought to lie in economics, it is clear today that these contributions lay instead in sociology. Marx is one of the two or three individuals most responsible for the general theoretical direction taken by sociology in Europe. Above all, it was his immense emphasis on the *social-class* character of society that took root. From the time that he and Friedrich Engels wrote the *Manifesto of the Communist Party* (1849), through such works as *The Class Struggle in France* (1850), *Critique of Political Economy* (1859), and *Capital* (1867), Marx believed that the class structure of a society played the strategic role in shaping the rest of its social organization and culture. All history, he declared, is a history of classes and of class struggles. In the ancient world it was master and slave; in the feudal world, lord and serf; in the modern world, it is the capitalists or bourgeoisie and the workers or, as Marx referred to them,

the proletariat. The intellectual culture of a society, including its science, art, and literature, is essentially a reflection of the interests of the
dominant class, thus forming what Marxism calls an *ideology*. The
dialectic of historical change dictates that, through internal conflicts and
contradictions, each form of society dies in time and is replaced by a
higher form. Through its internal conflicts, Marx argued, capitalism
will be destroyed in time from within; so will the two classes be destroyed. Then, for the first time in history, a genuinely classless society
will emerge—socialism, eventually to become communism—under which
exploitation, conflict, and the worker's alienation from work will terminate forever. Although it is this millennialist philosophy of history that
has had the greatest revolutionary and worldwide impact, it is Marxism's
stress upon economic determinism in the study of social behavior and
upon the class character of human culture, social organization, and social
change that has left the greatest influence on the social sciences. It
would be impossible to explain the strong emphasis in sociology, contemporary and recent past, upon social stratification apart from Marx's
powerful influence in the late nineteenth century.

Frederick Le Play (1806–1882)

Whereas Alexis de Tocqueville was generally liberal in political
sympathy, and Marx deeply radical, Le Play was a political conservative.
Like these two, he was, however, profoundly influenced by the effects
of the industrial and democratic revolutions on Western society. He
began as a businessman and engineer but devoted most of his life to
the study of social institutions, particularly the family, local community,
and social class. His greatest work was a comparative study of these
institutions as they were to be found in Western and Eastern Europe
and also in parts of the Orient. This study, *The European Workers*
(1855), sought to demonstrate that the major outlines of any society
are set by its underlying type of family. Three dominant types of family
were discovered and classified by Le Play: *patriarchal*, *stem*, and the
modern *nuclear*. The first is authoritarian-traditional in character; the
second is free of the authoritarianism of the first but still rooted in tradition; and the third is the small, conjugal or nuclear type, strongly individualistic, mobile, and secular. Le Play thought the last type to be
inherently disorganized and the prime cause of modern social disorganization generally. Although Le Play's political overview had little effect
on sociology, his system of kinship classification was to prove important,
most especially through his so-called budgetary mode of analysis of

family structure and function. This was, at bottom, an effort to apply the techniques of the then emerging science of social statistics to the family. Le Play deserves the title of the first quantitative sociologist, however primitive his uses of statistics were by contemporary standards.

Ferdinand Tönnies (1855–1936)

Like Marx a German, and influenced in many ways by Marx's emphasis upon class and the economic structure of society, Tönnies drew nevertheless from a broad and diversified tradition of social and legal studies. His *Community and Society* (1887) made explicit and systematic a distinction that has survived significantly to the present day in sociology—the distinction between what he called *Gemeinschaft* and *Gesellschaft*. The words are roughly translatable as "community" and "society," respectively. But their full significance is much richer. The first refers to types of society or periods in history characterized by strongly personal, communal, traditional, and stationary social ties. Kinship is the archetype of all forms of association. The second refers to a general type of society that is characterized by emphasis on territorial-political ties, commercialism, profusion of interest associations, loss of primary kinship and religious traditions, and by strong tendencies toward individualism and secularism. Tönnies applied his concepts of *Gemeinschaft* and *Gesellschaft* chiefly to the successive phases of European history, medieval and modern, but they have been widely used in the interpretation of non-Western societies as these are undergoing modernization today. More concretely, a friendship group, a close-knit family, or village community is, in Tönnies' framework, *Gemeinschaft*, whereas a shopping center, large industry, or labor union is *Gesellschaft*. What is crucial is the degree of involvement of the human being.

Max Weber (1864–1920)

Weber is one of the two preeminent influences on contemporary sociological theory, the other being Emile Durkheim, whom we shall consider next. Undoubtedly the most learned and imaginative of sociologists, Weber touched all aspects of social behavior, ranging from the minute and interactive to the large and institutional. His profoundest and most influential work is *Economy and Society* (1922), which appeared in four volumes shortly after his death. The most widely read of his writings, however, are *The Protestant Ethic and the Spirit of Capitalism* (1904–1905), in which Weber, in reply to Marx, demonstrated the noneconomic and partly religious origins of capitalism, and two magnificent addresses, published as essays, *Politics as a Vocation* (1919) and *Science as a Vocation* (1919), in which the humanistic and deeply liberal texture of his mind is to be seen.

Most of contemporary sociology's conceptualization of *social stratification* (in terms of class, status, and power) and its principal classification of *types of authority* are attributed to Weber's work. Weber's distinction among *charismatic, traditional,* and *rationalist* types of authority is by all odds the most influential of his many theoretical contributions and is clearly the basis of contemporary political sociology. We shall have frequent occasion in later chapters to refer to this typology, for its usefulness goes well beyond the study of authority as such to include social organization generally and also religion, law, education, culture, and government. Of all sociologists Weber has undoubtedly had the most far-reaching effect not merely upon sociology itself but upon other social sciences as well, including political science, economics, administration, and anthropology.

Emile Durkheim (1858–1917)

Rivaled only by Weber in breadth and depth of influence upon sociology and the other social sciences, Durkheim is responsible for the first clear-cut scientific study of a single social problem in modern sociology. This was his epochal *Suicide* (1897), in which he accounted successfully for the varying incidence of suicide in society through explanations which were both empirical and theoretical in character. For all its technical limitations by contemporary standards, the study remains a model of what scientific imagination can achieve in the way of verifiable, testable results. Durkheim's earliest work, *The Division of Labor in Society* (1893), made use of a typology akin to that of Tönnies. Durkheim referred to the two great types of social organization as "mechanical" and "organic," the first analogous to Tönnies' *Gemeinschaft*, the second to *Gesellschaft*. Although Durkheim never again made use of this typology of mechanical and organic solidarity in his writings, his subsequent interest in the nature of the social bond as well as his derivation of morality, law, and religion from the social community sprang directly from his early interest in the two major types of social organization. His initial conception of mechanical solidarity, with its emphasis upon the elements of cohesion, authority, and consensus, developed into such works as *The Rules of Sociological Method* (1895), *Suicide* (1897), and *The Elementary Forms of Reli-*

gious Life (1912). These outlined Durkheim's conception of the very nature of society generally. The radical character of his work, by the standards of his day, arose from his virtual dismissal of the individualistic factors favored by utilitarianism and his stress upon the role of group organization and disorganizat'on in accounting for differential human behavior in society. His *Suicide* and *The Elementary Forms of Religious Life* remain persisting influences on sociological research to this day.

Georg Simmel (1858–1918)

Simmel is unquestionably the most readable of all the great sociologists, as brilliant in style as in thought. In Simmel is to be found a deep and far-reaching concern with the *microscopic* elements of social behavior. No one in his day wrote so perceptively about the nature and processes of small groups, the nature of social interaction, or about the social roles that form any social organization or group, however large or small. More than any other sociologist, he deals with the underlying elements of the social bond. And it is for this reason that the American sociologist Everett Hughes was led to call Simmel "the Freud of sociology." Simmel's study *The Secret Society* (1906) reveals more readily than any other of his single works the combination of his interest in the individual human being, in the small face-to-face association, in the nature of social ties, and in the larger groups which form a society. But this book is far from the only one. His studies of the nature of power in society, its types, its settings, and its processes, rank Simmel almost with Weber in this realm. Simmel's difference from both Weber and Durkheim chiefly in his more vivid sense of the reality of the individual person. But Simmel was not insensitive to the social roles and statuses in which individuals are to be found. Neither did he take refuge in the idea of a set of imagined social "instincts" within the individual. Simmel was a sociologist, in as full a sense as any of the others cited here, which meant for him, as for the others, a study of the forms, structures, as well as the content of social relationships.

Herbert Spencer (1820–1903)

Along with Auguste Comte, Spencer is one of the two great *systematic* sociologists of the last century. All knowledge, for Spencer, formed a consistent and interrelated whole, given unity by the idea of development or evolution. Spencer was a contemporary of Charles Darwin, and although the two men arrived at their theories of evolution independently, they had much in common. For each the evolutionary principle was the means of providing a single and unified explanation of all the diversities revealed by observation. Spencer applied the principle of evolution to all aspects of nature and society, but he is best known for his voluminous evolutionary studies of social institutions such as kinship, religion, property, and the state. In his books we find an immense amount of illustrative material drawn from primitive peoples for the purpose of reinforcing the succession of stages that Spencer set forth for each institution he dealt with. Much of this is today thought to be of little use by sociologists because of Spencer's assumption—which was a common one in his day—that there is a single sequence of stages of development for each institution and for society as a whole. There is, however, more than social evolutionism in Spencer. In such works as *Social Statics* (1850) and *Principles of Sociology* (1876–1896), we find some approaches to problems of social structure, social stability, and also to the mechanisms of social change, which stand up very well indeed in terms of the perspectives of contemporary sociology. Spencer regarded society as being in some respects similar to an organism. From his organismic analogy he drew principles of functional interdependence of parts which compare favorably with the central propositions of contemporary functionalist theory in sociology and anthropology.

Vilfredo Pareto (1848–1923)

An Italian, Pareto is equally famous as an economist and sociologist. In the first role he is the author of *Cours d'economie politique* (1896–1897), a work regarded with high respect even today by economists for its pioneering uses of mathematical techniques, its original treatment of the problem of economic equilibrium, and its theory of economic demand. Pareto was one of the first to give theoretical focus to a uniting of social and economic data. It was his early interest in the social aspects of economic materials that led him to his monumental *The Mind and Society: A Treatise on General Sociology* (1916). In this remarkably learned and original work Pareto set forth his theories of nonlogical behavior, of residues and derivations, and of circulation of elites. By nonlogical behavior Pareto did not mean illogical. He was reacting to the heavy utilitarian emphasis in his day on reasoned or self-interested behavior by indicating the powerful influence in human lives of customs, mores, rituals, and other forms of acquired behavior which are, by their nature, neither logical nor illogical—but nonlogical. His theory of residues and derivations is a massive effort to classify social actions into universal types, relating these actions to what he called the underlying residues, basic forces in human nature. Pareto's theory of circulation of elites is a fascinating effort to show how in history there is an endless, cyclical circulation of two broadly different types of men of power: "the foxes," men of innovative and speculative character, and "the lions," those of conservative, stable disposition.

Gabriel Tarde (1843–1904)

A French sociologist, contemporary with Durkheim, Tarde was in almost total opposition to the central principles that Durkheim advanced. Rivalry between the two men was sharp, and controversy between followers of each was often bitter. Whereas Durkheim began with the priority of society in the study of social behavior, Tarde made the individual his point of departure. What Durkheim declared to be irreducibly social, Tarde explained through his all-important doctrine of *imitation*. Society, Tarde contended, is simply an aggregate of individuals given unity by the instinct in each person to imitate. It was Tarde's further contention that all new culture traits arise from highly creative individuals who alone are the sources of change in society, and that these traits are in time imitated by the "crowd." Although imitation is the primary doctrine in Tarde's work, he was not blind to the existence of other, related, processes, notably those which he called *opposition* and *adaptation*. Broadly speaking, Tarde believed that society consists simply in what he called the "inter-mental" behavior of discrete individuals united by imitation of one another. Change is the consequence of the opposition and fresh forms of adaptation contributed by innovative individuals. Although Tarde has had nothing like the influence upon contemporary sociology that Durkheim has, his *The Laws of Imitation* (1900) is still worth careful study, for it is a brilliant and lucid corrective to theories of society in which the role of the individual tends to be lost.

William Graham Sumner (1840–1910)

One of the founders of the discipline of sociology in the United States, Sumner is chiefly famous for his classic *Folkways* (1906).

This book is very probably one of the best studies of the nature of institutions, customs, conventions, and manners ever written. "Folkways" was the single generic term Sumner used to cover all such modes of behavior. Within this largest category falls that special type of folkways that Sumner, borrowing from the Latin, called mores. Mores are folkways which have a higher and more sacred importance to a society. They are the folkways, Sumner declared, that form the substance of a given society's system of morality. Mores make anything right: this was Sumner's pithy and wholly secular explanation of the nature of morality. Sumner also coined the term "ethnocentrism" to deal with the recurrent phenomenon of contrasts in history between "in-groups" and "out-groups" and the powerful tendency of each group or society to think its ways sacred. Although *Folkways* is primarily directed toward the mechanisms of order and persistence in society, it is equally valuable as a study of the conditions of change, which Sumner saw largely in the evolutionary terms of adaptation and response to new environmental circumstances.

Charles H. Cooley (1864–1929)

Like Sumner, Cooley remains one of the very few early American sociologists whose works are still widely read and influential. He was primarily concerned with the nature of human association. His most famous contribution is probably his concept of "the primary group," a term that he employed to cover not merely family and neighborhood but any type of close, face-to-face relationship in which the individual belongs as a whole person rather than in one or another of his role aspects. This concept has proved to be one of the most fertile in the entire history of American sociology. First set forth in Cooley's *Social Organization* (1909), where it is made a part of a well-articulated theory of the social order, it is the sociological means of explaining the development of the self, conscience, and personality. In his earlier *Human Nature and the Social Order* (1902) Cooley, working largely from systematic observation of his own children, had set forth the essential elements of his theory of the self and its indissoluble relation to the ties of primary association. Both of these works are invaluable, even at the present time, for the lucid accounts they give of the maturation of the self in society. In his *Social Process* (1918) Cooley extended his analysis to other parts of the social order, dealing with some of the conditions of change in society.

George Herbert Mead (1863–1931)

Although Mead was not a sociologist by profession (he was a professor of philosophy at the University of Chicago for many years), it would still be hard to find anyone whose impact upon the discipline in the United States has been any greater than his. His prime interest was what he called the *social act*, and from this essential and highly empirical unit Mead worked toward those principles of social psychology for which he is best known. His study of the social act—which he defined as any processual relationship involving two or more persons, in which some degree of division of labor exists—led Mead to the importance of the *social role*. Human beings become members of society insofar as they assume one or more of the various roles which are, so to speak, the social molecules of groups and associations. Individual social growth is the means by which human beings, beginning in infancy, learn to take roles. Through this role taking, Mead suggested, they become gradually aware of society as a kind of "generalized other." Unquestionably, however, Mead's greatest and most brilliant contribution to sociology and to social psychology was his whole theory of *symbolic interaction*, through which he explained not merely the development of the self but the character of human culture and society. Communication in the unique form of interaction through accepted symbols was, for Mead, the best way of resolving the ancient problem of the alleged antinomy of the individual and society. It is fair to say that at the present time Mead's theory of symbolic interactionism is the reigning theory in sociology of the nature of the self and its relation to the social order.

William I. Thomas (1863–1947)

Thomas is the fourth and last of the early American sociologists whose works remain as relevant and important today as when they were written. No one before or since has united as fruitfully the prime requirements of theory and empirical research. He always worked empirically in his study of society but never without explicit utilization of theoretical concepts. A number of these hold lasting importance. His greatest work was *The Polish Peasant in Europe and America* (published in successive volumes from 1918 to 1920), done in collaboration with the brilliant Polish sociologist Florian Znaniecki (1882–1958). This work is at once a study in comparative institutions, ethnic groups, social organization, and social psychology. Its point of departure was the authors' desire to explain the relatively high incidence of delinquency in the Polish section of Chicago. From this, the authors worked their way to all of the key changes and dislocations which had been involved in the movement of Polish people from their old country to the new one. Not least among the book's great and seminal contributions is its pioneering in the field of the technique or method of studying social behavior. It was in this book that skilled use really began of such documents as diaries, letters, and native-language newspapers. Thomas also pioneered in the use of interviews and surveys. He was as interested in the problem of change as in the conditions of order and stability. His use of the concept of "crisis" for the first—emphasizing the crisis character of all change involving social behavior—matched in importance his formulation of such concepts as "definition of the situation" and "primary group norms." Above anyone else Thomas gave fertile emphasis to the fact that in human behavior it is *not* the objective situation that leads to social action but the individual's perception and *definition* of the situation. This definition is itself shaped by the norms of those groups in which he has been most closely involved. There is a straight line from Thomas' concept of definition of the situation to contemporary reference group theory.

Florian Znaniecki (1882–1958)

Polish-born, Znaniecki came to this country as a young man trained primarily in philosophy. Under the influence of W. I. Thomas he changed his interests to sociology, first achieving note as collaborating author with Thomas of *The Polish Peasant in Europe and America*. It detracts in no way from the genius of W. I. Thomas to say that much of the theoretical and conceptual structure of that work was the consequence of Znaniecki's own philosophical brilliance. In the 1920s Znaniecki returned to his native Poland where he became a professor of sociology at Poznan and where he began the succession of remarkable works in theoretical sociology that was to establish him as one of the major figures in modern sociology. He returned to the United States in the early 1930s, and the final years of his productive scholarly life were spent at Columbia University and the University of Illinois. Among his most original works are *Cultural Reality* (1919), *The Method of Sociology* (1934), *Social Actions* (1936), and *The Social Role of the Man of Knowledge* (1940). Of the distinctiveness and originality of his mind there can be no question. One need but look at some of the strongest of still-emerging tendencies in contemporary sociological writing to realize the profoundly anticipatory character of much of his work.   We see this in the large number of studies going on in the nature of social norms, patterns of interaction, small groups, social roles, and reference behavior.   Znaniecki is one of three sociologists, all foreign-born, who did much of their distinguished work in the United States.   All three had considerable influence in introducing Americans to the wealth of sociological perspectives and insights contained in the European tradition.   We shall conclude the chapter with the other two.

Pitirim Sorokin (1889–1968)

Born in Russia, Sorokin was a notable scholar in Russian academic circles before the Communist revolution in 1917.   His political differences with the triumphant Bolsheviks led to his departure from Russia and his eventual settling in the United States.   His *Contemporary Sociological Theories* (1928) was published while has was at the University of Minnesota and did much to put the resources of European social theory before American sociologists.   It is more than a survey of sociological theories.   Strongly rooted in Sorokin's own sociological convictions, this book can be seen as an important step leading to the work for which he is most famous, *Social and Cultural Dynamics* (1937–1941).   Here, in four volumes, Sorokin drew upon sociological, philosophical, and historical studies to write one of the notable works of the century.   Whether it is thought of as philosophy of history or historical sociology, it is that rarity among American-written sociological studies, a work set in a vast comparative-historical framework.   Although it is perhaps best known for its cultural categories of "ideational," "sensate," and "idealistic"—categories which Sorokin employed in historical analysis of several societies—the book is rich in other areas of sociology as well.   Nor should Sorokin's role in the study of social stratification be overlooked.   His *Social Mobility* (1927) can be seen in retrospect as the key work in generating American sociological interest in this now central area of research.   Immensely learned, Sorokin brought to the already existing interests of American sociology—rural-urban studies, for example—comparative materials drawn from numerous other cultures which went a long way toward offsetting a kind of parochialism that was threatening in the 1920s to seize American sociology.   He was, finally, the founding figure of sociology at Harvard University (where he went from Minnesota in

1930) and the first head of what was in a short time to prove to be one of the most fertile of sociological centers in this country.

Robert M. MacIver (1882–   )

MacIver must be regarded as the first in this country to fashion the field of research known today as political sociology. As much political scientist as sociologist, MacIver, like Znaniecki and Sorokin, brought ideas and perspectives to American social science from European thought which were, in their time, strongly needed as freshening influences in theory and research. MacIver, who was born in Scotland, was educated at Edinburgh and at Oxford University in England. He launched his teaching and scholarly career in the United Kingdom. In the early 1920s he came to this continent, first to Canada where he held a professorship at Toronto, then to Columbia University in this country. Of all the major sociologists he is the most gifted in literary style, but this fact does not detract from the power and originality of his ideas. Americans owe to him the introduction of the vital problems of associations in their relation to political power (a theme he drew in part from the English pluralists under whom he had studied), the nature of the state conceived as an interest association, and, perhaps most important, the nature of the community, conceived not merely as locality but as a form of association encompassing many spheres of culture. His major works include *Community* (1917), *The Modern State* (1926), *Society: Its Structure and Changes* (1931), *Social Causation* (1942), and *The Web of Government* (1947). Strong interest in social change, specifically in social development, is a persisting feature of almost all MacIver's numerous writings. This, like his interests in the nature of community, of power, of association, and in the methods by which we study social phenomena, gives him the kind of continuing currency in sociological thought we have found in the other major figures. One final important point about Robert MacIver is the fact that his has been a profoundly "linking" role in sociology from the very beginning. More than any of the others mentioned, he has joined the first generation of major sociologists—Weber, Durkheim, Simmel, Tönnies, and others—with contemporary schools of thought. His own superb classical education has been the means of linking the "two cultures" of science and humanism in his work.[1]

These, I believe, are the principal makers of the sociological mind as we find it today. Any inference that they alone are responsible for sociology in its rich diversity today would be false. Sociology, like any science, is the product of many minds. I have limited myself, doubtless with personal bias that is inescapable in these matters, to those whose contributions are clearly major in the period leading up to the present age of sociological thought. Nor should the fact be forgotten that there are others today, some of like distinction in their thought, who maintain and deepen the sociological imagination. These we shall occasionally refer to in succeeding chapters.

Note

1. I am indebted to Charles Page for this insight into both MacIver and the persisting needs of sociological thought.

II
THE
SOCIAL BOND

3

The Nature of the Social Bond

THE REALITY OF
THE SOCIAL

In this central section of the book we shall examine the major elements of the social bond, the mechanisms and processes through which human beings become members of the social order and by which they remain members. Just as modern chemistry concerns itself with what it calls the chemical bond, seeking the forces that make atoms stick together as molecules, so does sociology investigate the forces that enable biologically derived human beings to stick together in the "social molecules" in which we actually find them from the moment, quite literally, of their conception.

Note this last point carefully. We do not really see "individuals" in the sense of discrete, elemental human particles in the world around us. We no more see "individuals" in this sense than we see the smallest elements of matter with which physicists work. We do indeed see human beings. In fact, that is all we see. Any theory or system of sociology that forgets the priority of human beings and of concrete human behavior in the study of the social bond in its varied, multiple manifestations must be regarded as suspect at the very outset. The fundamental and inescapable subject matter of sociology—and of all the social sciences—is human beings and how and why they behave as they do.

But it is equally true that we see human beings only in the roles, statuses, and modes of social interaction which are the stuff of human society. And these roles, statuses, and modes of interaction are *social* —that is, they belong to an order of reality that is every bit as solid and differentiable as are the atoms dealt with by physicists, the molecules and substances by chemists, and the tissues and organs by biologists.

To insist upon the distinguishable reality of the social is not, of course, to endow it with metaphysical separateness or to declare it removed from the behavior of human beings. Not at all. We simply insist that when, as sociologists, we undertake to study social behavior, we are confronted by elements, processes, and mechanisms which cannot be dissolved or translated into the elements, processes, and mechanisms of, say, psychology, physiology, chemistry, or physics. To insist that in some ultimate, far-reaching philosophical sense all matter is one—as philosophers since the earliest days of Greek rationalism have claimed—is beside the point. From the strictly empirical and scientific point of view there are (for all the possible metaphysical validity of monism) different, or at least distinguishable, spheres or levels of matter and behavior. They must be recognized and respected.

One of the oldest and commonest of errors is *reductionism*, the stratification of reality into "levels," with explanations of "higher" levels derived from one or another of the "lower" levels. From such efforts at reductionist explanation have come, in the past as well as the present, systems of thought that seek to reduce all society or social behavior to the operation of some complex of psychological instincts, physiological needs, or even chemical and physical processes. Invariably such efforts have proved to be either ridiculous or so bland in the order of their generality as to be meaningless. What usually happens is that some constant, such as a claimed instinct toward some goal, is made the means of explaining behavior so diversified in its character as to negate the importance and even the reality of the claimed instinct or physiological force. Suppose one were to say that the "instinct of aggression" found in all organisms is sufficient to explain the myriad conflicts of human beings which we find in the social world. Our "explanation" would be at a level of generality so vast as to be nearly useless for what is concrete, distinctive, and varied in social life. The dangerous habit of reductionism makes psychologists on occasion think that in psychology lie the really fundamental explanations of behavior that manifests itself as social, or physiologists think the same with respect to psychological behavior, or chemists with respect to physiological behavior, and so on.

Of course we cannot, in any total view of the matter, neglect the various spheres or levels of reality. And of course social behavior is the behavior of beings who are at one and the same time psychological, physiological, chemical, and physical. It is equally true that no social behavior can ever go beyond the clear and absolute limits set upon behavior by one or another of these spheres. That man cannot by waving his arms and legs fly through the air successfully clearly imposes limits to his social behavior. That all human beings have certain physiological functions and needs inevitably affects the substantive character of social and cultural life. Think only of the elaborate folkways and mores that surround eating, sleeping, sex, and so on. Political and social schemes which overlook the physiological or psychological character of man are fated to disaster or futility.

The fact remains, however, that social behavior cannot be explained in terms of its peculiar differences and varieties except through concepts which reflect the *distinctiveness* of this behavior. There is, in short, as much distinctiveness of identity in the realm of the social as there is in the realm of the psychological or the physiological or the physical. None of these areas is a watertight compartment and that fact is attested to by the frequent phenomenon in the history of science of insights drawn from one field proving useful in the problems of another. But while remembering this constantly in our work, we do not commit the reductionist fallacy of obliterating the identity of one body of data by submerging it in doctrinaire fashion in another and different body of data. Here some words of the social anthropologist A. R. Radcliffe-Brown are salutary.

> *One may say that the characteristics of a society are determined by two things: first, by the simple fact that the society is composed of human beings; and second, by the internal nature of those human beings. No amount of investigation can explain the characteristics of society by simple reference to the nature of human beings; but by an investigation of human beings arranged in a certain order, yes. The social scientist is studying the structural arrangement of the units and takes the internal structure of the units for granted.*[1]

As Radcliffe-Brown goes on to point out, if we were to take the view that one cannot study a society or mode of social behavior until one had exhaustively studied the individual, then we should have to say that it was senseless for chemists of earlier times to have studied molecules before they had found out what atoms were like. Happily, eighteenth-century chemists did not think that way; and, as Radcliffe-

Brown notes, the whole system of modern chemistry was built up without knowledge of the internal structure of the atom.

Radcliffe-Brown correctly writes: "It would be perfectly possible to build up a social science without paying the least attention to the internal relations of human beings."[2] He is referring, of course, to *intraindividual forces* and elements, those we commonly think of as psychological or physiological. Obviously he is not referring to the microcosmic internal processes of social groups or patterns of social interaction. For these, however concealed they may be to ordinary observation, are the very stuff of what we call the social bond.

Let us be very clear at this point on the utter falsity of the ancient distinction between "society" and "man." I have said, and will repeat from time to time in relevant context, that the *social* is as distinct and irreducible a subject matter as any other in the realm of modern science. I have said that it is impossible by internal analysis or dissection of the single, discrete human being to arrive at the kind of elements and processes that form the social bond. But I have *not* said, nor could any responsible sociologist, that the individual and society are separated, that society is something "out there," autonomous, substantive, and separable from the actions of human beings.

To be sure, there are and have been distinguished sociologists, including Emile Durkheim, who occasionally seem to be suggesting that there *is* a kind of metaphysical reality to society that separates it from the behavior of individuals. We may generally charge such statements, however, to excess zeal or ill-advised terminology in their worthy effort to emphasize the irreducibility of the social bond to forces which are purely psychological or physiological. As the following passage makes clear, not even Durkheim believed, really believed, that society was something which could be detached from concrete human beings in interaction.

> *On the one hand, the individual gets from society the best part of himself, all that gives him a distinct character and a special place among other beings, his intellectual and moral culture. If we should withdraw from men their language, sciences, arts, and moral beliefs, they would drop to the level of animals. So the characteristic attributes of human nature come from society. But, on the other hand,* society exists and lives only in and through individuals. If the idea of society were extinguished in individual minds and the beliefs, traditions, and aspirations of the group were no longer felt and shared by the individuals, society would die. *We can say of it . . . : It is*

real only insofar as it has a place in human consciousness, and this
place is whatever one we may give. . . . Society cannot do without
individuals any more than these can do without society.[3] *(Emphasis*
added.)

These words, as I say, were written by a sociologist, one of the two
or three greatest of modern times, who is often charged with failure to
recognize the fact that apart from human beings and their interactive
behavior there would be no society, no culture, no social order. But
Durkheim was indeed aware of the priority of human beings and so must
we be. To recognize the priority of human beings is not, however, the
same as recognizing or declaring the priority of human psychological or
physiological elements when it comes to the study of social behavior.
Given the nature of the human mind, it is not merely possible, it is
necessary to say that when human beings interact with one another,
social elements, forces, and mechanisms are established which are no
more capable of being reduced only to supposedly underlying psychological forces within human beings than to physiological or chemical
forces. Assuredly, the levels overlap and interact. But each has its own
conceptual reality.

THE ELEMENTS OF THE SOCIAL BOND

Now let us turn to the cardinal
elements, the principal manifestations, of what I have called the social
bond. My intent is to provide a preview of what we shall examine more
intensively in the seven chapters that follow. And the reason for the
preview is to set these elements in as tight and compact a format as
possible in their necessary interrelationships. For it is not really possible
to understand fully any one of the elements except in terms drawn to
some extent from the others. As George Homans has written, "It is
really intolerable that we can say only one thing at a time; for social
behavior displays many features at the same time, and so in taking them
up one by one we necessarily do outrage to its rich, dark, organic unity."[4]

What Professor Homans writes is as correct as it is felicitous, and
we must make the best of it. We have no alternative so long as we think
and write with the words at our disposal and seek to eschew neologisms
which, although they may seem pure and aseptic to their authors, serve
usually to confuse rather than clarify. We are much better off with
words that are well accepted, even when each of these is in some degree

dependent for its meaning upon other words whose full import cannot be made clear until later in the discussion. Nevertheless, it is still binding upon an author to do his best to make clear at the outset, however briefly and tentatively, the meanings of the terms which will be crucial in the chapters following.

The central elements of the social bond are *social interaction, social aggregates, social authority, social roles, social statuses, social norms,* and *social entropy.* No brief definition will do any one of them justice. Each deserves, and will receive, a full chapter of explication and clarification of its relation to ongoing sociological inquiry. But it is extremely difficult, for example, to make clear the nature of social interaction without at least tentative and operating knowledge of the meaning of social roles and social norms. For this reason, then, we shall devote the remainder of this chapter to short, prefatory treatments of each of the central elements of the social bond.

Social interaction

First and foremost of the elements of the social bond is that form of interaction we call social. Not all interaction of human beings is social in the precise and vital sense that sociology gives to the phrase "social interaction." My life may be dependent for its nutrition upon, say, an Argentine wheat grower, but never having met or otherwise communicated with the Argentinian, my "interaction" with him can hardly be called social—not even if he is equally dependent upon some commodity I produce that goes to him through international trade. Social interaction is that type of human interaction which Herbert Blumer, following George H. Mead, calls *symbolic.* That is, it is interaction of human beings which is mediated by symbols, mutually and incessantly interpretative, and, on each side, literally responsive to the reactions of the other. Social interaction is inseparable from *meaning*, meaning endowed by the symbols through which the interaction takes place. Proceeding from this symbolic character of social interaction are several key patterns of interaction to be found everywhere in human society, among them, *exchange, cooperation, conformity, coercion,* and *conflict.* These processes or mechanisms may be thought of as the microelements of the social bond. There is literally no form of social interaction among human beings in which one or more of these elements are not to be found. They, together with the context of symbolic interaction in which each of them is alone found, are, so to speak, the molecular cement of society.

Social aggregates

Everywhere we find human beings clustering together in aggregates of one kind or another. I use the word "aggregate" as the largest and most generic possible term to cover a range that extends from the tiny, intensely personal dyad based upon friendship or love all the way to the mammoth organizations of modern political and economic society. Social aggregates may be as transitory as a picnic or cocktail party or as durable and long-lasting as a modern nation-state. They may be as informal as the neighborhood get-together of housewives for morning coffee or as formal as the State Department or General Motors; as binding upon human allegiance as the feudal tie in the Middle Ages or as loose and undemanding as a contemporary social club. They may be primary or secondary, direct or indirect. What is important is the fact of the aggregate itself and the fact that although it is indubitably but a collection of human beings it nevertheless exerts upon each single human being who belongs to it influences which can be found nowhere else in the universe. Social interaction and its several mechanisms make possible social aggregates. But it is through the existence of the aggregates themselves, and especially those of close, primary, and binding types, that the social bond most directly reveals itself to human observation.

Social authority

From one point of view human society is a tissue of authorities. There can be no social group or social relationship of any kind that is not characterized by, in however slight or diffuse a manner, some mode of authority. No mistake would be greater than to conceive authority invariably in the pattern of the sovereign power of the modern state, the military or police command, or the elaborate, highly ramified structure of a large corporation. These, to be sure, are forms of authority, or, if we like, of power. But they are not the only forms. There is the authority of religion over its communicants, of the family over its members, of the labor union over its members, of the business enterprise, the political association, the organized criminal or conspiratorial group, and even the small, primary types of relationship which spring up informally and spontaneously in society. Authority is not necessarily something external, something manifestly coercive and based upon the use of force, either latent or actual. Authority, as we shall see in Chapter 6, has many types and many degrees of intensity. There is the authority of syntax in a language or of scientific achievement and greatness. There is, indeed, authority of human distinction in whatever field it may be found, ranging from the military band to modern professional football and its luminaries.   There is the authority that proceeds directly from mere participation in a common enterprise or function.   Authority may be defined as simply the inner order of a human association, whether this be the mutual trust in a friendship, a business contract, or of civil society.

Social roles

I said above that we never encounter individuals, in the sense of analytically independent, free-roving, and discrete entities or atoms. Human beings, yes; individuals, no.   And the reason for this is that we never encounter others except in the roles which, in a sense, the social order has thrust upon them.   Not, obviously, in any mechanical way. What has already been said about the nature of social interaction makes plain that there is no more gulf between human being and role than there is between human being and the social order.   Let us merely say at this point that human beings are to be found *in* social roles and that social roles are to be found *in* human beings.   From the strictly behavioral point of view, what else is history about and what else is society composed of but the myriad roles in which we find human beings? There are the universal roles of father, mother, son, daughter.   Each of these roles is a bundle of normative expectations and of actual performances.   There is very little difference in meaning in the word "role" as we find it in drama and as it is used in sociology.   To assume the role of Hamlet for a theater run of a few months may not be as fundamental and constitutive in one's makeup as to have assumed the role of father.   But it is a difference in degree only.   None of us holds just one role in life.   Each of us, considered as a human being involved in social interaction and belonging to one or more social aggregates, is a constellation of social roles.   Sometimes our several roles fit harmoniously and in a more or less integrated structure within our personalities. At other times we find ourselves involved in what is called role strain and role conflict.   The demands of one role may exact toll from other roles, which leads to agitation of mind and occasionally to deep-seated personality disorders.   Roles are indispensable in the process we commonly call "growing up."   Whether we grow up in healthy and effective fashion or whether we find ourselves—in Paul Goodman's matchless phrase—"growing up absurd" is in large measure the consequence of our relationship to social roles, our ability or inability, our desire or our lack of desire, to assume these roles in normal social interaction.

Social status

Here we are brought face to face with the universal fact of *hierarchy*. "Stratification" is the word which sociologists most commonly apply to the phenomenon; but under either term, what is crucial is the *unequal ranking* of human beings, social aggregates, social roles, systems of authority, and social norms. No society has ever existed, nor in all probability ever could exist, without inequality. But societies and social groups vary enormously in amount of inequality, in the types of inequality permitted, and in the degree to which inequalities are ascribed or achieved. Plainly, there are relatively equalitarian societies and relatively inequalitarian societies. And one would be foolish indeed to rob the Western ideal of equality of all meaning. But this said, the indubitable fact remains that every social aggregate, whether it be the nation, a university, a totemistic clan, or a labor union, ranks its members differently in their varied roles. The services and functions of a social order are also ranked unequally—that is, in a stratified or hierarchical way. When we refer to social roles we *may* (or may not) be visualizing them in any measure of vertical relation. It is possible to refer to the role of professor without automatically implying anything with respect to the position of professor in any hierarchical distribution of roles. But when we refer to the *status* of professor, we summon up instantly a context of higher and lower—that is, of vertical distance. It is difficult if not impossible to refer to the status of a person or a function or a role without prefacing it explicitly or implicitly with the words "high" or "low." We may think of status in the discrete sense of a given role occupied by an individual in a hierarchical order of such roles in a social organization. Or we may think of status in the more generic and classificatory sense of system of hierarchy or stratification that is to be found in human society. There are innumerable complexities about status, some of which we shall seek to resolve in Chapter 8. It is sufficient at this point merely to be aware that status, in the sense defined here briefly, is a vital and indispensable aspect of the social bond.

Social norms

Basic to social interaction in whatever degree of intensity, and basic also to every type of social aggregate, system of authority, social role, and social status, is the *norm* or *value* that gives it meaning and orientation. When we speak of norms we have reference to a dimension of human existence we have not yet reviewed. This is the vital and dis-

tinctively human realm of the "should" or "ought." In an earlier section
we noted that the human being does not ever really confront the natural
order face to face. His approach to the natural or factual order is always mediated by the normative order, by that order which is composed
of the values, symbols, and norms which reflect the myriad rules, regulations, disciplines, "oughts," and "shoulds" that the human being has
been exposed to from the moment he was born. Norms quite literally
cover every aspect of human life. They are by no means limited to the
area we conventionally term the "moral"—that is, the area of conduct
relating to honesty, virtue, chastity, and so on. All systems of thought,
behavior, belief, and organization are built around culturally acquired
norms. Science and technology both are and contain norms. Objectivity is as much a norm as is discrimination; respect for the individual,
as much as is cannibalism. Norms are the culturally acquired ends or
guideposts of social interaction and social order. Probably the greatest
single difference between the social organizations of the "lower" orders
of life such as ants, bees, and chimpanzees and the social organization of
man is that the latter alone is oriented to norms rather than to basal,
biologically inherited needs and drives. Not one of the concepts we have
thus far dealt with in this chapter is fully comprehensible save in terms
of its relation to norms. Human behavior is overwhelmingly *normative*
behavior, normative in the strict sense that it is not primarily directed to,
or even actuated by, the physical or biological or "natural"—to use a
word here once cherished in philosophical discussions of morality. Instead, human behavior is governed by those symbols, values, and norms
which we acquire as members of the social order *through social interaction*.

Social entropy

The last of the essential components of the social bond is what I
have chosen, for lack of a better word, to call "entropy." In modern
thermodynamics this word has a very precise meaning. It is defined as
the amount of energy unavailable for work during a natural process.
Social philosophers, such as Henry Adams and his brother Brooks, have
occasionally used the word to suggest the tendency of all civilizations
to decline or to run down in the kind of human energies required to
keep civilizations vital and durable. I shall use the word here in a somewhat different sense, though one that draws from both the technical
meaning it has in physics and the more metaphoric meaning that Henry
and Brooks Adams gave it.

By "social entropy" I refer to processes of behavior which are endemic in all forms of human association in at least slight degree and which have a "negative" quality that arises from their being in opposition to the norms, roles, and authorities making up a social order. The major types of social entropy are *alienation*, in which we see a kind of withdrawal of human energy from the roles, statuses, and norms of the social order; *anomie*, characterized by conflict of socially accepted norms in an individual; and *deviance*, in which more or less conscious opposition to the roles, statuses, and norms of society is to be seen. There is overlap among the three terms, as we shall see, but their conceptual distinction is nevertheless important. What we shall call "social entropy," in its three principal forms, is often characterized by such words as "antisocial," "immoral," "disorganized," or "pathological." The chief difficulty with these words, however, is that they leave the impression of the exceptionality, even abnormality, of the processes involved. In fact, these processes are as socially constitutive in their way as are processes of opposite character. Above all, in whatever degree, they are universal in human society.

It would be a serious mistake to think of any of the above elements of the social bond as a mere specimen, so to speak, in a sociological showcase. Each of them is and should be constantly regarded by the reader as a means of illumination of the social scene. As I stressed in the first chapter, the fundamental concepts of sociology form its essential and lasting method. The method of sociology is to approach the world of human behavior through such concepts as social interaction, social roles, or social statuses. We may invoke all kinds of ancillary techniques: statistical, experimental, comparative-observational, mathematical, and so on. Each of these, in proper place, can be a valuable, even indispensable, assist to the method of sociology. But the method, I repeat, lies in the fundamental concepts, each of which is a source of understanding of human behavior. To see a given incident in the community— a black-white confrontation, for example—in terms of such vital elements as social interaction, social norms, and social authority is, at one and the same time, to employ a *method* in reaching an understanding of the incident, a method and an understanding that would not be available were we to seek to explain the incident simply in the terms of physiology or geography.

One other point must be stressed. The elements of the social bond that we are about to examine are far from being static and fully understood. Instead, these elements constitute a very dynamic sphere of constantly ongoing research in contemporary sociology. That we already know much about the nature of the social bond is true enough. One need but open any recent issue of a standard sociological journal, however, to become aware of how central each of our elements of the social bond is to scientific research. Similarly, each of the elements is a recognizable aspect of the life around us. Just as the student of linguistics studies in depth a language he has spoken all his life, so does the student of sociology find himself studying—in such concepts as social interaction, social roles, and social entropy—areas of experience in which he has been involved all his life.

Notes

1. A. R. Radcliffe-Brown, *A Natural Science of Society* (New York: Free Press, 1957), p. 49. (First published by the University of Chicago Press, 1948.)
2. *Ibid.*, p. 50.
3. Emile Durkheim, *The Elementary Forms of Religious Life*, trans. by Joseph Ward Swain (London: Allen & Unwin, 1915), p. 347.
4. George Homans, *Social Behavior: Its Elementary Forms* (New York: Harcourt, Brace & World, 1961), p. 114.

4

Social Interaction

SYMBOLIC INTERACTION

In our detailed inquiry into the nature of the social bond, we begin with what is from any strictly behavioral point of view the most fundamental of all the elements and forces of the social bond—symbolic interaction. Apart from the possibility of interaction among human beings that is maintained through symbols in contrast to mere direct emotions and acts, there could not possibly be either culture or a social order as we understand these. Only through man's capacity for interaction with other human beings that is, at one and the same time, possessed of *meaning*—meaning that may, in effect, be stored away for future recall and use—and *anticipation of intent* is it possible for the immensely complicated structures of human society to come into existence and to remain from generation to generation. The behavior—which we often call "social"—of lower orders of the biological world (ants and bees, for example) is biologically fixed and is not varied through processes of social interaction, symbolic or other. But man's behavior is inseparable from his capacity for symbolic and social interaction.

By *social* interaction we mean something very distinctive. Social interaction is not the same as physical or human interaction. There are many encounters in our life that are not social, as we shall use this term in the present chapter. For one person in a crowd to bump into another by sheer accident is no doubt a form of interaction. As we noted in the preceding chapter, the relation between the auto worker in Detroit and the wheat grower in Argentina, in which each may be dependent upon what the other produces, is also a form of interaction. But neither of these is a process of *social* interaction in the strict sense demanded by sociology.

The essence of social interaction lies in the very nature of social action, strictly defined. Let us use the definition of social action given by Max Weber: "Action is social in so far as, by virtue of the subjective meaning attached to it by the acting individual (or individuals), it takes account of the behavior of others and is thereby oriented in its course."[1] The crucial words in Weber's famous definition are "subjective meaning." Much human behavior is not by any means social in the sense of its being possessed of "subjective meaning." Behavior may be purely random, elicited by some passing stimulus that is devoid of the significance required in the social act. It may be no more than a more or less mechanical response to physical pressure or some other kind of disturbance.

Actions and interactions become social only when the element of subjective meaning is present, only when in addition to the mere mechanical act there is present a sense, however dim and fleeting, of the *meaning* of the act to the person or persons primarily involved. Herbert Blumer, who has dealt most perceptively with the nature of social interaction and its importance to the social bond, gets us off to an excellent start here with his insistence: "Human society is to be seen as consisting of acting people, and the life of the society is to be seen as consisting of their actions." Bear in mind that the acting units may be concrete human beings in physical separateness, aggregates whose members are purposefully acting in concert in a given objective, or organizations acting in behalf of others. Fundamentally, Blumer goes on to stress, group action is a fitting together of individual lines of action. "Each individual aligns his action to the action of others by ascertaining what they are doing or what they intend to do—*by getting the meaning of their acts.*"[2] (Italics added.)

The vital and indispensable part of the foregoing is, of course, *meaning*. It is this that has led Blumer, following George Herbert Mead, to deal with social interaction as *symbolic* interaction. Social acts are mediated by symbols, symbols which we possess in common with others. The most obvious and important form of symbol is language. It is language, spoken and written, above any other symbolic element that makes human culture possible. And it is language alone that makes possible the development of the human mind, the sense of self, the consciousness of personal identity, and that very fundamental capacity, unique in mankind, of being able to adopt one or more of the social roles that confront each newborn infant in human society. Verbal language is by far the most important of all forms of symbolic communication, but it is not the only form. Music, painting, sculpture, and physical mannerisms such as the raising of an eyebrow or the shrug of a shoulder, the whole of what has well been called "silent language," are also modes of symbolic interaction.

The importance of symbolic communication or interaction to human learning and culture is perhaps obvious enough. It is only because of the existence of more or less fixed symbols for things, ideas, values, thoughts, and sentiments that it becomes possible for man to live other than by native physiological and psychological resources. Culture is, in the classic definition of the nineteenth-century English anthropologist Edward B. Tylor, "that complex whole which includes knowledge, belief, art, morals, law, custom, and any other capabilities *acquired by man as a member of society.*" (Italics added.) So dependent is the ordinary human being upon his cultural (as distinguished from his physiological) heritage, that if by some unimaginable catastrophe the human race were to be suddenly cut off from all that is cultural, all that had been learned, accumulated, and, as it were, stored through symbolic communication, the vast majority of us would be dead within a matter of days or weeks. It is no denial of the essential role in human life of biological reflexes, instincts, and drives to say that man lives, uniquely lives, through the learned and accumulated ways of thought and behavior which in their entirety form culture. And at bottom culture is rooted by and inseparable from what we call symbolic interaction: the interaction of human beings in terms of symbols with shared meanings.

But the importance of symbolic interaction goes beyond culture. It is easy to think of culture as something external to the human mind, for no infant possesses it at birth. The whole experience of growing up is essentially the assimilation and internalization of values, ideas, techniques, and ways of behavior that are already in existence when each of us comes into the world. But we must think of symbolic interaction as forming the very stuff of human personality, character, self, and identity. Only through communication in terms of shared symbols is it possible for each of us to acquire his sense of self, character, and identity.

The seventeenth-century philosopher Descartes thought that each human being is born with the sense of self, with the feeling of "I am I." From this, Descartes concluded, man works his way intellectually and socially to awareness of the rest of the world and society. In fact, however, as the great pioneers in the study of symbolic interaction, G. H. Mead and Charles H. Cooley, both stressed, Descartes actually had the matter backward. Each of us acquires his sense of subjective being, of "I am I" first from observation of, and then assimilation of, *the identities of others around us.* The self, as both Mead and Cooley stressed in their seminal writings, is not something the individual is born with, not something that emerges, as do, for example, his secondary sexual characteristics, from organic growth alone. Above all the self is not something that can be located within the discrete human body. The self, individuality, the distinctively human sense of "I-ness," is inseparable from the process of symbolic interaction which begins from the moment the infant first becomes aware of the identities and actions of others around him who are addressing their attentions to him.

Cooley used the vivid phrase "looking-glass self" to describe the process through which, by close personal interaction with others, we gradually acquire a sense of self by what we see reflected in the answering words, gestures, and responses of others. The "other" will at first be the mother, or whoever ministers most directly and constantly to the infant's needs and wants. In time additional "others" will become important to the child—sibling, father, teacher, and so on. And finally, as Mead put the matter in his great work on the self, each of us becomes aware of a kind of "generalized other," that is, society at large. We acquire our sense of self, in short, in virtually parallel fashion with our sense of "otherness."

Fundamental in the mechanism of symbolic interaction is the process of role taking. We shall have much more to say about this vital matter in Chapter 7. It is enough to note here that were it not for the infant's gradually acquired capacity for assuming—for "playing at"—the roles of mother, father, and each of the others with whom he is in frequent association in the primary group of which he is a part, his sense of self would be nonexistent, as nonexistent as would be his sense of society.

There is nothing mechanical or one-sided about acquiring a sense of self. It is not a simple matter of the social order forcing, conditioning, and shaping, as certain rather mechanistic theories have it. It is, from the very beginning, an interactive process, one in which the individual projects himself into the surrounding scene, affecting those in the very process of projection who also affect him. We should not think of a passive, absorptive, and malleable human being on the one hand and, on the other, a social order or culture that does the imprinting and shaping. The process is always interactive, that is, *symbolically* interactive. For, as we have seen, the very essence of human interaction is that it takes place in terms of symbols—the symbols which are the dynamic elements of culture.

Apart from symbolic interaction, the very conception of the human self is impossible. Nothing is more distinctively human than consciousness of self. As Cooley explained, there are three fundamental elements in the self, all of them social in the sense that they are derived from interaction. The first element is the imagining of our appearance to other persons—at first members of the family, then playmates and companions, and, finally, that vague but powerful sense of the social order as a whole. The second element in the self is the imagination of others' *judgment* of our appearance: approval or disapproval, admiration or contempt, like or dislike. And third, following almost instantaneously from these two elements, is our reaction—pride, confidence, poise, shame, insecurity, awkwardness. One's conception of self is something that develops slowly, always in the context of symbolic interaction, and it is as the result of difficulties or impediments in this process of symbolic interaction that in some persons the sense of self, of identity, can be weak or wavering.

We also owe to symbolic interaction the uniquely human faculty of being able to get outside ourselves, so to speak, to see ourselves as objects in much the same way we see others around us. As Mead emphasized, the self is both subjective and objective. The subjective "I" is able to deal with the objective "Me." This capacity, itself nurtured by interaction with others, is, above anything else, at the core of what we commonly call conscience. That a person can know the sense of shame, guilt, abasement, remorse (and who does not at some points in his life?) means no more in terms of symoblic interaction than that he has acquired the ability to see himself in the objective, examining, censuring terms that he first knew in interactive situations with other persons. They examined, judged, and then censured or praised him; he did the same with them. In time, with the development of the self, the process becomes an internal, reflexive one. The roles of others whom the person encounters, the roles he finds himself on occasion assuming—borrowing, we might say—and the roles he imagines himself occupying, whether exalted or ignominious, are all crucial to the development of the self, of that "I am I" feeling that was once thought to be a very part of one's germ plasm and then, later, thought to be something merely stamped on an individual by the social order.

The final point to make about symbolic interaction as a mechanism in society is that in a very real sense it separates us from the purely

factual or empirical order of things. Here W. I. Thomas' phrase, "definition of the situation," will be useful. We never react to our environment or to other persons in a strictly mechanical way, in an unmediated
way. No matter what the object in front of us—another human being,
a flag, a piece of wood, a gun, or a mountain—we see it as part of a
situation that is inseparable from what we, as human beings, bring to
the external object. It is, in fact, not really external at all. For, from
the moment of confrontation, we have already begun defining it *and
hence seeing it* in ways which are bound up with the symbols and norms
that are already in our minds. A hostile encounter between a black
and a white is not even *seen* the same way by a Black Panther and a
white supremacist. How one reacts, what one does, what one really
sees, are all bound up with a "definition of the situation" which involves
norm, symbol, and role. Two members of the same primary group or
culture are more likely to define or otherwise give meaning and structure
to a situation in the same way than are two individuals drawn from different groups or cultures. When we discuss social aggregates, we shall
see how indispensable to the individual's "definition of the situation" is
the complex of ties and the particular set of norms which form the
aggregate that may have, for this particular situation at least, dominating significance. Again let us emphasize that the impact of the group
on the life of the individual is never a purely one-sided, mechanical, and
necessarily coercive influence. Let us keep in mind Durkheim's words
that "society exists and lives only in and through individuals." The
very essence of group life, however external and coercive it may sometimes seem to the individual in his moments of subjective withdrawnness
or alienation, is interactive.

     The really crucial and decisive processes of symbolic-interactive be-
havior occur in infancy and childhood when the human self is being
formed through these processes. It would be a major error, however,
to forget that symbolic interaction continues throughout the individual's
life. What we find is that this interaction becomes ever more complex,
ever more fraught with meanings of an increasingly subtle type, ever
more charged with symbols that have been drawn from widening and
diversifying areas of experience. Symbolic interaction, considered as
a concept for illumination of human behavior, remains as useful in the
understanding of the behavior of adults in their developed and multifold roles and statuses, or of adult groups and organizations, as it does
in the understanding of infants, children, and adolescents. For through
symbolic interaction the sense of self and the sense of the generalized

other come first into being, and through this kind of interaction, both senses are maintained and reinforced.

TYPES OF INTERACTION

From a purely empirical point of view there are doubtless as many types of interaction as there are interactive encounters among human beings. No one of these encounters, obviously, is exactly like another. But, as we saw in the first chapter, uniqueness of direct experience does not prevent us from perceiving experience in terms of general categories and types. Thus, however unique each manifestation of exchange or conflict may be, there is clearly more in common among manifestations of exchange than there is between those of exchange and those of conflict. Five modes or types of social interaction are probably the most basic and universal ones: *exchange, cooperation, conformity, coercion,* and *conflict.* Each is worth careful examination.

Exchange

This is the process in which one person or group acts for the express purpose of receiving a reward. For a long time exchange was considered almost exclusively an economic process. But, as such contemporary sociologists as George Homans and Peter Blau, and before them Simmel, have made evident, exchange is in fact a part of the social bond. Even in the smallest and most intimate of social relationships—the relationship, for example, of close friends or lovers—we find the exchange principle not infrequently at work. This is not to say that one person loves another merely to receive the other person's love. Such a characterization would be hedonistic psychology carried to a ludicrous degree. Rather, even granting the irreducible ties of love or friendship in a relationship, there are nevertheless times when the act of one member is predicated upon his confidence that from that act there will flow a reward —in the form of some desired expression of love, gratitude, or simple recognition.

Exchange is found among groups as vast as modern nations or ancient empires and as small as elemental dyads. And exchange among larger groups, economic exchange or exchange of any other type, is not confined to modern peoples. Among many preliterate peoples there exists a mode of exchange known as "silent trade." It is a means whereby two separated tribes or communities, each jealous of its own cultural identity and fearful lest open trade between the two groups result in an intermingling of individuals that would lead to corruption of their respective customs, nonetheless effect exchange of goods. Some common, equidistant point, long since agreed upon by the two tribes, is the scene of the exchange. On a particular day one of the tribes goes to the agreed-upon place, leaves its goods, and then returns to its home. The next day the other tribe goes to the same place, picks up what has been left for it, leaves in turn what it contributes to the exchange, and departs. On the third day the first tribe goes back to the scene and gets what has been left for it by way of exchange. Obviously, at some earlier time, a direct means had to be worked out for exchange of this type, but once established, it could thenceforth be, as the ethnographer's phrase has it, "silent trade."

Our concern in this section is not, however, with exchange in the obvious sense of economic or other types of trade. Rather, our concern is with the subtler, more microscopic, types of exchange that are to be found in the interactive process among individuals, especially in small groups. It is here that contemporary sociology is finding one of its richest fields of study in the larger enterprise that is the exploration of the social bond. Let us keep constantly in mind that our task in this chapter, and indeed in this entire section of the book, is illumination of those elements that are crucial to the social bond. Exchange is one of these vital elements.

Although recognition of and insight into exchange is very old in social thought, we are primarily indebted to Georg Simmel for its contemporary place in the study of social interaction. The works of Blau, Homans, and others now working intensively in this area are in very large degree built upon Simmel's pioneering observations on the role of gratitude in human interaction, and on the function of exchange in effecting gratitude. Gratitude, as Simmel expresses the matter, is a *subjective* counterpart of the kind of exchange among two or more individuals which we find *objectified* commonly in goods and money. Exchange, Simmel points out, is the objectification of social interaction when its units are substantive and more or less measurable.

Gratitude originates, Simmel continues, *from* interaction and *in* interaction, specifically the type of interaction we call exchange. But in gratitude we have *subjectified* exchange, or rather the subjectified product of exchange, instead of the objectified kind to be found in the more tangible forms of goods. Simmel defines gratitude as the sentiment which, for inner reasons, effects the return of a benefit where there is no external necessity for it. For example, I may find myself in a dangerous or ticklish situation; another person stops long enough to help me out of it. In an objectified form of exchange I should pay him with goods or money. In the more likely subjectified mode, however, my end of the "exchange" consists of the gratitude I experience, convey to my good samaritan, and, in a very real sense, store up in my own consciousness. Did the good samaritan come to my rescue because of his desire for gratitude? Such an ascription would be too simple. But were I to reward his assistance to me with chilly indifference or hostility a vital exchange relationship would have been ruptured. My ingratitude would be exchange, no doubt, but of a sort not likely to aid the social bond.

"All external and internal motives that bind individuals together may be examined with respect to their implementation of the exchange which not only holds society together once it is formed but, in large measure, forms it."[3] Simmel's words are by no means limited in their validity to those simple and immediate modes of exchange which we see in direct forms of social interaction. As he notes, much of what we call "higher culture" consists of the exchange between the gifted artist or scientist and the rest of us who, although not acquainted with the particular artist or scientist, nevertheless respond with a gratitude that is inseparable from our admiration or appreciation.

Nor is exchange limited to what someone *does* with answering gratitude. The feeling with which we sometimes respond to the mere existence of another person can, Simmel thought, be thought of quite properly as gratitude. "We are grateful to him because he exists, because we experience him. Often the subtlest as well as the firmest of bonds among men develop from this feeling."[4]

In sum, there is no opposition between social exchange and even the closest and most loving of relationships between two people or between social exchange and feelings of profoundest admiration, respect, and gratitude. Every relationship, however intimate it may be, however deep its roots in passion, in love, or in friendship, has its aspects of exchange, with the act of one person predicated upon expectation of reward from the other.

Exchange by no means limits itself to relationships of the sort I have just been describing. As Peter Blau has stressed, a paradox of social exchange is that it can establish not only bonds of friendship among peers but create status differences as well. Nowhere in the European social order was this more evident than during the long period of feudalism, the very essence of which was exchange and, at one and the same time, of profound status inequality. Feudalism was a complex network of exchange relationships among individuals belonging to very unequal strata in society. Whether it was the manorial lord promising protection to the serf in return for a share of his crops or the deeply ritualized oaths of great barons promising aid to one another in the event of attack, the exchange relationship was fundamental.

This analysis suggests the relation between exchange and differentiation of power in society. A person who gives things or services to another person that cannot possibly be reciprocated in value places himself not merely in a superior status position but, assuming gifts and services continue to be accepted by the second person, in a position of power. As Blau points out, a person who has control of services that others need or desire and cannot get on their own, and moreover who is himself in no need or want of any services or things they can give is without competition with regard to his services and is plainly in a position of power. For here exchange consists or could consist in the utmost compliance or obedience by those receiving the services.

Such an exchange relationship can and frequently does generate disaffection. Montesquieu once said: "I cannot understand why that man dislikes me so; I have never done anything for him." Among peers or among citizens in general in a society where the ethos of equality is strong, one-sided and unequal relationships of exchange produce tensions and can lead to sheer hatred on the part of the beneficiary. And this is almost wholly the result of the power that lies in, or is implicitly claimed by, exchange relationships where there is no clear mutuality or equality.

But whether productive of friendship and love or resentment and hate, the exchange mechanism is one of the most important among all the elements that go into the social bond. Most obvious and visible in the larger forms of economic exchange and legal contract, the exchange mechanisms is just as important, just as vital, within the small and intensely personal relationships of human beings.

Cooperation

Second among the crucial elements of social interaction is cooperation. We may define this as joint or collaborative behavior toward some goal in which there is common interest. It may be spontaneous or directed, voluntary or involuntary, formal or informal, large or small.

As with other modes of interaction, I must emphasize that we are concerned solely with *social* cooperation, which, in accord with what we have called symbolic interaction, involves reciprocity of intent, capacity for taking the role of others, and behavior that is in response to what others expect either directly or through norms.

Cooperation, like exchange and other forms of interaction, has its analogues in the physical world. One may speak of the "cooperation" of the tree that provides shade for the shrubs at its roots and of the shrubs which help to conserve moisture for the tree. There are similarly, even in the human world, forms of conjoint aid in which one set of people who concentrate on food getting "cooperate" with those who concentrate upon shelter building, or in which one people who grow wheat "cooperate" with others at a great distance who manufacture iron products, each needing the other's product. Cooperation so described exists between great nations, as in an organization such as NATO, between large industries in the form of cartels, between small groups, as when families in an agricultural area cooperate to bring needed water into the area for irrigation of crops; and, of course, cooperation exists between individuals when there is some object or goal desired by each but unattainable save through joint activity.

We properly distinguish between cooperation and competition. The latter is evident when the same goal or object is desired by several individuals or several groups and where, instead of a uniting of the desires into a single joint or cooperative effort, each individual or each group goes after the object or goal through his or its own efforts alone and in rivalry with the others. Thus in a learning situation in the schoolroom the teacher may present a problem of some kind leaving the pupils to compete with one another in reaching the answer. Or, by contrast, the teacher may present the same problem but suggest instead that the students pool their talents and energies in reaching the answer.

It is easy to distinguish between cooperation and competition, but in terms of actual social situations we rarely find one wholly without the other. Indeed cooperation and competition may have an actual contributory relation to one another. Competition requires at least the degree of prior cooperation that is necessary for the setting of rules and imposing of sanctions without which competition would burst into unorganized conflict or war. I shall have more to say about competition as an element of social interaction under our next heading, which is *conflict*. For the moment it is important only to make clear that however distinguishable cooperation is from competition and conflict, in practice it is rarely separated from these two interactive processes. We are even justified in referring to *competitive cooperation* in which individuals or groups associate and cooperate in laying down conditions without which each would fail. But, within these agreed-upon conditions, there is competition for rewards.

There are several main types of cooperation, and four of these require identification here. First, there is *spontaneous* cooperation, undoubtedly the oldest, most natural, and widespread of all types. Unprescribed by tradition, norm, or command, spontaneous cooperation is situational in character and is found wherever there are reasonably close forms of association among human beings. Everything we know about cooperation indicates that it is most likely to be found as a mode of spontaneous interaction where there is a prior basis of amity or congeniality. Spontaneous cooperation is universal and timeless as far as mankind is concerned, and is to be found, of course, not merely in small, face-to-face groups but within even the most formal and bureaucratized of organizations. Its real nature is its essentially unpremeditated, unplanned, and undirected character.

A second type of cooperation is *directed*. Here the same jointness of behavior toward some common goal is involved but the cooperation is not spontaneous, not the simple outcome of a suddenly manifest situation involving two or more persons but rather the result of direction from above. A great deal of modern large-scale organization is unintelligible except in terms of cooperative behavior at all levels that has been planned in advance and requires constant leadership for its effectiveness. Military organization is probably the oldest and most universal type of directed cooperation, but in modern society military organization is rivaled by a host of organizations—political, economic, religious, educational, recreational—in all of which, direction of cooperation is fundamental.

A third type of cooperation is *contractual*. In this case terms of interaction are specific and conditional upon the will of the participants or governed by legal sanctions. Such cooperation is precise both in terms of the length of the relationship and of what is specifically required by it. Contractual cooperation may be directed or undirected, but it is not, cannot by its nature be, spontaneous. Contractual cooperation is invariably the result of forethought, of planning, and of prior delegation of responsibility and function, the whole made detailed and determining. In modern industrial society a vast amount of cooperation is contractual. Contractual cooperation commonly increases in historical periods during which the close ties of community are supplanted by the more individualistic and utilitarian ties of open society. We are most likely to think of contractual cooperation in terms of such large-scale entities as economic cooperatives, credit unions, and profit-sharing plans, but we should not overlook the rich profusion of that more informal type of contractual cooperation that is to be found in such customs as baby-sitting and car-pools. These and their many analogues make clear that grass-roots contractualism is far from dead in modern society.

Fourth and last is what we call *traditional* cooperation. It is regulated neither by instinct, volition, nor legal norm; except in the most incidental sense, it cannot be said to be directed; and it is anything but spontaneous. It is an ingrained part of the mores, of immemorial custom, of convention. Prime examples of traditional cooperation are the joint family of India, the Chinese clan, the village community of medieval Europe and of much of contemporary Asia, and craft and merchant guilds the world over. The Hindu family—"joint in food, worship, and estate" —is an excellent example of a cooperative relationship that is under no contractual sanction, no mode of direction from above. Where it is still intact, however, it is as binding a form of interaction as any to be found in the world. In this case the family is conceived indeed as a cooperative relation among the dead, the living, and the unborn. Mutual aid is the most exalted possible ethic in such a traditional relationship. The same is true with respect to the agricultural village community, by all odds the most universal mode of agricultural endeavor in the history of mankind. Here such matters as the planting, cultivation, and harvesting of crops are dealt with cooperatively by the villagers. The depth and extent of the cooperativeness involved are frequently to be seen in the way the fields are laid out. They are in the form of strips of cultivable land, with any of one family's number of strips spread out and mingled with those of other families. Such cooperation is traditional.

Conformity

No social organization, no culture, no form of institutionalized relationship whatever could exist without the process of interaction we call conformity. From it come all the uniformities which provide the sinews of human society. Fundamental to conformity is the norm or value to which the human being adapts his behavior (thus, as we say, conforming). It is common and easy in ordinary discourse to refer to some persons as "conformist" and others as "nonconformist." There are indeed differences along this line, but they are minor by comparison with the overall reality that everyone conforms at any given moment to something—to some value or norm, however variant the value or norm may be with respect to the generalized consensus around him. In the next chapter we shall be concerned with the phenomenon known as the "reference group." For the moment we shall note merely that any individual may be nonconformist by the standards of the group most immediately evident to the outsider's observation. Yet, at the same time, the individual maybe highly conformist with respect to that group —however distant in space and time it may be—to which he is prone to "refer" his actions for judgment (including self-judgment). It is the distant group whose symbols are most imperative in that individual's consciousness.

Much of the behavior that an older generation of sociologists, including Tarde, categorized as *imitation* proves to be more comprehensible when it is regarded as a manifestation of the type of social interaction we call *conformity*. The reason for this is that conformity, as a concept, directs attention more simply and precisely to the group character of social behavior than does the concept of imitation which rests—and nowhere more clearly than in Tarde's own work—on an implicit denial of the centrality of the group.

The classic experiments of such social psychologists as Muzafer Sherif and Solomon Asch in recent times have taught us not only about the mechanisms of conformity generally but about the crucial role of social interaction, and specifically the group nature of this interaction. From these experiments it is plain enough today that a good many individual perceptions, evaluations, and modes of consciousness are in fact largely the result of the operation of another element in the situation—the subject person's dependence upon, his conformity to, the perceptions, evaluations, and modes of consciousness of *others around him*, or others to whom he relates in some manner. What Sherif and Asch were able to demonstrate with respect to perceptions and distortions of perceptions involving a person's relations to physical objects naturally takes on even greater cogency when we consider the social, cultural, and moral symbols to which human beings react. Sherif's and Asch's experiments reveal, with pinpoint accuracy, the *continuing* dependence of human perceptions of objects upon those processes of interaction that we epitomize in the word "conformity." It is clear that when we are thinking, not of suddenly arranged experimental groups but those groups and symbols which occupy long and persisting influence in the individual's life, the mechanism of conformity assumes all the greater significance.

Conformity, in sum, is simply our way of conceptualizing in sociology one of the most universal and timeless of all processes of social interaction—the process by which the individual adapts his behavior, adapts *himself*, to some norm that is preexistent to the situation and does this in ways in which the influence of the social group is either manifestly or latently evident. No doubt conformity as a process could, through what I have called reductionist analysis, be made to be simply a manifestation of some other, more-encompassing process or mechanism. Some might say it is no more than a manifestation of symbolic interaction generally; and so it is. Others might see in conformity a mode of interaction governed primarily by considerations of exchange. By conforming we receive a reward: approval, esteem, success. Still others might wish to reduce the process of conforming to coercion, which is the element of social interaction we shall examine next. We conform, it may be said, because we are coerced by the group or by the norms around us. Such reasoning is generally plausible, but it is to be as much disregarded as are all other efforts at reductionism where, in the process of the reduction, what is vital and distinctive in the process to be explained becomes lost. Let us grant that there may be interrelations of exchange or cooperation with conformity at any given moment. The process itself is nevertheless a distinguishable one among the several processes of social interaction and must be considered as such.

In conclusion, let us note again the fact that not all human beings have like tendencies toward conformity. There is, on the evidence— experimental and historical—reason for regarding some personalities as more easily given to conformity, irrespective of what the norm is, than other personalities. There are all manner of variations of intensity of conformity. But conformity is itself one of the universal modes of social interaction, and it is safe to say that literally no one is exempt, or could possibly be exempt, from its manifestations.

Coercion

Here we have reference to modes of interaction which rest ultimately on compulsion, often, though not necessarily, with the threat of force behind such compulsion. At first thought, coercion may not seem to be a form of *inter*action but rather of action that is unilateral. We are prone to think of coercion from the point of view of a force or compulsion from the coercer—the person, organization, or code that "does the coercing."

But no matter how external or one-sided coercion may appear, it is, in the first place, inseparable from the person or group that is being coerced. But of more central importance is the fact that what the coercer does is in some part conditioned by what he expects the effect of coercion

to be on the one coerced. Similarly, the response of the coerced is in
some degree conditioned by the effect he expects it to have on the person
doing the coercing. Even in the most extreme case of coercion—domination of a slave by his master—there is, as Simmel has told us, still
an inescapable element of association that robs the domination of the
unilateral character we ordinarily ascribe to it. The element of association given to the relationship by the one dominated may, of course, be
self-abasement, groveling, or some form of fawning or self-ingratiation
into the mercies of the master. An element of association is still involved, and the relationship, for all the power possessed by the master,
is one of social interaction.

As Simmel points out, nobody, generally speaking, desires that his
influence completely determine the fate of another individual, as such
influence might determine, for instance, the shape of a piece of wood
that one is carving. "He rather wants this influence, this determination
of the other, to act back upon *him*. Even the abstract will-to-dominate,
therefore, is a case of interaction. This will draws its satisfaction from
the fact that the acting or suffering of the other, his positive or negative
condition, offers itself to the dominator as the product of *his* will." [5]

One may coerce himself. It is the peculiar character of the human
self, as we have already seen, that it can be at one and the same time
subject and object: "I" and "me." The symbolic interaction that is
the indispensable context of the formation and consciousness of self contains mechanisms of coercion as well as the others we have looked at.
What we call "will power" is a form of coercion in which subject and
object are one and the same person. In these terms, coercion can be seen
as a form of mental or spiritual exercise, as when one tests himself by
denying himself some value or by imposing upon himself some unde-
sired value. The history of abstinence, of asceticism, and of self-morti-
fication in religion is a history, of course, of forms of self-coercion.
Some of these forms (from a conventional point of view) are very bizarre indeed.

It would be difficult to find a relationship in social behavior that is
by its nature free altogether of coercion, or at least of the possibility
of coercion. For there are numerous ways in which coercion manifests
itself in social interaction. Force, in the physical sense of the word, is
by no means the invariable way of giving sanction to coercion. Coercion
may be imposed when the penalty for failure to obey is ridicule, ostracism, excommunication, denial of love or protection, the withholding of
recognition. There is the coercion of parental and filial love, of a religious community, of the school, of a value that one believes in but on

occasion finds uncongenial to immediate desire, and so on. Thoreau's civil disobedience and the nonviolent techniques of Gandhi or Martin Luther King were, as the record shows, important forms of coercion. What is alone essential to coercion as a form of social interaction is the fact of domination, of compulsion.

Few persons enjoy the consciousness of naked coercion. Throughout the history of human philosophy much ingenuity has gone into forms of legitimation of coercion or of rationalization. We shall have occasion to see some of these in Chapter 6, where we discuss authority. The coercive power of the absolute state was rationalized at one time through the idea of some primordial social contract by which people exchanged their freedom and insecurity for the protection that an absolute rule could give. Thomas Hobbes, in the seventeenth century, was so enamoured of the idea of contract as a means of legitimating power that he even applied it to the family. The father's coercive power over the child, Hobbes declared, rested upon a tacit contract between child and parent in which obedience from the one was granted in return for the knowledge and security possessed by the other.

There is no question that other forms of social interaction—exchange, cooperation, conformity—permeate the types of coercion we find around us. But coercion is, nevertheless, as distinct and irreducible a form of social interaction as is any of the others we have seen. However mixed it may become with other relationships, however it may be justified, coercion, in the sense of superordination and subordination, is a universal reality in social behavior.

Nor, in all probability, could we live without it, or even wish to live without it. That sense of "ought," which we have seen to be one of the distinctive products of symbolic interaction, is clearly a form of coercion in itself and the consequence of interactive coercion in the lives of human beings. The child acquires his sense of the "oughtness" of certain things only from the repeated experience of coercion, whether negative or positive. Gradually one reaches the sense of oughtness about such matters as civility to others, respect for privacy, respect for property, and the numberless other elements of what we call morality. But to reach this sense of self-coercion implicit in the word "ought," we are obliged to go through innumerable experiences of coercion in which domination from the outside is crucial. It was this aspect that led Durkheim to declare that the single most vital element of morality is coercion: first, the coercion of the group over the individual, then the absorbed, internalized coercion that is but another way of referring to what we call conscience.

Simmel writes: "Occasionally the consciousness of being under coercion, of being subject to a superordinate authority, is revolting or oppressive—whether the authority be an ideal or a social law, an arbitrarily-decreeing personality or the executor of higher norms. But for the majority of men, coercion is probably an irreplaceable support and cohesion of the inner and outer life." [6]

There is, in short, a functional importance to coercion in the development of human personality just as there is in the other mechanisms we have examined—exchange, conformity, and cooperation. True, it does not at all follow that simple exposure of an individual to the coercions of a given social organization automatically result in the internalization of these coercions—in the formation, that is, of what we call self-discipline. Of all forms of social interaction, coercion is one of the most varied and complex, with actual results that are least predictable. Nevertheless, it is true that self-discipline, where it exists, is the consequence, through social interaction, of external discipline—whether this be personal or impersonal.

Could there be, as many have dreamed, a form of society utterly free of coercion? Could there be a society in which relationships of cooperation, exchange, and simple conformity rendered unnecessary any relationship predicated upon compulsion or the latent threat of force? We shall come back to this point in the chapter on authority. Not that there is any final answer to the question within the province of this book. But unquestionably there are relationships among human beings in which the element of coercion is so minimal as to invite the dream of a coercion-free existence. And there is no question that coercion, which has been a univeral process in human history, has varying intensities among human beings and among various cultural groups. But whatever may be the possibilities of a coercion-free society, simple observation makes evident that among the basic and timeless forms of social interaction, coercion is in the forefront.

Conflict

So, of course, is conflict. As there is the dream of the coercionless world, so is there the dream of a world without conflict. Most religions—those at least in which the idea of an afterlife, a heaven, is strong—define blessedness and salvation in terms of the individual's final escape from all forms of conflict and suffering. When secularized, such visions result from time to time in utopias, real or imagined, in which conflict as a process is extinguished altogether. But when closely examined, such dreams of utopia turn out usually to be dreams of elimination of certain types of conflict—national, tribal, class, and the like—and the subtlization of these grosser forms of conflict in types less injurious to human beings and less destructive. Thus Marx and Engels could look forward to a time when, private property having been abolished, conflict of social classes would be ended forever. It is unlikely, however, that either Marx or Engels thought that conflict in every possible form would also be ended. This point is very important: whereas conflict may well be a universal, something ineradicable by the very nature of man's relation to man and man's relation to diverse norms, it does not follow, as certain philosophers have argued, that therefore any given form of conflict—armed war, for example—is inevitable.

In simplest terms, conflict is the process of social interaction in which two or more persons struggle with one another for some commonly prized object or value. There can also be conflict within one's self. Again we come back to the indispensable role of symbolic interaction in human life. The mere fact of the self, of those reflexive feelings when one becomes an object to himself, with division between the "I" and the "me," means the ever present possibility of internal conflict. One aspect of one's being desires a certain objective; another aspect resists, or wishes to resist. The result is conflict within one's self. Through the repeated experience of such conflicts the personality gains much of its character, its motivations, and the general configuration that makes one person seem more conflict-ridden by nature than another.

Our concern here is not, however, with psychological conflicts but rather those more overt ones in which conflict is a process of social interaction. We are generally prone to think of conflict among individuals or groups as necessarily negative, as destructive of unity and amity. But as Simmel emphasized many years ago, and as Lewis Coser has stressed more recently, conflict can as often be positive, that is, integrative, as it can be the opposite. How, for instance, can we explain the cohesion *within* a certain group except—in part, at least—through the conflict that exists between this group and its enemies or antagonists? It is an old story that nothing is so likely to reduce conflicts within a given social relationship as the threat of conflicts between that relationship and other, possibly hostile, organizations or individuals on the outside.

But the integrative aspects of conflict can be seen in ways which are somewhat more subtle. The social world abounds in contrasts and differences. These, to be sure, are not identical with conflict. But the mere presence of such contrasts as status, power, privilege, or wealth can often generate tensions. As Simmel writes: "Conflict itself resolves the tension between contrasts. The fact that it aims at peace is only one, an especially obvious, expression of its nature: the synthesis of elements that work both against and for one another." [7]

Conflict can be, and very often has been in history, the means by which quite extraordinary achievements have taken place. The Latin word *hostis* means both "stranger" and enemy." Given the powerful tendencies in human history toward conformity within the group, conflict among groups has often been the principal means whereby ancient orthodoxies have been dissolved, old tyrannies loosened, and individuals in a manner released, however briefly, to achieve new and higher goals. Conflicts of norm and value within a complex culture are frequently the setting for acts of thought and behavior that lead to betterment. Given the historic status of the Negro in American culture, who can doubt that conflicts between blacks and whites have had inestimable importance in the cultural advancement of the American people?

There is no group or relationship, however small and intimate, in which conflict does not occasionally occur. However devoted two friends may be, two lovers, a husband and wife, brothers, or fellow workers in a common cause, there cannot help but be conflict from time to time. The conflict may so subtle, so infinitesimal as to be unobservable by outsiders; it may be tacit, not acknowledged by word or gesture between the participants; but it is there. The famous German philosopher Immanuel Kant referred to the "unsocial sociability" of human beings, by which he meant the allied tendencies in one and the same relationship toward cohesion and toward dissolution.

Competition and ambition are both, in a manner of speaking, forms of conflict. We refer to competition as the struggle between two or more persons for a given object in which the emphasis is entirely on the object itself rather than the persons themselves as antagonists. Ambition refers to an individual's or group's efforts to improve position in terms of a given value—status, wealth, esteem, and so on. But in both forms of behavior the element of conflict is present, however muted it may be by comparison with the more overt and naked forms.

Conflict is the diametric opposite of cooperation, but rarely if ever is either seen in total absence of the other. Threat of conflict from the outside can strengthen tendencies toward cooperation within a group. Less obvious but no less real is the degree to which observed cooperation within one social organization can generate tendencies of conflict toward that group from other persons or groups.

Whether between two individuals, however intimately woven their lives and affections, or between two groups such as classes, communities, and nations, conflict is a persisting aspect of social interaction. Conflict in the social world has something of the same function as friction in the physical. In each instance it is a means, if not *the* means, whereby immobility is transformed into mobility or action. As Simmel points out,

> *An absolutely centripetal and harmonious group, a pure "unification"* (Vereinigung), *not only is empirically unreal, it could show no real life process. The society of saints which Dante sees in the Rose of Paradise may be like such a group, but it is without any change and development; whereas the holy assembly of Church Fathers in Raphael's* Disputa *shows if not actual conflict, at least a considerable differentiation of moods and directions of thought, whence flow all the vitality and the really organic structure of that group. Just as the universe needs "love and hate," that is, attractive and repulsive forces, in order to have any form at all, so society, too, in order to attain a determinate shape, needs some quantitative ratio of harmony and disharmony, of association and competition, of favorable and unfavorable tendencies.*[8]

Coser has emphasized that what is important from the point of view of sociology with respect to conflict is the sharp separation of objective from subjective elements. Even if we grant that conflict among human beings is a universal, one rooted in psychological dispositions, the fact remains, and it is an important fact, that it is the *objective base* of conflict that largely determines the most vivid and generally decisive elements of conflict. We may concede, indeed, stipulate, that there will be conflict among human beings irrespective of the form of social organization men live in. But it is surely of more than passing interest whether such conflict is of the sort that produces events such as the French Revolution or the contemporary black-white situation in the United States or whether it is the sort that some Eskimos engage in when they hurl derisive epithets at one another in lieu of physical combat. There is also, as Coser has stressed, the fact that the type and intensity of conflict are functions of the kinds of social structure within which conflict is to be found. In a large, loose, pluralistic type of structure, conflict has far more likelihood of performing an integrative function, of resolving differences. When conflict occurs within a rigid, closed type of social organization it is more likely to be of the deadly, unconditional, and relentless sort. It has been said that the bitterest of conflicts and hatreds are to be found *within* the close community or family, just as the bloodiest of wars are likely to be civil wars.

These, then, are the five principal forms of social interaction to be found in human behavior: *exchange, cooperation, conformity, coercion,* and *conflict.* All, as we have seen, are manifestations of what we have called symbolic interaction. All of them, as found among human beings, involve the vital element of reciprocity. There can be no social action or social interaction in which the element of reciprocity is not present in some degree. What one does is affected by his estimate of probable response on the part of the other; and how one responds is affected by his estimate of what the cause or real nature is of the precipitating act. In all of these forms of social interaction, human beings participate, not as physical or psychological atoms, but as members of social groups or aggregates, as holders of roles and statuses, and within the contexts of acquired norms. These are the subjects to which we shall now turn, for they are the more visible manifestations of the mechanisms of inter-action we have just considered.

It is of the utmost importance that the student of social behavior keep in mind the sheer impossibility of dealing with any one of our central concepts except in terms which at least partially involve use of other terms not yet fully explored. Again we are forced to agree with Professor Homans: It is really intolerable that we cannot say every-thing at once. But we can remember that each of our central concepts is a perspective, a parameter, through which we are enabled to observe single aspects of what is in fact, in Homans' words, "rich, dark, organic unity." This, to be sure, is the method of all science, but it is nonethe-less difficult and nowhere more difficult than in such a field as sociology.

Notes

1. Max Weber, *The Theory of Social and Economic Organization,* trans. by A. M. Henderson and Talcott Parsons (New York: Oxford University Press, 1947), p. 88.
2. Herbert Blumer, "Society as Symbolic Interaction," in Arnold Rose (ed.), *Human Behavior and Social Processes* (New York: Houghton Mifflin, 1962), pp. 179–192.
3. Georg Simmel, "Faithfulness and Gratitude," in Kurt Wolff (ed. and trans.), *The Sociology of Georg Simmel* (New York: Free Press, 1950), p. 389.
4. *Ibid.,* p. 389.

5. Georg Simmel, "Superordination and Subordination," in *The Sociology of Georg Simmel, op. cit.*, p. 181.
6. Simmel, *op. cit.*, p. 299.
7. Georg Simmel, *Conflict and the Web of Group-Affiliations*, trans. by Kurt Wolff and Reinhard Bendix (New York: Free Press, 1955), p. 14.
8. *Ibid.*, p. 15.

5

Social Aggregates

THE NATURE OF SOCIAL AGGREGATES

We have thus far been concerned with the processes or mechanisms of interaction through which individual human beings—the raw material of society—become functioning parts of the social order. We have seen that the process of becoming a social being, in contrast to a merely physiological being, is inseparable from human interaction through symbols and in the varied patterns which we have called exchange, cooperation, conformity, coercion, and conflict.

But social interaction itself, including its symbolic foundation and its regular and recurrent patterns, is never present among human beings except within the contexts formed by social aggregates. I am referring to those specific clusters, assemblages, gatherings, and groups within which social behavior is to be found in the human species.

Here it must be emphasized that we shall be concerned with *social* aggregates, not aggregates of human beings as these might be constructed either through fancy or statistical artifice. All the human beings in the world who measure exactly six feet in height or who have red hair or who eat turnips no doubt form an aggregate. But such an aggregate could hardly be called social, for it lacks what we have seen to be the minimum and indispensable attribute of social behavior—interaction of a symbolic and mutually determinative character. Social aggregates may be as large as nations, as small as intimate dyads. They may literally serve any function or purpose imaginable, however broad in scope, however specialized, however bizarre. They may draw their essence from the fact of common territorial residence, from kinship, from religion, from war, from peace, from love, from hate, from good, and from evil. They may be as long in duration as the Japanese Empire, the Roman Catholic Church, or the Jewish people. They may also be as short as the cocktail party or the church picnic. They may be as loose and tenuous as the crowd at a football game, as cohesive and binding as the clan in a preliterate society.

But what is essential to the *social* aggregate is the sense of mutual awareness, either directly in a face-to-face manner, as in the small primary group, or through common possession of symbols, as in a vast nation or world-wide church. A Roman Catholic living in isolation among Mohammedans in a village in the Middle East is nonetheless a member of the social aggregate we call the Roman Catholic Church. His behavior may indeed be more directly responsive to the symbols of the Church and to the sense of belonging to the Church than the behavior of a Roman Catholic surrounded by fellow religionists but for whom the Church is but a weak and wavering influence in his life. What is vital, in short, is not the fact of numbers, not the fact of commonness with respect to some selected attribute, not the fact of propinquity within some arbitrarily delimited area, but the fact of belonging to, being a part of some relationship with others that is, by its nature, a consciously shared relationship. Tribe, clan, nation, business enterprise, church, family, mutual-aid association, criminal conspiracy, town, social class, play group, gang, neighborhood—each of these is a *social* aggregate for the reason just given: each is composed of members—however far-flung in area they may be—who, either directly or indirectly through common symbols, are aware of each other and are influenced by each other.

Obviously, social aggregates are not fixed, as are valleys and mountain ranges. What was but yesterday only a numerical aggregate may be today a vital, profoundly felt, social aggregate. Blacks in the world population are a vivid case in point. It was not many years ago that the blacks of the vast continent of Africa existed as a numerical aggregate; so, for that matter, did the blacks in other parts of the world who had moved from or been taken from the African continent. There were, without question, many influential social aggregates in the lives of blacks, ranging from isolated tribes to slave plantations in the Deep South. But only slowly did the attribute of blackness, of common membership in the Negro race, become, as it so plainly has in our day, the binding symbol of a *social* aggregate.   The peoples of India are another, though different, case in point.   Until a century ago, possibly even more recently than that, the several hundred millions of people occupying the subcontinent we call India had neither awareness of, nor interest in, the social bond that is today so strikingly reflected in India as a political nation. The social aggregates of tribe, caste, village, family were the binding unities in the lives of Indians.   The opposite can also be the case.   Once, a few thousand years ago, the people living in that area roughly bounded by the Mediterranean, the Danube River and the Rhine thought of themselves, for the most part proudly, as members of the Roman Republic and, then, the Empire.   What could have seemed more permanent than the Eternal City, more binding than the tie of Roman citizenship in this great area?   By the ninth century A.D., as we know, this social aggregate had become nothing but a dim memory in the minds of a few monks and other scholars.

In sum, what we have found to be true of social interaction is no less true of social aggregates.   For the word "social" to apply there must be some sense of mutual awareness, of affinity, of symbolic, if not direct, interaction, and a feeling of membership or belonging.   Two people, unbeknown to one another and dropped by parachute into a wild and uninhabited place do not form a social aggregate, however close by they may be.   The same two persons *aware* of one another—irrespective of feelings of hostility, fear, gratitude, amity—do form a social aggregate. Black persons in the United States aware of themselves only in terms of their individual relationships to family, church, or to plantation form a numerical aggregate but not a social aggregate.   Black people today in the United States very obviously form a social aggregate—one that is for many of them a far more implicative and evocative unity than other, older forms of social relationship among them.   The difference clearly consists in the fact that whereas blackness of skin is a very old physical fact in the human race, only recently has it become a profoundly important symbolic fact, one around which deeply absorbing, implicative social unions and movements are formed, one around which an entire culture is in the process of being formed within Western society.

We turn now to the *types* of social aggregates that are fundamental in the discipline of sociology.   This is perhaps a good point at which to emphasize again that when we talk about sociological types and attributes of social aggregates we are not referring primarily to family, local community, church, school, labor union, or social class, although these are institutional areas within which much sociological work has been done. Such institutional areas are, however, the common domain of all the social sciences. My observation holds equally for ethnic groups, political associations, and business enterprises. Sociology has worked in these areas also, and worked creatively. But they are the common area of all the social sciences.

When we refer to the types of social aggregate in which sociology has a distinctive and uniquely identifying interest, we must use criteria that have to do not so much with the content or purposes of social aggregates—kinship, religious, ethnic, and so on—but, rather, with the *type of social interaction* that is to be found and with the conditions and forces which affect the varying intensities of social interaction. Purpose or content in any social aggregate is indeed vital. People do not come together merely to *be* together, as the old saying has it, but to *do something* together. To pretend that any social grouping is not strongly influenced by whether its central norm or norms are economic in contrast to political, recreational, religious, or related to kinship would be to pretend nonsense.

Although all of the foregoing is true, it is equally true that the norms themselves are powerfully affected by the *social* character of the groupings or aggregates within which we find them. From the sociologist's point of view it is important to know what the motivating purpose, the content, of an aggregate is. But, knowing this, it is then of primary importance to find out further what the strictly social or sociological properties of the social aggregate are and how these interrelate with the norms around which the aggregate is formed.

From the sociological point of view there are several crucial factors, all social, which influence the different types and intensities of social interaction we have just considered. These factors are our means of distinguishing types of social aggregate in society. First is the factor of *size*—whether the aggregate is small or large; second, whether the aggregate is *open* or *closed;* third, whether it is *personal* or *territorial;* fourth, whether it is *Gemeinschaft* or *Gesellschaft;* fifth, whether or not it is a *reference group.* These are not the only types of social aggregates, even from a strictly sociological point of view.[1] They are types, however, which clearly are important and vitally affect the nature of the aggregate, irrespective of whether its purpose is religious, political, economic, or ethnic.

THE FACTOR OF SIZE

No matter what the purpose of a social aggregate, or what larger institutional area it may fall in, size (that is, number of members) directly affects its nature and the behavior of those participating in it. A small group, merely by virtue of being small, involves certain sociologically determining considerations that are not found in large groups. Georg Simmel first developed this point. Although much has been added to Simmel's pioneering observations, they are still worthy of direct note.

The Dyad

Let us begin with what Simmel called the dyad, the union of two persons. Dyads may be marital, political, economic, or religious; they involve friendships, love affairs, and also animosities and hatreds. In the dyad, Simmel noted, are to be found all of the essential interactive patterns, the social materials, and the basic elements of structure that are present in all social aggregates.

The dyad, obviously, is the smallest social unit within which social interaction can take place, within which the several mechanisms of interaction can be observed. In the whole, vital, and expanding study of the microaspects of association that today forms so important a part of the science of sociology, the role of the dyad is crucial.

The importance of the dyad to human personality is apparent in many ways. Take, for example, the sensations of freedom and of isolation. Nowhere else in the individual's life are these two feelings so vivid, so dominating, at least temporarily, as when the individual has suddenly become disengaged from a dyadic relationship in which he has participated for a considerable period of time. If the dyadic relationship has somehow become oppressive and suffocating, release carries with it a sense of freedom that cannot be matched in intensity by release from other and larger forms of relationship. Conversely, if the dyadic relationship has been a deeply gratifying one, one in which the individual has felt a profound sense of his own fulfillment, release from it—as the result of the other's death, removal, or rejection of the first individual—can lead to agonizing feelings of isolation, feelings which, as we know, are hardly assuaged by the presence of others, however physically close or beneficently inclined they may be.

It is also within the dyad that we experience the most intense feelings of intimacy with others. The reason for this, as Simmel noted, lies in the fact that the dyad is uniquely the form of relationship which never becomes, in a manner of speaking, superpersonal. Even in the triad, the group of three, it is possible for one person to remove himself and for the group to go on. Thus, from the individual's perspective, there is a feeling of intimacy in the dyad that arises from his own absolute indispensability to the relationship. The dyad, not possessing any identity whatsoever apart from the presence of the single person, that is, each of the two persons, achieves a degree of intimacy that is the result of its being almost pure social interaction. Signs, gestures, words, mannerisms, and glances assume a significance and degree of importance hardly possible where more than two persons are involved. Communication is possible in a degree of perfection, of fullness, that is scarcely even imaginable when more than two persons are involved. The dyad is, above any other form of social interaction, the context of the most exalted feelings of love, understanding, trust, and devotion.

By the same token, however, the dyad is the setting for the most extreme feelings of hate, of jealousy, of distrust, and of the agonizing sense of betrayal. It is possible, of course, for one to feel that he has been betrayed by a very large group, even by a nation, when one has been its leader and has been repudiated. But such feelings of "betrayal" are as nothing in their true intensity compared with the feeling of betrayal one has when the other member of a close, intimate union says or does something that destroys an inner understanding, a love, or a secret. It is the nature of the dyad, Simmel wrote, to invite intimacy, to evoke the release of feelings, tastes, beliefs, and hopes of the most private nature. And since it is within the scope of the dyad that these are released to another, it is within the dyad also that grief, agony, and hatred can attain their maximum shapes in social interaction.

That the dyad is in a sense the most "natural" of unions, the most elemental in terms of size, does not mean that it is the least complex or the easiest to sustain. Nowhere is this more obvious than with respect to marriage—monogamous marriage. It is usually during the earliest weeks and months of marriage (at least in societies such as our own where romantic love is commonly the basis of marriage) that there is the strongest desire to give the other all of one's self, to admit the other to the deepest recesses of one's own individuality. Love and its continuing demonstration demand, it is often thought, such giving of self, such interweaving of innermost sentiments and beliefs. But it is not easy, as many a couple has learned the hard way, to sustain this kind of intimacy, and, from being the means of unique self-fulfillment in the early stages, such intimacy can become burdensome, can become almost impossibly difficult to maintain in the accustomed manner. By very virtue of the affinity between the dyad and feelings and sentiments of deepest unity, intimacy, and separateness from the rest of the world, the dyad can become, where surrounding contexts fail to give it reinforcement and nourishment, the most precarious and fragile of all relationships. But of its centrality and universality in the human race, and of its profound importance to the social bond, there can be no question.

The Triad

Next in size is the *triad*. Simmel tells us that with the introduction of the third human element a kind of quantum change has taken place, a change much greater than what might be signified by the mere arithmetic of the matter. For among three elements, writes Simmel, "each one operates as an intermediary between the other two, exhibiting the twofold function of such an organ, *which is to unite and to separate*." [2] (Italics added.)   Where three persons comprise a relationship, there is something substantially different from the direct relationship between *A* and *B*; now there is the *indirect* relation of *A* and *B* through *C*. The fact that two elements—any two elements—are connected now not merely by the straight line of direct interaction but, in addition, by the "broken line" created by the presence of *C* makes, very obviously, for a richer relationship—measured, that is, in strictly sociological terms. Observe the possibility that now exists for the triad to make possible modes of communication even between *A* and *B* that may have been lacking while *A* and *B* formed a dyad only. The most obvious and common example is what happens to the dyad of a marriage when a child is born and the relationship becomes triadic. Clearly something now prevents the dyadic relation from being the exclusive relation it was. Equally clearly, with the disappearance of the exclusive and direct-line communication between *A* and *B*, there arise other forms of communication between the two parents through the very existence of the child. Moreover the presence of *C*—whether within a kinship triad or some other kind—makes possible communication between *A* and *B* when some rupture of the relation between them has occurred. *C* becomes the common object of attention for *A* and *B* and also the means of communication and, as such, the means of repair of the ruptured relation between *A* and *B*.

Plainly, however, the presence of *C* can also present a threat or interference to the desired intimacy between *A* and *B*. The hoary folk saying "two's company, three's a crowd" has in it exactly this possibility of the third person's becoming an intruder. To return to our kinship illustration, it does not necessarily follow that it is always the child who is most likely to assume the role of "intruder." Far from it. There may immediately be generated such a degree of intimacy between one of the parents and the child as to make the other parent the intruder.

It is far more difficult for the triad to achieve perfect community of interrelation and of relation to some external object or value. Whereas two persons who become deeply united and profoundly responsive to one another find little difficulty in achieving almost perfect uniformity of reaction to some experience—say to a painting or political event—it is much less likely that three persons will. The same thing is true when the number is increased to four or five or more. *But* the difference in uniformity of response is not nearly so great between the group numbering three and the group numbering four or even five as is the difference between the dyad and the triad. This is why I referred above, following Simmel's keen insight, to the fact that there is a kind of quantum jump from two to three; a jump not even approximately equaled, in sociological terms, by the jump from three to four or four to five.

The possibilities of diagramming the relationships among three persons, if it were possible to diagram sentiments and feelings as we should like to, would be very great. What we call sociometry—the spatial and functional relationship of elements within a pattern of social interaction—is a rich field of investigation for the quantitatively minded. And of all the sociometric possibilities here, the greatest, the most historic, and longest-lived come from the fact that within the triad there are inevitably the two roles of mediator and of what Simmel called *tertius gaudens*—literally translated, "the third who enjoys." The nuances in both roles are nearly endless. We begin with the clear fact that the mere presence of a "mediator" invites the creation of matters to be mediated that would not, in all probability, have been created were the third person, the mediator, not present. But irrespective of this fact, the third person finds himself not infrequently serving as mediator between *A* and *B*, and by virtue of his mediatorship he wields a degree of power over *A* and *B*. Here the role of mediator in the triad shades into the role of *tertius gaudens*. At any given moment the third person in a triad may stand to benefit by being outside the relationship of *A* and *B*. Whereas *C* as mediator seeks to hold together the triad, possibly gaining power in the process (power directly related to cohesion of the triad), *C* as *tertius gaudens* has a stake in the continuation of strife between *A* and *B*. *C* may now favor *A*, now *B;* in the process he adds to his stock of whatever it is he is seeking—esteem, love, power, money, or superiority.

Let us not make the mistake of supposing that either the *mediator* or *tertius gaudens* necessarily seeks his role in the triad. It is often thrust upon him by the interaction of the other two. Either role can often be an unconscious one, as in the case of the competition between two parents for the love of their child, and the child's capacity, in whatever degree of consciousness or unconsciousness of the situation, for either mediating or exploiting the situation.

Dyads and triads are eternal and universal. No matter how vast the scale of organization of a society, how formalized or bureaucratic, how deeply rooted in law or tradition, all human associations are composed of dyads and triads. Theoretically we may say that a larger organization—be it a clan, a tribe, a military unit, a department in government, or a business enterprise—is composed of individuals, each fulfilling a stated function, each directly related to the whole of the organization. In fact, however, dyadic and triadic relationships spring up within, and sometimes these relationships and their internal dynamics can hold the actual clue to the nature of the environing organization. Anyone who has observed or studied prisons and the informal organizations among prisoners that exist within the tight structure of the prison organization knows the degree to which dyadic and triadic relationships among prisoners can spell the character of the prison as a whole.

Small Groups

From dyads and triads we move to the phenomenon of the small group generally, the group with a membership of sufficiently small size for the members to be known to each other, to be in more or less constant association, and to be the scene of the large number of interactive relationships, responses, feelings, and sentiments that the human mind is capable of. Unlike the precise quantity involved by definition in the dyad or triad, the smallness of the small group is relative. It may contain two or three persons; it may contain a dozen. What is crucial is the intensity of interaction among the component individuals. When we speak of "the small group" in contemporary sociological research we may have in mind the conjugal family, a play group, a military squad, the working group in an assembly room of a factory or in an office, an academic department, or a jury.

Throughout human history the small group has, in a sense, held the clue to the formation of human personality and to the diversities of personality and conduct that we see from one culture to another. It was with respect to the small group that Charles H. Cooley formulated his notable concept of "the primary group." Cooley was referring to the group that, in the processes of symbolic interaction, of socialization of the individual, is small enough to permit face-to-face contact in more or less durable and persisting fashion. In the primary group, Cooley observed, are developed the successive awarenesses of membership in the social order; of relation to the fundamental values of the larger society and internalization, through interaction, of these values, thus forming the sense of self, of character, and identity. Although Cooley gave greatest attention understandably to the family, the small neighborhood, and village—the small groups which have been "primary" for the largest number of people throughout human history—he by no means confined the term "primary group" to these. Nor do we today. There is almost no area of human behavior within which the small group cannot be found.

During World War II we learned that the fighting effectiveness and morale of whole armies depended to a large extent upon the degree to which small groups were permitted by military policy to flourish. Studies showed that in military replacement systems in which not lone individuals but small and continuing groups were the units the morale consequences were large. Analogous studies of morale and productive efficiency in factories, of success of political parties and other organizations in government, and of learning effectiveness in schools have depended to a considerable degree upon the extent to which small and informal but nevertheless close, cohesive, and identifiable groups can exist within the larger structure of organization.

No matter how vast and impersonal, how regimented and externally directed a society may be, close investigation reveals that it is quite literally honeycombed with small groups that can become influential in the lives of their individual members. Although the leaders of both the Russian and German totalitarian political orders made every effort to eradicate or neutralize *traditional* small groups—on the ground that their continuation could easily harbor sentiments of a subversive nature—no effort was spared by either Bolsheviks or Nazis to develop on a wide scale *new* small groups in the population, each organized in one sphere or another around the values central to the controlling political policy. No matter how large, impersonal, and bureaucratic an organization may appear to be from the outside, careful examination usually reveals the existence of whole networks of small, informal, social groups within the larger structure. Often these can prove decisive to the success of the large organization.

It is possible that certain types of objectives and values are attainable or preservable only within very small associations. Simmel wrote that socialism—using this word in the strict sense of complete equity in distribution of production and reward—is possible only within the small organization. The larger the association, the greater the likelihood of loss of the socialist objective through dispersion. Although the *ideal* of socialism might remain luminous from afar in the large association, the possibility of its achievement would wane with the necessary rise of differentiation of function, of division of labor, and of the inevitably unequal valuations which would in time come to be placed upon work and rewards. The same is true, Simmel tells us, with respect to religion. Where the nature of the religion is such that perpetual assent, absolute devotion to dogma, extreme discipline of behavior, and marked differentness of dress, manner, and belief from the environing population are vital, then smallness of the religious group is essential. It is an old story in the history of religion that those small sects answering the description just given lose a great deal of their religious character when they become large church organizations. The kind of discipline—or devotion, assent, and faith—possible in the sect is far less possible in the great church. Such is the case, as Simmel tells us, with respect to aristocracies also. The essential sociological element of the aristrocracy is not its domination over the mass of people but rather the internal connections and interactions whereby it remains conscious of itself and possessed of the desire to maintain itself through intermarriage, emphasis on family, common patterns of speech and dress, and of life style generally. The larger the aristocracy becomes, the greater the difficulty of maintaining the cultural values that are essential to the aristocracy's identity in the population.

This situation is similar in what we call *elites*. An elite may be drawn from almost any sphere of human behavior: scholarly, military, artistic, athletic, and so on. Let an elite, whether it be the elite that is formed by professional football players or that formed by cardinals in the Roman Catholic Church, become too large, too diffuse, too amorphous, and the character of the elite is bound to change. The elite may even erode away as the consequence of change and dispersion of its numbers. There are, in short, certain values and structures in human society that are inseparable from smallness of size.

There is a flexibility, a creativeness, and a capacity for radical innovation within the small group that is not as likely to occur in the large group or the mass. Great ages of philosophic, artistic, literary, and scientific achievement turn out to be, when studied minutely, ages in which small groups of like-minded human beings predominate. Despite what we call the "individualism" of such ages as Athens in the fifth century B.C. or the Renaissance in European history, the social contexts of this efflorescence of individual creativeness must not be overlooked. And what we discover repeatedly in such ages is the profusion of small groups of artists, writers, and scientists. These groups have a quality of informality, of autonomy, and of high intensity of personal interaction within, and often among, them. No aspect of the study of the great ages of cultural history has more often been neglected or more often buried under the correct but wholly insufficient word "genius."

What close inspection of history reveals over and over in the clusters of genius which mark such ages as ancient Athens, Augustan Rome, Elizabethan England, the New England of mid-nineteenth-century America, and the astonishing efflorescence of creativity among Jews in Western society during the past half-century or so is the crucial role of small aggregates, of "circles," of more or less constant "gatherings." In short, they are unions characterized by enormous individual ability, of course, but individual ability released and given stimulus and intensity within contexts small enough to put a high premium upon interaction. Whether in the history of art, music, philosophy, imaginative literature, or of modern science, we shall find, whenever we look closely at the lives of such men as Plato, Michelangelo, Shakespeare, Goethe, Bach, or a Niels Bohr or Enrico Fermi, not that any one of these was lacking in what we call genius, but that without exception, this genius was heightened, given intensity, and, often, direct stimulus, by the mode of social interaction possible within small, informal, more or less autonomous social aggregates.

A sharp word of warning: there is no magic in smallness. Dullness multiplied by two or three or ten is still dullness. Nor are small groups, any more than dyads and triads, the invariable settings of love and understanding. Hatred, brutality, viciousness, and torment or misery are more likely to be found, in their extreme forms, within small groups than large. From the viewpoint of social interaction, the small group can as easily heighten feelings of hatred or misery as it can feelings of friendship and mutual agreement. It is an old saying that tyranny at close quarters is much harder to bear than tyranny at a distance. The sense of freedom gained from release from a small group grown intolerable to a single individual is greater than the sense that derives from release from a large-scale organization.

Large-Scale Aggregates

We shall be brief here, for much that is pertinent is scarcely more than a kind of inversion or reversal of what has just been said about small groups. If the essence of the small group is its personality, its intensity of interaction, its informality, and its incessant face-to-face character, the essence of the large-scale aggregate is usually found in greater impersonality, diminished intensity of personal interaction, greater formality of character, and a minimum of face-to-face association in which the participants are "whole personalities." The larger the association the greater the likelihood that it engages but a single aspect, a single interest or objective of the individual's life.

Without going into the details here, it can be said that large aggregates tend to be, in Simmel's theory of association, either *organizations* or *masses*.

The *organization* is, by its very nature, formal, differentiated in terms of more or less precise roles of its members, impersonal in that it sets greater emphasis upon role or upon office than it does upon the whole personality of the individual involved, and characterized by more or less rational and calculated division of labor. We shall have much more to say about the organization as a large social aggregate in the next chapter. There we shall discuss what Max Weber called "rational authority" or bureaucracy. We are concerned here solely with the factor of size. True, there is no inherent or necessary reason that the organization be large. There are certainly instances of numerically small groups organizing themselves in terms of the characteristics just cited: differentiation of function made explicit in idea and form, division of labor, precisely assigned duties, and so on. But even when these instances occur, it is the nature of the small group to neutralize such characteristics through the operation of the kind of interaction that is inseparable from the small aggregate. And even within the very large, formally organized, and calculatedly impersonal organization, there are usually many small, informal, and highly personal groups. These smaller groups, which occupy the interstices of the larger organization, can variously implement or sabotage the goals of the larger organization.

The larger the aggregate is, generally speaking, the greater the necessity to rely on formalized and rationalized procedures and the greater the likelihood of a sense, on the individual's part, of impersonality. He may, of course, as often find the exhilarating feeling of freedom, of liberation from custom at close quarters, as he does the feeling of anonymity, of being a mere cog in a large machine. We err grievously when we assume that formality, impersonality, and anonymity are invariably distasteful to human beings or out of keeping with the proper exercise of certain functions in society. It is an almost monotonous refrain today in much writing that the individual is made alienated, estranged, given a feeling of loss of identity by virtue of large-scale organizations. And it is true that such are sometimes the consequences. But it is equally true that not only would much vital work fail to get done apart from large-scale organizations but that for most human beings today life lived exclusively within the interaction patterns of small groups would seem intolerable.

Moral judgments regarding small and large aggregates are not the point here, however, nor anywhere in the science of sociology. We are interested primarily in the fact that size of aggregate vitally affects the way human beings interact with one another and behave or think with respect to the values around which the aggregates come into being in the first place. Essential dogma may remain the same over a period of centuries, as for instance in the Christian Church during it first ten centuries of history. But the mere fact of change in the social character of Christianity—that is, its development from sect, or rather a congeries of loosely united sects, in the earliest period to an increasingly large aggregate of believers in the later period—meant inevitable and profound changes in the nature of the religion and the relation of its essential dogma to its members. The growth of formalized roles, the increasing differentiation of function, authority, and work within the Church, the development of a bureaucracy with the Bishop of Rome at its apex could not help but be the consequences of large-scale aggregates of Christians in contrast to the small, sectlike communities around which the intellectual character of Christianity first emerged. What is true so evidently in the history of Christianity is equally true of other religions and, for that matter, of other institutions, whether political, economic, or educational, and of other values, whether anarchist, socialist, or capitalist. Size of aggregate is a vital aspect of the nature of social interaction, which in turn is a vital context of the function or value that is central to the aggregate.

The other type of large social aggregate is the *mass*. I use this term, following Simmel and certain other writers, to refer to those aggregates which are not organized but which nonetheless manifest a certain unity, a certain sense of mutual awareness, and an occasional capacity for acting in unison. No mistake could be greater than to suppose that the *mass*, in the sociological sense of the term, is confined to lower-class persons, to the poor or the propertyless, to the illiterate or politically disenfranchised. Unfortunately, a whole mythology that is about equally divided between the laudatory and the pejorative has grown up around the word "mass" or its analogue "masses." Either word becomes as often a term of romantic political fantasy as of elite-conscious contempt.

But all of us are, at one time or other, in one connection or another, members of those large aggregates we call "masses." The mass is a large aggregate of people, which may or may not be in physical union, in which the unifying force is some single, usually simple, interest or idea. The television public is a mass; the crowd at a football game is a mass; the people brought together in part of a city by an incident, or report of an incident, are a mass; political parties, as we find them in the United States at least, are masses. It is the essence of the mass, as Simmel observed, that it is built around a single interest or aim, one involving but a part of the individual's whole nature, and that it is animated or guided by only *simple* ideas: "What is common to many must be accessible even to the lowest and most primitive among them. *Even nobler and more differentiated personalities in relatively large numbers* never meet on complex and highly developed ideas and impulses but only on those that are relatively simple and generally human."[3] (Italics added.)

The mass may be quiescent, it may limit itself to the spectator role, or it may become, as it does frequently in history, extraordinarily active, its members given the sudden sense of almost intoxicating unity and purpose. If it is a mass that is found at football games, it is also the mass that is found storming the Bastille, a university building, or the central offices of the government. When a mass is in physical proximity, Simmel writes, and when an event occurs that arouses attention, "innumerable suggestions swing back and forth, resulting in an extraordinary nervous excitation which often overwhelms the individuals, makes every impulse swell like an avalanche, and subjects the mass to whichever among its members happens to be the most passionate."[4] A familiar phenomenon in the mass or crowd, as many students—Simmel, Le Bon, Tarde, and Michels among others—have noted, is the ease with which leaders are displaced by the seeming demand of the mass for ever more vigorous and radical action. To speak of the mass as devoid of sociality, as nothing but a horde, would be a mistake. It does possess a social character that flows from the mutual excitation, from the idea or desire that gives it unity. It is, however, by its nature, a rather precarious and usually short-lived unity. For it is the essence of the mass that it is without the kind of organizational framework that holds large organizations together for long periods and without the face-to-face intimacy based upon multifold interaction that is the essence of small groups.

It is one of the common errors of much writing about modern society to suppose that "mass society" is peculiar to the nineteenth and twentieth centuries in Western Europe. But there have always been masses in human history—in the Athens of Pericles, the Rome of Seneca, the Middle Ages, the England of Shakespeare, and the France of the *philosophes*. Again let us emphasize that the identifying characteristic of the mass has nothing to do with mere size of total population. A country as vast as India can be, and during occasional periods has been, virtually devoid of masses simply because during these periods all of the Indian people were engaged, were socially identified, with traditional joint family, village community, and caste, all of them unities of a profoundly committing nature. When traditional unities such as these become weakened through change, when the formal governmental organizations—whether public or private—lose their hold upon members, when considerable numbers of human beings become conscious of themselves as an aggregate given social unity by some single theme or idea that does not arise out of the old order, the mass tends to make its appearance.

The mass movements of the late Middle Ages—all of them millennialist in inspiration and most of them given on occasion to acts of terrorism and extreme violence—were formed by individuals who had become detached from the ordinary unities of village, guild, town, kindred, and church. As Norman Cohn tells us in his *Pursuit of the Millennium*, these masses were composed largely of the uprooted, the disinherited, the atomized. Given the climate of culture, it was inevitable that the themes around which these masses were organized would be religious: simple but powerful and galvanizing themes of impending salvation for the good once the wicked had been exterminated, of the return of Christ, of the imminent destruction of the world, and so forth. Despite our conception of medieval European society as a quiescent and highly organized period of history, mass movements were by no means uncommon.

In more recent times political themes have joined religious ones as the sources of the unity around which masses are built. As a number of able students of Nazism have pointed out, the great strength of this movement lay in the political mass. By that we do not mean the mere numerical majority of the German people, but those sectors of the population within which traditional norms had become weak, where traditional norms were thought to be threatened, where ordinary social bonds had become tenuous and meaningless, or where these bonds—

religion, family, job, and so on—were thought to be threatened by enemies from either outside Germany or from within. A mass began to form, at first relatively small in size, then, through a combination of skillful manipulation by Hitler and his lieutenants and grassroots apprehensions which spread in ways peculiar to the mass, of constantly increasing size.

The mass, as all students of the subject have emphasized, is a universal type of social aggregate in history, no more limited to modern times than to areas of high population density alone. It remains true, however, as such writers as Ortega y Gasset, Emil Lederer, William Kornhauser, and Hannah Arendt have pointed out in vivid detail, that modern and contemporary history is richer in the forces producing masses than perhaps any prior age.[5] The reason for this is, first, the sheer intensity and scope of social change during the past two centuries and, second, the character of so much of this change. Under the spur of political centralization, democratic equalitarianism, the factory system, and the whole thrust of secularism, a great many of the traditional communities of membership and belief have been weakened in the eyes of their members. Kinship, religion, the local community, and traditional social class are among these. Paralleling this process of dislocation or atomization is that through which more and more of the organizations of state and economy—and also religion, education, and leisure—have become large, seemingly impersonal, and unrelated to ordinary social interaction. The result, it is argued, is an increasing number of persons who, lacking traditional contexts of meaningful association, are repelled by the impersonality of the large-scale organizations in society. These persons form a mass—the anonymous, faceless, atomized mass, as so many writers in our day have described it.

There is much merit in this perspective from the point of view of social and political analysis. One would be blind indeed to fail to see in a great deal of popular behavior in Western society today evidences of the mass, using the word in the strict sociological, and nonpejorative, sense. And, as suggested above, there appears to be little doubt that it was the formation of the mass in this sense that lay behind the success of Nazism in Germany. It also lies behind the appeal of Marxism in many areas of the world today. With the traditional contexts of membership and belief eroded away, with feelings of anonymity and alienation rife, it would be strange if those involved were not lured by political doctrines promising the sense of community—at whatever cost to freedom or morality. As we shall see in Chapter 10, there is little doubt that alienation and anomie are considerably more in evidence in mass society than in those societies characterized by small, cohesive, and continuing unities of social life.

But no careful student of the subject will take the above picture as the sole perspective for the understanding of mass society. There is much truth in the view, given appropriate time and place. But it can be a serious distortion of reality. As the sociologist Joseph Gusfield has impressively reminded us,[6] we are obliged by much of the data to see a rather different perspective of mass society. If we take those people who, by virtue of type of job, life style, suburban setting, proximity to large-scale organizations, and so on, meet the criteria of belonging to mass society, we find a high percentage of them who do *not* evidence the facelessness, the frenzied searching for community, and the quick responsiveness to extremist politics that the mass society perspective might lead us to expect. Moreover, as Gusfield points out, the conditions of mass society can mitigate against extremist politics by virtue of the very sterilization of sharp and divisive socioeconomic differences, which so often are the root contexts of extremist ideologies. Mass society provides sources of direct attachment to supralocal, supraethnic, and suprareligious institutions. In so doing, this type of society can reduce the intensity of social and cultural conflicts and provide framework for consensus on the norms required for a pluralistic society.

Until a few years ago there was a strong tendency to picture metropolis and suburbia almost exclusively in terms of the mass society perspective, with emphasis upon atomization, alienation, political conformity, and general diminution of close cultural and social ties. More recent studies, however, such as Scott Greer's *The Emerging City* and Herbert Gans' *The Levittowners*, have a rather different picture of "mass society"—one reconcilable with the *persistence* of kinship, friendship, and other ties, as well as of the cultural differentiation and social heterogeneity that the mass society stereotype does not incorporate.

The mass and mass society, like other sociological concepts, are perspectives or parameters. Neither one can be used undiscriminatingly. Each is valuable and throws much light upon social behavior when properly used, but each is far from foolproof.

CLOSED AND OPEN AGGREGATES

Just as the character and type of internal social behavior of aggregates are affected by numerical size, so are they affected by the degree to which their membership is closed or open. Each of these words, "closed" and "open," is of course relative to some specific norm or other attribute. We will follow Max Weber here in defining an aggregate of persons as open when membership is not denied to anyone who wishes to participate in whatever function or norm or idea is the reason for the aggregate's existence. A closed social aggregate is one in which, irrespective of an outsider's desire to join, membership is denied on the basis of some rule or consideration or sharply limited by special conditions.

It is well to avoid treatment of extremes that might easily come to mind and think instead of the terms "closed" and "open" as dimensions or parameters assignable in varying degrees to all forms of social aggregates. No doubt there are still groups in the world which are totally and unvaryingly closed and others which are totally and unvaryingly open. But the overwhelming majority of social aggregates, whether small or large, fall somewhere between these extremes. Whether a social relationship is open or closed, Weber writes, "may be determined traditionally, affectually, or rationally, in terms of values or expediency." Limiting considerations may be those of birth, marriage, legal naturalization, achievement, honor, race, nationality, belief, morality, and so on. There is literally no type of consideration that is not somewhere at sometime operative as a condition of membership. Tribes are closed to all not related by comon descent; clans, to all not related by some norm of kinship, whether common blood or marriage; religions, to all who do not, by some kind of ritual affirmation, indicate acceptance of laws and canons; nations, to all who do not meet quotas or legal standards of naturalization; colleges and universities, to all who do not meet minimal academic requirements; clubs and fraternities and analogous groups, to those not of prescribed race, nationality, or acceptable degree of honor or renown; elites, to those who lack the intellectual or cultural characteristics deemed essential; and so on. Few indeed are the social aggregates which are not closed in some degree or, conversely, open in some degree.

But this said, there is still a high degree of differentiation possible in sociological terms among social aggregates with respect to the relative amounts of considerations that close and open membership to outsiders. That all sociological concepts are relative and are best seen as parameters does not mean that they lack substantive importance. An organization closed to all who are not white, Anglo-Saxon, Christian, and Republican is, patently, a "closed" organization by comparison with one, such as Phi Beta Kappa, which normally is closed merely to those unable to achieve a certain grade average in their academic studies.

Phi Beta Kappa is, just as is the National Academy of Sciences in this country, or the Royal Academy in England, a fairly exclusive organization. But one would not ordinarily think of any one of these as "closed" organizations, for, at least in theory, membership is open to anyone who, by achievement, meets the clearly stated conditions of membership, almost all of which are those of an achievement character.

Social groups in primitive, folk, and highly traditionalized cultures tend to be relatively closed. Considerations of hereditary descent, common blood, kinship, and caste are likely to be paramount. Strangers are not welcome, and membership is made possible only through rare and highly ritualized means of adoption. There is no lust for numbers as such in these societies for a variety of reasons: food supply, religion, mutual aid, distrust of alien or exotic ideas and beliefs. Numbers remain small by preference, and there is the distinct atmosphere within such societies of an intellectual and cultural, as well as social, world closed to outsiders.

One of the most fascinating and important of all social changes or historical transformations is that involved in the passage of a society from "closed" to "open," as occurred, for example, in the century preceding the fifth century B.C. in Athens. This was the century culminating in the Cleisthenean reforms, when membership in the city-state was no longer closed by virtue of limitations of kinship and race and became a matter of simple residence, with naturalization procedures open to all. Athens, as we know, became as open a society as the ancient world knew in the fifth century B.C. This openness accounts for much of the spectacular efflorescence of philosophical, artistic, and political genius of that century. True, the sudden passage from closed to open status of a group or social order may often be attended by consequences of a very different sort: sensations of disorganization, alienation, and modes of aberrant behavior that are destructive rather than creative. The modern history of Africa is filled with illustrations of the latter: members of tribes find themselves separated from their traditional memberships through the opening up of job opportunities in distant cities dominated by Europeans. But the tribesmen are not accepted as members of the political or social order in those European-dominated cities. What social anthropologists call "detribalization" is little more than simple passage from closed to open society, with consequences often measurable in terms of high rates of deviance.

There is still another sense in which the word "closed" may be used with respect to a social aggregate. I refer to mental asylums and prisons. Here the attribute of "closed" exists, we might say, in reverse fashion.

Such associations are closed to the exit of their members, and the entry of outsiders is carefully screened by those in authority. Although prisons and mental asylums are the most obvious examples of closed aggregates in this sense, there are others which share many of the characteristics of these two types: hospitals, monasteries, and certain types of schools —usually, though not necessarily, religious or military in emphasis. In all of these, even if original entry is voluntary and exit not a matter of legal permission as it is in the case of the prison or the mental asylum, a closed character is manifest. As Erving Goffman has pointed out, there is a *total*, even totalitarian, character to such institutions. Not merely is the full range of human activities to be found within one of these institutions, but there is commonly an effort, at least implicit, to remake the individual, to dislodge prior values and ideas and ways of behavior, to replace old statuses with new, to institute new sanctions in the individual's life, and, through total control of the individual— penological, medical, psychiatric, pedagogical, as the case may be— to give him a new, or largely new, "personality."

PERSONAL AND TERRITORIAL AGGREGATES

In terms of human history and of social change on the large scale, the distinction between personal and territorial aggregates is of utmost importance. On the one hand we are dealing with groupings that derive their primary identifying attributes from essentially *personal* qualities—qualities of kinship, religion, and ethnicity being perhaps the major ones in human society but by no means the only ones. On the other hand we are dealing with groupings that derive their nature and *raison d'être* not primarily from qualities inhering in persons but rather from the fact of *territory*. The political state and its innumerable subdivisions of provinces, counties, districts, villages, and towns are the most obvious examples of the second, or territorial, type.

At first glance the distinction between the two types may not seem vital. In fact, however, whether a human being, or a people, tends to give primary emphasis to the first or the second type of aggregate tells us much about the nature of that person's or people's general type of social organization. And, of even greater importance, is the transition that takes place recurrently in history from the one type to the other.

The oldest of all types of relationships is personal—manifest in clan, kindred, tribe, religion, war band, and the like. There is no major people known to us that was not organized in the beginning solely in terms of kinship and around religious and moral values which were inseparable from the people itself and which had, basically, no connection with the territory in which the people lived. As readers of Homer know, the Greeks identified themselves by particularizing blood relationships, not by reference to place or area. So did the most ancient Jews, and so, later, did the Germanic peoples who came gradually to occupy what is today Western Europe. So have peoples everywhere identified themselves, at all times, including the present day in a few, though diminishing, parts of the world. What is fundamental in the values, life styles, authorities, and functions of these peoples proceeds directly from the structure of personal relationship. The notion of a culture or an authority or an identity that springs directly from the piece of ground on which life is lived is totally alien to such peoples.

One of the most fateful and decisive of all changes in the history of human culture is the change involved when a given people ceases to identify itself exclusively in personal terms and begins to attach significance to the area or territory. Consider the momentous Cleisthenean reforms at the very end of the sixth century B.C. As the result of tensions of a political and economic nature which had been accumulating for a century, the Greek city-state of Attica was brought into being. Personal ties, of course, remained in the forms of family, kindred, clan, and social class. But now, with the Cleisthenean reforms effected, there were new unities—those of the territorial deme or township and, above all, the unity of Attica as a whole.

The striking and really important aspect of this change lies in the transformed locus of authority over the lives of the Greeks involved and the transformed locus too of the sense of personal identity, of rights and freedom, and participation. The momentous concept of citizenship arose. Thenceforth what was *politically* crucial in the life of the individual sprang from the fact of territorial residence rather than from kinship or religion. With this change went also, as we noted above, a change from a relatively closed society to a relatively open one. By virtue of diminished emphasis on the close and personal ties of clan and social class and, equally, of enhanced emphasis upon those rights and privileges that accrued from residence rather than from lineage, a much greater degree of mobility, of economic, intellectual and cultural, as well as political individualism, and, in time, of secularism was possible.

The change from a social order based primarily upon personal ties to one based upon territorial ties has occurred, quite literally, hundreds and even thousands of times in human history. Nor is the change always evidenced by the qualities just cited with respect to the ancient Greeks. The most striking consequence may not be freedom and cultural efflorescence as it so plainly was for the Greeks after the Cleisthenean reforms; it may be sheer repressive power, social atomization, and political despotism with economic and cultural inertia all too evident. The consequences vary.

The history of modern Europe is one of the gradual replacement of tribe, kindred, and clan as the decisive social aggregates in the lives of the peoples who were to become the English, French, Germans, and others by such territorial unities as county, parish, province, and political state. The change is never sudden, of course. Elements of a personal or kinship nature extend into the symbolism and authority structure of the territorial aggregates. Feudalism—which, far from being a distinctively Western European phenomenon is a well-known type of government in world history—may be described as a combination of the personal and territorial or, depending upon one's historical vantage point, as a transitional period in the replacement of personal by territorial ties. The personal element in feudalism lies in the binding ties that exist from man to man, as from vassal to liege lord. The increasingly important territorial factor is to be seen in the fiefs, some of which became, through aggrandizement, the nuclei of the modern states in Europe.

Naturally, the transition does not eradicate the personal ties. Families, clans, social classes, and religious and economic groups continue in the areas, forming a large part of the social organization of the people concerned. But gradually the sense of membership in a territorial unity —county, province, and eventually the country as a whole—becomes more vivid and evocative. Gradually the political authorities contained in clans, guilds, and church—once nearly absolute—pass, in their sovereign form at least, to the territorial aggregate. Words, concepts, and statuses which were in the beginning primarily personal in their reference gradually become territorial. The original significance of "king," of "law," of "liberty," and of literally hundreds of other words in Western languages was personal, inseparable from persons and their direct interrelations, as is, say, "Roman Catholicism" or "Methodism" today. Gradually, however, each of these words became increasingly territorial in reference. For example, the king was no longer king of the Franks, but of France.

Today, in many parts of the world, Africa, Southeast Asia, Oceania, and elsewhere, transitions analogous to those just described are taking place, with, of course, an immense variety of results. Only slowly, and with difficulty, does the transition take place, does the sense of clan or tribe recede, to be replaced more and more by the sense of the territorial unit in which one finds himself living.

It should not be thought that the distinction between personal and territorial is one of historical importance only. After all, we live, all of us, in both types of social aggregate in even the most civilized and modern parts of the world. However much of our lives are lived through the relationships of state, county, township, administrative or electoral district (territorial relationships that have authority over us as citizens), it is obvious that much more of our day-to-day lives is experienced through the personal relationships of family, religious or economic association, ethnic group, social class, and so on.

And for all the usefulness and importance of the distinction, there is no necessary separation between the two types. The village community, for example, to be found throughout the world in history, is at bottom a territorial entity. So is the neighborhood. But, as we all know, these entities can and frequently do become personal as well. The ties of kinship, religion, and class can become thoroughly interwoven with those of place. In the beginning, as the distinguished historian Pirenne has emphasized, towns were not places so much as they were personal associations, with membership limited to those of special, usually economic, characteristics. Only later did towns, like states in general in Western Europe, become essentially territorial forms of social aggregate.

It should also be stressed that it is a rare territorial aggregate that is not influenced, in some degree at least, by social unities of a personal kind: kinship, religious, ethnic, and other. The strategic influence of certain families, of leaders of religious organizations, of ethnic groups, and of both lower and upper classes in a given city, town, or state is a recurrent aspect of the contemporary political power scene. Theoretically, all citizens are equal in a township or other territorial-political unit—and the underlying residual strength of this theoretical equality should never be overlooked—but it is only too plain that some citizens, in Orwell's classic phrasing, are more equal than others. Some are made superior through ties of kinship or class or ethnicity or occupational association. None of these counts in strict constitutional rendering, but all exert influence that can be decisive in the actual workings of organizations and governments.

It is probable that for the most part personal ties are more intense than territorial ones. One clearly is more devoted to his family, let us say, than to the electoral or irrigation district of which he is a part. But these are the extremes. It would not be wise to overlook the intensity of what we call "patriotism" in modern society: the allegiance that is given, often at the expense of property, religion, and even life, to the territorial state. Nationalism is one of the most powerful of sentiments and ties in the contemporary world, and basically it is no more than the expression of territorial solidarity and allegiance. Many a citizen today gives to his country an intensity of devotion and willingness to sacrifice that was until fairly recently in history reserved for kinship or religion alone. Still, with the exception of modern nationalism, it is probably accurate to say that personal social aggregates are more likely to manifest depth and continuity of cohesive relationships among individuals than are territorial aggregates.

We shall come back to this distinction in the next chapter, for exactly the same kind of differentiation must be made between types of authority in human society. There is the authority that arises from such personal groups as clan, caste, tribe, and guild and the type of authority that arises from the mere fact of residence in a given territorial domain. One of the most striking features of the political change that is found today in such parts of the world as Africa, Asia, and large parts of Oceania is the shift taking place from the ancient allegiances and authorities of personal groupings (such as kinship, caste, and religion) to those allegiances and authorities which are bound up with the territorial political state and its numerous subdivisions. The shift, as we know, is a far from easy and simple one. It is attended by numerous and deeply complex tensions and conflicts. Nor is it ever a clear-cut and sharp change. Almost always the past continues into the present and future.

Conflict between personal and territorial allegiances is by no means confined, however, to the historical past or to the non-Western parts of the world today. Periodically we see this conflict in our own social order, as when the social bonds of kinship, or religion, or cultural association seem to conflict, in the minds of individuals who are, so to speak, caught between, with the social bonds embodied in the political state or one of its subdivisions. We see this most dramatically and vividly perhaps in the flag-salute cases in law or in the refusal, for religious or personal reasons, to submit to the military draft. The conflict reached its height in modern times in the rise of the totalitarian states of the twentieth century when every effort was made by leaders of the political state to dissolve or thoroughly subordinate traditional personal unities in the population and to make the territorial state itself serve as the single, total, manifestation of society.

But quite apart from totalitarianism and from the more dramatic types of instance seen in flag-salute and related cases in law, the conflict between personal and territorial aggregates within a single society is always latent, for the obligations of membership in the one can frequently seem prejudicial to obligations in the other type. At the present time *ethnicity*—the social demands of being, for instance, a black, or a Mexican-American—is one of the most influential of expressions of what is by its nature a personal type of social aggregate. In a whole variety of matters—education, and administration of welfare funds, among others—we are witnessing conflict between powerful, deeply evocative *personal* social aggregates (in this case racial or ethnic) and those aggregates, such as municipalities or states, which are *territorial* and which are the official units of government in these matters. Again let us emphasize that, first, this type of underlying conflict is not new in history—it is one of the oldest we know anything about. Second, here as elsewhere, the conflict is based upon allegiances, loyalties, and authorities that are the very stuff of human society.

GEMEINSCHAFT AND GESELLSCHAFT

I use the German words for the two types of social aggregate which are the subject of this section because there is no single English word that expresses the distinctive nature of either one. The nearest we can come is "community" for the first and "society" for the second, but in neither case is the full meaning expressed by the English word. We owe to Ferdinand Tönnies primarily the sociological interest in these types of relationship.

When we refer to groupings of a *Gemeinschaft* character, we have in mind relationships encompassing human beings as full personalities rather than the single aspects or roles of human beings. These are relationships characterized by a high degree of cohesion, communality, and duration in time. The most obvious and historically persistent types of *Gemeinschaft* are kinship groups, village communities, castes, religious organizations, ethnic groups, and guilds. In each of these the whole personality of the individual tends to be involved, and in each of them the claims of the social unity upon the individual tend to be nearly total. *Gemeinschaft* types of social aggregates may spring from personal or territorial attributes, be religious or secular, small or large. What is essential is the quality of strong cohesiveness of persons to one another and the quality of rooted, persisting collective identity. The kinship group serves as the archetype of *Gemeinschaft*. It is by all odds the oldest form, and its spirit, its sense of communal membership, even its nomenclature, tend to become the image of other, nonkinship types of *Gemeinschaft*. In any genuinely *Gemeinschaft* type of social grouping there is a profound ethic of solidarity, a vivid sense of "we *versus* they," and of commitment of the whole self to the *Gemeinschaft*.

If we speak in moral terms, it would be a great mistake to label *Gemeinschaft* as necessarily "good." Bear in mind that examples of genuine *Gemeinschaft* include the ethnic ghetto as well as the village community, the totalitarian nation as well as the family, extreme social caste (as in India) as well as the guild or religious parish. *Gemeinschaft* is a neutral, descriptive term so far as ethical preference is concerned. *Gemeinschaft* cannot be subsumed under any of the types of social aggregate we have thus far considered, for it may be either small or large, open or closed, personal or territorial. Like each of these, it is a distinctive perspective for examining social behavior and a social order.

Gesellschaft may also be either small or large, open or closed, personal or territorial. What is crucial to this type of aggregate, irrespective of anything else, is the fact that, whether small or large, personal or territorial, it engages the individual in only one of the aspects of his total being, or, at most, only a few aspects. From the individual's point of view his relationship with others in *Gesellschaft* is more tenuous, loose, and less deeply rooted in his allegiances or commitments. *Gesellschaft* is commonly founded around a few specific interests or purposes, whether religious, economic, recreational, or political. In contemporary Western society there is a vast abundance of *Gesellschaft* types of relationship among individuals, types in which human beings are to be found linked more or less casually or else contractually, in terms of some specific interests. Such types do not and, by their nature, cannot command depths of loyalty or become the focus of motivations, as do those in *Gemeinschaft* groupings.

Just as the shift from personal to territorial types of human relationships is a momentous one in history, so is the analogous shift from *Gemeinschaft* to *Gesellschaft*. A given period in history, or a given area of the earth's surface, may be rich in *Gemeinschaft* groupings—whether personal, such as kinship, or territorial, such as village community or town. Then, through profound events and changes, that historical period or area may see the number of *Gemeinschaft* groups diminish relative to the number of *Gesellschaft* types. Or, as is common in periods of change along this line, *Gemeinschaft* groups may become altered by the rise within them of motivations, ties, and incentives which are more of a *Gesellschaft* character. In business, a generations-old family form of enterprise, one in which employees are either literally or symbolically members of the family, may become, as the result of competitive pressures, more and more of a *Gesellschaft* type. As a result, the spirit of contractualism, individual competition, self-interest, and loose, specific-interest-oriented motivations will replace the older ones. The same kind of change is witnessed in the history of the school, the university, the church, the village or town, the guild, and so on. It is one of the most universal types of social change to be found in the history of human society.

Sometimes, of course, the change works in reverse fashion. A relationship that begins as a *Gesellschaft* type—whether a business enterprise of the modern age, a military bond in early feudalism, or a political association—may in time become increasingly characterized by *Gemeinschaft* relationships among the members. The history of the modern political state is a striking example of an association that in the beginning encompassed very little of the ordinary human being's life and was limited to the sole functions of military defense and civil order. Gradually, through the growth of modern nationalism, a more and more *Gemeinschaft* type of social relationship arose. Today the political nation commands from most persons an allegiance, a sense of rooted membership, that a few hundred years ago was given to kindred or church. One of the most impressive aspects of the history of the modern business corporation is the extent to which it has developed from what it was a century ago. At that time, it was a specific-interest, *Gesellschaft* type of enterprise holding no responsibility whatever to its workers beyond payment of wage for work rendered and commanding little if any loyalty from them. Today, the corporation has developed into the multi-functioned, often paternalistic, more nearly *Gemeinschaft* entity that it is, or at least tries to be, in so many quarters today.

REFERENCE GROUPS

Any type of social aggregate or group may be a reference group: small or large, open or closed, personal or territorial, *Gemeinschaft* or *Gesellschaft*. A reference group may be organized around kinship, religion, social status, ethnicity, economic interests, or political values. It may be near at hand, the scene of an individual's incessant participation in its activities, or it may be distant and dispersed. A reference group can be deeply influential in an individual's life even when he is not a member of it.

What is essential in the concept of reference group is that it is the group or social aggregate to which an individual "refers," consciously or unconsciously, in the shaping of his attitudes on a given subject or in the formation of his conduct. It is the social aggregate toward which he orients his aspirations, judgments, tastes, and even his profoundest moral or social values. Once we clearly know, with respect to a given individual and his behavior, what the dominant reference groups are in his life, we are put in a better position for understanding and for predicting that individual's behavior.

The reason why the reference group must be distinguished from the types we have thus far considered is that the groups or aggregates within which a person may be seen living or participating need not be the entities that exert the greatest amount of influence upon his day-to-day behavior. The importance of this observation is the greater the more complex and differentiated the social order in which an individual lives. In a very simple society, one for example characterized solely by the tiny village community or kinship group in which the individual lives, thinks, aspires, and dreams, his reference group is in all probability that village or kinship group. If he is living within a social caste or ethnic ghetto and *knows*, at least to his own satisfaction, that there is no possibility whatever of his living anywhere else, of ever moving outward or upward in social terms, the probability is high that this caste or ghetto is his overwhelmingly dominant reference group. He is likely to shape his attitudes and life style almost exclusively to the norms of that group, the group in which he lives, to which he belongs.

But the more complex the social order, the larger the number of other social aggregates within the individual's ken, and the larger the possibility—even if it is but theoretical possibility—of the individual's exit from one and entry into another social aggregate, the less the probability that the group within which we actually find the individual is necessarily so powerful a reference group.

Actually, it is not a matter of exit and entry at all when we consider what is really crucial in the reference group. The black may, so far as his own definition of the situation is concerned, take it for granted that he will never escape his black enclave and still, in one or another situation, find himself powerfully motivated by norms he sees at a distance in white society. The mass media put us all in touch with life styles, values, and ambitions which may not be resident at all in the groups within which we live from day to day. The phenomenon of the aristocrat or upper-class man of wealth directing his political energies toward goals that are foreign to his own class is, while perhaps not a common one, certainly far from unknown. The upper-class individual who works for, votes for, and even provides leadership for lower-class sectors of the population, who is motivated by considerations utterly alien to those of his own family, his neighborhood, his church, or social club, is an individual for whom some outside set of norms, some external social aggregate, has become crucial in the shaping of his attitudes and life. His principal reference group, it is then possible to say, is largely separate from the group or groups within which he ostensibly lives.

From the strict point of view of understanding social behavior, the concept of reference group, or reference individual, or reference norm[7] is a vital consideration. We may say that, from the sociological point of view, the first requisite is discovery in a given individual's existence of what his reference group or groups actually are. They *may* be the visible group or groups immediately around him. But they may not. Deviant behavior—narcotic, sexual, political, legal—is sometimes, unthinkingly, declared to be behavior in which the individual concerned has lost all contact with a social group or a given set of norms. In fact what may have happened is that the individual has moved outside the sway of the obvious group—his family, his church, for example—and into the sway of a social aggregate or a set of norms that is not visible to the investigator until he has made a searching study of the individual's beliefs, his attitudes, his definition of the situation.

What Simmel wrote about social groups is exceedingly relevant at this point:

> *The groups with which the individual is affiliated constitute a system of coordinates, as it were, such that each new group with which he becomes affiliated circumscribes him more exactly and more unambiguously. To belong to any one of these groups leaves the individual considerable leeway. But the larger the number of groups to which an individual belongs, the more improbable is it that other persons will exhibit the same combination of group-affiliations, that these particular groups will "intersect" once again.*[8]

Hence the high correlation in the history of civilization between periods that exhibit an extreme individualism and those exhibiting an extreme profusion of groups and associations. Actually, what we are prone to call "individualism" is not so much anything that may be seen to emerge from the individual, considered as a discrete entity, but, rather, from the individual's relation to a considerable number of groups or other types of social aggregate. His powers of thought, imagination, and action may be heightened by the experience of living at one and the same time on the peripheries of many groups, as well as values and themes. Not one but several social groups may be his reference groups. These sometimes occur in rapid sequence, sometimes at the same time. There is a very close relation in history between high rates of intellectual mobility and the proliferation of reference groups in the lives of individuals.

The reference group may be a means of stimulating an individual to move out of his native circumstances, to desire strongly to move upward socially and culturally. What Robert Merton calls "anticipatory socialization" is a form of socialization that takes place in an individual when the norms of some reference group to which he can only aspire to belong to in the future are dominant in his life. He may live in the circumstances, for example, of a close combination of kinship, religious, and lower-class norms and yet, by virtue of a fresh exposure, perhaps through television or through frequent visits as an "outsider" to some very different part of the social order, become deeply influenced by the norms of a social group alien to that in which he actually lives.

Conversely, a person's reference group can be the means of reinforcing conduct and belief systems he has acquired natively in his family or religion, leading him to remain oblivious to socializing influences of the groups and associations to which he becomes exposed in later life. In short, the reference group may act as a powerful buttress to conservatism or, under different circumstances and in different individuals, it may become the source of radical break with native conditions.

There is much reason to believe that the widely different responses of individuals to extreme pressures or torments from the outside are accounted for in terms of the varying intensities of reference groups in the lives of these individuals. The capacity of certain individuals to resist torture or brainwashing techniques imposed by the enemy in time of war has much to do with the role that persisting reference groups occupy in the lives of these individuals. On the other hand, to be able to dissolve, as far as possible, the influence of old reference groups and to substitute the norms of new ones is the obvious aim of those administering torture or the techniques of brainwashing.

In a sense, the whole process of socialization is no more than the internalization of norms of successive reference groups. In his fascinating book *Growing Up Absurd*, Paul Goodman argues that it is the absence of clear-cut adult models—that is, of clear-cut adult reference groups, reference individuals, and reference norms—which goes the furthest to explain the frequently confused, anomic, and alienated behavior of youth in our present culture. A variety of economic, technological, and social influences has succeeded, Goodman contends, in separating the growing child from the kinds of adult reference groups which normally act to provide him with goals and models.

In summary we may say that the reference group serves as both a standard for *comparison* of one's self with a set of norms, that is, for self-appraisal, and also as the *source* of the varied norms and values which operate in a given individual's life. The concept of reference is one, obviously, that may be applied to authority, to culture, to morality, to social norms in general, as well as to simple groups or aggregates. What is fundamental in the concept of reference is the degree of social interaction, of *symbolic* interaction that is involved.

This element of interaction is, to be sure, what is fundamental in the study of all social aggregates. As we have had frequent occasion to observe, our primary task is that of explaining the social behavior of human beings. Such explanation carries us immediately to the several processes of social interaction, and these, in turn, to the several types of social aggregate in which these processes are to be found. Although there may be excellent reasons for the study of social aggregates in and for themselves as aspects of the social order, it is their relation to social behavior that alone justifies the scientific interest of sociologists and social psychologists.

One final reminder is in order. Each of the types of social aggregate we have examined briefly is a perspective or a parameter. Small groups, for example, do not exist in separation from what we have called closed groups or territorial groups or reference groups. A given group that has strong influence in the lives of individuals in a certain setting, may be, at one and the same time, small, open, territorial, and of *Gemeinschaft* character. Or it may be large, closed, personal, and of *Gesellschaft* character. The variations are, quite obviously, numerous in possibility.

Notes

1. One immensely important type of social aggregate not discussed in this chapter is that founded upon *status*.   However, I defer treatment of this type of social aggregate to Chapter 8, where we deal with the concept of status.
2. Georg Simmel, *The Sociology of Georg Simmel*, trans. and edited by Kurt Wolff (New York: Free Press, 1950), p. 135.
3. *Ibid.*, p. 93.
4. *Ibid.*, p. 93.
5. This is the central theme of my *The Quest For Community* (New York: Oxford University Press, 1953).
6. Joseph Gusfield, "Mass Society and Extremist Politics," *American Sociological Review* (February 1962), pp. 19–30.
7. To which should be added Charles Page's valuable concept of reference *area*, still evocative in human consciousness.
8. Georg Simmel, *Conflict and the Web of Group-Affiliations*, trans. by Kurt Wolff and Reinhard Bendix (New York: Free Press, 1955), p. 140.

6

Social Authority

THE ROOTS OF AUTHORITY

Any social order is a tissue of authorities. In contemporary society these authorities range from the mild and provident authority of a mother over her infant to the absolute, unconditional, and imprescriptible authority of the national state. Some system or pattern of authority is involved in any continuing social aggregate. The moment two or more persons find themselves in a relationship that involves, in whatever degree of informality or formality, the distribution of responsibilities, duties, needs, privileges, and rewards, a pattern of authority is present.

The authority may be wielded by one person or two, or more. It may be held to lie simply in the principles or purposes of the relationship. It may be formal or informal, tight or loose in character, free or despotic, legitimate or illegitimate. But in any regularized, persisting social relationship involving several human beings there is always authority. From a sociological point of view, the transition from the social aggregates we have just examined to social authority is both logical and necessary.

In this chapter we shall consider first the sources or roots of authority, then its principal types in society, the problem of conflicts of authority, and the relation between authority and power. We shall conclude our discussion with the nature of legitimacy of authority.

Let us begin with a simple but profound question: Why do human beings obey? Granted that not all people obey all authorities, that there are measurable differences in the degree of obedience that is found from one individual to the next even within the same social group, and that there are some persons—those said to be incorrigible—who, in appearance at least, rarely obey. Still, considering any single human life in its entirety and taking all human lives in a social order in the aggregate, it is plain that even the most recalcitrant of individuals spends the greater part of his life obeying the rules, regulations, signs, symbols, orders, and directions that form so considerable a part of any organized society. Moreover, even the person who is ostensibly flouting authority may turn out to be obeying the authority of some reference group that is not in the foreground. Those who, in Thoreau's great phrase, "march to a different drum" may still be seen marching, still obeying an authority of some kind, however distant from the immediate scene.

In answering our question, we must first rule out force as the universal and unvarying basis of authority. There are, without any question, types of authority that *are* based upon force and that in all likelihood would not long survive apart from force, either actual or potential. But these, although by no means inconsiderable in a society, are far from the whole story. There are many manifestations of authority in human lives, sometimes very strict and uncompromising authority, which are not rooted in force or fear of force. Any kinship system, religion, university, labor union, social club, athletic team, profession, or cultural association has a system of authority. For example, no one observing the behavior of any devout member of the Roman Catholic Church can doubt that he is obeying a whole host of injunctions, orders, and ordinances. So is the student in the university, the member of a labor union, or the employee of a business enterprise. But to try to explain obedience to authority in these instances merely by invoking the idea of force is clearly futile.

Moreover, even when we are dealing with the authority contained in the innumerable subdivisions and agencies of the political state, which is the one organization in modern society that may *legitimately* use force to buttress its authority, it can hardly be said that the state depends solely upon its force-resources—its police, military, courts, and the like. A citizen's instantaneous acceptance of the authority of a red light at an intersection, his willingness to drive on the proper side of the street, to pay taxes, to yield to a military draft, to refrain from breaking the laws against murder, theft, and arson, has much more behind it, obviously, than knowledge that the state possesses force. Even a prison—

one of the few organizations in our society that would undoubtedly dissolve instantly except for the residual force that holds it together—does not depend wholly upon the use or threat of force to command order. And as a large number of studies of prison riots show, it is only when a prison reaches the point of coming very close to depending solely upon force that social explosions become probable. Day in, day out, the authority of the prison rests upon factors other than force in the lives of the prisoners. If it didn't, the numbers of guards would have to be multiplied enormously. Force, then, is insufficient as an explanation even in those organizations of modern society where it is legitimate. And force is largely irrelevant when we are dealing with the great majority of groups and associations in society, all of which plainly wield authority in some form.

It may be remembered at this point that in Chapter 4 on social interaction we identified *coercion* as one of the major mechanisms of social behavior. It would be simple and pleasant if we could refer the matter of authority to this one process of social interaction—to the undoubted and frequent exertions of compulsion that we call coercion in day-to-day behavior. But we cannot. For there are innumerable manifestations of authority in a social organization—both the exercise of and obedience to authority—which cannot be reduced to coercion. Not, at least, without expanding the meaning of the word "coercion" to the point where it ceases to be precise and definite. Coercion may indeed be involved in many if not all instances of authority; but it is not exclusive. It is attended by other factors that have to be distinguished sharply from coercion: exchange, cooperation, and conformity, for example. My affirmative response to any given authority may be conditioned solely upon exchange: the obedience I give in exchange for the protection inherent in a certain type of authority.

We go farthest in reaching an answer to our question of why human beings obey if we recall at this point two major elements of what we were considering in the two preceding chapters. First, the existence of *social roles* and, second, the *nature of social aggregates*. Full discussion of social roles will have to await the next chapter, but enough has been said about social roles to get us started in the discussion of the nature and roots of authority.

Implicit in any role is a set of norms that define and give it identity. In so doing, the norms provide guidance or direction in individual conduct. Moreover, it is the nature of any single social role that a large part of its significance in the individual's life comes *not* simply from what is contained normatively in it alone but rather from certain other roles whose existence is made necessary by the existence of the role in question. Thus when one assumes the role of religious communicant, of devout believer in a church, he cannot escape the interaction of his role with the roles of others in the same religion whose role demands are to issue instructions or commands just as his own role demand as communicant is to obey or follow these. How can one be a genuinely committed communicant and, at the same time, fail or refuse to obey the varied injunctions issued or mediated by those in the church, such as priest or minister? How can one hold the role of student and not be involved (however rebelliously at times) in a pattern of authority which includes the role of teacher, and no doubt the roles of others whose business it is to exercise authority in the form of grading, assignments, and so on? Similarly, the role of child cannot be understood save in terms of role fulfillments which cannot possibly be achieved except through the existence, *and through the role demands*, of others in the family—father, mother, older brother or sister, and so on. The role of citizen in a political state, by mere virtue of its existence, puts the individual in a position in which fulfillment of the demands of the citizen's role automatically requires a substantial measure of acceptance of the roles of others in the state whose role tasks involve the wielding of authority.

There is no need to multiply examples. It is clear that the individual, simply because of the fact that from infancy on he finds himself in a succession and plurality of social roles, is involved in interactions with other roles. And within the complex of these role interactions lies some kind of authority. The role of member of the most tradition-defying, law-violating gang or criminal organization imaginable does not exempt the individual who is holding the role from what has just been said. He may have flouted all other authorities in society in the process of becoming a member of the criminal organization. So far as possible, he may have abdicated all other roles in society. But his role as member of the criminal organization is, from the strictly analytical point of view, no different from the other roles. He cannot hold this role without remaining a member of the organization concerned. And this, obviously, means subjection to authority.

This consideration brings us to the second major element of authority, the *social aggregate* itself. It is impossible to conceive of a social aggregate possessed of even the loosest and most tenuous organization in which a pattern of authority is not present. Although the organization may be the least demanding of authorities, one in which the individual member feels utterly free, it remains true that to the extent that he is a member of the aggregate, he is also subject to its authority. There is, in short, a *conditionality* to authority. There is also an element in all associations or groups in which membership is not compelled absolutely (as in prisons or asylums) that can only be called *consent*. Authority, writes Robert Bierstedt in a brilliant essay on the subject, is a property of social organization:

> *When there is no organization there is no authority. Authority appears only in organized groups—the associations—of society, never in unorganized groups or in the unorganized community. An absence of organization implies an absence of authority. There is authority only within an association, never in the interstices between associations. The exercise of authority, furthermore, never extends beyond the limits of the association in which it is institutionalized and which gives it support and sanction.*[1]

Professor Bierstedt, with good reason, puts the matter in these terms. But, without dislodging any part of his argument, it would be possible to state it in reverse, so to speak, commencing with authority rather than organization. We can say that where there is no authority there is no organization. Or we can say that without authority there can be no organization. The locus of authority may or may not be in an individual or plurality of individuals; it may lie solely and undifferentiatedly in the group as a whole, or in a set of principles—a constitution—that each member is theoretically free to interpret for his personal guidance. The point is that even in these more or less utopian social unities there is a system of authority operating.

Why do human beings obey? The answer is surely plain: they obey because, holding roles of one kind or other, they can hardly escape the normative demands of the roles; and, belonging to one kind of social aggregate or another, they can hardly escape its pattern of organization.

I mentioned the properties of *conditionality* and *consent* above. By the first we have reference to the fact that any system of authority is binding solely upon those who are members of the association that contains the system of authority. Authority is therefore conditional upon membership. The authority of the national state may be absolute, but only upon those who are its citizens. The same is true with respect to religions, communities, business organizations, and so on. There are as many systems of authority in a society as there are groups, associations, and social aggregates generally. The single individual may be— and frequently is in modern, complex society—a point of intersection of several systems of authority, and sometimes these systems can conflict in such a way as to create intense problems. We shall expand this point in a later section of this chapter, for it is a vital one.

The attribute of *consent* is a more difficult one to handle in any discussion of authority. For the vast majority of authorities to be found in contemporary society, consent is as obvious an element as is conditionality. One consents to the authority of the university, or the family he has formed through marriage, or the labor union, or his profession, or any of a vast range of associations and groups in modern life. That is, he consents by his initial choice of entering the association or, if by birth he finds himself a member, his choice to remain. Obviously, this does not mean total or invariable consent. He may feel that any given edict or ordinance of the association is oppressive, that it became effective over his strenuous opposition. Nevertheless in this vast range of associations consent is still operative because the individual consents to remain a member and, consenting, to suffer occasional or even frequent onerous acts of authority in return for other, possibly larger benefits.

When, however, we come to those authorities that are absolute and unconditional and have behind them a monopoly of force, the case is quite different. Consent is hardly the essence, not in the full sense of the word. A person may feel that he is consenting when he remains a citizen of the United States. He would not wish to be elsewhere, and he may say to himself that, broadly speaking, he agrees with the American way of life. Consent, however, is still lacking in the full sense. For if a person were to exercise his consent negatively by refusing to grant it to a specific law, he could be forced to, or else imprisoned or otherwise punished. Moreover, there is no way a person can choose to withdraw from membership in the modern political state except by express permission of the state itself. Therefore, consent in the modern state—and this includes democracies as well as despotisms—is not an obvious attribute, no matter how much one may in actuality desire to be a citizen of a given state.

We shall return to aspects of this point in the final section of the chapter when we deal with the matter of legitimacy of authority and the different ways of assessing it. However, we must now move to some of the more influential types of authority in society. Although we have been able to see the roots of authority, its full nature can become manifest only in some of the types of authority.

TYPES OF AUTHORITY

From a purely empirical point of view, there are as many types of authority as there are groups, associations, and other forms of relationship in society. Thus we may speak of the authority to be found in the family, political state, church, social class, local community or neighborhood, profession, business, school, army, organized athletic team, and so on. Such empiricism would help us little, however, for obvious reasons. What we require is a distinction of types of authority that is drawn from the central concepts of sociology: social interaction, social aggregates, and social roles, among others. Just as we discovered that from the sociological point of view the nature of a social aggregate can be properly and usefully distinguished from its particular content or purpose, we shall now see that it is possible to do the same with social authority. Inevitably, given the nature and roots of authority, our types of authority will be closely linked to the types of social aggregates described above.

Informal and Formal Authority

Whether the social relationship is the simple dyad or triad, the gang or club, the business enterprise, or the modern nation, there is, to some degree, a pattern of authority to be found. One of the most important questions to be asked of any such aggregate relates to the degree of formality of such authority. The *informality* of much authority sometimes creates the illusion of nonexistence of authority, and the *formality* of much other authority often creates the illusion of its despotic or oppressive character. Irrespective of anything else, the very character of authority can be changed in the individual's definition of the situation merely by change in the relative degree of formality or informality of the authority.

Informal authority is most likely, though by no means necessarily, to be found in small social aggregates, just as formal authority is most likely to be found in large and complex aggregates. Informal authority is characterized by its relatively spontaneous, situational, and usually face-to-face nature. It lacks, by its very nature, the continuity of character that we would expect to find where authority is made a matter of systematic rule or calculation. In informal authority there may well be clearly understood sources of the authority—in the father or mother in the family group, in the foreman of a working group, in the teacher of a class in school, in the minister of a church, and so on.   But such authority—and it may at times reach despotic proportions—is inseparable from the situations in which it becomes manifest.   That is, it arises in, and assumes its specific nature from, a concrete, interpersonal situation in which rules or laws previously set forth no longer exist at all or else are few and flexible.   There is often a high degree of inconsistency in informal authority.   Such inconsistency is the product of its situational character and its being rooted in the face-to-face, interpersonal type of relationship among individuals.   Informal authority tends to be unstructured, often relaxed and loose, seldom perceived as authority by those participant to the situation, and strongly colored by the personalities of those participating.

Formal authority is of a more systematic, calculated, regularized character.   It is more often found in the large association than the small. It exists when numbers of members become too large, when functions become too complex, or when its importance to the social order as a whole becomes too great to be left to the simple and ad hoc decisions found in informal authority.   Formal authority makes plain, usually through written rules or laws, exactly where the sources of authority are to be found, what the varying levels of authority are, who reports to whom, who gives directions, who follows them, who sets policy, who executes it, what the penalties are for failure to abide by the rules, and so on.   Rights as well as duties are clearly defined, as are the several spheres within which authority operates.

The extremes of informal and formal authority are clear enough. One would hardly expect a college friendship group, a small family, or two or more buddies in the army to govern their relationships by formal rules and avenues of appeal, by specification of who issues instructions, and the like.   No more would one expect a giant corporation such as General Motors or a large labor union to be run other than by highly formalized rules and regulations.

But the last sentence suggests the possible difficulties that are involved when one makes the mistake of trying to explain a given type of authority *wholly* in terms of either its formal or informal features.   For, when we speak of "running" a large and complex organization and of the fact that formal rules and regulations are indispensable, we should not make the mistake of supposing that this organization is run solely through these rules and regulations.   The informal, rule-stretching, regulation-bending, out-of-channels relationships among key executives may have far more to do with organizational success than the formal rules and channels.

Equally important is the network of informal authorities which may be found within the organization, usually in the interstices of departments and divisions. Often individuals whose formal role in the authority structure is slight—such as an unusually able secretary in an executive office—exert very considerable influence and authority. Innumerable studies of work groups have shown the degree to which morale and work effectiveness are dependent upon the informal authority of a particular individual or group of individuals rather than upon the formal authority of foreman or manager. Sometimes, as in an occasional badly run prison, the informal authority exerted by powerful inmates can outreach the formal authority of warden and guards.

One of the commonest patterns in social history is the persistence of purely informal modes of authority in an organization when, for reasons of accumulated size and complexity, formal modes of authority are required. The whole modern field of administration has largely grown out of the rising need for persons trained in the mechanics of formal authority, formal organization, and formal function. Even when a given organization is made formal, or more formal, older and highly informal ways of authority frequently will hang on and sabotage the formal ways. Conversely, though much less often, aggregates long accustomed to formal authority will find themselves forced to rely upon more or less spontaneous and informal patterns of authority as the consequence of breakdown of the formal through disaster or mere erosion. Finally, we may note that occasionally we find social aggregates small enough and interactive enough in terms of personal contact to warrant informal authority but where, for one reason or another, rather systematic and formalized types of authority are found. Such authority may be the result of strong internal conflicts among key individuals, or it may be the result of mere preference for the formal, no matter how grotesque the consequences.

The contrast between informal and formal, the transition from the one to the other, the conflict between the two types in any given social situation, and the varying dependence of one on the other are all vital matters of sociological inquiry into the nature and functions of authority.

Traditional and Rational Authority

We are indebted primarily to Max Weber for clear identification of these two contrasting types of authority. Although there is a slight degree of overlap possible in some circumstances between traditional and rational (as well as between formal and informal), the differences are overriding. We are dealing with quite different perspectives. Thus informal authority may be either traditional or rational, and formal authority is as often one as the other.

Traditional authority derives its efficacy from being handed down from the past. According to Weber, traditional authority draws its legitimacy from belief in the special sanctity attached to the old. That which is "traditional" is quite literally and etymologically that which has been transmitted from generation to generation over a long period of time. The authority may be religious in theme or it may be economic, political, legal, or related to kinship. Its context may be the church, the village community, the labor union or industry, the political government, or the family. It may be written or unwritten. What is central is none of these but the fact that the primary reason for obeying authoritative norms is simply that they are old, that they "have always existed," that they are a part of time-tried experience.

Strictly speaking, any kind of authority that is handed down from one age to another may be called "traditional." It is common in sociological writing, however, to limit the word to the innumerable types of authority that are embedded in customs and traditions and that tend to exist not primarily because of any obvious legal utility or pragmatic rationality but because they *are* and because they *have been*. The effectiveness of traditional authority varies from people to people and from period to period. Nothing is more common in history than the phenomenon of traditional authority giving way and being altered or transformed by the impact of events or alien ideas. But a people or group in which some degree of traditional authority was not present would be hard to find.

When we speak of *rational* authority and contrast it to traditional, we do not mean necessarily that the former is more "rational" in the sense of being intelligent in conception or is superior by virtue of being the product of "reason" instead of mere historical tradition. It *may* be these, but it may not. Rational authority, in the sense in which Weber and contemporary sociology use the term, refers to all authority that derives from conscious and calculated effort to make the authority correspond to the express needs of the situation and to the norms of reason and logic. Such authority dispenses, so far as possible, with the nonlogical, nonrational criteria of mere antiquity or the sanctity produced through age. A rational law, like a rational approach to any problem, would be one in which the criteria of instrumental experience and logic would be dominant rather than the criteria of simple antiquity and hoary conventionality.

Weber introduced another attribute of rational authority that is vital to sociological understanding. This is the attribute of "legality." Here we have in view authority that exists, Weber writes, "by virtue of the belief in the validity of legal statute and functional 'competence' based on rationally created rules. In this case, obedience is expected in discharging statutory obligations."[2]

What is perhaps most important about rational authority, when seen through the prism of "legality," is that unlike traditional authority, it is regarded as something capable of being established, enacted, or decreed. This fact introduces us to one of the most striking of all transitions that any people can undergo in its history—the transition from a condition in which all authority is held to be rooted in the past, unchangeable, and not capable of being established or contrived by any living generation, to a condition in which the pregnant distinction is made between *tradition* and *law* and in which law is deemed something within the rational powers of living man. Whether we are dealing with the ancient Greeks of the fifth century B.C. or modern peoples in Asia and Africa, this transition is invariably a fateful one, for with it goes the larger, encompassing, transition from a largely passive, acceptance-oriented outlook on world and society to an outlook that is active and change- or reform-oriented. Great periods of intellectual achievement in history are quite commonly periods in which this transition may be found. The same dynamism that is a part of the view of law as something to be made, through reason, is likely to express itself in other areas as well—economic, cultural, artistic, and so on. Once the aim of law is deemed to be its rationality, the same impulse not infrequently goes into a consideration of the entire social order. Hence in the fifth century in Greece as well as in certain contemporary, emerging new nations, a spirit or process of *rationalization* is to be observed at work. The merely inherited, the merely traditional, is converted through calculation and conscious effort into the rational and systematic.

Weber regarded rationalization, in the sense just described, as one of the master principles in history. It occurred most vividly, perhaps, in modern Europe during its emergence from the tradition-dominated medieval period. But it was by no means confined to modern Europe. We may see the principle or process of rationalization in different periods and in different places throughout mankind's long history. What we see most often is the traditional authority of kinship, religion, and local community being replaced by the kind of authority that is most often—though not exclusively—found in the political state, with its gradually developing emphasis on enacted law. But, as a process, rationalization may be seen in the institutions of religion, education, economy, and culture generally, whenever the notion of authority-by-enactment supersedes, or rivals, the notion of authority rooted solely in the past.

A final manifestation of rational authority that is among the most obvious in the contemporary world is bureaucracy. As Weber—and before him Tocqueville—noted, it is the common character of rational authority to express itself *through the office rather than the man*, to be hierarchically organized through the relative importance of office rather than the man, and to seek to obliterate all distinctions within the organization that flow from the man rather than directly from the office. This is what Weber called the *ideal type* of bureaucracy. Obviously no large organization has ever functioned solely in terms of its bureaucracy, its official and formal relationships. What was said above with respect to formal and informal authority applies equally here. No matter what the degree of rational organization of offices and channels in even the very largest structures, the elements of the nonrational, the purely traditional, and the informal enter the day-to-day workings of the system. What Charles Page noted with respect to the wartime American navy, in a now classic article on the real workings of bureaucracy, would be just as applicable to departments of government, to large universities, and to private corporations. Apart from the *unofficial, informal* types of function and authority within the system, efficient solutions to many of the problems would not be possible.[3]

Page's point is both sound and important. False inferences, however, should not be drawn from it. To recognize the actual dependence of rationalized authority upon traditional or informal types or both is in no way to discount the historical importance of rationalization that Weber gave to it in Western authority. The tendency of more and more types of association, from the early modern era on, to seek rational and bureaucratic modes of authority is a clear one in Western history, as it is today in a great many non-Western parts of the world. And with the advance of bureaucracy—however incomplete it must always be in actual operation—has everywhere gone the familiar accompaniments of centralization, leveling, and channeling that Weber, Roberto Michels, and many others have described.

We should not conclude this discussion of bureaucracy and the organizational revolution in modern Western society without noting the degree to which bureaucracy has fallen under attack from the political left in our day. There is nothing novel in this. In Marx's writings are to be found some devastating criticisms of the political bureaucracy forming in European governments in his time.   And from the very beginning the political anarchists—Proudhon, Bakunin, Kropotkin, and others—declared political bureaucracy as much the enemy of man's freedom as any other element in the society.

But the fact remains that *most* of the attacks upon bureaucracy in government and large-scale organization generally came, until very recently, from political *conservatives*.   In the widespread extension of bureaucracy that modern humanitarianism in government has necessarily involved, the conservatives saw threats to both private property and individual liberty.   And although socialists tended to deny that the advent of socialism would carry with it any intensification of bureaucracy (the orthodox Marxists to this day deny that under socialism there can be any problem of bureaucracy), the conservatives saw in socialism and allied doctrines the absolute certainty of a bureaucratic paternalism that would stifle individual initiative and seriously circumscribe human freedom.

At the present time, however, radicalism rather than conservatism has become the principal context of attacks upon bureaucracy and upon hyperorganization in general.   This is particularly true in the radical movements springing from militant youth, both in the United States and Europe.   Without relinquishing historic opposition to capitalism and private property, the New Left has made bureaucracy its major target: bureaucracy in political government and also in university, church, industry, and the mass entertainment world.   This is not the place to assess the significance of the New Left in present-day Western society, much less the degree to which its varied doctrines are correct or false in their analyses.   However, we can observe that the greatest single difference between the New Left and most of the radicalism of the past century in the West lies in the central position the New Left gives to *bureaucracy* rather than to capitalism, private property, or laissez-faire as the object of its strongest opposition.

Personal and Territorial Authority

The importance of these two types of authority flows directly from the contrasting characters of the social aggregates involved.   Personal aggregates, it was noted, are those such as kinship, religious groups, ethnic groups, and certain types of association which derive their identifying nature from attributes belonging to *persons*.   Territorial aggregates are those of local community, political state, and nation which take on their outstanding character from the *territory* on which they are found, territory that is consciously separated from other territories by boundaries.

The oldest forms of authority in human history are personal— primarily related to kinship, religion, and ethnic group. Authority is made legitimate for any given individual by the kinship, religious, or ethnic group that he belongs to. No authority from the outside may claim the individual except with the consent of whichever personal group he belongs to. Law follows the individual precisely as does family- or ethnic-relatedness. In the ancient world wherever personal authority was strong—as in earliest Greece, Rome, India, China, Persia—and where the sense of territorial authority was weak, human beings were quite literally tried when offenses were committed requiring punishment, by their kinship groups, their ethnic-tribal council, or their religious courts. Rights, justice, and punishment were all defined in terms of personal relationships rather than of the territory where the person happened to reside.

Personal authority is by no means confined—that is, where it is ascendant over territoriality—to the ancient world. The European Middle Ages is a period rich in the supremacies of the laws of personal aggregates—clans, kindred, the Christian religion, and the whole assemblage of peoples and races that had settled in the area once dominated by Roman law. Even today there are large parts of the earth where the personal authority of kinship, religion, and ethnicity is still great, even though these areas are presently undergoing the same kind of revolution in the nature of authority that Greece, Rome, and Europe went through many centuries ago—the revolution involved when personal authority is superseded by territorial.

Personal authority, by its nature, strongly emphasizes the corporate solidarity of the group or aggregate from which the authority is derived. The sense of individualism tends to be weak. The individual is held to have duties rather than rights. The structure of authority is concentric, moving out from the authority of the household group (regarded as sovereign within its domain) to the successively wider circles of clan, kindred, caste, tribe, and so on. Each circle of authority is deemed to be absolute within its sphere. The strenuous effort of the Church in the Middle Ages to maintain its own authority against the competing claims of, first, kinship and, later, the territorial state is one of the major aspects of medieval and modern history.

Personal authority thus tends to be decentralized and plural, with the sanctity of the personal groups forming it held inviolate within the legitimate sphere. Justice tends to be group justice. The notion of group responsibility is strong. When an individual commits an offense, the social group of which he is a member is regarded as guilty by the larger community until the group has, so to speak, purged itself of guilt by punishment of its own member. In ancient Rome, until late in the Republic, only a person's own family could legally put him to death, no matter what the type of offense. Justice tends to be a process of negotiation among groups, sometimes resulting in the blood feud, rather than a matter of impersonal decision by nonpersonal tribunals. The distinction between "private" and "public" offenses is a strong one. Many offenses which in modern society are regarded as "public," as quite literally crimes against the state, such as murder and assault, are regarded as "private" offenses where personal authority is strong. Such "private" offenses are subject to adjudication between the two groups involved, with the rest of the community maintaining its distance.

Old age is usually venerated profoundly in societies dominated by personal systems of authority. The family is the archetype of such authority. Its own nomenclature and symbols—"father," "mother," "brother," "sister," and so on—are widely borrowed, with such terms as "elders," "alderman," and a host of others reflecting the esteem in which the older members of the family are held by custom. From this veneration of age comes the naturally hierarchical character of personal authority. There is little notion of "all men equal before the law," a doctrine that comes later in man's history. Wherever personal authority is ascendant there is a built-in stratification of rights, privileges, and duties. Almost always it is to the oldest individuals, the oldest family lines, the oldest ethnic or religious strains that the greater share of honor, privilege, and responsibility goes.

Although traditional and personal types of authority must be distinguished, there is no mistaking the fact that personal authority is usually strongly traditional rather than rationalistic. Tradition instead of rationality, contract, or individual right tends to be dominant. Max Weber was so impressed by the interrelation of the personal and the traditional that he made "personal" one of the chief identifying attributes of what he called traditional authority. The two, however, must be kept distinct, for tradition can be equally prominent in nonpersonal, territorial aggregates such as the village community and also certain forms of political state. Nevertheless, Weber's point suggests something of clear importance—the strong position that tradition tends to hold in all systems of authority, such as kinship, religion, and caste, which are personal by nature rather than territorial.

There is another aspect of personal authority that must be stressed.

This is *charismatic* authority, the kind that proceeds from individuals who are regarded as possessed of some special spirit, grace, or divinity that leads others to follow and obey. Weber made charismatic authority a distinct type in history, one rivaling his categories of "traditional" and "rational." I do not. Important as it may be, charismatic authority is simply a heightened form of personal authority, one that takes its initial form in some individual, known or unknown. This type of authority may then extend itself through descent (biological or purely social) to others who in some manner share the charisma. There is an element of the charismatic in all personal authority—hence the special quality that most persons like to think lies in their family descent, giving them at least some interest in their genealogy. And charismatic authority is personal to its core—even though it may imprint itself through tradition and legend upon *things*, such as the cross or types of food and drink, or become routinized as in the papacy.

When we turn from personal to *territorial* authority we confront something very different in all major respects. As indicated above, in the judgment of many great jurists of the past century such as Henry Maine, Paul Vinogradov, and F. W. Maitland, one of the most momentous changes in all history is that which occurs in a people's existence when the basis of its life is transformed from personal to territorial ties, from personal to territorial authority. Ancient Athens underwent this change in the late sixth century B.C. (just before its magnificent fifth century.) Rome underwent it in the first century B.C. The breakup of the Middle Ages is, at bottom, the breakup of a system of primarily personal authority and its gradual replacement by a primarily territorial system—that is, the modern national or territorial state. The emergence of the new nations of Asia and Africa today is founded on the replacement of ancient personal authorities of clan, kindred, caste, and religion by the kind of authority that is held to be resident in a given area. The new authority is represented by political government and is deemed by its possessors to be sovereign over the ancient personal authorities.

That a man's primary identity should flow from *where he lives* rather than *from whom he is descended* does not come easily to human consciousness. The history of law is filled with incidents of conflict between the two types of identity and the two types of authority. When, at the end of the sixth century B.C., the famous reformer Cleisthenes founded the political state of Attica, with its component territorial demes or townships, and declared that thenceforth the basic rights, privileges, and duties of all Atticans would flow from the fact of Attica as a sovereign territory, he delivered a death blow to the previously ascendant tribes, clans, and kindreds of the Atticans. Their authority was rendered secondary, derivative, purely social, or traditional. The seat of sovereign authority was the city-state itself. This Greek transition, from the personal to the territorial, is one of the most celebrated and consequential changes in all human history, but there have been countless transitions of similar or identical type. They go on indeed at the present time.

Certain direct consequences of the replacement of personal by territorial types of authority are important. In the first place, territorialization of authority has *individualizing* effects. We have noted the strong tendency of social organizations that are exclusively organized in personal terms to be cellular and concentric: the group subordinates the individual. With the territorialization of authority a kind of liberation of the individual from the kinship, religious, or ethnic group is effected. By virtue of the fact that the seat of law is now the area rather than anyone of the personal groups composing the social organization, it is possible for the individual to achieve a discrete identity as citizen, or at least as unit of the government. This identity was less possible when all authority was resident in kinship and other types of personal groups. As the history of the Western world makes plain, this establishment of individual legal identities does not take place overnight, at least for many individuals. For long periods slaves, members of certain ethnic groups, women, children, and servants may remain confined within the authorities of groups that intermediate between individual and state. But, as is equally plain from the record, once the process of territorialization of authority—and, with it, of rights, liberties, and equalities—begins, it rarely stops short of inclusion of nearly all individuals in the area. Much of the history of human freedom can be written in terms of the achievement *by individuals* of rights, privileges, and responsibilities which, prior to the rise of the territorial state, were functions solely of tightly knit kinship and ethnic groups, or of social classes and churches.

Second, territorialization brings with it a certain degree of *centralization* of authority. Whereas personal authority tends to be diffuse, plural, and decentralized by its very nature, the process of territorialization tends to eradicate group immunities. Such eradication flows necessarily, even if mildly for long periods, from the transfer of the locus of authority from the plurality of personal groups in the area to the single agency of territorial authority, the political government, as we call it. Whereas personal authority tends to maintain intact the several concentric circles of expression of this authority (with clan authority, for example, stopping short of the household, tribal authority stopping short of the clan, etc.), it is the character of territorial authority to cut through these immunities and to reach the individual.   The central point is this: the same overall process that includes individualization also includes the kind of centralization that makes possible a sufficient degree of displacement of group authority to permit individualization.

Third, the *mass*, or at least the beginning of the mass, is produced by territorialization.   I follow Simmel here in referring to the mass as an aggregate of individuals, of whatever size, that is devoid of kinship, religious, ethnic, or other types of social and traditional relationships.   Or, if not altogether devoid, the mass at least is lacking largely in the functional influence of these relationships.   When we speak of *mass society* we have reference to a high degree of social atomization.   Now, it is precisely the transfer of sovereign authority from the personal groups of a given area to the new agency of government *representing all the individuals, irrespective of social grouping, cultural tradition, and social interest*, that makes possible the emergence of the mass.   For unless there were a system of authority—and, with it, of function, of service, of allegiance—that transcended the identities of the traditional personal groups in the area, it would be quite impossible for the mass to maintain itself, or to be maintained.

It is impossible to exaggerate, in sociological terms, the significance of the contrast between personal and territorial types of authority and the historical significance of the transition from one to the other in innumerable areas of the world.   Although there were manifestations of the transition many thousands of years ago in China, Egypt, Greece, and Rome, there are continuing manifestations today.   These, as I have suggested, are vivid in the new nations of the world.   But these manifestations are also vivid, in perhaps less dramatic terms, within nations where the fundamental change took place centuries ago and where territorial sovereignty as a principle became established by the sixteenth or seventeenth century.   In these nations the process of absorption of all human beings (peasants, women, children, Jews, blacks, and others) into the rights, privileges, and equalities of territorial authority has been going on continuously for centuries, down indeed to the very moment.

One other aspect of the distinction should be mentioned.   I noted above when discussing the two types of social aggregate that, in one form or another, they are to be found coexisting in all parts of society.   So are their respective modes of authority.   Consider the United States, or any one of its numerous territorial internal subdivisions.   Of the sovereignty of these subdivisions over purely personal types of authority there is no question.   We all know where the law lies.   But who will deny that purely personal types of authority continue to exert their power? This is evident in such personal types as political party machines, some dominant and wealthy families, well-organized ethnic groups, the members of certain elites within a community, and so on. Once *sovereign* authority lay in kinship, class, or ethnicity; and in a few fast-vanishing parts of the earth it still does. Today sovereign authority generally lies only in territorial types of social aggregate. But personal types of authority, for all their lack of sovereignty, do continue, in certain circumstances, to exert profound and sometimes decisive influence in human affairs.

Limited and Total Authority

This is another dimension of authority that overlaps some of those we have already discussed. But the distinction is as important as was the distinction we made in the preceding chapter between open and closed types of social aggregates.

When we speak of limited authority we have reference to authority that is restricted to some given form of association, to a single relationship, or to a single function. By its nature it does not encompass all aspects of the individual's life. The authority of Jewish dietary injunctions, of the Roman Catholic confessional, of the Democratic party in the United States, of the university, or of any business group is obviously limited to those who belong to the associations involved. Generally speaking, such authority is limited in the further sense that it pertains to but a single aspect of the individual's life. The authority of church or labor union or business enterprise is limited to that aspect of the individual's life that is given to the association: faith and morals with respect to the church, work with respect to labor union and business enterprise, and so on.

We observed at the beginning of this chapter that there is, to a certain degree, an element of conditionality, of limit, in all authority. If one's role, his membership in an aggregate, is discontinued, so also is the particular authority over him. Thus whether with respect to the small friendship group or the totalitarian state, we say correctly that authority is conditional upon membership. This is an important observation so far as the roots of authority are concerned.

But, very plainly, there are profound differences in the degree of exertion of authority from one aggregate to another and also in the capacity of the individual member to withdraw from the aggregate. The authority of any church today, or labor union, or university clearly is limited by the fact that it touches but a single aspect of the individual's life and by the further fact that he is, generally speaking, at liberty to withdraw when he chooses. Even if we grant that under certain circumstances the individual's effective freedom to withdraw from a labor union may be limited by reprisals of an economic or even forcible kind, it remains true that a higher degree of conditionality is to be found in the labor union or church than in the modern political state.

There are, however, other types of authority from which, for one reason or another, the individual is not free to withdraw, not free to escape the authority contained, and which, far from touching but a specialized aspect of the individual's life, touch his entire existence. Here we are in the presence of total authority.

There are various manifestations of total authority. That of the modern national territorial state is total, at least in theory and in potentiality. In even the most democratic state, if a sufficient majority of the people, working through proper constitutional channels, were to seek to extend the authority of the political state over literally all aspects of the individual's life, there would be no limit to its effort save that of sheer expediency. Even constitutional guarantees, such as bills of rights, can be set aside legally by proper political action. For the most part, however, what we call the liberal or democratic state (and this was equally true of the old, tradition-bound monarchies of early Europe) remains relatively limited in its authority in actual practice. Irrespective of what it might do in purely theoretical terms, the democratic state does not prescribe religious beliefs, fix individuals in their respective social classes or jobs, or superintend all details of family life.

The totalitarian state of the twentieth century is—at least in theory and design—the unlimited extension of political power and the political bond into all areas of human behavior. Nothing is held to be morally or legally exempt from the scope of political government. Religion, family life, labor, industry, profession, and education, as well as music, art, and literature, are deemed to serve their highest function in direct service to the specific ends around which the totalitarian state is formed. Fascism in Italy, Nazism in Germany, and Communism in Soviet Russia, Maoist China, Albania, and Yugoslavia, among other places, all exemplify the totalitarian state in some degree. It is the very nature of the totalitarian state that autonomy of association, freedom of culture, and rights of individual dissent are forbidden, for in them would lie ever-present possibilities of divergence from the aims of the state.

I have been describing the theory and design of the totalitarian state. In actuality such states are somewhat different. A considerable number of studies of the totalitarian state in operation make clear that between ideological design and actual fulfillment lies a gulf—sometimes narrow, sometimes broad.   In part the gulf is the same type we have seen to lie in all human behavior between the ideal type and concrete reality. No matter what the group and its norms, actual patterns of behavior are bound to deviate somewhat from the ideal.   Totalitarian rulers also face the problem created by individuals whose cherished traditions, personal ideals, and hopes serve to make reality somewhat different from the totalitarian ideal. Hence the incessant effort of totalitarian governments to root out divergent ideas and ideals before they can attract followers.   The problems faced by every large-scale, formal, and bureaucratized organization are greatly intensified in the totalitarian state, especially the large one. We may go back to what Simmel said about the factor of group size: the smaller the state, the eaiser for it to become absolute in near fact and total in political scope.   All evidence suggests that the sheer organizational problems faced by Germany under Hitler had become nearly insuperable and would very probably have swamped the regime before the end of the 1930s had it not been for the onset of World War II with its inevitably centripetal effects.   The same seems to have been true of Russia under Stalin.   Whatever the personal and ideological factors involved, the death of Stalin and the ascendancy of Khrushchev and his succesors meant a considerable lessening of the organizational rigidity that was beginning to paralyze certain economic and political sectors of Soviet Russia.

But for all the gulf between totalitarian ideal and practice, no one familiar with the totalitarian states of the twentieth century would wish to depreciate the differences between them and the limited political orders which, as in the cases of Germany and Italy, preceded them and which continue to characterize the liberal democracies of the world. One may grant that the totalitarian state is but an intensification of tendencies present in the modern limited state, an extension of political powers possessed under the doctrine of sovereignty even by democratic states.   There is still a profound difference between a political order in which power stemming from government *is* limited and significant areas of intellectual, cultural, and economic autonomy *are* left intact, and a political order whose aim is systematic extermination of these areas of autonomy.

No matter how free and democratic the political state in the contemporary world, its *residual* authority is, in constitutional theory, absolute, unconditional, and imperscriptible.   For example, by the standards of the early nineteenth century in the United States, even the freest of present-day democratic states can seem repressive at times.

Through a variety of constitutional amendments, laws, and changes in popular consensus since then, the political order now assumes far greater authority in the various sectors of society than it once did. (But it also assumes far greater responsibility for human welfare.)

Immigration laws are a fair measure of the degrees of limitedness imposed by political authority in successive decades. United States government authority in this respect was much more limited in the early and middle nineteenth century, when any number of people could move to this country. In the early twentieth century, the authority of government became strict as far as quotas of immigrants, conditions of entry, and conditions of residence were concerned. Even so, the authority of the United States remained far more limited as far as prescription of conditions of immigration and emigration were concerned than did the authority of the Soviet Union from the early 1920s on.

The difference between limited and total authority is perhaps clear enough when we are considering liberal and totalitarian political states. But the interest of sociology in these two types of authority does not stop with the state. For there are several other forms of total authority to be found in society, all of them in the liberal or democratic political order as well as in the totalitarian. I refer to such patterns found in the asylum, the prison, the military organization, and, from the point of view of the small child at least, the family. In each of these the authority of the organization—what we referred to in the preceding chapter as a "closed aggregate"—is total in its reach, fully encompassing the individual's life. Within each of these patterns there is, in effect, a disappearance of limits to authority except those that are set by the organization itself. The individual, plainly, is not free to withdraw from the prison or asylum or military organization until his term is up, even if its authority comes to seem oppressive. And, within the organization, he is subject to the full sweep of its authority.

Inevitably, patterns of social interaction, definitions of situation, and conceptions of self differ when we move from a system of limited authority to one of total authority. Consider a school in which (as is the case, or used to be the case, with many private schools), authority over the pupil extends through all hours of the day and ranges from instruction to what he eats, where and how he sleeps, what he may do with his free time, and so on. We do not commonly think of the school as a manifestation of total authority. But, taking it from the vantage point of the pupils, within—and this may include many public schools as well as the old-fashioned and still prestigious residential private school—the authority of the principal or headmaster may be total in effect. Whether, in actual practice, schools reflect total or merely limited systems of authority depends largely upon the norms of the surrounding society. The same is true of the family and its discipline of members, especially the children.

On the evidence of history and comparative study, there is literally no type of social aggregate that has not at some time been total in the scope of its authority. Today, "totalitarianism" is a word we confine to the political state. But there can be and has been religious totalitarianism in which the authority of the religious faith, the church or sect, has been without limit in the lives of the individual members and in which escape from that authority was impossible or at least very difficult. Kinship systems can be equally total in their authority, as in those social orders in which a single family or family line governs all aspects of the lives of the individuals in a community or region. As Frank Tannen-baum has wisely observed, every institution has the theoretical possibility of being total in its authority. Whether authority is in fact limited or total depends upon norms of freedom and authority in a population and also, perhaps of greatest significance, upon the degree to which that authority is checked, limited, challenged, and countervailed *by other authorities* in the social order. This observation leads us to the important matter of conflict of authority in society.

CONFLICTS OF AUTHORITY

Earlier we found conflict to be a persisting and universal pattern of social interaction. Nowhere is conflict more evident than with respect to types and systems of authority. Only in a society where every part is harmoniously fitted to every other part and where perceptions of discordant relationships among authorities and norms do not, through some magic, ever enter the minds of human beings, could there be a setting altogether free of conflict of authorities. Obviously, given the nature of the human mind and the interactive character of social life, such a society must remain forever imaginary, a product of utopian fancy.

The omnipresence of conflicts of authority derives from the nature of authority and its relation to social aggregates. There can be no social aggregate apart from a system of authority, and it is impossible for one to be a member of an aggregate without standing in some degree of obedience to its authority. If each of us belonged to but one social aggregate, itself undiversified and unramified, we might quickly reach some limit to our perception of conflict. But most of us live not in one but in a plurality of authority systems. We do, that is, once we have escaped the total dependence of infancy.

What begins as the simple and largely accepted authority of family alone becomes complicated by the intrusion in our lives of other and sometimes conflicting authorities: school, play group, gang or club, possibly church, and then business enterprise, labor union, profession, and so on. For the most part, most of us keep these conflicts, or potential conflicts, within bounds. We learn more or less unconsciously to arrange, to stratify the several demands of the groups and associations we are a part of. Generally, we have no great difficulty in perceiving one authority as ascendant over all others; or else we find ways of harmonizing several authorities that might otherwise conflict. At one age the authority of the family takes precedence over that of the peer group. At another age, however, it may not, and then some kind of resolution of conflicting demands is necessary.

As almost everyone knows, however, there are times when resolution of authority conflicts is impossible. One comes to feel deeply disturbed, literally torn by an inability to resolve the conflicts. The conflict may be between demands of school and those of family, between family and the friendship group one belongs to, between one's religion and the military demands of the political state. In a plural society such as ours, especially inasmuch as a high degree of individualism accompanies plurality in our society, conflicts within the individual personality can occasionally be profound. The plight of the member of the ethnic minority is often one of deep conflict of authorities in his life. He may feel a strong pull toward the traditional authority represented by family, language, and religion. At the same time, he may feel an almost equally strong pull toward the patterns of the majority culture in which he lives, a culture represented most powerfully, as we know, by the public school and the groups formed around it.

The importance of conflict of authority is not limited to the socialization of the individual. It is an inescapable part of human history in the large. From one point of view the history of human society is a history of the successive conflicts among authority systems. For long periods in the existence of societies the dominant system of authority may be kinship as represented by tribe, clan, family. The headship of the housefather is unquestioned in all matters of individual life. Matters of community significance are dealt with by the family elders. Then, as not infrequently occurs, a challenge to the authority of kinship appears. It may be military. By virtue of the tribe's exposed position, it has become subject to frequent attack from the outside. The structure of kinship society is insufficient to the demands of war, and the war band arises. Naturally, the military organization has its own imperatives, its own criteria of rank and effectiveness. And naturally, too, it has its own demands to make upon those who serve within it. These demands may in time come to rival and even challenge the demands upon individual lives in the kinship system. A deadly conflict within ensues, one that is not terminated until one or the other of the two conflicting authorities is triumphant. Much of the early histories of Greece, Rome, India, Persia, and other ancient countries can be written in these terms.

Or the conflict may be between kinship and church, as was the case in early medieval Europe. Among the Germanic peoples who occupied so much of Western Europe after the collapse of the Roman Empire, the authority of kinship was sovereign in ordinary civil life. Matters of birth, marriage, death, disposition of property, and religious worship were all under the authority of the family. Marriage, for example, was commonly effected by arrangement between the two families concerned, without outside influence from either a church or political authority. But with the spread of Christianity among the Germanic peoples there was bound to be a conflict of authorities. For many of the same matters which fell within Germanic kinship authority, such as baptism, marriage, and death rites, were central elements of Christian dogma and liturgy. Conflict in these and other areas went on for centuries in early Europe; indeed in parts of Northern Europe conflict between religion and kinship persisted until the modern era. Eventually, the authority of the Church won out over kinship in the greater part of Western Europe. The prestige and influence of the housefather waned before the rising power of the priest. But, despite the fact that marriage, for example, was from the very beginning a *dogma* of Christianity, it was not accepted by the Germanic peoples as a *ceremony* of the Church until relatively late. Not for a long time were families willing to recognize the Church's right to perform, and thus seek to legitimize, marriage of their members. In their view as in the view of their ancestors, marriage was an exclusive prerogative of the individuals and families concerned, not of any outside authority. The so-called common-law marriage is a manifestation of the right claimed by individuals to unite themselves in marriage without the intervention of outside authority. Its roots are deep in European history and, of course, within the history of conflicts of jurisdiction.

The Christian Church became the dominant influence on nearly all social, moral, and intellectual matters by the twelfth century in Western Europe. A large number of issues that had once been the sole concern of kinship organization became subject to the authority of the Church: issues of kinship itself but also of law, economy, taxation, education, and many others. There was scarcely a part of any human life for several centuries that was not decisively touched by the authority of the Christian religion. An immense variety of conditions and events that fall today within the sovereign contemplation of the state alone fell then within the structure of the Church.

Soon the authority of the Church was rivaled by still another type of authority, that of the political state. In the early Middle Ages the political state hardly existed except, in some measure, symbolically. Then, as the military requirements of society became greater—in response to the growing incidence of wars among feudal nobles—the political state become an ever more encompassing institution. At first limited to the needs of war, the state began to take on more and more of the civil, social, and economic functions of the Church in the lives of people. And as the state came in time to capture more and more of the allegiances of the peoples of Europe and to monopolize authority within its confines, struggle between it and the Church was almost inevitable. A large part of the social and intellectual history of modern Western Europe can be best understood in terms of the innumerable conflicts between the authority of the Church and the authority of the burgeoning state over supremacy with respect to the myriad aspects of human life and belief. For a long time the state's authority did not touch the more personal aspects of individual life; these were left to the Church and to what was still left of kinship authority. But in time, as the modern nation-state became ever stronger as the object of human allegiance, ever more deeply involved in economic, social, and legal issues, ever more powerful in its armies and police systems, it became what it has essentially been since the seventeenth century in Western Europe—the one authority system in society possessed of what we call sovereignty. The modern nation-state is the absolute, unconditional, and imprescriptible authority over human lives.

Even today, however, the conflict of authority continues. For although the absolute sovereignty of the political state became established in law and jurisprudence by the seventeenth century, it did not in fact extend itself to all areas of human life until the advent of the totalitarian state in the twentieth century. Today, occasional conflicts respecting the saluting of the flag, the custody and authority over children in a family, the claimed right to resist military draft on religious or ethical grounds, and the right of an association to organize and exist autonomously vividly attest the struggle between political and other types of authority in society.

It is precisely this type of authority conflict that is so evident in many of the new nations. Here, all within the period of the past three or four decades, we can see repeated some of the great conflicts of authority that fill the pages of histories of Western Europe. In the new nations of Africa and Asia, in the still-developing nations of Latin America and Oceania, we can see convulsive conflicts between kinship, religious, and political authorities.

The rise of the totalitarian state in Russia, Germany, and, more recently, in certain East European countries and in China brings the process of authority conflict to its dramatic height. For the principal aim of the totalitarian state is to replace through its own agencies the several authorities of nonpolitical society: the authorities of family, religion, guild, profession, business enterprise, labor union, and even of small cultural, social, and mutual-aid groups. No totalitarian state, as we observed above, ever succeeds fully in its aim. Divisions of some kind and degree always persist and, with them, conflicts of authority. But obviously, the stronger and more successful the totalitarian state by its own criteria, the greater its capacity for exterminating or subjugating all authority systems except its own. As a process, totalitarianism is in essence the reduction of all competing authorities within the boundaries of a given state and the substitution of its own single authority in their place. The normal diversity and plurality of authority, like the normal plurality and diversity of social aggregates themselves, is replace by a structure that is, in aspiration at least, monolithic.

Put in these terms, it is possible to see conflict of authorities, at least in moderate degree, as one of the functional requisites of what we call free society. For if freedom of choice has anything to do with the nature of a free society, then, plainly, it can be maintained only through the existence of competing values, functions, and authorities. And where there is competition among these, there is bound to be occasional conflict.

AUTHORITY, POWER, LEGITIMACY

There are, as we observed, many elements involved in one's obedience to any given authority—elements of role performance, structure of the group or association involved, tradition, the sense of utility, and so on. *Legitimacy* is also a major factor.

Broadly speaking, we *spontaneously* and *willingly* obey those authorities in which we can sense, however dimly, even subconsciously, their *legitimacy*. The religious communicant obeys the commands of his church because, within the realm of religion at least, he regards them as legitimate. Or his continued membership in the church is sign of a probable feeling of legitimacy. The same is true—or was until recently—of most university students in this country, of the members of the labor unions, and, for the most part, of the citizens in the modern state. For most persons, most of the time, in most places, the authorities they obey are perceived as legitimate authorities. Obedience is willed, or at least not checked, in light of this legitimacy.

What is legitimacy of authority? This is one of the central problems of modern political sociology, discussed with great insight and learning by such socoliogists as Tocqueville, Weber, Simmel, Michels, and MacIver. We can answer our question tersely, if somewhat unsatisfactorily, by saying authority is made legitimate by the mores, by all the customs and folkways with which authority is commonly surrounded. But this answer, although acceptable perhaps on the empirical level, still leaves unanswered another question: Why and when do people *consciously regard* a given authority as legitimate?

In a highly religious or sacred society the answer may lie completely in a person's religious belief system. If he believes that the holders or wielders of authority are descended from a religious being, or are the agents of a religious being in whom he devoutly believes, the legitimacy of authority, however tyrannical it might seem to the outsider, is assured for that person. Or, if one believes that time and age confer wisdom, one may derive legitimacy from either the ages of those who wield authority or from the antiquity of the tradition that is being obeyed. Legitimacy, in short, is perceived as an attribute of religious belief or sacred tradition.

As Weber emphasized, however, one may also derive legitimacy from the rationality of a given authority. If one believes that the rationality of any given function or authority is its supreme, or even exclusive, justification, then one tends to regard those authorities as legitimate that meet the test of reason and logic. A legitimate authority is a rational authority. Other criteria such as justice, equality, and humanity have been closely associated with rationality as the test of legitimacy in modern history. Legitimate authorities, we say, are by definition just authorities before which all persons are equal. And, perhaps above all, legitimate authorities are humane.

To these conceptions of legitimacy we may add one that is not excluded by the others but deserves its own identity here. This is the test of *function*. We are prone to regard authority as legitimate if it arises necessarily from discharge of a given function in society. The authority of the teacher is legitimate as long as it is confined to the function of teaching; so is the authority of the parent, the priest, the playground supervisor, the plant manager, the village squire, the tax collector, and even the police. The authority of the traffic light is legitimate because it is so clearly functional. The ordinary authority of the policeman is legitimate because, as everyone recognizes, there are malefactors in any society, and the presence of the policeman is vital to the function of maintaining order. As long as what is demanded or commanded appears relevant to the function involved, authority tends to be regarded as legitimate and, hence, as properly to be obeyed.

It is when authority ceases to be, or to seem to be relevant, to an accepted function that the question of legitimacy tends to rise. Suppose the teacher extends his authority from curriculum to matters unconnected, or *perceived* by the students as unconnected, with curriculum —to outside behavior, to dress, to political values? Plainly, the possibility of illegitimacy has entered. Or suppose the police, instead of discharging their function of protecting the public order, extend their authority—or are *perceived* to be extending it—to spheres of personal behavior that do not in any way constitute a threat to public order, public safety, or to public health and decency. Then the issue of legitimacy is likely to arise.

Philosophers from antiquity to the present moment have speculated on the possibility of a society in which all authority proceeds directly from function and from function alone. No authority would be exerted over anyone that was not contained within an association whose function was a part of the lives of the individual members. Anarchists are popularly regarded as believing in the absence of all authority. This is not true. From the writings of the greatest of the anarchists—Kropotkin, Proudhon, Thoreau, among others—it is clear that they respect authority, believe in its necessity and inevitability, but argue for a society in which authority and function are indissoluble. Proudhon argued that man would live under the authority of family, of local community, and of economic cooperative because each of these is possessed of a vital function in human life, and each is capable of a degree of human participation that makes government within equitable and just. But Proudhon also held that the authority of social class, of the political government, of church (Proudhon was an atheist) is not legitimate and cannot become legitimate, for each is devoid of legitimate social function.   And, he concluded, because each is devoid of function, its authority can be maintained only through the use of external *power*.

The above discussion brings us to the distinction between authority and power.   The two words are often used interchangeably in political and sociological writing, as in ordinary discourse, and will no doubt continue to be so used.   It does not matter.   The important point is differentiation of the two forms of social interaction involved.

We have found authority to be inseparable from any organized social aggregate.   The roots of authority are in the roles, the statuses, and the norms of the aggregate.   It is impossible to be a member of a school, church, university, family, or state without participating in a system of authority.   Merely to follow the specifications of one's role— whether as communicant or clergy, as citizen or official, as child or parent—is, as we have seen, to engage in and to be a part of a pattern of authority.

Power, or at least the type of behavior to which we shall affix the word "power," is very different.   Consider several clear examples of power in our own time: black power, student power, and flower power. To these might be added such examples from another period in our history as labor power and feminist power.   All alike refer to forms of control, pressure, or significant influence over other persons and circumstances.   All have plainly affected the course of American history during the present century.   The behavior of untold millions of persons has been in some way altered by the sheer impress of the powers mentioned.

Although the force of each example is different, what is common to all of them is the effort to exact obedience or compliance of others to the will of one or more persons in a way that, however moral or right it may be in some ultimate ethical sense, is *not* derived from the recognized norms of the social aggregate concerned, that is *not* perceived as legitimate by those who come under the brunt of the power, and that does *not* flow directly from the established patterns of role behavior or from the common and normal patterns of role and status interaction.   No matter how correct, progressive, and humane the goals of a given outburst of power may prove to be in the long run, power is, as MacIver has stressed, *without legitimacy, without mandate, and without office.*

Power often tends to arise within the interstices of organization and authority.   The conflict of authority and power in history is a familiar one.   By humane standards authority may be evil, obsolete, and repugnant.   The "power" of a slave revolt led by a Spartacus or a Nat Turner may well have the elements of lasting good.   This does not affect the matter. We are referring to sociological, not ethical, matters. When established authority becomes weak or corrupt, or when it is challenged by ends and purposes that have superior appeal to a significant number of persons, power is likely to arise. It may be "good" power as it was among the American revolutionists after the Declaration of Independence was signed and the war with England begun. It may be "evil" power as it was with Hitler and the Nazis in their challenge to the authority of the Weimar Rupublic.

Power and force are not the same. Force may often be utilized in support of authority, as in the case of the spanking of a child for an infraction of family discipline or the imprisonment or execution of the felon. Conversely, there are abundant examples of power in history without the utilization of force. The whole point of Gandhi's *Satyagraha* was the mobilization of an irresistible power of the people against British authority without the use of violence in any way. This, as we know, was also the approach of the Negro civil rights leader, Martin Luther King. The sheer power of massed nonviolence can sometimes be enough to cause the forces of authority to break discipline, to abandon authority, as it were, and turn to the use of power manifest in unauthorized beatings of the nonviolent petitioners or demonstrators.

The political state is alone among modern associations in its *sanctioned* use of force. Other associations—labor unions, clubs, business enterprises—may resort to force as a means of gaining compliance. But only the force of the state is legal. The state, we may say, has a monopoly on force in modern society—for both internal and external purposes. In a very real sense the political state began in force—military force. For a long time use of military power was the sole function of the state. The king's chief reason for being, indeed, was at first solely to lead troops into battle. Only later, as the king's power became sanctioned, fused both functionally and symbolically with other spheres of life, and as the outlines of the modern state began to be dimly apparent, did military power become the authority of the state in late feudal society. The gradual conversion of what was at first power into the diffuse and variegated fabric of political authority is, in a very real sense, the history of the modern European state.

Power is a common element of change in history. There is something about authority that makes for persistence of types and roles. It could hardly be otherwise because of the intimate and reciprocal relation between structure and authority. But power, whether in communal or associative form, as in black power, or in individual form, as in what Weber called charisma, is by its nature prone to effect change in societies and institutions.   And, as Weber pointed out, when charismatic power becomes routinized, when it becomes normatively sanctioned and assimilated into a continuing pattern of roles and statuses, it becomes another authority in that complex of authorities that is society.

One does not have to subscribe categorically to the "great man" theory of history to be able to recognize the frequency with which the really substantial changes in the histories of institutions and cultures are associated with the individual powers exerted by preeminent human beings.   Whether, in full analysis, the change comes from the sheer force of individual personality, genius, or charisma, or from the chance association of a human figure with the right combination of circumstances, or, as is probable, from both is not at issue here.   The vital point is that power, in the sense of human behavior aimed at non-sanctioned influence upon, or control of, others, appears very often in the shape of extraordinary human beings.   The histories of the arts, letters, and sciences are no exception.   The authority that can be formed in art or science by some set of established norms, roles, and statuses is, history tells us, very great indeed.   The criteria of excellence and of the intellectually significant contained within this established cultural authority can be every bit as dominant—and for long periods—as those found in religions or kinship systems.   Often very great power is required—the kind of power we associate with the names of Pasteur, Einstein, Picasso, James Joyce, Stravinsky, and Schoenberg—to break through the established authorities of schools, styles, and fashions in the arts and sciences.   We shall come back to this immensely important point in the final chapters of the book when we consider the problem of change.   For now, it is sufficient to say that whereas authority is the very essence of the stationary and the persisting in culture and society, power of some kind is a very common element of change.

It would be erroneous in the extreme to make power and the individual human being (prophet, genius, or madman) synonymous.   Power can be exerted in moments of crisis by small groups, by social movements, by political parties, and by disaffected members of a given structure of authority.   In the same way that a Buddha or Jesus, a Caesar or Napoleon, can challenge the legitimacy of a given system of authority by using his individual powers and acquired followers to effect the disruption of the established norms, so, as present events in the American academic scene make clear, can groups of individuals.

Outbreaks of student-sponsored movements designed to effect changes in the traditional authority of universities are by no means new.

Such a work as Hastings Rashdall's *The Universities of Europe in the Middle Ages* tells us in great detail of "student power" in the early history of the university. Nevertheless, in the United States at least, the authority of the university over students was recognized for many decades as legitimate for the most part, however repressive it might occasionally have been. The professor's right was to examine and grade, even to fail the student. The organized faculty's right was to create all curricula and courses, to set rules of student behavior, and to appoint, promote, and dismiss their own members. The administration's right was to govern in matters of finance, business, buildings, student discipline, meetings on campus, and living arrangements in dormitories. All of this was a structure of authority regarded by nearly all students and their parents for many decades as legitimate authority. Onerous and painful the authority could be; but it was still regarded—when administered fairly—as legitimate.

But in many European, Latin American, and Asian universities such authority was not always regarded as legitimate. Outbursts of student power in opposition to universities were far from uncommon in the nineteenth century in these areas and even, though less frequently, in the United States. Sometimes the demands of students were accepted and became assimilated into the structure of university authority. Sometimes they were not.

Today, in the United States and in nearly all areas of the world where there are universities and where civil laws are not as repressive as they are in certain totalitarian countries, a veritable revolution is under way on the part of students. Granted that it is a revolution participated in largely by only a minority at any given time. This is true of all revolutions in history. The important point is well enough exemplified by the United States alone. Within the past decade, much of the historic legitimacy of faculty and administrative authority has been challenged by student power in a host of ways, by no means all violent. Just as the condition of legitimacy of university authority had earlier been the right of the faculty to participate in it—at least in those areas central to faculty concern—so now the condition of the university's legitimacy of authority is the right of students to participate in it as it affects the areas of greatest concern to them.

No one living, studying, or teaching in the contemporary university needs to be reminded of the often dramatic, occasionally violent, clashes between established authority in the university and student power. From the point of view of students, or at least of their militant representatives, the historic authority of the faculty alone over courses ceases to be legitimate authority and of a sudden takes on the guise of sheer power.   Against it are arrayed the forces of student power—with strikes, sit-ins, and other forms of campus disruption their weapons. Out of the confrontations often come negotiations resulting in a novel inclusion of students in the structure of authority, thus endowing it, at least for a time, with legitimacy.

Nothing in the foregoing should be construed as suggesting that all eruptions of power, anymore than all outbreaks of social change, are "good."   No society could live without established authority and, when necessary, without the sanctioned force required to reinforce established authority.   If there are readers so naïve as to believe that student power is by its very nature unvaryingly good or progressive in consequence, let them be reminded of the vital role held by Nazi student power in the German universities during the 1920s.   Much of Hitler's success in suffocating the intellectual life of the German university after the Nazis came to office in 1933 was based upon the prior success of Nazi student power in intimidating the faculty, administration, and students alike and in effecting a considerable number of "reforms."   There is, in short, no guarantee of ethical or cultural improvement when we talk about either student power or power in any other of its forms through historical time.   Our only concern here is the frequent phenomenon of confrontation of power and authority in history and the indisputable fact that power is a frequent element in processes of social change.

It is unlikely that any form of association could exist for very long on the basis of power alone, anymore than it could on the basis of force alone.   One need but witness the difficulties of military forces occupying hostile territory, or police trying to maintain order in slums or ghettoes filled with persons who have built up a hatred of police and other representatives of the "establishment."   Almost always one finds in history that power early seeks to legitimize itself, to incorporate itself into the roles, statuses, and recurrent patterns of social interaction of an aggregate or territory.   History is filled with instances of eruptions of power —whether by charismatic individuals or by collective movements— that made temporary impact but failed for one reason or another to become institutionalized or, in Weber's word, routinized.   The power of Jesus became in time institutionalized into the vast and complex authority of the Christian Church.   The power of the American revolutionists in 1776 became similarly incorporated—first in the Articles of Confederation, then in the Constitution—into a system of state authority.   For every one of these "successes," however, there must be literally hundreds of eruptions of power that "failed," that did not become the points of departure for new institutions and systems of authority.

Notes

1. Robert Bierstedt, "The Problem of Authority," in Morroe Berger, Theodore Abel, and Charles H. Page (eds.), *Freedom and Control in Modern Society* (New York: Van Nostrand, 1954), pp. 67–81.
2. Max Weber, *From Max Weber: Essays in Sociology*, trans. and edited by H. H. Gerth and C. Wright Mills (New York: Oxford University Press, 1946), p. 79.
3. Charles Page, "Bureaucracy's Other Face," *Social Forces*, 25 (1946–1947), pp. 88–95.

7

Social Roles

PERSONS AS ROLES

"All the world's a stage, and all the men and women merely players. They have their exits and their entrances; and one man in his time plays many parts. . . ." So wrote that masterful sociologist William Shakespeare more than three centuries ago. He was perhaps echoing what the essayist Montaigne had written a little earlier about man's life in the world: "A noble farce, wherein kings, republics, and emperors have for so many years played their parts, and to which the whole vast universe serves for a theater."

From Montaigne and Shakespeare down through the modern sociological writings of Mead, Thomas, Znaniecki, and Goffman, the analogy between social life and the theater has often suggested itself. The metaphors of the poet and dramatist easily become the linguistic tools of the sociologist. For much of social behavior is role behavior, behavior that appears to us as does the behavior of actors on a stage. Except from the existentialist's point of view, we do not really see "individuals." We see *persons*. "Person" is another word deriving from the theater; originally a *persona* was a mask. And the concept of person is inseparable from that of role.

We find roles waiting for us in society. They are, as it were, parts that have already been written by time and circumstance before we are

148

born. To be sure, new roles in society are forever being created through the processes of change, and old roles are forever being modified in their character. But the fact remains that there are roles which are central in the lives of most of us: infant, child, adolescent, student, husband or wife, father or mother, worker, grandparent, the aged, these—which include Shakespeare's seven ages of man—are preestablished in larger outline when we come into the world. And, as we noted in the chapter on social interaction, socialization, that is, the process of growing up and becoming members of the social order, is largely the individual's learning to follow the lines of his successive parts in life.

Not that this is the whole story. We also noted in the treatment of social interaction the falsity of any view of human development that sees it as solely one-sided, a matter of environment mechanically making impress on a totally receptive organism. The process of *interaction* is always at work, with the individual modifying, shaping, and adjusting the successive roles he encounters in life. A great deal of what we commonly think of as the friction, the maladjustment, the occasional turmoil of growing up and of living with others is a consequence of strains which are so often precipitated by our efforts to take on roles whose lines do not seem to have been written for us specifically. We protest, we rebel at times, and in every age there are the few who seem never to be able or willing to adapt themselves to a society's central roles. Bear in mind, of course, that even the hermit, the bohemian, and the outcast occupy social roles that have long been known to mankind. Truly, no man is *merely* an individual.

But roles are nevertheless persons, and this is just as true as any of the observations above. We never see roles except as they are personified, although we sometimes imagine them. It is well to think of role-in-person and of person-in-role rather than run the risk of introducing any false antinomy between role and person. As we had abundant opportunity to discover and rediscover in the three preceding chapters, especially in the discussion of social interaction, it is unrealistic to deal with either role or person except in the context of the other.

The first point to be made about social roles is that they are aspects of behavior. More precisely, roles are *ways of behavior*, distinctive, more or less prescribed, and handed down from generation to generation. In the history of mankind innumerable ways of action have made their appearance, and still do, that have not, do not, become converted into recognized roles. Through some kind of natural selection in social history, some ways of action become fixed through usage, become more or less widely recognized, and are even venerated and ritualized. These, of course, are the ways of behavior to which each of us is exposed in the process of his own socialization.

Second, social roles embody *norms*. There is no recognized role in society that is not linked to the normative order. We shall have more to say about social norms in Chapter 9. For the moment we shall deal with them merely as "ideal types," to use, in slightly different focus, a phrase of Max Weber. We are surrounded, no matter what our society or specialized participation in a society, with evaluative points of reference by which we assess ourselves. Some of them, as we saw above, are so fundamental that they become deeply internalized, providing substance for feelings of guilt, shame, pride, dignity, and, above all, conscience. One feels elated or depressed by his greater or lesser approximation to some cherished norm, some vivid ideal type, in society. It may be the mother feeling herself the good mother, and hence proud or smug; or the same mother feeling herself the bad mother, and hence guilty or ashamed. It may be the university professor feeling by turns confident and insecure as the result of the subtle, largely unconscious but puissant impress on his life of the ideal type of professor he carries in his mind—or, possibly, as the result of the varying degrees to which he meets or fails to meet the expectations of others. So too with the child, the student, the carpenter, the priest, or the physician; even, no doubt, the pickpocket, the prostitute, or the prisoner. Each of these is a social role, long known to human society, and each, in addition to being a more or less routinized way of behavior, is also defined by certain norms.

Third, a social role is invariably a part of some structure or system of interactive relationships. It is an element of what Simmel and others have called the *social circle*.[1] Only a moment's reflection is necessary to make clear that no social role can exist that does not take on its identity from its interactive, its complementary, or its reciprocal relation to other roles. How could there be the role of professor except in a social circle or system that by very definition includes at least the role of student? Similarly with the role of husband, wife, child, physician, beggar, prostitute, business entrepreneur, king, or slave. Each is, depending upon the larger social order and its norms, an established, recognized role that is quite inseparable from the behavior of concrete individuals. But each is also necessarily part of a circle or network that goes beyond the single individual in his role. For the social role to exist, in other words, there must be other, complementary or reciprocal roles that alone can give the particular social role meaning as well as function.

Fourth, and very strong in any established social role, is the element of *legitimacy*. We considered this important word above in connection with authority. It is no less vital in the understanding of social roles. Broadly speaking, we will accept almost anything in the way of conduct from another person *if* it proceeds from a role that we regard as legitimate. A punch in the jaw is one thing coming from another individual in anger or anyone from whom we do not expect it; it is something else coming from one with whom we are engaged in a boxing bout. Invasion of one's physical or mental privacy can be a repugnant experience when such invasion comes from one whom we do not consider legitimately entitled to it. From one's physician or psychiatrist or lawyer, however, we do not even consider it as invasion of privacy. We take it for granted that the physician, in his role of physician, is entitled to make the most intimate of examinations, to handle our bodies in ways that would be entirely offensive were the same individual dealing with us outside his role of physician. Even in our present, relatively liberated age, nudity is a subject of many taboos. Nudity—our own or another person's—can make us acutely uncomfortable when it is out of role, when it does not belong to a given situation. But nudity in the artist's model, in the stripper and actor on the stage, in the patient undergoing medical examination or being bathed by the nurse in the hospital ward, to use but a few examples, is nudity-in-role and is regarded as legitimate. Demands of extreme nature from another person will be accepted if we believe them to emanate from that person in a role that we regard as legitimate. The priest or professor, each in his religious or academic role, can impose very considerable hardships on us in our own roles of communicant and student. We accept them just so long as they seem to proceed legitimately from the priest and professor in their roles. However, when either oversteps role and uses it perhaps as the basis for demands of clearly nonreligious or nonacademic nature, or the basis for inquiries that apparently have nothing to do with the role relationship, we are likely to balk.

It is difficult to think of any single form of behavior that is not, or has not been at some time, regarded as moral within the recognized limits of role. For most persons, killing other human beings is legitimate *if* one is in the role of soldier or policeman; breaking into secret archives is legitimate *if* one is in his role of spy or secret agent; sexual intercourse or other intimacy is legitimate *if* the individuals are in their roles of husband and wife or, in other times, other places, *if* the individuals are in their roles of prostitute and customer; electronic invasion of privacy through "bugging" is legitimate (at least in the view of a good many people) *if* done in one's role of policeman or FBI agent; cutting another person's head off is legitimate *if* one is the royal executioner in the age of Henry VIII. And so on. To quote William Graham Sumner's famous apothegm, "the *mores* make anything right." Almost any form of behavior is acceptable to us if it results from a role in society that we recognize as legitimate.

Fifth, there is in every social role the strong element of *duty*— that is, perceived duty, whether with respect to oneself or another person. From the point of view of role theory, the idea of duty is a manifestation of the larger system of authority that exists in any social aggregate. We noted above the dependence of any system of authority upon the roles that constitute it. We can put the matter in reverse now and say that the vitality of any social role is in large measure correlated with the degree of duty or obligation one feels in his performance of the role. The sense of obligation that one feels—as mother, soldier, professor, physician, or theatrical performer—is the consciousness one has of the normative requirements of his role, its legitimacy, and also its relation to other roles in what we have called the social circle.

Many a social relationship has been kept going indefinitely, even in the absence of any degree of amity, simply by the strong sense of duty that is held by the principals. The wife may have long since ceased to love or even like her husband; if she has a strong sense of duty to the role of wife, she is likely to remain—even to desire to remain— married to her husband. It is the sense of duty in the role of mother quite as much as, often more than, the sense of continuing love of children that will produce extraordinary acts of self-sacrifice and dedication. There must be few holding any role in any society who are not attacked from time to time by feelings antipathetic to performance of role—going to work, keeping the house in order, looking after wife or husband, children or aged parents, going to one's study to write if one is a professional writer, or approaching still another manuscript if one is an editor. But all do in fact keep at it from a sense of duty.

There is another aspect of the matter. Duty to a social role explains much of the familiar phenomenon of the human being "rising above himself," as the well-known phrase has it. An individual not known for qualities of imagination, leadership, or bravery may find himself, for whatever reason, in a role that calls for these qualities. Just as the actor may reach new heights of excellence through assignment to a dramatic role that is better than any he has ever had before, so do many of us rise to a challenge in social life. The history of politics is rich in accounts of individuals who, through the circumstance of having had a new and higher role thrust upon them—that of king, president, governor, councilman, mayor—reveal excellences not previously suspected. The mere assumption of the role of soldier in wartime can bring out qualities of courage and intrepidity in a human being that neither he nor his fellows suspected he had. In a sense, he *did not* have the qualities until assumption of an appropriate role permitted their expression.

Role theory has taught us much about the actual dynamics of learning, especially the formalized kind of learning found in schools. Until the child, however unconsciously, has accepted or come to feel a part of the *role* of pupil, instruction by his teacher is made difficult. In many families the process of the child's adaptation to the role of pupil begins before he enters school. For if these families are, by culture and habit, strongly oriented toward education, it is highly probable that the child will have anticipated his role of pupil by playing at it in the circles of family and play group before he begins school. Here the role of pupil is in considerable degree formed before the period of formal schooling begins, and the work of instruction is made correspondingly easier.

Very different, as we have learned, is the situation of the child who comes from a family that by reason of ethnic, religious, or social class is not strongly oriented toward formal education, that may even have a strong bias against it. The child may not readily take to the role of pupil and his process of learning may be affected. He may be thought to be mentally inferior to those who learn more easily. That inequalities of innate mentality exist in every schoolroom is not to be doubted. But neither is the fact of role inequalities in the context of the school.

Much of deviant or delinquent behavior on the part of children in the school commences when, because of inability to assume the role of pupil, other, more easily assimilable roles are assumed: the roles of truant, troublemaker, and so on. Once a role is fully accepted—whether by child or adult—the world is perceived differently. What we have on several occasions referred to as "the definition of the situation" is strongly affected, even determined, by the role one has achieved or had thrust upon him. Studies of delinquent children make clear that once the child comes to feel himself identified with the role of delinquent, the work of guiding his behavior into more constructive or creative channels is made the more difficult. Thus successful conversion of delinquent behavior into constructive behavior involves first a breaking of a role, an emancipation of the child from his own role conception of himself, and then the beginning of the process of interaction and of socialization

by which a new role is acquired. Many a delinquent thought to be
incorrigible is in fact approachable through proper understanding of
roles.

Much behavior in society that we are prone to think of as "natural"
behavior, as behavior springing directly from organic or psychological
states, is in fact either wholly or partly role behavior. The behavior
of the "romantic" lover in our culture is an excellent case in point.
That there is a biological basis of heterosexual love is true enough, but
nothing in man's biological constitution predisposes him to the role of
romantic lover, which is as much a social role, requiring as much
learning and socialization as any other. Similarly with physical illness.
Obviously organic factors are involved in illness. But the unwell
person immediately assumes a social role; he acquires, while he is ill,
certain social exemptions and privileges and also a certain authority.
Organically, illness may be the same from one society to another. The
sick *role* varies enormously, however, from society to society, culture
to culture.

In the foregoing paragraphs we have described social roles in terms
of certain fundamental attributes: patterned behavior, correspondence
to social norms, relation to a social circle or structure, the felt sense of
duty, and authority. All are vital to any genuine social role in society,
and all are capable of objective analysis as microelements of social organization.

We must not, however, lose sight of the person, of the personality.
I said above that what we see in society are persons-in-roles and roles-
in-persons. The two dimensions are crucial to an understanding of
roles. From the sociologists's point of view, the person is a bundle
of roles. How else—sociologically, that is—do we describe and identify
people except through their varied kinship, local, economic, religious,
and political roles? Admittedly, each of us feels himself to be something
more than the sheer numerical total of the roles he holds in a social
order. And, of course, he is. The whole is indeed greater here than
the sum of its parts—when the parts are conceived as roles. For,
as we learned in the chapter on social interaction, there is always the
thinking, acting, meaning-oriented, purposive human mind at work.
No one who loves—or, for that matter, hates—another person deeply
is likely to think of the other person as simply the totality of his social
roles. This is obvious enough; one does not have to take the route here
of the phenomenologist or existentialist to recognize that the human
personality's psychological mechanisms of integration effect results that
cannot be described solely in terms of component roles. At no point in

this book, it should be emphasized, have I claimed that the sociologist's view of man is the complete view.

Still, with all qualifications made, it is necessary to stress the profound relation between social role and *human identity*. We tend to identify ourselves to others and to ourselves alike by reference to our social roles and the greater or lesser success we feel that we have in these roles. What Peter Berger has written is as profound as it is succinct: "Identities are socially bestowed. They must also be socially sustained, and fairly steadily so. One cannot be human all by oneself and, apparently, one cannot hold on to any particular identity all by oneself. The self-image of the officer as an officer can be maintained only in a social context in which others are willing to recognize him in this identity. If this recognition is suddenly withdrawn, it usually does not take very long before the self-image collapses."[2]

True, there are great variations among individuals in their capacities for sustaining social roles and self-images under circumstances of pressure. The type of personality that David Riesman has called, in now classic phrasing, "inner-directed" is far more likely to maintain a sense of persisting role identity irrespective of pressures from the outside or withdrawal of recognition by others than is the type that Riesman has called "other-directed." The military officer, biologist, father, priest, or president who believes powerfully in his own identity *as* officer, biologist, and so on, is not likely to have his self-image weakened by ordinary accusation, stigmatization, or ostracism. This is to say that some roles are more deeply set in their bearers' personalities than are others in human society.

The close relation between role and identity remains, nonetheless, and so does the relation between role and social circle—or reference group. When those we most respect withdraw their recognition, a vital support to social role or identity is dissolved. A person may maintain himself indefinitely through what might be called accrued recognition, or through identification with either the dead or the unborn—which in effect is what the archaist and the futurist do. But always there is some level or degree of identification with a reference circle, whether the circle be composed of those near at hand or distant, of those living, dead, or unborn.

How we choose to identify ourselves—that is, through what role or roles—depends largely on history. We shall come back to this point in the final section of the chapter. Let us say now that at one point in history one might find his kinship role the single most important thing about himself. At another point, with great social changes having taken place, one might instead find his religious or his racial or his political role the ascendant one in his life. And, of course, our sense of the ascendant role varies a good deal within the duration of our individual lives.

ASCRIBED AND ACHIEVED ROLES

One of the most valuable and instructive ways of comparing societies and cultures is with reference to the varying degree to which they rest upon *ascribed* and *achieved* roles and the varying degree to which they give functional significance and honorific character to these two major types of social roles. Much of what is central in the recent history of Western society comes directly from shifts in the amount of significance that successive generations assigned to ascribed and to achieved roles.

By ascribed role we refer to one that proceeds from such characteristics as age, sex, race, and (depending upon the larger context of circumstances), even occupation, religion, and social class. No one of these, as a moment's reflection makes evident, *need* be the basis of a recognized social role in society with all the attributes of social role which we have just examined. On the face of it, there is no absolute reason why the biological fact of sex, the racial fact of blackness or whiteness, or the fact of whether one is a youth or old man should be associated with a whole complex of social duties, restrictions, privileges, and other means of social identification. In point of fact, however, as is only too evident, each of these—sex, age, race—is very commonly the basis of a role. That role is ascribed to one through biological heredity combined with a society's implicit insistence that the role is an important one, to be made manifest through suitable types of dress, performance of occupational function, life style, language or speech, attitudes toward others and oneself, and so on. Depending upon the society or the period in a society's history, the single most important role one possesses may well be one or another of his ascribed roles—his old age, his color, or his sex. The first may connote wisdom and, with it, prestige, making the role of old age triumphant over any other. The second—and this has been all too true of American society—may remain the triumphant, that is, the supremely identifying role for an individual irrespective of age, achieved wealth, status, or learning. The third, sex, may, if the individual concerned is a male in a profoundly masculine-oriented culture, put him ahead of any female no matter what her superior endowments of mind, character, and ability might be.   Race, sex, and age are the greatest and most universal bases of ascribed social roles, but others have existed.   When, in the later history of the Roman Empire, all economic guilds were made hereditary, one's economic role was thus ascribed.   Today in the traditional sections of India many an occupation is still hereditary, fixed by caste, thus making it an ascribed role for one born in it.

An achieved role is one that is open, at least theoretically, to one who possesses the required degrees of skill, luck, cunning, mentality, learning, and overall agility.   In our society there is a vast abundance of achieved roles, as any newspaper classified ad section readily suggests.   One achieves the role of carpenter or professor, businessman or beggar.   True, as suggested above, it is possible, and not without precedent, to be born in the guild of carpenters or beggars and thus to have that particular role ascribed from the beginning of life.   But in our society such roles, and countless others, are the consequence of achievement: achievement through native acumen, education, luck, or whatever.   A girl is not able to escape the ascribed role of woman in society, but she may or may not seek to achieve the role of housewife, mother, career woman, or leader in her community.   A black is unable to discard the ascribed role of black in American culture, but, all other things equal, he may seek to achieve any one or more of the various roles in the social order which are open to achievement.

All other things equal.   In that pregnant phrase lies a vast amount of import to our subject.   For, quite obviously, all things are not equal and rarely (if ever) are in the distribution of ascribed and achieved roles in a culture.   Nothing can disguise the hard fact that holding the *ascribed* role of black, or female, or youth, or aged can and commonly does profoundly affect the degree to which achieved roles are open to an individual.   We may, at this critical juncture in our history, be most vividly aware of the limits imposed by the ascribed role of black.   But, for historical and comparative purposes, it is well to bear in mind also the limits imposed by the ascribed role of the female.   A great many achieved roles are in effect closed to females simply by virtue of femaleness, not of physical strength, intelligence, or temperament.   The arrangement works, of course, in reverse direction also.   A great many achieved roles in our social order are open primarily to those with the ascribed role of female: secretaries in many business organizations, nurses, clerks in women's-wear stores, and so on.   The same arrangement applies to the role of the black.   For a long time certain achieved roles—that of Pullman porter, for instance—were open only to those

with the ascribed role of black. With the gradual rise of the blacks
in America to political power in certain voting sections (Harlem, for
instance), the ascribed role of black is profoundly important in seeking
the achieved role of councilman or state assemblyman.

Nothing more need be said to make clear that one of the most valuable insights into the nature of any social order, and also into its history,
is the constantly shifting relation between the ascribed roles and the
achieved roles in that social order. A little later in this chapter we shall
glance briefly at the role of the woman in Western culture as a means
of giving illustration to this important point and also to certain other
vital aspects of social roles. For the moment it suffices to say that one
could write the history of modern Western Europe in the concrete terms
of all that has affected the woman's role in Wesetrn society.

ROLE CONFLICT AND STRAIN

Our discussion of roles has so
far been oriented toward the elements that make for stability and consensus in the social order. Relatively fixed ways of behavior, adherence
to social norms and ideal types, functional interdependence or comple-
mentarity, legitimacy, and duty—all of these qualities suggest order
and harmony in society. But social roles are also intimately involved in
social and psychological conflicts, in disharmonies, and in social in-
stability. We have before taken note of conflict as a universal and
persisting mechanism of social behavior. Nowhere is conflict more
likely to be seen than with respect to social roles: conflict among roles
in a social aggregate and conflict or strain among roles within the individual personality.

In a sense, conflict—in at least mild degree—is built into the very
nature of roles and their interrelation. Only if an individual held but
one role in life and this role were somehow insulated from the roles
held by others would it be possible to imagine the complete removal
of conflict from role behavior. What we find in fact, of course, is each
individual holding a plurality of roles. In very simple societies—kinship, agrarian, folk—where social differentiation is primitive, no person is likely to hold more than a very few roles, and usually no great
effort is required, either by the individual or by the society as a whole,
to keep role conflicts at moderate degree. Granted that even in a small
society founded entirely on kinship there are bound to be occasional
manifestations of role conflict—between father and son, between chief

and tribal member, between older and younger brothers, and so on—
it is evident from the common fixity of role types from generation to
generation that no extreme difficulty is involved in keeping such conflicts
within the boundaries of the social order. Only when such small and
simple societies are undergoing substantial change, as when they come
in direct contact with the norms and behavior patterns of some other
society, are role conflicts likely to become severe. After all, if it is sharp
enough, social change cannot help but become a matter of change in
social roles as well as in the social aggregates within which the roles
exist.

Whatever may be the normal intensity of role conflict in simple
societies, it is mild by comparison with what we find more or less
regularly in a society as complex and differentiated in structure as our
own. In the simple society, roles tend to be almost wholly ascribed
roles. Moreover, they are few in number—few in the social order as
a whole and even fewer when seen within the limits of the life organization of the single individual. But in any modern, Western society
there are bound to be—by virtue of the high level of social differentiation
in such a society—many more possibilities of role conflict. We may see
these possibilities not merely abstractly, as when we contemplate the
number and interrelations of ascribed and achieved roles in our society,
but also concretely, and more significantly, in the life organization of the
individual, in his day-to-day behavior.

Role conflicts begin rather early in the individual's life in our society. There is the role conflict that each of us gradually becomes aware
of during adolescence: when our role of child in the social circle that
is our family begins to conflict, in our own consciousness and in the
awarenesses of others, with the role that one is preparing himself for
—the role of adult. The kinds of social strains that Paul Goodman has
so vividly described in *Growing Up Absurd* derive basically from this
type of conflict—greatly heightened, as Goodman emphasizes, by the
diminishing number of opportunities for early and clear awareness of
the adult role and also by the blurring of both the adolescent and the
adult roles in our present social order.

Most societies in the past have taken the role aspects of growing
up very seriously. In almost all traditional cultures and even today
in religions where the "crises of existence"—birth, marriage, death—
are central and matters of explicit ritual, the passage of the child into
the role of manhood or womanhood is signalized by appropriate ritual
and festivities. Where the outlines of both roles, childhood and adult-
hood, are reasonably clear in terms of the norms and expectations of

each, there is bound to be less conflict between the two roles. There is
less conflict between two individuals holding these roles and less conflict within the single individual passing from one role to the other. It
is hard to imagine any society—however simple and stable, however
ritualized a person's relation to his successive roles in life—in which
there is an absence of conflict altogether. But it is a matter of verifiable
observation that far more role conflict of this sort exists in some societies
and ages of history than others and that in such a society as ours the
number of role conflicts within the kinship group is bound to be high.
What has just been said about the conflict between the roles of child
and adult in the process of socialization could be elaborated greatly by
reference to other roles within the kinship group: that of husband and
wife, of parent and child, of the aged and the young, and so on. It
is inevitable that role conflicts within the family will proliferate where
the outlines of roles become rather indistinct as the result of changes in
the relationship of the family to the larger social order, as the result
of substantial increase in the number of achieved roles which can at
least beckon and tempt, and as the result of profound alterations in
the authority structure of the family, most particularly those alterations
of the close relation of the immediate conjugal family to the extended
family.

These conflicts are far from the whole story. Even during the
period of one's life when he is growing up, when he is still under the
authority of family and his principal role is that of child, there are conflicts of another type, those flowing from his simultaneously held roles
of pupil in the school and member of one or another type of peer group.
Ordinarily, in middle-class sectors of our society at least, the first of
the conflicts is likely to be moderate. Most middle-class parents reinforce as best they can the child's role of pupil, providing encouragement and supporting the norms of the school. Only in certain ethnic
minorities and among those who share the "culture of poverty," where
antischool norms may still exist, is there likely to be severe conflict
between the role of child and the role of pupil. But in our present
society we are increasingly aware of the kind of conflict—notable in
all classes and ethnic strains—exemplified by the appeal of the peer
group. Because childhood and youth are more visible today in popular
culture, more celebrated and more honored, it is inevitable that the role
of child is going to conflict frequently with the role of member of peer
group. Such conflicts of role follow directly the conflicts of authority
involved.

Role conflicts accompany us throughout our lives. The more

diverse one's life, the more roles one holds, and the greater the number of norms and aspirations one is exposed to, the larger, quite obviously, the number of role conflicts in one's life—potential and actual. The matter is complicated by the fact that in a complex society each of the major roles breaks down commonly into a plurality of subroles. The role of mother in American middle-class society is anything but monolithic. By very virtue of the fact that she is the mother in the household she is also likely to hold the subroles of housekeeper, nurse, bestower of love upon her children, confidante, adviser, disciplinarian, den mother, PTA member, ad infinitum. Her central role of mother thus becomes in fact a complex of interacting and often conflicting subroles. Add to this the inevitable possibility of conflict between her role of mother and her role of wife, which also breaks down into a complex of subroles: lover, companion, homemaker, hostess, club member, and so on.

To itemize roles and subroles in the fashion of the preceding paragraph is to perhaps make the situation more difficult in appearance than it actually is. For just as we resolve the famous paradox of Zeno by actually getting to a distant object, so do we in actual life resolve most of the role conflicts without being especially aware that there are conflicts. The process of socialization, as we saw before, carries with it certain mechanisms of almost instantaneous adaptation and assimilation. Still, no one contemplating the position of the middle-class wife or mother in American society can be unaware of the ease with which potential role conflicts become actual ones and the occasional difficulty involved in resolving them. Sometimes the conflicts can reach the point of neurotic intensity. The person, through his or her own efforts, may be unable to resolve them; they are manifested in distortions of behavior and of growing inability to define a given situation adequately. The immense number of professional counselors in our society is probably evidence enough of the number of role conflicts. A good deal of such counseling concerns itself directly with the subject's variable relation to his or her roles and is designed to facilitate what can properly be called *role taking*—that is, the taking, for purposes of insight, the roles of others in the social circle. Some of our most valuable analytical understandings of roles and their relation to human consciousness have come from detailed observations of individuals who, either for experimental or therapeutic purposes, *take* the roles of other persons. As we noted at the beginning of this chapter, there is more than merely terminological similarity between social roles and dramatic roles.

One other aspect of role conflict should be emphasized—the capacity of any given role for accumulating strains and tensions as the result of changes in the relation of that role to the social order. There is no better and more immediate example of this than the role of the professor in the American university. Until about thirty years ago, the role of the university professor was defined almost universally as that of teacher-scholar. The primary and, generally speaking, most lauded aspect of this role was the teaching aspect. One made his most enduring reputation on a campus as teacher. With the activity of teaching went the less visible but hardly less important activity of research, of scholarship. Such research, however, was usually conducted within the professor's own study or laboratory, and almost without exception it was intimately engaged with the professor's teaching. His scholarship was commonly done by himself alone, as was his teaching. Far from creating any conflict, the two activities were generally regarded (I am referring to universities here rather than colleges) as mutually dependent.

What has happened, however, within the past three or four decades is the increasing participation of the university itself in the larger domain of society through consultative bureaus and institutes for giving advice to agriculture, business, local government, national government, and other areas. World War II saw the proliferation of scientists-in-government, at first physical and biological scientists, then social scientists. The era of large-scale, heavily funded research began. Such research went beyond the confines of the professor's study or laboratory to include others in great research organizations frequently stretching across the country. Large grants from foundations, industries, and government became increasingly common. With them and with the swelling of research generally, the role of researcher became either detached altogether from that of teacher or else union between the two became more and more unstable. There was also the rising influence of academic consulting. The prestige of the university in business and government meant also the prestige of the university professor as adviser to business and government. There was, finally, the ever-higher degree of importance of *profession*, disciplinary profession, in the life of the professor. Where his loyalty had once been given to his campus alone, now there was the added loyalty to profession—to engineering, to sociology, to political science, to chemistry, and so on. Most recently we have seen the spreading phenomenon of professors-as-businessmen. These are members of universities who conduct research and consultative businesses on the side with their own research eminence the marketable commodity.

The result is a degree of role conflict for the professor that his forebears in American universities could scarcely have imagined. To be a professor today in any one of a great many academic fields—that is, to be a successful professor, one who acquires prestige in the eyes of students and colleagues alike, as well as those outside the university, and who earns the salary and promotions that go today with success—means a fairly diversified, conflict-ridden, professional existence. He is teacher, yes, though the diminution of this role or aspect of role is very evident in universities today. He is also scholar or researcher in an academic department. He is, beyond this, a member of, possibly a director of, an institute or bureau concerned with the marketability of organized, corporate research. He is often a consultant in not one but several areas—industrial, professional, governmental. He is expected to be active in his own professional organizations and to remain high in esteem in his profession. He may at the same time be the president or chairman of the board of a consulting business, with full-time employees. Finally, given the ever-larger salaries that go today to professors in universities as well as the outside income from his consulting, his royalties on textbooks, and the like, he may find himself in the historically unwonted role of investor in the stock and bond market—for large incomes produce responsibilities for the care and handling of the money involved. Much of the recent history of the American university, its conflicts and turbulences, is deeply rooted in the role conflicts of the professor.

HISTORY AS SOCIAL SELECTION OF ROLES

From the sociologist's point of view, the history of human society can be seen most resplendently as the changing prominence that is given to the major social roles in society. At one point in history, it may be the kinship role that is most decisive for a society, with supreme honor accorded the patriarch or matriarch, and with family, kindred, clan, and tribe correspondingly the most honored of social aggregates. At another point in history it may be the religious role that receives the highest recognition and exerts the greatest influence. At still another point it may be the role of warrior or soldier; or it may be the role of scholar, business entrepreneur, explorer, technologist, or the political role of king or bureaucrat.

Earlier in the chapter I suggested that in the history of human society a process of selection has almost always been at work through which some ways of human behavior are fixed, conventionalized, and then passed on generation after generation. The number of possible ways of human behavior is nearly infinite, but the number of social roles is very clearly limited. It is limited by the needs and functions of human beings in their interaction with one another—needs for sustenance, protection, shelter, sexual gratification, companionship, knowledge, and so on. Not that each of the major social roles in man's history is the direct outcome of some biological need or instinct. We do not know what the ultimate origins of any of our major roles and institutions are, nor do we need to know for present purposes. It is enough to be aware of the fact that there is a close and continuing relation between man's most fundamental needs and those social roles that are found as central elements in all social orders and ages as far back as historical data permit us to go in time.

The remaining pages of this chapter describe a few of the major social roles in man's history, with special emphasis on Western man. Each role has a line of continuity in human history, one that connects the relatively simple and undiversified early age of human society with the highly complex and almost infinitely diversified age present in Western society. Finally, each role is a concrete element in which and on which are written the experiences of human beings in many phases of their social history. The English historian F. W. Maitland once said that the whole history of modern England could be written in terms of what happened over six centuries to the role of sheriff. It would be possible to write the history of mankind in terms of any of the roles that I shall describe very briefly in the paragraphs that follow.

The Patriarch

He may have been preceded, as far as exertion of ultimate social authority was concerned in primitive human society, by the matriarch. Some anthropologists have declared the matriarchal form of social organization to be an earlier one than the patriarchal. But if we limit ourselves (as I propose to do in all of these vignettes) to Western society as it comes into historical view about a thousand years before Christ, it is the patriarch who governs. True, the matriarch was not without vital social influence. But the supremacy of the patriarch is beyond doubt as we look at the oldest writings in the Western record.

What are the essential attributes of the patriarchal role? First, masculinity, of course—masculinity defined by hereditary accession to power that almost always went to the oldest living male in the kinship organization and by possession of the full name of the tribe or other kinship group. Second, the quality of wisdom, real or not, that was always held to be a derivative of age, experience, and of legitimacy of descent within the kinship circle. Third, the vital position of keeper of the records, traditions, and rituals which belonged to the kinship groups. The patriarch was also interpreter of these records, traditions, and rituals, for he was always the court of last resort, so to speak, in all matters falling within his organization. There was no outside power that could justly invade the circle over which he presided. Fourth, and flowing directly from these three, he had absolute power, at least in principle, over all the lives, property, animals, goods, and belongings of the kinship group.

Whether in the books of the Old Testament or in the Homeric epics or in the earliest records of Babylonian or Roman law, the figure of the patriarch is a resplendent one in Western history. He was the personification of wisdom, law, legitimacy, identity, and order on this earth, and, oftentimes, of the individual's relation to all that preceded him in time and all that would follow him, in this world and the next. In earliest times the patriarch had the power of life and death over all within his circle and the right to exile offenders, confiscate individual property, tax, legitimize births, permit marriages, and give ritual blessing to the dying. Between the once nearly limitless functions and authorities belonging to the patriarch and the presently limited and attenuated influence of the father, or "Dad" in the Western social order, lies a long history of displacement and transfer of role attributes to other types and relationships in society. As a form of social governance, however, patriarchalism has not been confined rigorously to kinship aggregates. It is found as a role model in many other forms of social aggregate: in villages, in guilds, in monasteries, in religion as a whole, in professions and business enterprises. It is also found in almost all forms of social interaction where at any given time the essential personal qualities of the patriarch have ascendancy: qualities of masculinity, advanced age, presumed wisdom through experience, legitimacy through descent (kinship or other), and mastery of lore and tradition. Even today one will occasionally speak of the patriarch of a given academic department or school, or of a profession, community, or business enterprise.

The Matriarch

Despite a common belief that it is only in modern, democratic and industrial times that the woman has achieved personal influence in society, the role of matriarch has been an impressive one for many millennia. It is entirely possible, as we noted above, that her eminence goes back indeed to a time when she, rather than the patriarch, was supreme in the kinship order. This position has been argued by a number of anthropologists, among them the late Robert Briffault in his *The Mothers*. But for our understanding of the prestige of the role of mother, we need not go back beyond the literature of ancient Israel and of Greece and Rome. Even in those preeminently patriarchal societies enough power, prestige, and functional importance were attached to her role to merit her the title of matriarch.

From the historic role of the matriarch, as we can uncover it in ancient literature and in timeless tradition, have flowed most of the role qualities which we make fundamental even today in the activities of women and in the norms surrounding anticipatory socialization of girls and young women in Western society. The classic virtues of the woman, especially of the "lady," go back continuously in time to the position of the matriarch in early kinship society in the West. Such virtues are repeatedly described in the books of the Old Testament.

For the original qualities of the matriarch we do not have to rely upon supposition of what may have lain in the powers of the especially gifted, strong, and aggressive female. We need rely solely on what we know of the role of mother, grandmother, and great-grandmother as we find it vividly set forth in history. It was, and is, a role compounded of a few of the same elements we found in that of patriarch: age, wisdom by virtue of age, and descent, among others. Whatever the patriarch's ultimate rights of control over children and grandchildren and their further descendants, and whatever the monopoly of genealogical identity in the patriarch's name, the matriarch (or the matron as Romans called her) plainly had a strong influence in day-to-day decisions affecting all aspects of family life and related activities. As far back as we can go in Western literature we find indications of the profound respect in which the woman—the woman, that is, in role of mother and matriarch—is held. The intimate, direct, and easily perceived relation she had to the all-important fact of procreation, of issue of children, especially sons, would doubtless have been enough to guarantee her elevation into matriarchal roles of even religious and political majesty. But beyond this, as the early testaments and sagas make clear—even those dealing for the most part with the patriarch and with other male-ascribed roles—there was early recognition of a distinctive quality of wisdom and moral influence in the woman that was not to be found in the male. And when the patriarch died, when governance passed by hereditary descent to the oldest son, the patriarch's wife, when she survived him, often retained much of her former husband's authority. The older she became and the larger the number of descendants around her, the more likely was her influence to increase. Even today, the role of the matriarch can be immense in importance, irrespective of patriarchal themes and symbols. This is especially true among those ethnic or religious groups in which kinship ties are strong or in which, as among American Negroes historically, the role of father has been a fluctuant one, the result of circumstances arising out of slavery in this country. And, as Conrad Arensberg has shown us in his masterful study *The Irish Countryman*, despite both a kinship and religious system that supports the patriarchal theme, the power of the grandmother is substantial. Nor is the influence of the matriarch in history limited to the circle of family. As with the patriarch, this role has become the model of matriarchal roles in government—the great queens in history—in religion, and other areas. One thinks of the founder of Christian Science, Mary Baker Eddy. Prophet she may have been in the full religious sense of the word, but she was also a matriarch, and matriarch-prophet she remains to this day. Few areas of social history have been spared the influence and impact of a role that began, and still is most universally to be found, in the kinship circle alone. But that role has passed into other areas where the attributes of the matriarch have proved to be functional through historical social selection. And what we noted above with the patriarch is as true today of the matriarch. Between the magisterial presence of, say, a Homeric or Old Testament matriarch and the diminished, if nonetheless popularly sentimentalized, role of mother or "Mom" in present-day, middle-class Western society lies a vast amount of political and economic, as well as kinship, history.

The Prophet

We do not know when it first occurred to *Homo sapiens* to wonder *why*, to fear the invisible and unknown. But it is certain that it was long before the age of man reflected in even our oldest records and artifacts. Granted that in earliest times the patriarch was perhaps the commonest source of spiritual as well as physical protection, there were bound to be certain individuals—certain highly endowed patriarchs, if we like—who provided spiritual refuge in their words. These men were given a unique position and status in their societies. They were the prophets. There has probably never been an age in human history in which the role of prophet has not existed in some form. Prophets exist all around us today. They may be religious prophets —the millennarian, for example—or the prophet in the guise of scientist or historian, of political ruler or social critic or august financier. What is central to the prophet role is conviction on the part of others that in him lies some special charisma or other superlative human essence that enables him to speak with authority about the spiritual unknown, about the existential, about the past, present, and future of mankind as a whole. All major religions in the West—and in other parts of the world as well—go back to some original prophet. The list could include a Moses, a Buddha, a Jesus, or, in more recent times, a Joseph Smith or a Mary Baker Eddy. The original role of prophet is not only that of interpreter of the sacred records, but inter- preter also of the myriad uncertainties of life that plague the existence of mankind. Sometimes the prophet is the exemplar of the virtues and wisdom that are presumed to lie in their ultimate perfection in the deity that is worshiped by a people. At other times the prophet is a moral spokesman for the best of the traditions that may lie in the history of a given people. But in whichever capacity, and whether as one primarily "religious," in the usual sense of that word, or as one whose life has been lived for politics, for knowledge, or for com- munity, the role of the prophet has been a central one in human history. And it is today, though the most imposing of prophets in recent history, such as Karl Marx, may have been attached to no body of religious precept at all but rather to an ostensibly nonreligious writ in which, however, the elements central to prophecy remain in full glory. It was from the charisma belonging by definition to prophets—religious, primarily, but also political and military—that Max Weber derived, as we have already seen, the category of "charismatic" for certain types of leadership or authority in society.

The Magician

This word has become identified in our present-day society in the West with the prestidigitator, the man who makes the visible disappear or gets rabbits out of a hat. The function of the magician in our society is wholly that of entertainment. But the magician has not always held this relatively minor function, nor does he even today in many parts of the world. His role and eminence go back in time at least as far as that of the prophet. In some ways he is related by role to the prophet. Both are believed to possess arcane powers not given to ordinary people; both assume importance in times of collective crisis or personal difficulty. But whereas the central function of the prophet is that of interpretation of the sacred tradition and of gaining access to the deity in ways denied the bulk of the populace, the central function of the magician is that of effecting exceptions to the natural order. The magician is able to bring about rain when long drought threatens the crops, to put his hand upon the kind of poison or weapon guaranteed to dispose of the enemy, to find the elixir that will preserve the life of the dying child, to assure the permanence of buildings that might normally succumb to disintegration in time. The magician's role is that of the doer—but what he does is reserved for times of crisis and for activities which are affected by risk or uncertainty of outcome. His role is the outcome of special knowledge that he holds to himself and to his legitimate descendants. The number of persons —Christians and other religionaries included—who go to magicians (though they usually are called by different names today) is still substantial in Western society. Most who go are doubtless of minimal literacy, people who are steeped in superstitions of one sort or another. The vast majority of us have transferred to modern science and technology the needs, hopes, and lay beliefs that at an earlier point in Western history were given directly to the magician.

The Warrior-Chief

With the appearance of this role we find the first historical onslaught against kinship society and against the roles of patriarch, matriarch, and prophet. The warrior-chief's reason for being is, of course, war—or the threat of attack from the outside by violence-prone enemies. A social order, if sufficiently isolated from possibility of invasion, may endure indefinitely under the governance of patriarchal and prophetic rule. The kinship-religious order is sufficient and all-encompassing. The authority of the patriarch or prophet is unchallenged. But history shows that isolation of a social group has frequently been invaded by the foreign host, armed and ready to kill, lay waste, and capture. Or, conversely, the social order in question may for its own reasons—for food, minerals, women, slaves—decide to engage another people in war. For whichever reason, however, it is war or the threat of war that leads to the rise of the warrior-chief in history.

The role requirements of the military leader are plainly very different from those of the patriarch or prophet. Were a people to go into battle under the headship of the man who had attained his position of rulership in society solely by virtue of age, knowledge of sacred custom, ritual, and tradition, and simple hereditary accession of office, the consequences might be disastrous. For war demands a very different set of qualities. Chief among them are youth, strength, agility, cunning, and, when necessary, ferocity. Hence, among all peoples known to us, the transfer of ultimate authority over the males who form the war band or militia goes from patriarch to warrior-chief. That is, for the duration of the hostilities. In ancient Rome for many centuries the militia returning from foreign war was compelled to halt outside the city gate and divest itself of military garb and weaponry. From the moment the militia members entered the city they were once again under the full authority of their respective patriarchs. The authority of the warrior-chief expired with return of the militia to the city.

It has been the fate of most peoples known to us, however, that wars, once they began in the life of a people—Persians, Egyptians, Greeks, Romans, and others down to the present day—assumed progressive frequency and intensity. War, at first a merely sporadic and relatively mild military activity requiring only civil militia and leadership of qualified young civilians, tended to become a more or less perpetual activity. There is no major people known to us in the West that has not, in time, under spur of increase in wars, seen the military become an ever more permanent establishment and the role of the warrior-chief, the military leader, an ever more firmly based role in society.

The result in purely social terms was, and had to be, unremitting conflict of role. The role of the patriarch and his lineal role descendants, supported by tradition, civil and kinship norms, and the kind of conservatism that goes with such societies, was in conflict with the role of the warrior-chief and those who, by electing the life of the battlefield, lived in terms of altogether different norms and role requirements. Throughout most of human history war has been the principal occasion for challenge to tradition and patriarchalism. Thus, quite literally, the warrior-chief is the first in history to manifest the kind of personal assertiveness that is the beginning of individualism, in however primitive a degree. All that puts premium upon youth, virility, cunning, and ferocity, that is, upon the life of the warrior and of the warrior-chief, is in deadly conflict with all that puts premium upon old age, wisdom, tradition, and conservatism. True enough, in times of prolonged peace, with a military organization in continuous existence, the lack of the kind of challenge that is embodied in war can lead to assumption by the military organization of qualities—seniority, traditionalism, and the rest—historically associated with patriarchal societies. Then when war comes suddenly with all its built-in challenge to age and patriarchalism and its inevitable favoring of the young, strong, and cunning, there is commonly the same kind of toppling of military rank, and the sudden replacement by new, vigorous minds.

History, especially Western history, reveals an incessant waxing and waning from age to age of the influence of the military role. One period, that of feudalism in the West, for instance, may be inseparable in its political structure from the dominance of the military. In another, such as the nineteenth and early twentieth centuries in Western Europe and the United States, the military role, although far from reduced to nullity, is overshadowed by other roles, those of businessman or politician, for example. Our own age, especially since World War II, is one of renewed ascendancy of the military in political and social affairs. In the United States alone, for example, it is impossible to miss the degree to which the military has risen, within the past thirty years, to positions of eminence and direct power in government that would have been inconceivable as recently as the 1920s. And the role of the military is not confined to formal government. There is scarcely a major industry today that does not have a retired high military officer securely placed in its management structure. The late C. Wright Mills, in his *The Power Elite*, may have exaggerated his contention of the overriding *unity* of contemporary military, industrial, labor, and technological elites in government. But he did not exaggerate the continuing influence of each, most especially that of the military, from one political administration to the next since about 1939.

Political Man

Call him citizen or politician, elected official or divine-right monarch, bureaucrat or magistrate, the role of political man is inseparable from the political realm of the territorial state and its various subdivisions. Historically, the state arises through war, more or less continuous war. The circumstances we have just seen with respect to the conflict between patriarch and warrior-chief are the common, if not universal, circumstances of the beginnings of the political state. Like every other form of human relationship or institution, the political state has arisen not once but many times in history. In its most primitive form the state resembles the military tie between warrior-chief and soldiers more than it does the patriarchal tie. But when a state becomes more or less permanent in an area, and when the demands of war begin to subside, the state commonly begins to take on the characteristics it can borrow from patriarchalism. Then the military leader becomes the king, the emperor, the "father" of his people. Traditions can then begin to accumulate, and authorities become hereditary or based on succession and seniority.

The political *role*, however, remains substantially different from the role of kinsman, religionary, patriarch, or prophet. For whereas these are inseparable from what we have described as *personal* types of social aggregate, the role of political man always arises when the *territorial tie* comes into existence. The great Cleisthenean reforms in ancient Greece, which we have referred to in other contexts, were the immediate occasion of the rise of the political role—the role of member of the territorial deme and polis, the role of citizen, of elected official, of politician, of bureaucrat. Each of these manifestations of the political role is inseparable from the territorial unity, the political reality, of the state as it comes into existence repeatedly in the separate histories of the numerous peoples whose careers make up the subject matter of Western history. Just as the prime responsibility of the patriarch or matriarch is to kin group, of the prophet, to the religious community, and of the warrior-chief, to his war band, the prime responsibility of political man, whether as citizen, governor, politician, or bureaucrat, is to the entity we call the state. The role demands are inherently different from the others, and in their differentness lie myriad possibilities of conflict with others—the kind of conflict that can be seen from time to time within a single person in his separate roles of kinsman, religionary, and citizen. The role demands may also create the kind of conflict that can be seen so vividly between patriarch and political ruler, between prophet and political ruler, and sometimes between warrior and political ruler.

The Man of Knowledge[3]

Originally this role was fully contained within the role of either the patriarch, the prophet, or the magician. The time came, however, when knowledge for its own sake began to be valued, began to assume an autonomous position in a social order. Without question the most momentous of all times when this happened was about the sixth century B.C. in Greece. The exact circumstances are unclear. Certainly this could not have been the very first time the man of knowledge came into existence in man's already long history. But there could not have been many such times, and no matter how many there had been before, it was the coming into prominence of the philosopher and scientist in Greece that made the vital difference in the part of the world we call the West. These archetypes of the man of knowledge persist to this moment.

Knowledge had figured in the existences and roles of patriarch and prophet, but there it had been purely ancillary. What is vital to the role of the man of knowledge is what Simmel has called "cognitive autonomy." Only when knowledge is valued for its own sake or when direct pursuit of knowledge is regarded as the unique and indispensable condition of virtue, of mastery of self and of others, can the man of knowledge be said to have a distinct social role in society. That the hunter, the peasant, the artisan, as well as the patriarch and prophet, must have some "knowledge" in order to fulfill function is plain enough. But there is no cognitive autonomy of knowledge here; it is inextricably embedded in the function of hunter, peasant, and so on. Only when the role of sage, philosopher, technologist, or scientist is recognized in and for itself, is defined as such by society, and is supported by society, can the role of man of knowledge be said to have emerged in society.

Whatever an Empedocles, a Heraclitus, or Anaximander may first have been in social life—politician, soldier, civil functionary—they enter our historical ken as philosophers and scientists. And it is in this capacity of man of knowledge that we encounter Socrates, Plato, and Aristotle later on in Greek history. So too in Rome were found, in long succession, men of knowledge regarded by their contemporaries (and by all since who have absorbed any of the classical tradition) as scholars, philosophers, or scientists who are respected accordingly. It is possible for the social role of the man of knowledge to disappear entirely for long periods. This seems to have been the case in Western Europe during at least a few centuries after the collapse of the Roman Empire in the West. Once again knowledge became the ancillary pursuit of the prophet, the patriarch, and the political ruler and not an end in itself. When the man of knowledge reappeared in the West, it was first in the garb of the theologian—the follower of prophets. Then the successive extrications of knowledge from other functions and the increasing envisagement of knowledge as a proper end in itself began to take place. Once again the man of knowledge assumed his social role in society. What we call secularization as a historical process in Western society, from the late Middle Ages on, is, at bottom, the extrication of the man of knowledge—and also of the artist whom we shall next depict—from the role assemblages of the church. Since, in this prolonged process, the influence of the political state was great—arising from its own conflict with church—an affinity between the state and the man of knowledge began very early and has persisted to the present. Whether as political philosopher, as intellectual, or as scientist, the man of knowledge has had to depend to a very considerable degree upon the environment of territorial rights and protections that the state could best offer. The natural law philosophers of the seventeenth century, the empiricists who followed Francis Bacon, the physical scientists of the seventeenth and eighteenth centuries, the *philosophes* in France just before the Revolution were all, in their preferred roles at least, men of knowledge.

The single most continuous context of the man of knowledge during the last eight centuries has been, however, the university. For, from the very beginning of the university, in centers such as Bologna, Paris, Oxford, and Salamanca, its prime institutional function was that of discovery and dissemination of knowledge. Of all types of the man of knowledge, therefore, the professor, attired in medieval gown, was without any question the best known for many centuries in Western Europe. His essential function was that of discovery of knowledge and the dissemination of knowledge through teaching and writing. So it has remained to the present—with due allowance for the normative and role conflicts of the professor that we observed briefly in the preceding section. One point in this connection should be emphasized, however. Although the university is today the major and at times the seemingly exclusive habitat of the man of knowledge, it has not by any means been so in all ages of the West since the university first came into being as one of society's institutions in the Middle Ages. There have been periods, such as the eighteenth century and much of the nineteenth, when the greatest contributions to knowledge were made by those who were not merely outside the university but who frankly condemned the universities of their day for what were considered to be intolerable academic ritualism and aloofness to all that was intellectually vital in society. The man of knowledge has been, in short, a nonacademic figure oftener than he has been a member of the academy.

The Artist

There is evidence that at least as far back in time as the Cro-Magnon man art has been a recognized activity in human society. It is entirely possible that the distinguishable *role* of artist is one of the oldest in human society, as old perhaps as any nonkinship role. For art is, and has been for many millennia, one of the principal manifestations of man's deep desire to understand, to interpret, and to communicate his sense of both the known and the unknown. Whether as painter, dramatist, musician, teller of tales, architect, sculptor, or artificer, the artist has satisfied human cravings for understanding and interpretation that are not satisfied through other channels. We may say that beauty is the goal of the artist, but this is not enough by any means. The drawings in Cro-Magnon man's caves may have seemed beautiful to their viewers; we cannot be sure. But important they surely seemed —important as representations of whatever it was that Cro-Magnon man valued. This has always been the main function of art, in whatever form it may take. For this reason the role of the artist has always been one of the most honored roles in Western society—and all other societies as well. Although for long ages the tie between art and religion was very close (and at no time was this more true than during the Middle Ages) there have assuredly been ties between art and politics, between art and warfare, between art and mere human comfort. Once luxury became a prized aspect of life, art was bound to be regarded as a cherished contributor to luxury.

As there have been ages characterized primarily by the role of the patriarch, the military chief, the political leader, the scientist or technologist, so have there been ages in which the role of the artist has been dominant, valued, occasionally at least, over almost all other roles in society. The fifth century B.C. in Greece was such an age, although that age was rich in other roles as well—political, military, intellectual. The Renaissance in modern Western Europe was also such an age. Painters, sculptors, artificers, and architects competed with one another for the favors of wealthy patrons. And patrons often competed for exclusive access to the art of some highly talented creator. The relationship between the artist and his community of fellow artists was a close one, as the history of the ateliers and studios and schools of the period makes plain. There were apprentice and journeyman subroles in the artists' guilds just as there were in technology, business, war, and politics in the Middle Ages and Renaissance.

The artist today is sometimes regarded as being universally what

he often seemed to be in nineteenth- and early twentieth-century society
—rejected, misunderstood, even alienated.   Close study might show
how erroneous this view is even for the periods just mentioned.   It
is beyond any question an erroneous view for most of the history of
art.   The role of artist has, for the most part, been as closely articulated
with the rest of the social order as has almost any other role one can
easily think of.   Sometimes the artist's role has been closest to religion,
as it so obviously was in the earlier phases of Greek and Roman art and
was again in the Middle Ages when the artist's work was almost exclusively confined to what he did for the church.   At other times the
artist's role has been closer to politics.   After the seculariziation of
Athenian culture in the fifty century B.C., artists vied with one another
in celebration of the polis.   Many centuries later in Europe, the French
Revolution and its promise of universal democracy fired the imaginations of painters, poets, musicians, and others.   At still other times the
artist has been closer to the economic system of a social order, as when
he worked under private patrons, whether aristocratic or of the *nouveaux
riches*, and with themes favored by his wealthy patrons.   Sometimes the
artist's role has been rather highly individualized, eccentric, or bohemian,
as it was at the end of the nineteenth century in Europe.   Much more
often in history, however, his role has been as a member of a socially
recognized circle: church, guild, community, foundation, or university.
In this respect the artist has been like all others holding social roles.
It would be absurd to seek to explain the springs of artistic creativity
solely in terms of role elements.   But it would be as absurd to pretend
that the artist, for all his high degree of individuality, does not hold a
social role and is not strongly affected by whatever the role may entail
at any given moment in history.

The Entrepreneur

Although this word is commonly limited in its meaning to economic
entrepreneur, there is no reason why it cannot be applied to anyone who
organizes and directs an enterprise of whatever nature—economic,
political, technological, space exploratory, or dramatic.   History is
filled with exploits of the entrepreneur who, by virtue of extraordinary
energy combined with foresight, skill, and intrepedity, breaks free, so
to speak, of the social order he lives in.   His entrepreneurial role may
be that of the earliest trader in man's history, the individual who, seeing
the presence of a commodity in one tribal community (his own perhaps),
and an absence of this same commodity in another community, thought

of trading, of selling. Whenever, wherever this happened, a major type of economic enterprise was born. The entrepreneur need not, of course, be a single individual planning and directing. The role as well encompasses a group, a "company," as it came to be known in Elizabethan times in business, exploration, and theater alike. However, even in these circumstances, careful investigation usually reveals the presence of some unusual individual who provides the spark of inspiration and leadership. The academic man today who organizes, directs, and provides creative inspiration for some research institute or for some consulting business on the side is hardly less an entrepreneur than the man whose foresight and acumen result in a new electronics enterprise or some vast conglomerate.

One of the most vivid and exciting chapters in the history of the entrepreneurial role in human society is that formed by the exploits of pirates wherever seapower became ascendant, as it did in ancient Carthage and, even earlier, in some of the Aegean islands, or, later, in seventeenth- and eighteenth-century Europe. The pirate was the economic entrepreneur who worked outside the pale of the law, often with incredible daring and less often with great success. Much of so-called organized crime today in the United States and elsewhere is the work of the entrepreneur, criminal though we pronounce him. Such industries as those formed by the illicit sale of narcotics, the numbers racket, and off-track betting on horse racing are often characterized by entrepreneurial ability of high order.

There is also the entrepreneur-explorer—Columbus, Magellan, and, before either, Marco Polo. Much of the real, and essential, preliminary work of bringing the American continent under settlement in the eighteenth and nineteenth centuries was done by entrepreneurs. One thinks of the fur-trapping companies under entrepreneurs in the early part of the nineteenth century in the Rockies and across the plains to the Pacific. Only the uninformed or naïve will suppose that the American continent was explored, mapped, and then settled by amateurs.

There are, and have been for centuries, perhaps millennia, the art entrepreneurs, those who have in a sense advanced music, drama, painting, and other art forms through their organization of creative talents in the theater or opera company, or in the artists' guild. Shakespeare was a highly successful entrepreneur as well as an actor and playwright. His theatrical companies at the beginning of the seventeenth century were models for other entrepreneurs. What we call today "Broadway" and "off Broadway" in the American theater is essentially entrepreneurship expressed in dramatic terms.

The inventor is in every sense an entrepreneur—an entrepreneur in technology. The founder of a private school, an oil company, a great steel company, railroad complex, publishing house, or, to use the favored homely example, the inventor of a new and superior mouse-trap is an entrepreneur. If we are prone to think of this role in terms of the Fuggers, Rothschilds, Morgans, and Rockefellers in history, it is only because the word became prominent in Western writing at a time—the late nineteenth century—when the most conspicuous mani-festations of entrepreneurship were industrial and financial. But the entrepreneur, whether as freebooter, pirate, bandit, businessman, theatri-cal producer, explorer, technologist, research project organizer, or book publisher, is legion in human society. Wherever the role is found, in whatever social circle or subculture, it is made notable by the attributes of personal boldness, intrepidity, willingness to take risks, and usually, inability to endure the ordinary confinements of social life.

The Rebel

This leads us to the last of the social roles I shall deal with here —the individual whose social type was born doubtless when the first son (or daughter) challenged the supremacy of the patriarch and who, as a consequence, no doubt suffered the punishment many rebels in history have known. As most readers of this book know, Sigmund Freud made this act of rebellion, metaphoric though it may be in his work, fundamental in a whole system of psychology.

Everyone rebels at something or someone part of the time. The rebel, as a recurrent social role in history, is formed of more hardy and enduring stuff. He is the individual who puts as much thought, acumen, boldness, and intrepidity into rebellion as the entrepreneur does into his work or the artist, prophet, or warrior-chief into his. Whether from high ideal or from base motive, the rebel in history is the person who seeks to destroy a given social arrangement. In the Bible, Cain was a rebel as well as a fratricide. Spartacus, from all that we are able to learn about him, was a master rebel in history. His overthrow of his own master, his organization of other slaves, and his unbelievably successful military maneuvers for months against professional Roman legions cer-tainly earn him that title despite the horrifying end that he and his slave rebels eventually came to.

There are rebels in all spheres of society. Jesus was a rebel. The history of religion is filled with the acts of rebels, most of whom have been consigned to the ranks of heretics, sometimes to crucifixion, sometimes to burning at the stake, and only rarely to the elect company of founders of new and enduring religions. The line between the bandit and the political rebel, as Eric Hobsbawm has shown us, is often a thin line, as in Southern Italy and Sicily, especially in the nineteenth century but even, in some degree, today. We need recall only the cherished English legend of Robin Hood to realize that stealing can become more than stealing; it can be envisaged as political or economic rebellion both by those engaged in it and by those who witness it. Robbery or banditry thus becomes sanctified through its real or seeming participation in activity whose larger purpose is liberation of people from tyranny or injustice. Conversely the out-and-out political rebel—a Cromwell—is generally compelled to make robbery of some sort the basis of his economic existence.

In all ages everywhere, the rebel has always been feared. The distinguished novelist Richard Wright has, more than any other creative writer in our century, shown us the essence of black rebellion. In *Native Son* the protagonist, Bigger Thomas, is the rebel. He is a rebel in just as rich and full a sense as was Spartacus. All of his misdoings, delinquencies, and bitterness are shown by Wright to proceed from his role of black rebel in a social order dominated by white conventions. And, as Richard Wright has told us in an autobiographical account of his own youth, the black rebel in the traditional South was feared most by black people themselves, who could see in the act of the single black rebel the possibility of white reprisal that would encompass large segments of the black community.

Much so-called juvenile delinquency proceeds directly from the child's assumption of the rebel role: he or she becomes perhaps a rebel against parental authority that is hated or despised because it seems hypocritical. The youthful male rebel may act through car stealing; the youthful female rebel is more likely to act through her sexuality, which she flaunts, finding in sexual promiscuity no particular sexual pleasure perhaps but immense gratification in an act of revolt.

It would be fanciful to explain all rebellion in terms of any single area of causation. Doubtless it springs as often from mere boredom as from political or ethical principle. We are living in an age characterized by student rebellions in many colleges and universities. The student rebel has become, in some quarters, as much a hero as the slave rebel, the citizen rebel, or religious rebel has been at other times and in other quarters. And, of course, as much feared and hated by those who oppose student or other types of rebellion.

The greatest rebels are those who act either from profoundly held principle or from obscure psychological motivations that drive and press endlessly—or both.   There are as many sociologists who are prone to make the first of these categories include the second as there are to make the second all-inclusive.   In fact, however, both sets of causes are found in the history and distribution of rebel roles in society.   For every Bigger Thomas whose sufferings and rebellions proceed from social or psychological mechanisms he does not really recognize, there is a Spartacus or an Alexander Berkman whose signal rebellions are the direct outcome of political or moral principle deeply believed in.

Whatever the sphere in which the rebel is to be found and whatever the residual causation—ethical principle or sociopsychological process— the attributes of the role are universal and persisting in human history. But whether the rebel be a Cézanne, a Cromwell, a Martin Luther, a Eugene Debs, or possibly a Tom Hayden or a Jerry Rubin, he holds a role that was in a very real sense fashioned long before he was born.

Notes

1. This phrase and much of the thought in this chapter owe their orgin to Simmel and Znaniecki. The latter is the true founder of the systematic study of social roles.
2. Peter Berger, *Invitation to Sociology: A Humanistic Perspective* (New York: Anchor, 1963), p. 100.
3. The phrase is taken from Florian Znaniecki's superb study, *The Social Role of the Man of Knowledge* (Octagon Books, Inc., 1965), to which I am much indebted.

8

Social Status

PERSONS AS STATUSES

There is much in common between roles and statuses. Having begun the preceding chapter with a quotation from Shakespeare, we should do no less here. "Take but degree away, untune that string, and hark! what discord follows; each thing meets in mere oppugnancy."

The words are individual; the thought is as nearly universal as any that might be imagined in reference to human behavior. A desire for status, a belief in the necessity of some order of status, or rank, or hierarchical position, a conviction that status is as eternal in human affairs as is role—all of this is deeply embedded in human consciousness. It has been so throughout the long human past. Not even the present age of Western democracy, with its built-in values of equality and equity, has dislodged the importance of status in the human mind. The most passionate egalitarian usually turns out to have some system of rank in mind as an ideal. His egalitarianism is an ideological weapon against existing status arrangements, not those closer to heart and mind. Whatever a century and more of democracy have done to predemocratic structures of class and estate, it can hardly be argued that the democratic mind has become less obsessed with status. Whether in reference to oneself, one's family, ethnic group, job, or college, status is apparently a driving motivation for a great many Americans today. Democracy, as Tocqueville foresaw nearly a century and a half ago, is, of all forms of political government, the one most likely to contain within it—built into it as, Tocqueville emphasized—status desires, status apprehensions, and status anxieties. A preoccupation with status is often a consequence, indeed, of the erosion of fixed and clear class differences in a society.

When we refer to status we have in mind a person's position, or some social aggregate's position, or the position of a job or other role *in a vertical perspective that permits considerations of "higher" and "lower" to become relevant.* Hierarchy, stratification, and rank are the very essence of status. This is true whether we are referring to status in the concrete, as in *a* status, or generally, as when we observe that status is important to all people. And it is true whether we are describing the status system of a kinship group, an army, a university, a profession, or a society as a whole. When we say that status is important to human beings we mean that among other ways a person defines the situations he finds himself in, that of higher and lower, applied to persons, roles, and aggregates, is one of them.

Social statuses and social roles we noted, have much in common. We may describe a social status indeed in exactly the same terms we used for social roles. A status is first of all *a way of behavior.* We acquire and learn status behavior through social interaction, precisely as we do role behavior. Whether one conducts himself as a gentleman or as a peasant requires more than a little socialization during childhood and young manhood. And no one who has ever lived in a society that takes these status categories seriously is likely to have missed the fact that, all appurtenances of dress to one side, the gentleman behaves, thinks, acts, and speaks like a gentleman, and the peasant, like a peasant. We may say of the relation between status and person what we said of role and person. Statuses lie in persons and persons are viewed in statuses.

Second, a status is a part of a *social circle*, though it would be more exact to say pyramid or hierarchy. Just as there are interdependences of roles, with the meaning of one role proceeding from its relation to another, so are there analogous interdependences of statuses. The high status of patriarch in a strongly familistic society is inseparable from the lower statuses of younger brothers, wives, children, servants, and others. How, after all, would it be possible to be a gentleman except for the answering behavior of those below (or above in an aristocratic society) in status? In a memorable line George Bernard Shaw said the difference between a lady and a charwoman is how you treat them. True, but equally significant is how the lady and charwoman treat themselves and how their statuses reinforce one another. In a play by James Barrie, *The Admira-*

ble Crichton, we have the spectacle of an English yachting party ship-wrecked and forced to live on a desert island for a considerable period. The whole point of the play is the immediate rise to command of the butler, Crichton, and his virtually life-and-death dominance of the group—a dominance fully and gratefully accepted by the group itself. But with the rescue of the group the needs change, the circle resumes normal relationships, and Crichton, contentedly, goes back to being the gentleman's gentleman.

The third factor is that statuses are bounded and reinforced by *norms*. Apart from the social norms of the gentleman, of the peasant, of the lady, and of the charwoman, there would be little to give them substance. In status behavior, as in role behavior, there is almost always some kind of ideal type operating in the minds of those involved in the interactive situation. In the gentleman's behavior, as in the peasant's—where these two types are pronounced in a social order—there is to be seen some degree of self-conscious approximation of behavior to a normative ideal type. In any society characterized by recognition of status types, the process of socialization of the young rests to a large extent upon inculca-tion of this ideal type. And where the outlines of the types are clear, where, through a great variety of nuances of bearing, speech, dress, and life style generally, the status types are well recognized by the population, it is extremely difficult, if possible at all, for the outsider to assume one of the status types convincingly. However hard he may try, however clever at mimicry he may be, there will almost always be the tell-tale sign of his spurious credentials, his lack of the long, early period of ap-propriate socialization within which the norms of the status were made a part of his very being. And these words are as applicable to status types regarded by the surrounding population as low as they are to those held to be high. The norms that give definition to status are as many and subtle, objectively viewed, for the one as for the other.

Fourth, there is an element of *legitimacy*—that is, perceived legiti-macy—in status behavior just as there is in role behavior. No status will long survive widespread belief in its loss or lack of legitimacy. Ages that are truly revolutionary, in the social sense of the word, are ages in which the sense of legitimacy regarding the status system of a social order ter-minates rather sharply. The traditional prerogatives of high status in the society are challenged, and the traditional limits put upon low status are seen as so many illegitimate fetters, to be cast off. The high status of the patriarch, the man of knowledge, the businessman, or of the titled aristocrat will survive only so long as a determining part of the popula-tion in the social order regards each of these as legitimate, as properly entitling their possessors to the privileges which go with their statuses. The status of professor has been recently higher in our society than it was a few decades ago, which means, among other things, that there has been a clearer and firmer sense of the legitimacy of the professorial status.   However, this situation may be substantially modified by current events in colleges and universities.

Finally, there is in a status, as there is in a role, the sense of obligation, of duty, that proceeds from the relation of status to the larger system of authority in the social order.   The term "noblesse oblige" was drawn historically from medieval Europe, one of the most highly stratified social ages in history.   It reflects the sense, always strong in such an age, that status or rank his its obligations as well as its privileges.   Successful military organizations are those in which the obligations of rank are strongly inculcated in officers and enlisted men alike.   Comparative study indicates that one of the surest signs in history of the impending dissolution of a status system is the loss of sense of obligation to status.   This, as Tocqueville, Gaetano Mosca, and others have shown, was a vivid aspect of the behavior of the aristocracy in France, and much of the rest of Europe, during the century or two leading up to the French Revolution. It works, of course, at the other end of the scale too.   Behind peasant revolts, the uprisings of workers, and, in our own day, in the militant activity of many blacks and Mexican-Americans lies a progressive sense of being released from the obligation to behave in the manner that a social order has traditionally declared proper to one of a low status.   What we noted with respect to role in adaptation of behavior is equally valid with respect to status or rank.   To be able to convince the members of a class or caste that they do *not* have obligations to low status, that there is nothing legitimate in their low status, and nothing normatively binding when they are properly regarded is the first step in the active phase of any social revolution.   In periods of revolutionary social change, as in France in the eighteenth century, as in the United States at the present time with respect to the relations between blacks and whites, few things are clearer than the spreading erosion of any sense of obligation to status—that is, historically derived status.

So much for the criteria of social status.   I have said they are the same as for social roles.   What, then, are the differences between role and status?   Few questions have produced more confusion in contemporary sociology than this one.

The answer lies in the opening paragraphs of the chapter.   Whereas "role" does not carry with it any necessary implication of ranking in a vertical scale of "higher" and "lower," the term "status" assuredly does.

The essential character of *a* status in society comes directly from the meaning of status in more abstract terms: that is, of hierarchy and stratification. Precisely the same way of behavior can be, and usually is, *both* a role and status. However, distinction between them, from the point of view of social analysis, is vital. For example, the *role* of household father may meet substantially the same criteria in two different social orders with, however, the *status* of father in the social order higher in one than the other. In ancient Rome it was a very high status, a reflection of the preeminent position of the kinship group. In contemporary American society the status of father is, while clearly not as low as it might be in some largely matriarchal culture, not as high as it was in the Roman Republic or, for that matter, in an earlier period of American history when the functions of kinship were more numerous than they are today. The role of professor was substantially the same in American society a half a century ago as it was in Europe: this role was defined in terms of teaching and research in universities. But the status of professor in American and European society differed then rather markedly; it was considerably higher in Europe. This is merely to say that at that time the role of professor was more honored by society at large in Europe. It carried more prestige than it did in an America that was still dominated by pragmatic values and the norms of business and economic achievement.

I am not suggesting that the relation between role and status is always as simple as these two illustrations might suggest. Status is something that attaches, especially in societies where social class or caste is strong, to *specific* families and persons. Thus one born in, or who through adoption or marriage becomes a part of, a family with a highly honored name, with high status in a given society, would very probably be said to have high status as an individual, irrespective of whatever economic or social role he took on. And it would work in reverse. As anyone knows who has ever lived in a socially stratified community, it is quite possible for an individual, through education or extraordinary personal ability, to assume a role that is regarded as a high *role* but that does not materially affect his low status. The most vivid example of this for Americans is, of course, the traditional position of the Negro. In nearly all American communities, North and South, an individual Negro's capacity to assume the role of banker or lawyer or professor does not, as we know, substantially affect his status as a Negro. This status is inseparable from an American system of status ordering in which Negroes are categorically placed below whites.

We come back at this point to two terms used with respect to roles in the preceding chapter—"ascribed" and "achieved." There are ascribed statuses just as there are ascribed roles. The role of woman is ascribed; so is the particular status that womanhood may have in a society at any given time. A woman is the object of certain immediate normative expectations by others, men and women alike. Whether the behavior that approximates these expectations—becoming a wife, a mother, a nurse, homemaker, and so on—enjoys high or low *status* is, of course, inseparable from the role and how the role is regarded in terms of the criteria of honor and prestige in the specific social order. If, as a homely saying once had it, woman's place is in the home, then both her role and status will be determined by the functional significance of the kinship group. Save only for that of patriarch, there was no higher status in early Roman society than the role of matron. In our present society, where kinship ties are rivaled by those of business, politics, and others, the status of the woman is a kind of uneasy compromise between the still somewhat honored role she may occupy as wife and mother and the increasingly honored roles for her as political figure—citizen or office holder—business or professional woman, and so on.

Status is, like role or authority or any major element of social behavior, essentially a dimension or perspective. It is one through which we see ourselves and others around us. We may speak of the status of a given job in the economic system, of an age group, of either of the sexes, of a social aggregate, of a form of sport or recreation, of a given discipline or science in the university, of a specific university or a specific family in the community or a specific individual. In all instances we are referring to the position any one of these may have in a vertical scale more or less generally accepted in the social aggregate involved, that is itself a scale of esteem or honor. Despite a once common tendency in sociology to deal with status solely within the context of the kind of social aggregate we call social class or social caste, it is clear enough from the foregoing words that all kinds of status relationships are possible, especially in a complex society. Many different kinds of elements —individual persons, families, jobs, educational achievements, among others—all figure in the establishment of status. We shall return to this point when we deal with status consistency and status inconsistency. For now, it is necessary only to recognize that in a large, rather loosely organized, highly differentiated society, there are many status spheres, many possible scales by which status is assessed. Some are old, some are very new. Family may be crucial in one community, a matter of relative indifference in another where job, overt life style, or level of education matters more.

But however status may be prized or assessed, its governing importance in human affairs is not to be missed. Once a degree of differentiation of function emerges in any society, there is bound to be differentiation of regard, of esteem, of ranking of the differences of function. However dedicated a society may be to the ethic of equality (and societies assuredly differ in their degrees of overall equality), there is bound to be unequal regard for the roles that compose the society and also unequal motivation toward these roles.

SOURCES OF STATUS

In any full sense, the sources of status in a social order are as numerous and diverse as the social aggregates that form the order. One has greater or less status in his family, his peer group, his school or college, his club or professional society, his business, his neighborhood, and so on. In a complex society such as ours the spheres within which one may achieve high status or be held to low status are obviously large in number. Criteria that are vital to high status in one sphere are useless in another. Generally speaking, wealth is an important element of high status in most societies and ages of history. But it will not carry us all the way in any precise location of high status in a complex society. Wealth, quite obviously, is valueless as a criterion of high status in, say, the American Sociological Association. The status, that is, the professional esteem, one enjoys there is a function of research eminence for the most part. To be sure, such eminence in our present society very probably carries with it high annual income, if not great personal wealth, but it is still utterly irrelevant to any status ranking of American sociologists. The same is true of political power. A sociologist of high status ranking within his profession may or may not have considerable political authority within the profession or at some level of public government. Similarly with family of origin. This can be crucial in some areas of society, but is less so in such spheres as the professions, universities, large business organizations of national scope, organized athletics, the theater, the entire entertainment industry, and many other spheres central to the lives of contemporary Americans. There are many status spheres, and the qualities that give a certain theoretical physicist matchless prestige among physical scientists will be lost upon the many millions who live, so to speak, in the status sphere of professional football, or professional sports at large.

The multiplicity of status and of status spheres is, then, obvious enough.   Still, there are certain broad criteria of status in nearly all societies which operate at least most of the time for most people.   Among the broadest and most persistent are *sex, age, wealth, political authority, ethnicity, education, job*, and *kinship group*.   Few are the social orders in history in which these, in one or another combination, have not mattered significantly in the fixing of one's status in the social order.   It is hard to imagine today an individual *not* regarded as of high status in American society who is, at one and the same time, wealthy, influential in political government, white, highly educated, holding a job that society ranks high (lawyer or physician, for instance), and who comes from a family line long known either in the nation or in a given region.   Conversely, it is a fair statement that an impoverished, illiterate, Negro American or Mexican-American, who holds a job as day laborer, is politically passive, and comes from a wholly unknown family will be regarded by his surrounding society as of very low social status, just about at the bottom of the social pyramid.

The two examples are extreme perhaps, but they suggest the phenomenon we call *status consistency*.   This term refers to the strong tendency for certain status attributes to be interrelated in a person or aggregate.   Depending upon the society and the period in history, there is significant degree of interrelation among the status attributes described in each of the above, rather extreme, examples.   Knowing that a person comes from a notable family in New England or the South is enough to give us at least fair predictive probability that the same person is well educated, holds a good job, has some degree of political influence, and so forth.   And if we work from two or three instead of just one of the status attributes, we can feel very confident indeed of our predictive accuracy with respect to the remaining attributes in the list.   So too with the person in the other example.   If we know that he is Negro or Mexican-American with little and poor schooling, the probability is high that he is identified by the other attributes as well—or most of them.   There is never anything absolutely certain in sociological prediction (or scientific prediction generally).   But, obviously, the probability is considerable, in each of the examples given above, of consistently high and consistently low overall status.

The simpler, more stable and stationary the society or community, the greater the likelihood of high degrees of status consistency for persons and groups in that society.   On the other hand, in societies or historical periods in which a high degree of change is to be found—change linked with status mobility—it is obvious that status consistency will be lower in predictive degree.   That is, it will be less certain that merely because a person will be high in one or two of the attributes mentioned, he will be high in the others.

This brings us to *status inconsistency*. If we consider an individual low in education, low in wealth, of obscure family background, and, say, Negro, the probability is quite high that the other status attributes will be consistent with these, taking the population at large. But the probability is diminished if, through substantial changes in the social order, avenues of upward mobility are opened that were once nonexistent. Thus our individual answering positively to the attributes just mentioned *might* prove to be a young, fast-rising, extremely able professional football star—not yet wealthy but perhaps on the way. Or he might be a movie actor, singer, author, dancer, or, given current demand for Negroes on rosters of large industries and government departments, a minor executive. True, not many persons are likely to fit the dimensions just given of status inconsistency. But in our society status inconsistency is nonetheless rife. Individuals who rank high on a status scale with respect to wealth, education, political influence or power, distinguished family background, or any other single attribute of status are not as likely as they once were in Western society to rank high in all or most of the other attributes. In a very important sense the whole thrust of fundamental social revolution is to establish widespread status *inconsistencies*. What usually happens over a period of time through ordinary processes of restabilization, however, is that new patterns of status *consistency* are formed. Thus, if distinction of family or landed type of wealth ceases to matter a great deal and status inconsistencies begin to appear widely in which these traditional criteria are seemingly reversed, new kinds of status consistency are almost certain to manifest themselves. In our recent history, education, occupation, and wealth of any type have plainly succeeded the older sources of status as the key ones.

Now let us return to the fundamental and, on any comparative basis, universal sources of status in society. I listed them above as *sex*, *age*, *wealth*, *power*, *ethnicity*, *education*, *job*, and *kinship group*. We need to examine each in brief but appropriate detail. These have all been, and remain, allowing only for historically varying intensities, the sources of social status in human society and the elements of those status groups we call classes, castes, and elites.

Sex

This is, along with age, the most ancient of all sources of social status. To be born a male instead of a female is to be endowed at the very outset, irrespective of intellectual, economic, and social compensations, with certain advantages which manifest themselves in an immense variety of ways beginning in childhood. True, the female takes on in a generalized way the status of her father or husband. But this has to do only with the rather limited and specialized areas of family life as such and with the circles of association which proceed directly from family life. It has nothing to do with the large number of areas in contemporary Western society where female and male are put in positions of rivalry—actual or latent. Merely by virtue of being female, she has reduced educational, legal, political, and economic opportunities open to her. There is a vast number of jobs closed altogether to women or open only in small degree to them. Until very recently in Western history, women were not permitted to vote, to hold property in their own name, to retain outside earnings, to sign contracts, to enter the best schools and colleges, or to initiate divorce action. Punishments, deprivations, privileges, and rewards in society were, and to a large extent still are, stratified by sex. If this is the case in our relatively equalitarian Western society today, the extent of status inequality arising from sex can easily be imagined in earlier ages of history and in the immense number of cultures on the earth at the present time where not even the ethic of equalitarianism exists. Despite their usually slightly superior numbers in a social order, women form—in the sociological sense of the term—a "minority group" with their opportunities in life cut off or diminished, as is the case with any racial or religious minority group. As I noted above, the woman has one opportunity, theoretical at least, denied to members of other minority groups: she can, by fortunate birth or marriage, take on the high status of father or husband. But, as noted above also, the limits in the degree of social equality this confers upon the female are quickly reached. Sex is even today, and was overwhelmingly in past ages, a significant source of an individual's social status.

Age

The fact of one's age level is another universal source. To be an elder, whether male or female, can be, irrespective of all other qualities, the basis of high status in certain cultures—usually those in which kinship is predominant. The significance of age is not, however, limited to kinship. Until very recently in Western, including American, universities, age was a requisite for academic rank within the university that it is perhaps not likely to be again for some time. To hold the rank of full professor when one was below the age of about fifty was very unusual prior to the aftermath of World War II. In a variety of ways even at the present time in supposedly youth-oriented American culture, age level can be decisive, with youth deprived of certain opportunities which may have no basis whatsoever in mentality, physical strength, and character. Political constitutions, voting laws, employment laws, not to emphasize the great variety of nonlegal and nonpolitical spheres in our society, put a premium upon age as a status element.

Of course, as recent events in the world strongly suggest, there is another side to this. In more than a few situations at the present time— economic among others—youth carries with it a positive effect. Everyone is familiar with the disadvantage attached to old age, even middle age, in the job market. And, within the context of what is today called the generation gap, there is a degree of militant status consciousness that was hardly known a few decades ago in the United States. As Lewis Feuer has shown in his important work, *The Conflict of Generations*, there has been, however, a profound status consciousness in youth for well over a century in other countries. Feuer points out that a good many of the revolts and allied turbulences of the academic scene in Western Europe—all the way back indeed to the Middle Ages—were in fact emanations of the status of youth, status bitterly resented, rather than the primarily economic or political matters they are sometimes thought to be. We cannot go into all the consequences here of the dimensions of age level. The important point generally is that these, in whatever number, in whatever arrangement, in whatever degree of intensity, are the dimensions of status that we recurrently find in the historical and comparative study of society.

Wealth

It would be a very rare society indeed in which wealth was not one of the key criteria in determination of the status of an individual or social aggregate. No such society, surely, apart from some religious order consecrated to poverty, is likely to be found. Even where wealth is not a direct and immediate condition of high status, not a means by which high status may be achieved directly, the presence of wealth or the fact that one's lineage was at one time connected with wealth is taken commonly as a manifestation of high status. No matter how deeply an aristocracy may be rooted in other considerations, the historical evidence is fairly clear that by adequate gain of wealth, not many generations are required for passage from low status to high status in a society. In his masterly study of Elizabethan social structure, the historian A. L.

Rowse has shown in detail how many families peasant in status at the beginning of the sixteenth century had managed, through opportunities for increase of wealth coupled with skill or luck, to become distinctly middle class, even in a few instances nobility, by the end of the century. The Elizabethan age was, of course, one of extraordinary mobility in many spheres. So is our own age in the United States and much of Western Europe. For some time now wealth, measured either as annual income or as fixed capital, has been a major criterion used in the ranking of status in the social order. What we call upper class, middle class, and lower class—one may use either "stratum" or "level" in place of the word "class"—are all bounded primarily, though not by any means exclusively, by wealth considerations. Still, there are not a few instances of individuals moving suddenly and rapidly up the income scale who, in any given part of the country or in any given sphere, cannot be said to be moving up the social scale generally (as this social scale is commonly, if often confusedly, assessed in our society). And, as indicated above, there are assuredly individuals whom we would rank socially high in the population—university presidents, scientists, judges, members of old families—whose wealth is modest and irrelevant in any event to present status.

Political Authority

We should say here simply *authority*. For it may or may not be political in the formal, governmental sense in which this word is generally used. To hold high place in any authority system (and, as we have seen, all social aggregates are authority systems) is to possess a certain influence or power of determination over others that is often valued as highly as wealth itself. At certain periods in history it might have been true that all politically powerful individuals were wealthy. This is assuredly not the case today. Many an administrator in political government, many an elected official, exercises direct power over human lives greater by far than that to be found in divine-right monarchies of the early modern era in Europe or the imperial monarchies of Asia. But whatever the age or form of society, possession of authority has always been an indicator of status that is distinguishable from each of the others we are describing. Irrespective of amount of wealth, of advancement of education, or of family origin, the position of authority one holds, the degree of influence he exerts over others, is sufficient to rank him fairly high. And in those societies which have become highly politicized —with totalitarian societies the most obvious types—the degree of political influence one holds is nearly decisive in his status position in the whole society.   Certainly, in neither Hitler's Germany nor Stalin's Russia did other criteria matter significantly.

Ethnicity

This is, and has been throughout history, one of the most dominant criteria of status.   To be white rather than black, Gentile rather than Jew, Greek rather than barbarian can govern absolutely one's status in a social order, as present and past experience abundantly make plain.   No amount of achieved wealth, education, job, or authority in a given sphere will offset the status that ethnicity can ascribe for a person.   Not, of course, that possession of the favored ethnicity—whiteness, let us say, in traditional America—guarantees high status.   There are, after all, many low-status whites, some very low indeed in the rural South and elsewhere, just as there were (and still are) low-status Gentiles and low-status Greeks in ancient Athens.   But favorable ethnicity saw to it that one was not as low in status as was one of unfavorable ethnicity.   And possession of unfavorable ethnicity—in any age when ethnicity is as dominant as it was a half a century ago in this country—is virtual guarantee of low status, irrespective of all other criteria of the achieved sort.   Ethnicity— broadly defined—is most likely to be the basis of caste in contrast to class in society.   Even in relatively equalitarian ages, when ethnic militance and political law combine to reduce the extremer manifestations of status inequality, especially in the larger spheres of political and economic society, ethnicity continues to matter.

Education

A man may be very learned and still rank low in a society's status order.   One thinks of some of the towering Jewish scholars, those who migrated to this country from Eastern Europe early in the century, who, by virtue of ethnicity, could acquire neither academic renown in America's universities nor status of high degree in city or nation.   High education has been accompanied by low status for many Negroes and other representatives of minority ethnic groups.   Still, the evidence is clear— if not quite as clear as with respect to wealth and political authority— that for the most part in human history degree of education has mattered. With rare exceptions the role of the man of knowledge has been fairly high.   Today degree of education matters enormously in the population as a whole.   Whether one is a grade-school dropout or the graduate of a university very clearly matters with respect to income that may be predicted for an individual, and it matters, accordingly, with respect to social status.   The most advanced education or the most famous of academic intellects will not get one anywhere in the status system of a community that chooses to give family tie or wealth or absolute power precedence. But the correlation between education and social status in contemporary American society is nevertheless a very high one.   And of all means of rising in the social scale, educational achievement has been historically one of the most effective.   Even in the highly stratified, class- and estate-conscious Middle Ages, the learning that could be acquired within the Church or through one of the great universities was occasionally enough to carry an individual to papacy and rectorship and certainly to relatively high status in the social order.   Considering education in the broad sense, it is highly unlikely that any social order has ever existed in which an outright negative correlation existed between education and social status.

Job

What a person does occupationally is as important today in establishing his status as it has ever been in times past.   Many would say more important.   For it can hardly be overlooked that in those areas— rapidly expanding areas throughout the world—most characterized by industrialization and politicization, the job one holds threatens to supersede many of the historically prominent bases of status: family lineage, locality, ethnicity, and even wealth.   Precisely to the extent that society becomes industrialized, commercialized, and politicized, the jobs or functional positions involved in these momentous processes of change become vital in the status systems of society.   Still, whatever present levels of importance of occupation as an index of social status may be, it would not do to dismiss the importance of occupation in other ages.   No matter how vital family, ethnicity, and wealth were in the Middle Ages, or in the ancient world, the job one held—as merchant, as military figure, as priest or bishop, or as tiller of the soil—made a great deal of difference in his status.   It is parochialism of the first order to suppose that ours is the only civilization in history that has made occupation a central and even governing criterion of status.   It is perhaps sufficient to say that with the far-flung differentiation of jobs and the associated specializations in our society the sheer number of channels to status based upon occupation has gone up sharply.

In any event, what is important here is the capacity of occupation to elevate or lower social status in human society. For, as we noted above with respect to job, no civilization has yet been found that does not, however unconsciously or informally, rank the occupations which make up the framework of its economic system. Even if a people were to be found so simple in economy as to be organized solely around hunting, or tilling the soil, or picking berries from natural vines, there would still be some degree of gradation of responsibility and skill. And with this gradation there would be inevitably a gradation of status.

In a complex society, as countless opinion surveys make evident, the overwhelming number of persons in the society have a generalized consensus with respect to ranking of jobs in the economy. There may be, and generally is, disagreement on details—on whether, say, banker, lawyer, or physician stands at the top; whether ditchdigger or refuse-collector is at the bottom—but not on the broad categories. We rank jobs in our society just as we rank roles in general. And with the ranking of jobs there goes inevitably a ranking of the persons in the jobs— to some extent, at least. As has already been made clear, a society's generalized system of status is composite—based upon several of the elements we are now describing. The status assessment of bank president in a community may be profoundly limited as far as citizens of that community are concerned by the factors of ethnicity, family, education, and wealth. But no matter how limited, the bank presidency cannot be other than significant in some degree. The person holding the bank presidency may be black, of subcollege education, and possessed of very modest financial means. His status in the community is nevertheless significantly affected by possession of a job that Americans generally regard (as indicated by decade after decade of opinion surveys) as high in the ranking of occupations. And for all the magic that may be associated with the name of some great family in the history of the nation or of a given region, the actual status of a member of that family cannot but be affected significantly by the specific job he holds. The nearest Americans have come to royalty, it is sometimes said, is in the moving picture world, where actors and actresses have, for half a century now, provided much the same kind of fare for enchantment and for gossip that royalty traditionally did in Europe. And the moving-picture world, as the biographies of its principals makes very clear, is nothing if not job oriented—from the lowliest of extras to the most resplendent of stars.

Kinship

"What's his family background?"   Probably no question in all history has been asked more often.   If today parents of nubile daughters are at least as prone to ask instead about job or education, it will not be claimed that interest in family background has disappeared.   And even within the modern industrialized West there remain enclaves in which family tie, lineage, and descent are vital.   There are not nearly as many such sectors as there once were; in fact, taking the population at large, very few.   But they continue, and they are testimony to the immense importance that has been placed at other times on kinship line as the hallmark of social status.

The phrases "high birth" and "low birth" have little if any currency today in American society.   They once did, even in an age of American history (the first half of the nineteenth century) that Tocqueville and other European visitors thought to be transcendingly job-, money-, and achievement-oriented.   One need but go back to the novels that were being written throughout the nineteenth century—always a useful way of assessing and identifying crucial values—to see the degree to which social level of family line mattered.   The idea that moral as well as intellectual quality inheres in a kinship line is as old as any idea we can readily dig out of human history.   That there are noble families in contrast to base families is, when we reflect a moment, the very essence of the great tragedies that have been written in the West since Aeschylus. For the peculiar kind of horror that was evoked in the minds of those attending the tragedies of Aeschylus, Sophocles, and Euripides in ancient Athens, or the tragedies of Marlowe and Shakespeare in Elizabethan England, was rooted precisely in the contrast of men and women of high birth driven by some fatal flaw to crimes of base passion or intrigue.   It is our relative lack of regard today for high versus low birth that has led more than one literary critic to declare the unsuitability of tragedy, as a literary form, for democratic societies.

Even in contemporary American democracy, however, we find sections of the country in which family descent is vital to social status.   We know these sections best perhaps in certain areas of the South and of New England—the so-called First Families of Virginia, the Cabots, Lowells, and Lodges of Massachusetts, et al.   But there are still other sections in the Midwest and West that contain communities in which family line, irrespective of anything else, can grant one high status.   In his fascinating and important works *Philadelphia Gentlemen* and *The Protestant Establishment*, E. Digby Baltzell has shown, among other things, the vitality of kinship as a source and measure of social status. In the novels of William Faulkner we find obsession with family at the level of literary genius. Whether Faulkner is dealing with family in its upper or lower reaches (as in the repellent Snopes family who come as poor whites and stay on to dominate politically and economically), it is plain that the theme of family is as compelling in his mind as ever it was in the mind of a Marlowe or Shakespeare.

But it would be deceptive to end on such a note. In plain fact, for the bulk of American and Western society today, the claims of family ancestry take second place to wealth, job, education, or political power. In a large number of sectors indeed, family would rank very low as a source of the status that is prized generally in our industrial-democratic society. As a kind of last stronghold of traditionalism, the criterion of kinship is plainly on the defensive in our own society and many others.

In historical and comparative terms, however, kinship has been absolutely vital in status systems. For, above any other single element, it is family—that is, centrality of family in the social order and continuity of a family line from generation to generation—that forms the steel spring of social class and (usually with ethnicity added) of social caste. We shall turn to these now.

STATUS AND CLASS

When we turn to social classes we are once again in the realm of social aggregates. Whatever else social class is, it is—to the extent that it has substantive and sociological rather than merely statistical existence—an aggregate of human beings united by common ranking in terms of a significant number of the status variables we have just described. The anthropologist Walter Goldschmidt writes that class society is "one in which the hierarchy of prestige and status is divisible into groups each with its own economic, attitudinal, and cultural characteristics, and each having differential degrees of power in community decisions."[1] This depiction is excellent, for it draws our attention to the *social* character of class rather than to the mere listings of traits and variables that we are prone to get from the statistically minded. To Goldschmidt's description we can add Richard Centers' emphasis on *consciousness* of class. A man's class, writes Centers, "is a part of his ego, a feeling on his part of belonging to something; an identification with something larger than himself."[2] And, finally, it is useful to quote here some words of Maurice Halbwachs, a student of Durkheim, on the *culturally* distinctive character of class. Where we have social classes, Halbwachs writes,

> *each of these social categories determines the conduct of its members and imposes definite motivations on them; it stamps each category with such a peculiar and distinctive mark, so forcibly, that men of different classes, even though they live amid the same surroundings and are contemporaries, sometimes strike us as belonging to different species of humanity.*[3]

All of these descriptions get at the hard core of social class. Where it exists as a substantive social aggregate in a community, a region, or a nation, it is tangible, functional, and recognizable through the most ordinary processes of observation. Anyone who has ever lived in a locality characterized by social classes knows that their members are often distinguishable by appearance alone—through dress, bearing, language, and general life style. Closer or more informed examination may reveal in addition that members of the social classes of a given area are distinguishable in terms of persisting attitudes toward politics, education, job motivation, and life in general. There may even be what Marx and his followers characterized as an ideology—a more or less homogeneous set of motivations and attitudes springing directly from the class one belongs to and reaching all spheres of cultural, social, and intellectual existence.

That societies have existed, and do now exist, in which social aggregates answering to these descriptive criteria are found is indisputable. Quite apart from what has been yielded during the past century or two by direct sociological and anthropological examination, the world's literature, from Hesiod to the greatest writers of the present century, makes sufficiently clear that social classes have been among the most influential of social ties among human beings. And class differences have, beyond doubt, often furnished the stuff of political action ranging from simple reform legislation to revolution.

Modern interest in social class dates from the momentous impact of Karl Marx on European social thought in the late nineteenth century. Whatever may have been the extent of earlier interest in social class and its significance to social behavior—from Plato's *Republic* to the brilliant analytical accounts of social class that we find in the eighteenth-century writings of Rousseau, Adam Ferguson, and John Millar—it was minor by comparison with the immense burst of interest that followed Marx's powerful writings in the middle of the nineteenth century. For Marx, social class was primary in the social order, the essential source of an individual's whole way of life and thought. All history, Marx and Engels declared in their *Communist Manifesto*, is the history of classes and of class struggle. As the ancient world was divided between master and slave classes, so was the Western medieval period divided between noble and serf, with a middle class gradually arising that was to become in time the fateful bourgeoisie. The modern age, Marx and Engels declared, is chiefly notable for the convulsive struggle between the capitalist class on the one hand—the class of property owners and of all whose functions swept them into the vortex of this class—and, on the other hand, in dialectical and irrevocable opposition, the proletariat, the lower class of workers, without property, wealth, or political influence. A fundamental in Marx's philosophy of history was the idea that through relentless increase in numbers of proletarians, through equally relentless diminution of number of ruling capitalists, and through unresolvable contradictions in the capitalist economy, a revolutionary situation would in time be precipitated in which the proletariat would destroy the capitalist class and capitalism. The way would then be open, for the first time in history, for the possibility of a classless society—first, socialism, then, in time, communism.

Few ideas in all human history have been as historically directive as Marx's idea of social class allied, as it was so profoundly, with a theory of history and of revolution. A great deal of the present shape of mankind—political, economic, military—would be inexplicable apart from the direct influence of Marx's ideas on such leaders as Lenin, Stalin, and Mao Tse-tung. On this point there can be no argument.

The scientific utility of the Marxian doctrine of social class is cause for debate. This doctrine states very succinctly that men's productive (economic) relations determine the class structure of every social order and that all major social, cultural, and intellectual differences among groups in a population are the consequence of class differences. Putting the matter bluntly and in a degree of specific detail that is largely *implicit* in Marx himself but has been made *explicit* in countless writings by followers of Marx, we may say that social class determines the way men will live and think in society. In the long run social class will be the most powerful determinant of life style as well as of political allegiance, economic, religious, familial, and educational disposition, and of consciousness generally. It is in this sense that Marxists have used the word "ideology"—to refer to the sum total of beliefs and attitudes about world and society which, it is held, derive ultimately from the social class people belong to.

In their search for historical and social causation, Marx and his followers have quite obviously neglected or played down the multiplicity of other types of social aggregate, social authority, and social allegiance as significant contexts or causes.   They have focused directly on man's economic position and, with this, the single social entity, social class, that arises from economic position.   Political entities such as the nation-state, kinship ties, local community, ethnic caste or group, and religion— among other social aggregates—are thus declared to be secondary or derivative reflections of the primary reality, social class.

Although no one can take credit from Marx for having made social class very nearly the most widespread and obsessing of all interests in modern sociology, there are few if any non-Marxist sociologists today who would hold with the Marxian theory of social class and its relation to the social order.

If there is any one sociologist whose ideas are dominant in contemporary studies of social stratification it is Max Weber.   As I have shown in my *The Sociological Tradition*, it was Weber who, proceeding from the kinds of insights into the nature of European social stratification that had been set forth masterfully by Tocqueville, most clearly demonstrated the inadequacies of the Marxian theory of class when it is set against the complexities of modern Western society.   What Weber emphasized in his greatest works was not only the plurality of social causation (the impossibility, for example, of making religion a simple reflection of economic interests), but, more pertinently to our present interest, the necessity of distinguishing sharply among *economic class*, *political authority*, and *honor* (the last being "status" as the word is used here).   We cannot, Weber declared, make the political and social dimensions of stratification mere extensions of the economic.   Weber stressed that there are classes to be discerned in the economic order— classes differentiated by relation to production, by wealth, by nature of occupation.   However, he also insisted upon the incapacity of economic classes to explain phenomena of distribution of political influence in society and the gradations of social prestige we find in any given social order.   And, finally, Weber repudiated the Marxian belief that men's primary and lasting allegiances, their social and cultural consciousness, their "ideologies" are the direct (or indirect, for that matter) emanations of class.

Contemporary study of social stratification (and within it of social class as such) tends overwhelmingly to flow from the perspective Weber gave the matter. What Weber, and before him Tocqueville, realized so presciently with respect to modern society has been abundantly made manifest by subsequent currents of history and social change. Economic class or level, while assuredly a vivid reality and a profoundly important element in contemporary American society is not the primary and controlling force that Marxism makes it out to be. To seek to find in economic class, or occupation alone, the principal determinant of both human behavior and the varieties of social and cultural experience we observe around us is, as Weber realized full well, to turn one's back on those fundamental forces of politics—voting franchise, party, bureaucracy—and those innumerable, and ever-shifting, status spheres of modern life which can by no stretch of logic be made simple derivatives of economic class. There is, moreover, the independent, or at least sharply distinguishable, set of forces to be found in ethnicity, in religion, and in the whole vast educational system that is a part of modern cultures.

In short, although social stratification is ubiquitous, an ineffaceable element of all social orders at all times, it does not follow that the kind of entity Marx thought of as social class is equally ubiquitous. The sophisticated and rigorous study of social stratification was retarded for a long time in the social sciences by the assumption that social stratification and social class are one and the same. They are not. What modern sociology, beginning with Weber primarily, has found in the social order are not simply classes, approximating the Marxist layer-cake model, but a vast profusion of social levels, status spheres, interest groups, organized associations, elites such as the powerful scientific and academic group, political parties, the increasingly powerful and insistent administrative units of government, and, underlying the whole, the voting franchise. We live in a society of mass political electorates, and no one acquainted with the history of politics during the last century can be ignorant of the profound influence of these electorates in times of urgency and crisis.

Stratification and inequality are spread throughout the social order. Of this there is not the slightest question. All that is in question is the capacity of the concept of social class—especially the Marxian concept of class—to give satisfactory explanation or even satisfactory description of the patterns of stratification and inequality. One of the greatest stumbling blocks, until recently, to the informed study of stratification was the naïve ideological assumption on the part of many social scientists (though not the pioneers or the great ones) that, first, social class and stratification are synonymous terms and, second, that any questioning of the substantive reality of social classes in modern society was tantamount to a questioning of the existence of social inequality. Fortunately, sociology has in recent years gone well beyond this view. Status, not class, has become ever more surely the central concept.

Where social class is a major feature of the social order, however, the concept is, obviously, indispensable. Consider, for example, the famous English landed class which, beginning in the early modern era, was so conspicuous and powerful a feature of English history down through the nineteenth century. Indeed, with important extensions it persisted into the present century and formed a model of upper-class behavior for many non-English parts of the world, America included.

There was, first, the economic unity of this class, a unity founded largely upon a particular type of wealth—land. It would be inaccurate to say no other sources of wealth were involved. It is not inaccurate, however, to say that landed wealth furnished the economic identity of the class, that it was, so to speak, the *raison d'être* of the class. From generation to generation land tended to remain within the same family hands.

Equally notable was the political unity—and supremacy—of the class. Economic position and political power coalesced almost perfectly. This was evident in the vast number of parliamentary seats that went to the members of the landed class and in what the historian Sir Lewis Namier has shown to be the astonishing degree of interaction and consensus among members of the class with respect to political issues. It was also to be seen in the virtual monopoly members of this class held of administrative functions in local and county government. "The great unpaid," as they were to be called by a later historian, is an apt term. They were powerful but the very opposite of a bureaucracy, for not only were they not paid for the functions they performed, they also operated in an utterly informal, situational way outside the domain of regularized law or statute.

Just as economic and political attributes converged, so did those of education, ethnicity, and family tie. Except for the handful of intellectuals in London and others of the Oxford and Cambridge university establishments, the only people of education in England were the members of this class—all educated alike first in one or another of the distinguished public schools of England—Winchester, Harrow, Eton, and so on—then at either Oxford or Cambridge.

Of ethnicity nothing need be said beyond the vital facts that all members were of "solid English stock," with family identities going back several generations at least and, without exception, formally identified with the Established Church. There were, to be sure, some powerful and prestigeful Roman Catholic families in England, and it would be unfortunate to dismiss their influence altogether. But they were relatively few in number by the eighteenth century within the aristocracy, and they were, like Jews, limited by law in what they could do politically and even economically.

Family ties were powerful. There was much intermarriage within the landed class. In this respect it was, in effect, very close to an endogamous social aggregate. Family structure was reinforced by laws of entail and primogeniture: the first making it nearly impossible to separate property from a family line, the second tending to prevent dispersion of ownership into an ever-growing number of small families. The sense of family was profound, and whatever the number of internal conflicts, jealousies, and even hatreds, there was a strong tendency for the unity of the family—the formal or institutional unity—to hold together generation after generation.

Over the whole structure of the landed class hovered the conception of the "gentleman." Although the concept is hard to define in abstract terms, the reality of the gentleman in English society was nevertheless as vivid and unmistakable as was that of the land itself. In dress, opinion, reading tastes, physical bearing, manner of walking and sitting, style of language (including accent, intonation, and gesture), and common understanding of the hierarchy of life's values, the landed class set the image of the gentleman, and set it so deep in English consciousness that to this very day, despite the cataclysmic changes of English society in the twentieth century, the image is almost immediately recognizable. It was the gentleman, drawn from the landed class, who created the model of what was socially highest in English society. There were no significant challenges to his status until a very short time ago in England, and even now this status is an influential one.

The foregoing picture of the English landed class is admittedly somewhat purer, sociologically speaking, than all the records we have of it would bear out. But it comes as close to the sociological ideal type of class as any I can readily think of. In a whole host of ways it has left its heritage in the contemporary world. Much of what is today called "high culture" or "upper-upper" behavior in many parts of the world, not least the United States, is descended from the norms and social patterns of this highly influential class in England. From such novelists as Henry Fielding, Jane Austen, and William Thackeray we have been given pictures of it that are not too far from the sketch I have just made. And from more recent writers such as John Galsworthy, especially in his fascinating and sociologically invaluable *Forsyte Saga*, G. B. Shaw, and H. G. Wells have come useful insights into the strains and tensions involved in the passage of this social class into the dynamic twentieth century. And, as many a reader of this book will recall, the works of the so-called angry young men following World War II—novelists, playwrights, essayists—were largely about the agonies and resentments which have been incurred by remnants of the landed class, that is, its Establishment descendants, in the present age. In the United States, as novelists from James Fenimore Cooper to Edith Wharton have made vivid in their works, a clear reflection of this English class has been a reality from the early nineteenth century on.

I would not wish to suggest that only an aggregate answering to the descriptive elements of the English landed class is properly a social class. There are innumerable other types, all of which reveal in at least moderate degree the grounding in a type of wealth and the union of political, social, cultural, and psychological traits we have seen in the example given. In small or large degree, social class in this sense is to be seen in all societies at one period or other. The America that Tocqueville and other European visitors thought so dominated by equalitarian values was in fact a society in which social class was considerably more substantive, more visible, than it is in contemporary mass America.

What is crucial in theoretical terms about social class, as viewed in this discussion, is the *convergence* of a significant number of the status elements we have examined, the convergence of these not simply in a level or stratum in the population but in an aggregate possessed of some degree of collective self-awareness, of actual social interaction, and possessed of a degree of visibility that makes it instantly recognizable to the other elements in the population. Further, social class is an aggregate that has continuity in time. Family is crucial, crucial in preserving and transmitting the essential elements of class, as Joseph A. Schumpeter, in his remarkable and too little known *Imperialism and Social Classes* emphasized.

What do these descriptions and definitions of social class have to do with the contemporary realities of stratification in the United States? As I suggested above, very little. Taking the national scene generally, rather than the small, out-of-the-way communities in which most sociological studies of social class have been done, we find a picture of stratificaton that is far different from that just described with respect to the English past. It is a picture that is rich in thrusts of political power, in spheres as well as levels of wealth, in variety of life styles, in degrees of education, in varying emphasis placed on family, religion, and ethnicity, and, perhaps above all, in diversity of occupation. To try to derive from this rich and even kaleidoscopic picture the simple layers of social class which are inseparable from the Marxist view is an exercise in futility.

The terms "middle class," "lower class," and "upper class" have a great deal of use in American language, popular and scientific alike. Particularly is this true of the middle class and what is widely understood to be its culture and its spirit. The spirit of the middle class, it is often said, was born with the new nation in the American colonies; hence little approximating a lower-class or upper-class set of mind is to be found in significant degree in the United States. Most workers see themselves as potential members of the middle class, and many men of wealth and power take pride in middle-class rather than upper-class identity. This essentially was the view of American society that Tocqueville expressed in his classic *Democracy in America*, written a century and a half ago but still regarded by a good many scholars as the best single study of American social structure ever written. The same view has proved to be a profoundly influential one on subsequent interpreters of the American scene—among them David Riesman in his *The Lonely Crowd* and Max Lerner in his *America as a Civilization.*

Not that these perceptive observers of the American scene see simple equality. Whether it is Tocqueville in the last century or Riesman, Lerner, and scores of others in the present century, *inequality* is almost a point of departure for interpretation—as well it should be. Inequalities in wealth, power, education, and in each of the other status sources we examined are manifest and rife. No one could exceed Tocqueville in awareness of the phenomena of status competition, status conflict, and status obsession in American society. And, as a notable chapter makes vividly clear, Tocqueville was well aware of the contrasting political power of manufacturer and of worker. None of this is at issue in the work of any serious student of the American scene. Substantive *inequality* is as manifest as is the ethos of equalitarianism that hovers over the landscape.

What is at issue is simply the best way or ways by which to interpret, to explain, what is at bottom the social behavior of human beings from the point of view of status. The idea of social class will carry us nearly all the way in many societies, ages, and localities. But, considering national society as a whole in the United States—and other countries as well—we are obliged to turn to concepts other than that of social class for adequate explantion of today's status pyramids.

The plural in the last word above is calculated. There are many status pyramids, or status spheres, in contemporary Western society. Even if we omit reference to matters of wealth and political influence and confine attention solely to social prestige, we find that our present condition is as far from that described earlier with respect to the landed class in England as any that might easily be imagined. There is indeed a status sphere nationally in the United States in which descent from a Philadelphia Main Line family added to graduation from, say, Groton and then Harvard or Yale, and further reflected by membership in some highly prestigious law firm—or perhaps by no occupation at all, by simple membership in the leisure group—places one at the top. *But in that status sphere alone.* Such a background does not, surely, place one in the status spheres of science, technology, politics, professional athletics, the theater, the world of music, the steel or automobile industries, the publishing world, and so on ad infinitum. And as far as the acquisition of, or participation in, substantial political influence is concerned, the kind of social background just described can amount to a distinct liability in many places at many times. Nor, obviously, can that type of social background be easily assimilated, sociologically, for purposes of description or analysis, into the varied categories of wealth, relation to property, size of annual income, and so on.

We come back, in short, to what was described in the preceding section as *status inconsistency.* Mostly, the referent of this valuable term is the single person with perhaps low status in wealth, family background, and political influence, but very high status educationally. Or with any of the numerous other arrangements of these and other status elements. But from the point of view of the larger social order the referent of status inconsistency, as a concept, goes beyond the lone individual to the large number of *status groups* or *aggregates* in contemporary society. The multiplicity and inconsistency of these aggregates is at the heart of the matter of social class. As Max Weber saw long ago, we can stratify the population in terms of wealth and produce one set of classes or levels, stratify by occupation or professional membership and produce a different set, and so on with respect to education, ethnicity, family background, political influence, and finally, sex and age. That these criteria, or most of them, sometimes are united into sociologically homogeneous, persisting, and widely recognized horizontal aggregates in the population is clear enough, as our example from England showed. But to *assume* social classes in any large, industrialized, professionalized, political mass where widespread education has existed for a considerable length of time is as risky in scientific terms as it would be to assume the existence of influential ties of clan and kindred merely because there is evidence of family life.

Apart, then, from the smaller and older communities and regions, social class has less sociological utility as a concept today than do certain other concepts, among them, as we shall momentarily see, the concept of *caste*, with respect to the Negro in America. To repeat, the concept of social class—especially as applied generally and amorphously to "middle class" and, here and there, "working class"—will carry us a part of the way, scientifically. But to go all the way in sociological explanation of contemporary society, we require other concepts such as *level* or *stratum*, *elite*, and *status sphere*, none of which is precisely reducible to the concept of class.

We dealt at length with status spheres in the preceding section, and I shall have something more to say about elites in the final section of this chapter. A few more words about the concept of *level*, and about *level consciousness*, are, however, in order at this point. "Level" would appear to be the proper substitute for the word "class" in most discussions of stratification that relate to national, or even international society, especially Western. What we find in vivid reality is a hierarchy of levels in modern society.

A level is first and foremost a set of norms, more or less congruous and consistent with one another, relating to the several economic, social, and cultural spheres of social behavior. We have no difficulty in distinguishing several such levels, arranged hierarchically in the attitudes of most persons in society. Whether one wishes to distinguish three or more such levels is not of importance. It is sufficient to emphasize that there are several, with the middle level by all odds the most important at the present time in the life styles, opinions, and aspirations of those living in modern society.

Each level rests first and foremost, of course, on wealth or income. But each level has, beyond its economic substance, a larger sociological identity that derives from patterns of norms persisting from generation to generation which relate to such matters as family organization, child-rearing practices, orientation toward formal education, attitudes toward economic and social advancement in life, the use of leisure, extent of membership in associations, speech or language patterns, and life style generally. It would be deceptive to claim more than approximate coherence within each of these levels. Human behavior is rarely so consistent. There are many families with two or more of these levels of norms manifest in any given type of activity. Nevertheless, on the national scale, a hierarchy of levels is plain enough to be useful in sociological explanations of human behavior. Clearly, people do tend to conform to the norms of their level, even though there are striking exceptions, and most people are aware of the existence of other levels—those lower and those higher.

What is the difference between level and class?* The difference pertains largely to the factor of *consciousness* or, as we might better say, *definition of the situation* in social behavior. Unlike class consciousness (which, as we have seen, was for Marx vital to the long-run reality of social classes), level consciousness makes for a high degree of individualism with respect to life style and aspiration. Level consciousness does not promote, as does class consciousness, feelings of identification or collective involvement. The principal motive of the level-conscious individual is to pass up and out of the level in which he finds himself— except, of course, when he is, or imagines himself to be, at the top. The level-conscious individual is, so to speak, on the make. His number is legion in modern society—the characteristic hero, we are obliged to confess, of most of our novels, dramas, and popular songs, not to mention public speeches. We find him everywhere. He lives in an atmosphere of competition that is nourished constantly by education and ideology and by the substantive fact of a shortage of skill in the industrial and professional worlds and by an abundance of prestige and honor that society is willing to confer upon the successful. He ranges from the bowling champion to the newly arrived millionaire, best-selling author, or Ivy-League professor all the way up to the President of the United States.

Level consciousness creates awareness of one's differences from others, rather than one's similarities. In this respect the individual is constantly motivated by distinctions he finds or invents between himself (nowhere more charmingly described than in Tom Wolfe's *The Electric Kool Aid Acid Test*, for instance, or *The Pump House Gang*) and others, and by preoccupation, even gnawing anxiety, with these distinctions. As Mozell Hill has perceptively written, "One by-product of all this on the American scene is that people have come to feel that it is not so much a matter of destroying those on a higher level of consumption as it is of acquiring skills, strategies, and techniques which will enable one to surmount his level."†

* The intellectual roots of this distinction are clearly in Weber and Simmel. A generation ago Robert M. MacIver and Charles Page (*Society* [New York: Rinehart, 1937], pp. 358 ff.) gave the distinction important focus with their differentiation of "corporate class consciousness" and "competitive class feeling." I am personally indebted to the late Mozell Hill for the concept of "level consciousness."

† The quotation is from an unpublished manuscript on class and mobility. The best single treatment of the conceptualizations that are current

It is the concept of level, not social class with its old associations, that best enables us to deal with all the myriad, shifting, and complex patterns of social mobility in contemporary society. Social mobility, despite a general belief to this effect, is far from peculiar to modern mass society. As I suggested above, there have been other periods of Western history—among them some of the greatest ages of culture and thought —which were rich in the indexes of social mobility. Still, no one looking at the career histories of the persons who form contemporary elites— in the academic, technological, business, sports, and literary spheres, to name but a few—would care to deny the especially pronounced character of social mobility patterns at the present time. There are those who believe these patterns to be most evident in the United States. But it is by no means positive that other Western countries and also such non-Western areas as Soviet Russia and Communist China, are far behind, if they are behind at all. Social mobility can exist, and has existed, in societies characterized by social class. Social class is not—and was not declared to be by Marx—the same as caste. But whatever the rates of social mobility in genuine class society, they are minor by comparison with those we find in societies strongly marked by levels rather than by classes.

At the present moment, it would be absurd to claim level consciousness and level aspiration for all persons in America or any other society. There are more than a few whom attitude studies show to be content with whatever level they may occupy—occupationally and in other respects as well. Many of these show the same contentment at the prospect of having their children occupying their own level in society. There are also, as we have become profoundly aware during the past decade, the adolescent children of upper- and middle-level families—the beats, bohemians, and hippies, the dedicated members of the Student Left, among others—who, far from manifesting a desire to move upward in life, show instead contempt and sometimes hatred for the upper levels and their ways of life.

So much is true, and, in one form or other, will doubtless persist in mass culture, in industrial and democratic society. Nothing, however, in either the indifference we find toward middle-level or upper-level life or the current youthful hostility toward these levels suggests the utility of the concept of social class to the kind of mass society that

---

today in the study of social stratification is Charles Page's *Class and American Sociology.* See especially the valuable introduction, "Thirty Years Later," in the new edition published by Schocken.

exists at the present time. The word "class" is no doubt a permanent element of our vocabulary. For scientific and analytical purposes, however, we will do better to think in terms of concepts that are more flexible and more expressive of empirical realities of inequality and stratification.

STATUS, CASTE, AND ETHNICITY

Of all forms of status aggregate in society, caste is the most rigorous and encompassing of human behavior. The claimed base, or justification, of caste varies from area to area. In India, where caste reached a degree of omnicompetence not found anywhere else, the justification is theological, with members of the lowest castes—the untouchables—thought to be living out some kind of expiation for sins committed in previous incarnations. In the Deep South of the United States the quasi-caste relation of black and white traditionally has been defended on the ground of the Negro's biological inferiority. The explanation of caste by its participants is rarely the same from area to area. But the social structure of caste tends to be much the same wherever we find it.

Caste, wrote the late anthropologist Alfred Kroeber, is "an endogamous and hereditary subdivision of an ethnic unit occupying a position of superior or inferior rank or social esteem in comparison with other such subdivisions."[4] It is the combination of endogamy and hereditary base that gives to caste a substantive reality not found in any other form of status aggregate. Other types, social class included, rest on a set of attributes which are—theoretically, at least—within the reach of any individual or family possessed of ambition, skill, or good fortune. Even during the Middle Ages in Western Europe there was some degree of mobility among the social classes. The Church and the universities were important in this respect. And in the most celebrated of eulogies ever given the English landed class—that by Edmund Burke at the end of the eighteenth century—opportunity to rise to it from the lower classes was given emphasis. It is true that such opportunities were few in relation to the size of population (just as they must have been during the Middle Ages), but they existed nonetheless. More important, such mobility was not held antithetical to the nature of social class.

It is very different with caste. Only if an individual were able to obliterate every trace of his caste identity and then manage to take on the many and subtle marks of identity of some other caste would full passage from one caste to another be possible. Within the ethos of caste little possibility of such mobility exists. One is born into his caste; he is obliged to marry within it (the exception known as hypergamy is rare and insignificant); and he dies in the caste of his birth. No alteration of educational, economic, or political circumstances can affect his caste membership.

In India many of the castes are directly connected with occupations. The highest of the castes, the Brahmins, are the priests or theologians. One of the lowest of the castes is that of the scavengers. There are castes traditionally engaged in barbering, in well-digging, in silversmithing, in carpentering, and other occupations. But such occupational identity, whether high or low, is but a minor and unessential attribute. A man might change his occupation; it would not affect his true caste. He could not leave the caste of his birth; he would not be acceptable in any other caste. There are by now more than a few cases on record in which members of low castes have managed, through favorable opportunity united with their own ability, to found successful businesses, or to acquire educations at university level, to earn substantial incomes, or to hold key political positions, either in the civil service or in a political party. But their caste was in no sense altered. And beyond this, as we know in a number of poignant instances, these individuals were pursued all their lives by the calculated insults, humiliations, and discriminations of those of higher caste status who resented and often fought against proximity in working with low-caste individuals.

The members of the lowest, most depressed, of the castes are called (and with excellent reason) the untouchables. It would be difficult to find anywhere in all history a more extreme example of sheer social degradation than what is found even today in this element, which numbers many millions. Although the great and otherwise powerful Gandhi fought for many years to elevate their status in Indian society and often came close to death in his fasts undertaken in their cause, it cannot be said that their overall condition was much affected. The lower castes have been given at least the possibility of relief through the present political constitution in India, and the untouchables do have political spokesmen in legislatures. But in rural India, at the village level, the social position of the members of the lowest castes is about as degraded as it was a century ago when the British first began a few efforts in their behalf.

In some areas of India, members of the lowest castes may not come within twenty of thirty feet of Brahmins lest the latter be contaminated, forcing them to return immediately to their homes, to divest themselves of their clothing, bathe, and become ritually purified.   Untouchables are forbidden use of the religious temples.   They may not directly serve, or be in any way served by, members of the high castes.   Common eating is forbidden, as is common use of cooking utensils and eating implements.   Separate wells must be used by low-caste Indians when this is possible; otherwise, if water has to be drawn from a single source, caste rules govern time and amount of use by the low-caste individuals. Low-caste Indians may be forbidden the right to use certain streets or sidewalks, ferries, bridges, and public vehicles such as buses and trains. When the first factories were opened in India, special ways had to be found for segregation of functions to match necessary segregation of castes.   It is difficult to think of a single area of life in which the most rigorous of taboos or the most powerful of injunctions do not exist relating to the segregation of castes.

Interestingly, the lowest castes themselves are quite sharply divided. The higher among them tend to regard the lowest of the low castes as polluted in much the same way that *they* are regarded by India's high castes as being polluted.   When the Communists took control of the small state of Kerala in India, it was noteworthy that the leaders of the Communist government were mostly Brahmin.   No evidence exists to indicate that among the lowest castes in Kerala any expectation whatever existed of relief through efforts of Communist governors.   Caste is so rife in India as to seem a part of the air men breathe.   Caste is intimately enmeshed in kinship, village, religion, law, economy, and each of the other main institutions in Indian society.

Why has caste persisted for close to twenty-five hundred years in India?   Why does a system so manifestly hopeless to tens of millions of people continue century after century?   True, there are sectors of Indian society today where, as the result of technological and industrial and political impacts, caste is no longer as potent an influence as it once was.   But these sectors are still few and far between.   In India generally, especially the vast rural areas, caste is still omnipresent.   Why?

The answer lies in part in the religious system itself.   Caste is an inalienable aspect of religious belief which itself divides human beings in various states of blessedness and wickedness.   Nothing like the Judaic and Christian belief in residual spiritual equality of men exists in Hinduism.   But there are two other answers of a more sociological nature that also are highly relevant.   In the first place, as we have already noted, there are few Indians who cannot by their caste status look down on at least a few other Indians.   There are many hundreds of castes and subcastes in India, and the consequence of this is to endow most

Hindus with at least *some* status superiority.   And in a culture that is permeated by caste themes, this is no minor consideration.   Second, and perhaps even more contributory to the persistence of caste, each of these entities is, in some degree, a world of its own, with its own stated authority, its functions, its mutual-aid responsibilities, and even its cherished traditions.   Caste can be for the individual in India—even the lowest of castes—a means of succor in time of distress, a reinforcement to family bond, a collective source of identity that the individual would not otherwise have.   Suppose he were to leave his caste?   No other caste would have him.   He would be isolated.   His material existence would be precarious at best, and his spiritual existence damned.   Leaving spiritual considerations out entirely, caste is functional: its close relation to occupation, family, and community makes it so.   As is so often the case when we are dealing with social behavior, the problem is not reducible to mere ideas and opinions.   If it were, caste might have been banished long ago in India.   There have been many reformers, beginning with Buddha in the sixth century B.C., including more than a few Christian missionaries in modern times, and coming down to Mohandas Gandhi and his political successors, who have tried to exterminate or at least moderate caste in India.   None have succeeded.

This is not to say that caste is therefore eternal or even that no changes in its character and intensity are evident.   As I suggested above, changes in certain parts of India are taking place now—under the spur of new ways of organization and behavior (chiefly economic and political), which have no room in them for the principle of caste.   Consider only the problem of segregation of castes in modern transit systems, in great machine-based factories, and in departments of government which are forced to acquiesce in some degree at least to the provisions regarding caste in the new constitution of India.   The extent and intensity of caste are undergoing change in India.   But such change is still minor, sporadic, and widely separated.

Caste and Ethnicity

Although there are castes in India based in fact upon racial difference, this type of difference is not the essence of Indian caste.   It is, however, in other areas of the world, including the United States.   Not only do racial differences affect caste, so do ethnic differences in the more general sense that includes nationality, religion, and highly individualized culture.   In most parts of the world where caste is to be found in any significant degree, ethnicity forms the base of caste or quasi-caste.

From the strictly sociological viewpoint stratification of status in society provides the theoretical context for consideration of ethnic differences. We do not have to go outside the United States to observe the ease with which racial, nationality, and religious-cultural differences among human beings become invested with status significance that is more nearly caste in nature than either class or level—as we have previously described these terms. Caste, like each of the other major concepts in sociology, is at once a social entity and a *perspective*. It is not necessary to hold to a definition of caste that is as rigorous as is required for the study of social organization in India to see how clarifying it can be in the assessment of ethnic aggregates in the United States

The most obvious example is, of course, the Negro-white relation. It is not level or class difference that best explains this relation; it is, quite literally, caste difference. It would be extreme to suggest that anywhere or anytime in American society the position of the Negro has been as low as is the position of anyone of the depressed castes of India. But no one familiar with Negro-white relationships and interethnic customs in the United States over the past century will doubt that the perspective of caste is indispensable for understanding these relationships and customs.

Throughout most of that time—not to mention the earlier long period of Negro slavery—the social status of the Negro has been hereditary in most particulars. It has also been, as numerous state laws on miscegenation suggest, endogamous. Prior to a generation or less ago, marriage between Negro and white was either illegal or else attended by the most extreme forms of social intimidation and ostracism. A whole variety of other customs testify as well to the caste character of the relation between Negro and white. Segregation in education, housing area, the military, shopping opportunities, jobs, public transit, and in use of sidewalks, restaurants, parks, amusement facilities, and churches was the rule—a rule that was observed with rarest exceptions by Negroes themselves until a few decades ago and that was overwhelmingly insisted upon by a very large number of whites.

Class considerations such as education, wealth, political position, and career distinction did not help much when it came to elevation of a Negro's social status in the community. Even a half-century ago there were at least a few very wealthy Negroes, well-educated Negroes, and some indeed who had earned international distinction in science. There were others who had acquired, among Negroes at least, considerable political influence in local, state, and national elections. This mattered very little socially except within the Negro caste itself. No set of achieved criteria of distinction was sufficient to place the Negro other than below any white in the status scale at large—and this meant not just in the South but nationally.

There were even pollution customs. Admittedly, the Negro servants were free in most households, including Southern, to eat from the same utensils and plates that were used by white employers. And, especially in the South, it was almost common for Negro nurses to care for white infants and children—even to serving as wet nurses. Avoidance customs, in short, did not often reach the level in the United States that is common in India between the high castes and the depressed castes. Nevertheless, the lore of Negro-white experience in the United States has its due share of avoidance and pollution customs. When, through sheer political pressure from Negro leaders in cities such as Chicago, Los Angeles, and New York, the first ordinances were passed that gave legal permission to Negroes to eat in any public restaurant, a not uncommon early defense against these ordinances by restaurant or cocktail bar owners was the conspicuous smashing by whites of whatever glass or plate had been used by a Negro customer.

Further examples are not necessary to illustrate what is obvious enough in the experience of most persons above the age of thirty. Caste has been, and is even yet, though in altered degree, an indispensable perspective for the understanding of Negro-white relationships in the United States and certain other—though by no means all—countries.

The caste perspective is useful in the understanding of other ethnic differences. There is the historic position of the Mexican-American in the Southwestern part of the United States. In most respects this position has never been quite as extreme as that of the Negro in caste terms. But until very recently in this large area no amount of the ordinary attributes of social class status—wealth, education, occupation, and so on—was sufficient to lift the Mexican-American out of the semicaste status he was born in, and within which he married and died. Almost the only exception to this situation is provided by those relatively few Mexican-Americans who were and are descendants of some of the very early, wealthy, and politically powerful Mexican landowners of the historical era preceding American acquisition of California and other areas that had once been under Mexican sovereignty. In the fundamental sense of the term, caste has been the social status of the Mexican-American as it has been of the American Negro.

The status position of the Orientals in American society, whether Chinese, Japanese, or Filipino, has also been characterized by the themes of caste rather than class as such. Today the imperatives of caste are not nearly as striking for the Oriental in the United States as they were at the time when California enacted legislation designed to exclude Orientals and when avoidance customs were almost as severe for Orientals as for Negroes.

Nor is the situation entirely different with respect to Jew and Gentile in the United States. Here, to be sure, we are obliged to be more precise and discriminating in our analysis. The evidence suggests that prior to about 1870 there was little anti-Semitism in the United States, even in the East. Jews had figured prominently and with honor during the American Revolution and subsequent events in national history. They were small in number and overwhelmingly Western, chiefly Germanic or Spanish in national derivation. Then with ever larger numbers of Jews—though still a small minority relative to the rest of the American population—coming to this country from Eastern Europe and the rising visibility of their ethnicity along with rising influence in the economy, the arts, and the learned professions, Gentiles began to take extreme measures against them. Forms of exclusion from residential areas, hotels, clubs, and recreational facilities were practiced; quotas of admission into schools and colleges and professions were set; and a whole, complicated and subtle, but potent, set of exclusionary or avoidance customs became common in American Gentile society. Anti-Semitism was extensive in the United States and in some sections of the country almost as profoundly rooted as were negative sentiments against the Negro. Irrespective of achievement in business, politics, science, the arts, or learned professions, the fundamental status trait for the Jew tended to be his ethnicity, his relation to Jewish religion or culture. Caste is by no means too strong a term to use for a relationship that existed for decades in many parts of this country and has existed repeatedly, as every student of history knows, in a great many other parts of the world. To be sure, it is not caste in the nearly limitless sense that is applicable to the depressed castes of India. But caste in the sense that hereditary descent, endogamy, and other ascribed elements could often outweigh all the elements of status that are the result of achievement.

None of the above is meant to imply that the terms "ethnic group" and "caste" are synonymous. They are far from that. But as experience with almost all areas containing a multiplicity of ethnic aggregates makes plain (Hawaii is almost an exception here; also Southeast Asia, in parts) there is a strong tendency on the part of populations to give these ethnic aggregates ranking at least in *social* terms. And caste, with its emphasis on endogamy and hereditary nature, comes closer than the concept of either class, level, or elite in assimilating ethnicity into the conceptual framework of social stratification.

THE CIRCULATION OF ELITES

The heading of this final section on social status is drawn from Pareto's famous *The Mind and Society*. Although I shall use the word "elite" here in greater conformity to current sociological thought than to Pareto's own system of sociology, his view of history as an endless alternation of the powers of elites is a useful one to any student of social stratification. History, declared Pareto, is a "graveyard of aristocracies." The equilibrium of society, is constantly being threatened by the penetration of those of lower social status into the upper reaches of society and by the descent, through inertia or stupidity, of the high ranking into lower levels. When the individuals in power in a social order no longer have the motivation or resources (Pareto spoke of "residues," referring to ingrained components of behavior) to govern and when a decisive number of individuals out of power manage to gain it through higher motivation and resources, a turnover of elites is the result.

No social order, thought Pareto, is without its oligarchy, its power elite. It can maintain itself, he argued further, only through willingness to use force ruthlessly and quickly when the occasion demands. To seek alternatives to this readiness to use force—for humanitarian or rationalist reasons—can only lead to collapse in the long run. Much of Pareto's *The Mind and Society* is concerned with the instances he found in history to support his contention. He had little respect for, or confidence in, modern humanitarian, liberal, democracy. The values associated with this form of government could only, he thought, lead to incessant weakness of government and general social turmoil. There would be a constant cycle of strength and weakness in society, a constant succession of the two great social types which Pareto believed he had found in human history: the *speculator* and the *rentier*. The former is the type who depends upon his wits, his skill, or general manipulative abilities. He lives by income rather than fixed wealth. He is a "fox" in that he displays risk taking, shrewdness, desire for gain, and innovation. The *rentier* on the other hand is the type of human being who tends to follow tradition and routine, to become ensconced in land or other fixed wealth, to distrust individual sagacity or acumen, and to rely heavily upon historical experience and established values. He is a "lion."

History, Pareto thought, is marked by oscillation between these two types in rulership of government and also by oscillation among the many forms of aggregate that make up the social order—business, military, university, and church included. This view is, in a sense, Pareto's response to Marx and the latter's belief that history is unilinear, that conflicts among classes carry society to an ever higher level, with attainment eventually of the classless society. For Pareto, however, belief in the unilinear and progressive nature of history was absurd. Moreover, Pareto believed that no matter what the form of larger society—capitalist, socialist, monarchical, or democratic—there would always be this alternation of social elites, the alternation between the foxes and the lions.

Although Pareto's conception of the two elites endlessly alternating is much too simple for the complexities of modern society, it provides a useful offset to conventional theories of social class. Also, when expanded to meet the differentiation and specialization of modern society, the conception of elites is a valuable adjunct to our idea of stratification in terms of what was just described as social levels. For, to a very considerable degree, it is the presence of an elite—a visible, clearly ascendant elite, commanding in its appeal to large numbers of people—that sets the levels to which masses of people belong or aspire. For reasons given in the preceding section, "social class" is frequently an awkward term for the clarification of contemporary stratification in the West. But we could no more do without the concept of elite than we could do without the concepts of strata and level.

An elite is a relatively small number of individuals who possess a substantial amount of high prestige, wealth, or political influence—or combinations of these—in a given sphere of generally recognized social significance. A more precise definition is hardly possible. For there are many elites in contemporary Western society, ranging from political elites, official and unofficial, to the far more specialized but scarcely less imposing elites we find in theoretical physics, chess, professional basketball, and ballet. Given the reality, in whatever degree, of the sphere of activity, a corresponding elite in the sociological sense of the term is almost inevitable. As Mike Nichols, himself a member of the American (and also international) theater elite, recently noted, there are elites to be found in the dry-cleaning industry and in locomotive engineering. Much of the charm and also value of Tom Wolfe's vivid essays on elites in the American population is his demonstration of the exceedingly specialized and, by ordinary standards, even antic character of these elites. But elites they are nonetheless.

It would be absurd, however, to overlook the difference in appeal and sheer power of elites in society. Plainly, the elite of custom-car racing is not of the same order of importance as the elite that runs the United States Government—the President, his strategic advisers, key senators and representatives, the top military figures, and a few others. For all the constitutional division and delegation of political authority, no one acquainted with the actual workings of governments at all levels could doubt the significance of political elites which usually have little identification in the formal documents of government.

Almost equally important is the scientific-technological elite in several of the contemporary Western nations. Such is the dependence of modern military power and of modern industry upon the insights and skills of the scientist-technologist that this elite is a powerful one in its own right. What the highest ranking physical scientists and engineers in American society think of any given piece of legislation in Congress or any given program affecting national defense in the White House has, very plainly indeed, a great deal of influence.

There is also an elite in large-scale industry in the United States, and internationally for that matter. It is composed of the presidents and chairmen of boards and a few others in equally influential positions in the largest of the great industries, corporations, and banks. There is also a military elite, and, given the international situation prevailing since about 1938, the influence of the military elite upon national affairs is considerable. There is an intellectual elite, formed of the major writers, artists, and intellectuals in the country. This elite has shown in very recent years a large potential for influence on government and people when circumstances are propitious. There is the academic elite, composed of those who preside over, teach in, or study in, the half dozen or so top universities in America, chiefly, but not exclusively, those of the Ivy League.

There is a great multiplicity of elites, but obviously some are much more influential than others and much more widely recognized than others. Nor should one forget, finally, the social elite—those belonging to the international jet set, those who make the Social Register, and those in smaller communities whose names figure recurrently in stories on the society page of the local newspaper.

Elites are not easily given limit. One may belong to the academic elite and, through strategic board membership or a consulting position, also to the economic elite, even the political elite in Washington and, through the whims of Washington or New York hostesses, the social elite. Elites blur into one another, as do so plainly the academic, the scientific-technological, the political, the industrial, and the intellectual elites at the present time. To speak of a social class, in any substantive sense of the term, that is being formed by this spectrum of elites is absurd. There is too little continuity, too little sense of common membership, and too little ideological consensus for anything resembling social class to be designated. But the complex of these elites can, at any given moment, powerfully affect the fortunes and destinies of governments—and many other areas of modern society.

When the late Dwight Eisenhower, at the time he left the Presidency, warned against the power of the "military-industrial complex," he was, in effect, warning against a combination of two potent elites, that formed by top-ranking figures in the military establishment and that formed by leading industrialists in this country. C. Wright Mills' *The Power Elite*, to which I referred in Chapter 7 with respect to the military role, went much further in an identification of the elites exercising power at the national level. To the "big three" of the political, military, and industrial, he added that of the leaders of organized labor. Even if Mills did not give sufficient attention to the powers of the countervailing forces in national government—Congress, the judiciary, the electorate, and the whole amorphous but recurrently effective assemblage of what David Riesman has called "veto groups" in American society—Mills must still be credited properly with identifying the positions and activities of some highly effective elites in contemporary national affairs. Any view of modern democracy that did not include these elites would be a limited one.

Suzanne Keller, whose *Beyond the Ruling Class: Strategic Elites in Modern Society* is the most systematic work yet done by a sociologist on the subject of elites, has skillfully differentiated among four major *types* of elite in society. The first is *political*, formed by those elites whose primary purpose is achievement of certain goals in a national polity. The second type is what she calls *elites of adaptation*, formed by those falling primarily within the military, economic, diplomatic, and scientific sectors of society. Third are the elites containing high-ranking clergy, educators, certain intellectuals, first families, and others whose fundamental function is that of exerting *moral authority* in society. These are, in a sense, integrative elites. Fourth are the elites Professor Keller describes as concerned, whether consciously or not, with keeping a society knit together *emotionally, psychologically,* and *esthetically.*

These elites include the outstanding artists, theater and film stars, writers, musicians, and athletic figures.

How these elites—and others which may not easily fit within the classification just given—are formed, how they are recruited, what their integrating norms are, how they maintain themselves, how they exert influence in concrete ways, and, finally, how they are succeeded by others is very clearly one of the indispensable parts of any study of the social bond. Social class may be difficult to discern in a social order. The historian J. H. Hexter has demonstrated brilliantly and conclusively how hazardous the concept of class can be even for such a society as England in the sixteenth and seventeenth centuries. How very much more hazardous, theoretically speaking, is use of the concept of social class for the mass society we live in at the present time. But no such difficulties inhere in the concept of elites. Their specific ways and their interrelationships may be elusive to the investigator, but there can be no question of the existence of elites in any social order, however simple and isolated.

Notes

1. Walter Goldschmidt, "Social Class in America," *American Anthropologist*, 52 (1950), p. 492.
2. Richard Centers, *The Psychology of Social Classes* (Princeton, N.J.: Princeton University Press, 1949), p. 27.
3. Maurice Halbwachs, *Psychology of Social Class* (New York: Free Press, 1958), p. 4.
4. Alfred Kroeber, "Caste," *Encyclopedia of the Social Sciences* (New York: Macmillan, 1930), Vol. 3, p. 254.

9

Social Norms

NORMS AND CULTURE

We have had frequent occasion to refer to social norms in the preceding pages. Consideration of social interaction, social aggregates, roles, and statuses would be quite impossible without reference to the norms that supply the end and purposes of social life. All human behavior is normatively directed. Apart from the social norms which are, so to speak, waiting for us in the social order when we are born, behavior in any recognizably human sense (good or evil) would be hard to imagine. From the very beginning of life, one's interaction with others is normatively bounded, normatively inspired, and normatively maintained. What has been called, for thousands of years, "human nature" is human *normative* nature. All efforts to derive human nature and its modes of behavior directly from man's biological heritage are fallacious. This heritage cannot be overlooked, but between it and what we see around us in the way of social organization and culture lies the all-important structure of norms which, as we have seen, are the essential stuff of symbolic communication. No matter how spontaneous, how deeply intimate and seemingly unique one's communication with others may be—and this is true from the time one is a newborn infant—this communication is symbolic. It is symbolic because, whether through language, gesture, facial expression, caress or blow, it draws its meaning from symbols, signs, and norms which are the common stock of those living within a given culture. What Shakespeare called, in one of his loveliest sonnets, "the sessions of sweet silent thought" are not the less symbolic for taking place only within one's mind. Nor is what Shakespeare, in the words immediately following these, referred to as "remembrance of things past." All thought, all memory, all communication, all roles and statuses we occupy are given meaning by norms. Each personality, each social group, and each social order is given its distinctive nature by the norms which provide structure and which are given emphasis in the behavior patterns of any one of these.

Norms are the vital core of *culture*. The concept of culture is indispensable to any understanding of human behavior. We may think of culture as the aggregate or total of all the ways of behavior, feeling, thought, and judgment which are *learned by man in society*. Culture is to be distinguished from those ways of behavior—motor reflexes, sounds, basic drives toward food, sleep, and so on—which emerge directly from man's biological character and which would, in some form, exist even if everything man has learned in his long history were, by some miraculous blight, to be destroyed. Much behavior that appears at first sight to proceed unmediatedly from man's biological nature—expressions of joy, pleasure, pain, hate, violence, love, and others—in fact proceeds from culture and its ways of defining the ends which produce these ways of behavior, although of course man's *capacity* for them is biological, as is his *capacity* for thought and speech.

Strictly speaking, everything we find in man's behavior in society that is not the direct product of his biological structure is culture. That is, it has been learned through some process of socialization in the social order. Culture, thus considered, is coterminous with all society, all social organization, and all social behavior. A nuclear weapon, a high-rise office building, a pattern of family life, religion, friendship, morality, language, life style generally, as well as each of the prescribed ways we interact with others, is a part of culture. Beliefs, codes of law, systems of philosophy, esthetic, moral, and utilitarian values, all of these as well as the sundry machines, gadgets, and physical structures we find in all human societies are culture. Behind each is a way of thought or behavior that has been learned. In Malinowski's phrasing, taboo or canoe, each is culture.

But in accordance with much contemporary usage, and as a means of achieving greater analytical precision, we shall adopt a more specialized use of the word "culture." We shall consider culture as the total of *designs*, *themes*, or *ideal types* that is to be found in any social aggregate, small or large, that has continuing identity. We shall distinguish, in other words, between the *structures* of social behavior we find everywhere and the *ends* or *norms* which lie behind them or which give them their special identity.

It is possible to describe any social relationship solely in terms of what might be called its sociometry—the physical and social arrangements in space of the members of the relationship, the regularities of interaction, the roles, and statuses. But until we have brought into understanding the ends and purposes of these, we have not exhausted the nature of that social relationship. It is not only possible but common for social relationships and social aggregates to be highly similar in their structures but highly dissimilar in their cultures—using the latter word in the strict sense of the norms which give purpose to the relationships and aggregates. A great deal of loose thinking in social thought and social research has come from failure to recognize precisely this point—that two or more groups seemingly identical in structure or form may be wholly unlike when attention is turned to the ends for which the groups exist, that is, to their cultures. After all, the differences between an ordinary club and a criminal conspiracy may not be consequential until we turn to the norms that activate each.

Every social aggregate, large and small, moral and immoral, legal and illegal, has its culture in the sociological sense. We are justified in speaking of the culture of the French or the Russians, of a given region such as the Deep South in the United States or the Midlands in England, of an ethnic minority, a social class, an occupation, a sect or church, a family, or a delinquent band of youths. It is impossible for human beings to be in continued association and interaction with one another for long without a culture arising. That culture may in large part be drawn from the signs, symbols, and norms of the larger social order but it will, nonetheless, have its own distinctiveness, given enough time. Not only will special words be coined or common words given different signification, but gestures, looks, manner of dress, each with its own distinctive meaning to members of the group, will in time become a part of the consensus of the group. It is the diversity of *culture* in the world—a diversity fully reconcilable with the essential biological sameness of individuals and with the relatively few fundamental social types and roles to be found—that is the most striking aspect to all who travel or read. We may say that the conjugal family, for instance, exists everywhere, and is, by definition, that group composed of husband, wife, and immediate children. But what a major difference lies between this group as we find it in native Africa, caste-bound India, ancient Rome, the Kwakiutl Indians, and in middle-class America. And this major difference consists substantially in differences which are cultural, which are, in short, normative.

Norms are the adjustments which human beings in interaction make to the surrounding environment. We may think of them as solutions to recurring problems or situations. They may be ineffective, stupid, or evil solutions by our own standards. But any norm, whether small or large in social importance, whether sacred or utilitarian, is some form of adjustment to a recurrent problem. And once formed, the norm, if it seems to work at all, if it somehow gives a sense of protection or achievement, is likely to become a part of the culture of the group and to be transmitted by its members to all born in, or otherwise added to, group membership.

It is possible to classify social organizations (as Ruth Benedict did in her volume *Patterns of Culture*) in terms of variable norms and the dominating influence they have on a given social order. Thus, borrowing from Nietzsche, she labeled a certain type of primitive people Dionysian and another type Apollonian. In the first, exuberance, abandon, and lack of restraint predominate among the norms as does a strong sense of limitlessness of power and achievement. In the second, the Apollonian, the norms of order, balance, symmetry, and restraint predominate. Using a similar form of normative labeling, the German philosopher-historian Oswald Spengler characterized the modern Western order as Faustian—given to the same limitless ambition that Goethe built his great epic around—and in profound contrast to ancient Greek Apollonian society, which gave priorty to the norms of restraint and balance rather than those of achievement without limits.

The concept of culture and of norms is also useful in the understanding of a great deal of behavior that might otherwise be explained in terms of the biology of race or of that hoary abstraction "human nature." Everytime we hear someone say "It is Negro (or Italian or Jewish or English) nature to . . . ," we may be certain that we are about to hear an explanation in terms of race or inherited biological character that should instead be made in terms of social norms, of the culture that is transmitted socially. There may indeed be residual racial difference (beyond mere skin color) between black and white peoples. Countless whites have thought so; so today do certain militant blacks. But until we have made clea allowance for the cultural differences of *norms* that are transmitted through the generations historically, we are in no position to say very much about racially based differences of social behavior. This is not to imply that differences of social behavior are light and superficial merely because they are normatively, rather than biologically, based. People live by their norms, and the evidence of history makes clear that normative behavior can be very deeply rooted and very persistent indeed. One need but think of the extraordinary persistence through thousands of years of the residual normative elements of the Jewish people—a persistence often in the face of extreme persecution by non-Jewish peoples bent upon exterminating these normative elements. Every close student of English—or French or German or Kwakiutl—culture knows the extent to which a given set of norms regarding a great variety of recurrent situations can go on generation after generation and can shape the behavior of individuals born into, or otherwise assimilated into, each of these cultures.

A sense of the normative character of human behavior is indispensable in our attack upon social problems in society—poverty, ethnic conflict, drug addiction, alcoholism, and others. The juvenile delinquent is usually a member of a culture in just as real a sense as is the citizen of a nation. He and the other members of his gang or group are living largely in keeping with certain norms which represent that group's mode of adaptation to their environment. They may be—and usually are—aware of the norms of the larger social order, the norms against which their own are directed. But their own norms are serving, however illegally, the same functions of adaptation, cohesion, and achievement that are served by the norms of the larger order. We shall have more to say about this aspect of the matter in Chapter 10 where we deal with deviance. The points to be emphasized here are, first, the social, rather than biological, nature of the group norms and, second, the fact that in their aggregate these norms form a culture in as full a sense as that of Americans or Englishmen as a whole or members of a Hindu caste, or of a church or tribe.

Let us pass now to what is in many ways the most vital character of social norms—the sense of *oughtness* they inspire in human conduct. The moral order of society is a kind of tissue of "oughts": negative ones which *forbid* certain actions and positive ones which *enjoin* actions. What is true of the moral order in a society is largely true of personality. Personaliy, too, is a kind of tissue of "oughts," each reflective of some norm which is internalized in some substantial measure. What we mean sociologically when we refer to *conscience* is the individual's assimilation of social norms in a way that leads these norms to become arbiters of his behavior both generally and specifically in a concrete situation. "My conscience compels me" or "My conscience will not permit me" is in each instance a compact way of saying, in effect, "Because of the norms regarding right and wrong that I have somehow acquired and that have become almost indistinguishable from my perceptions of situations, I must, or must not, allow myself to do a certain thing." Hamlet's famous "Conscience does make cowards of us all" is testimony to the inhibiting effect upon impulse and raw desire that social norms can have when they have become strongly internalized in our individual beings.

However, like the norms it reflects, conscience is highly selective. Conscience might restrain me from killing another human being, robbing him, or subjecting him to oppression *if* the other human being were of my family, my religion, my race, or my nation. And, as we know, criminal laws back up conscience in these respects. However, conscience might or might not restrain me from killing, robbing, or oppressing another person *if* the context were different, if, for instance, a state of war were declared and killing and its related acts made legal, even mandatory. The most pacific and gentle and humane of individuals are found in what can only be called killer roles in time of war.

Thus, when internalized through socialization processes, the norms inspire or inhibit us through the sense of "should" and "ought" they convey. We observe, as a corollary to this concept, that the norms *legitimize*. Here we return to the discussion of role. It is *proper* that a man be in the presence of a nude female to whom he is not married *if* he is a physician or artist. So would say the large majority of even the most conventional of people in our society. But beyond such roles, with the norms contained in them, there would be fairly widespread disapproval in the minds of a majority of Americans today—and of many other peoples as well. *The mores make anything right.* This phrase from William Graham Sumner's *Folkways* is as succinct a way of expressing the relation between social norms and morality as any imaginable. And, as Sumner points out in rich detail, there is not a custom to be conceived that has not somewhere at sometime been regarded as right—just as right as any of the norms which exist in our culture. Torture, incest, cannibalism, infanticide, murder, theft, and a vast number of other forms of behavior condemned by our own codes have been, at one time or other, within *legitimating contexts*, deemed to be morally right.

Cannibalism exerts a certain degree of horror, or at least repugnance, upon most of us. The playwright-vegetarian George Bernard Shaw once described it ironically as meat-eating with the heroic dish left in. But apart from the role that cannibalism has in our more mordant forms of humor and in situations of extreme distress such as that of the ill-fated Donner Expedition, it is as profoundly taboo in most civilizations as any practice we might think of. But there are exceptions. Cannibalism has been pronounced moral by quite a few peoples in the world. All who have read *Robinson Crusoe* will remember Crusoe's horror when his companion, the native Friday, pointed with obvious anticipatory relish to the body of a recently slain invader of their island. We are perhaps less likely to remember Defoe's point in stressing Friday's dismay at the thought of allowing excellent, needed food to go to waste. In each case the mores made right.

Incest is another activity on which the mores have been firm in all cultures. Almost all cultures have had strict taboos against incest, but the range of variation on what constitutes incest is rather wide. Today, among the vast majority of peoples, certainly all those in the West, incest would be defined as sexual relations between parent and child or brother and sister. The circle within which incest is defined and prohibited is thus the small conjugal family. Marriages of first cousins in our society, although hardly common, are unlikely to be thought incestuous. Such marriages, however, and along with them marriages of second, third, and even fourth and fifth cousins, have been pronounced incestuous in other times and places. On the other hand the royal family of ancient Egypt was permitted a sacred form of incest in which brother married sister on occasion. And in pre-Western Hawaii the royal ruler was permitted to marry whomever he or she desired. Incest is always socially defined, and because it is so defined, we often find very large groups indeed—the huge clans of China, for instance—within which marriage is forbidden. Few acts appear to have so nearly universal taboos as incest. But as welfare department records make plain, especially in the United States where such records are more abundant, even "basic" incest—sexual relations of mother and son, father and daughter, brother and sister—is far from unknown in society, with participants often in full knowledge of both the moral taboo and the legal statutes involved.

Despite what most of us think of as an "instinctive" repugnance to incest of this basic type, there is no clear evidence that any biological basis of the almost universal proscription of incest exists. What does exist, and has existed almost everywhere for many millennia, is a recognition of the *social chaos* that incest can bring about in a community. Sexual relations between father and daughter, between mother and son, would lead, almost certainly, to sexual rivalries and jealousies of extraordinary intensity. Close ties of either conjugal or parental-filial type would be difficult to establish in such circumstances. Confusion of roles and statuses within the kinship group would be extreme. The son of a union between father and daughter would then be a brother to his mother. One may compound this by extending the confusion of relationships thus produced to the several degrees of kinship relationship in the larger family. Multiply the confusion by imagining other types of basic incest, such as brother-sister, mother-son, and so on, and any system of ordered authority, of legitimacy of descent, would be impossible. Given the historic and universal primacy of the kinship aggregate in human societies, one need not go beyond the fact of social and normative confusion for explanation of the almost universal prohibition of incest. *If* a society were ever to come into existence in which the kinship ties were absolutely nonexistent, with the problems of socialization, legitimacy of descent in the society, security, and authority met by other forms of organization, there is no great difficulty in imagining disappearance altogether of what is now general repugnance at the thought of sexual relationships among those biologically closely related.

There is still another aspect of the normative order which must be emphasized. It has been stated succinctly by Kingsley Davis: "The normative order makes the factual order of human society possible." [1] At least two vital points are made in this statement. The first and more obvious is that it is only through the normative behavior we acquire socially that we are able to deal with the "factual" order—that is, raw environment, discrete individual human beings, and so on. How, apart from socially acquired norms relating to food gathering, shelter construction, and protection from the predatory would we survive? But there is a second and equally profound, if subtler, point in Davis' sentence. It is only through what might be called the eyeglasses of the norms we live by that we perceive and interact with the factual order. Pure perception—that is, perception unfiltered by one's cultural norms—is hardly possible. And this is as true of the scientist, who must therefore devise special techniques, as it is of the rest of us.

We may be reminded, at this point, of W. I. Thomas' "definition of the situation." *Perceptually*, the situation is inseparable from the norms we bring to it. What we believe to be right and wrong and what we think *ought* to exist form a kind of translucent curtain through which we look at reality, especially social reality. Of course, objectivity is itself a norm in contemporary scientific culture. This norm exerts a sense of oughtness that in its way makes us seek knowledge of reality in which the effects of other norms are suspended.

There is not the slightest evidence that human beings have a moral conscience about anything that does not proceed from the norms that are dominant in their specific cultures. The norms may be operative in aggregates as wide as nations or civilizations or as small as family or peer group. So-called normless behavior among human beings is an impossibility. There are, to be sure, different degrees of assimilation and internalization of norms in the process of growing up. There may be behavior springing from norms in groups so small or so clandestine as to be unknown by those observing the behavior. The juvenile delinquent, the criminal, even the suicide, as Durkheim stressed, are behaving in terms of certain norms. But they are the norms of cultures inhering in groups or ways of behavior the rest of us may not be aware of. There is the fact too that the delinquent child or adult may be observing with extreme fidelity the very same norms we respect—loyalty, honesty, courage, and the like—but only with respect to the norms of the group or organization that lays claim to *his* loyalties, that is, the delinquent or criminal group. We are prone to say of delinquent behavior that it has somehow become detached from the norms most of us live by most of the time. So it has, in a way. But of greater motivational importance is the fact that such behavior is often oriented toward the same norms, but norms which have different functions or different contexts.

Are there certain norms which are so fundamental, so universal, as to be properly thought "natural" in contrast to "artificial"? Many have thought so. Whole systems of ethics have been propounded by philosophers in terms of certain norms—justice, for example, in the case of Plato's *Republic*—which were held to be so fundamental to human society, so natural to man as a thinking being, that their opposite or their neglect could only lead to anarchy or tyranny. There are very few persons today who do not regard some norms as more natural to man than others. *How* they make the distinction depends, of course, upon what culture or subculture they are a part of. A good many young people today appear to regard the norms of middle-class society as not merely repugnant to themselves but basically unnatural to man the species. Definitions of "sick" society or "healthy" society are predicated upon norms which are regarded as baneful or, as the case may be, salutary to man. From the sociological point of view, however, there is nothing any less natural or more "sick" in the norms of American middle-class society than in the norms of the communes of the "new youth," or those of Bantu tribes in East Africa.

We do not know, nor will we ever know, precisely what man's life was like, sociologically considered, at that point a million or so years ago when evolutionary differentiation produced the species we call *Homo sapiens*. Efforts to deduce what man's "natural" behavior is, or would be, have been wholly unsuccessful. Sometimes it is the behavior of some distant primitive tribe that is taken as a measure of what is natural; then it is the observed behavior of the so-called feral children, children supposedly lost from parents at infancy and who have somehow managed to grow up apart from the human community; then it is the behavior of some child isolated in attic or cellar by demented parents that is held to be evidence of what natural human behavior would be. But we do not know. Whatever lasting appeal the question may have, it is not in any sense a sociological or scientific question. Man, however we find him, wherever and at whatever age in the history of society, is engaged in normative behavior. Few societies are in fact more norm-bound than some of those primitive societies in the South Pacific that eighteenth-century philosophers thought so perfectly illustrative of norm-less and natural existence.

In everyday life we often distinguish between behavior we encounter that we regard as natural and behavior that we pronounce artificial or affected. Few things in life are more likely to stir amusement than the latter in its more flagrant manifestations. But the first, the natural type of behavior, is no less rooted in social norms and social roles than the second. It is simply that the norms involved are more completely internalized. The individual has lived with them longer and in a greater variety of situations, and they are not in comical contrast to other elements of his behavior. What we call "being natural" is, as Montaigne wrote in one of his essays, a very difficult art. It is basically not different in conventional society and in the theater. The highest praise some people give great acting is that the actor has made every motion seem utterly natural, whether he is playing the king or the peasant. But there is nothing natural about it. It is the result of endless training, experience, and, finally, full commitment to the role involved—and to its norms. And in ordinary society the difference between natural and artificial behavior is substantially the same. To achieve the kind of behavior one still finds in the English upper class referred to in the preceding chapter requires socialization of appropriate kind from infancy onward. The upper-class norms of language, dress, bearing, belief, leisure, life style, and philosophy generally have to be quite literally drilled, even beaten, into the subject—by family, church, the "right" school and college, and a host of other influences. The end result is one of the most seemingly effortless modes of behavior to be found in the civilized world, but one that is the despair of almost all who have tried to ape it without proper background.

We have been referring to *norms*. The question of how norms differ from *values* may be raised. They do not differ at all. It is a matter of different words which refer to the same aspect of social behavior. If there is a difference, it is not substantive but one of usage. Philosophers are more likely to use the word "value" in reference to one or another of the major norms of civilization—justice, freedom, equality, charity, and so on. Each of these is, however, no less a norm, no less a product of man's social heritage, than the most trivial of customs.

There is a great diversity of types of norms or values. We speak of moral values, esthetic values, utilitarian values, or religious values. All alike are elements of culture, products of the social heritage, and almost infinitely variable in the world's vast diversity of social organization. All alike are to be seen in *human behavior*. However external they may seem to the individual concerned at a given point in his socialization, however alien to the outsider, norms and values are nevertheless as inseparable from behavior as are roles and statuses. Norms are reflected in personalities; personalities form around norms. David Riesman's now famous distinction between "inner-directed" personality and personalities that are either "tradition-directed" or "other-directed" is a distinction well within the province of norms. The inner-directed personality behaves normatively, but the relation between norm and act—or judgment or belief or conviction—is so close, so profoundly internalized, that we think of this personality as driven by impulses which are as much a part of his inner being as his innate physical strength or agility. The upper- or lower-class Englishman, the nineteenth-century American businessman about whose entrepreneurial self-direction so much has been written, the religious fanatic, or the individual of seemingly unswervable political conviction, is each, if we like, inner-directed to a degree not found in the behavior of a great many of us. But we are still referring to behavior that is residually oriented toward a set of cultural norms, norms which are or have been "traditional" and which, finally, are the product of interaction with others.

Once again we come back to the underlying unity of social behavior and the impossibility of making *separations* among the several elements involved. Conceptual distinctions, yes; separations, no. Norms must be distinguished from social interaction generally and from social aggregates, social roles, and social statuses. But, as we observed in each of the earlier chapters, it is impossible to deal with any one of these realistically except in terms of the norms which give a certain pattern of interaction, or aggregate, or role, or status its distinctiveness. *Which* norms will be dominant in an individual's way of life is a function of what social aggregates he has been influenced by, of the status level he belongs to, of the social roles he occupies, and of the types of *social authority* that are strong in his life.

This brings us to *sanctions*. With every norm or value there is some kind of sanction. The sanction may be weak, diffuse, and without notable visibility. Or it may be as specific and visible as the penalty defined by a legal enactment. But in theory at least there is always a sanction, and even where no apparent sanction exists at a given time in reinforcement of a norm, a little investigation always reveals the fact that the sanction once was visible and effective. The sanction may lie in one's conscience. The sanction may be the opinion, the *favorable* opinion, one desires from others in the group or organization that contains the norm. To violate the norm would be thus to incur hostile or contemptuous opinion. Or, if we are dealing with a reference group which may well be far distant from the individual concerned, the mere thought or anticipation of opinion will serve as a sanction. Sanctions, basically, *are forms of retributive action* for violations of norms in a social group or order. Our fear or dislike of these forms of retributive action explains—though only in part—our observance of certain norms and our avoidance of others. Retributive action may be as mild as the mother's disapproving glance or as harsh as the sentence by a court of law upon a felon. It may be as concrete and explicit as the law passed against murder, robbery, or arson. It may be as general but as potent as any of the numerous modes of ostracism which all groups, in one way or another, visit upon violators of norms. Ridicule, contumely, avoidance, public scorn, and threat of publicity are all sanctions in just as full a sociological sense as are laws and police and courts of justice. The seemingly fearless iconoclast may be as subservient to a set of norms—those of his reference group, wherever it may be—as the assertedly conformist individual.

History has its own ways of selecting norms which now are prominent in public fancy and others which are but shadowy reminders of some earlier age. Norms are expressed in the forms of great institutions such as the nation upheld by patriotism, the church upheld by piety, or the capitalist economic system by the norms of private property and profits. But norms are expressed in many forms of behavior. They are inseparable from fashions, fads, styles, as well as customs and traditions of all kinds. In the same way that we have seen history well described as a process of selection of roles and statuses, so may it be seen in terms of the selection of norms. In one age the dominant norms may be religious, as during the Middle Ages. In another they may be political, military, technological, or economic. Because economic norms were ascendant in the nineteenth century in Western Europe, many economists thought them to be universal and timeless as incentives to human behavior. Largely through the works of such sociologists as Weber, Durkheim, and Simmel, however, we learned differently. Economic norms, least of all those of private property and profit, are far from universal in time and space. Today, clearly, organizational and technological norms outweigh all others in the higher reaches of Western society.

SACRED NORMS (RELIGION)

There are many ways of classifying social norms. All depend upon the purpose of the classification and the degree of detail desired. The most fundamental and far-reaching classification is, however, that which takes its departure from the difference between *sacred norms* on the one hand and, on the other, those called variously *secular*, *profane*, or *utilitarian*. The latter are justified by their demonstrable efficacy, their utility, or their rationality. Sacred norms require no such appeal to utility, efficacy, or reason. Their justification (although, strictly speaking, sacred norms by their nature require no justification) is drawn from the realm of the divine, the profoundly traditional, or what Weber called the charismatic. Norms are sacred to human devotion if they are products of, or have association with, an influence so powerful upon human allegiance as to seem suprahuman, suprarational, or supraterrestrial. Characteristically, sacred norms are the components of religions, and it is largely in their religious manifestation that they will be considered in this section. But before turning to religion and its role in the social order, it is well to be reminded that literally any idea, belief, practice, or material thing can be, in some degree at least, sacred. There is a certain element of the sacred in the devotion alumni may give to the numbered jersey of some legendary football player, such as Ernie Nevers at Stanford or Red Grange at Illinois or Albie Booth at Yale. So, too, is the rapt attention given by baseball fans to the bat of Babe Ruth or the glove of Ty Cobb at the Hall of Fame Museum in Cooperstown. And, as Durkheim (himself a professed atheist) noted with respect to many revolutionary and secular movements, it is very easy in time for leading figures and for implements associated with the leading figures to be regarded as sacred. In France in 1794 the selfsame Jacobins who had overthrown the Church in France in the name of individual reason had statues made of the Goddess of Reason, with even a liturgy and ritual to prescribe to the citizens of Paris for observance in the public squares. Few social movements in history have been as relentlessly antireligious as modern Communism which triumphed in Russia in 1917. But official proscription of religion as such does not keep Marxism itself from having a quasi-religious function in Communist populations nor a great number of people from passing through the mausoleum in Moscow that contains Lenin's remains.

There is nothing that is immune by its nature from becoming a sacred norm. Gods, spirits, and demons are sacred, obviously. But sticks, stones, brooks, fields, houses, clothing, trinkets—in short, anything—may also be considered sacred. The cross is highly sacred in Christianity. It became so through the form of execution to which Jesus was sentenced. Romans (and many other peoples) had used the device of nailing certain criminals to crosses to let them die in agony, slowly. For the Romans the cross had essentially utilitarian, normative significance. The death of Jesus, however, made this form of execution sacred and the cross itself the very symbol of the religion that was in time to be Christianity.

How does a sacred norm arise? Max Weber answered by noting the influence of some charismatic human being, such as Jesus or the Buddha or Moses, whose own suprahuman, supranatural significance is then transmitted to everything done or said by this being, and to everything touched by him or that can in time become associated with him. Durkheim, whose analysis of the sacred is the profoundest of any sociologist's and who views religion as at bottom human devotion to the sacred, did not really deal with specific origins. But there is nonetheless a theory of *source*, at least, in Durkheim's declaration that *the sacred is, at bottom, but the consecration of society* and its varied manifestations. A given relation, a given form of interaction, becomes so vital over a period of time, so inseparable from the very identity of a people, that there is a powerful tendency to make this relation supranatural, suprautilitarian, and to see in it what we would call divine or godlike characteristics. It was Durkheim's genius to show, through detailed examination of one primitive culture, Australian aborigine, not merely the residual elements of all religion, including the largest and most modern, but also the ineffaceable relation between these elements and the social bond. Rituals, sacraments, dogmas, liturgies, Durkheim stated, can all be shown to have their functional sources in man's desire to maintain the social bond.   Hence the not merely anthropomorphic but the *communal* character of all primitive, all early, and certainly most modern religions.

The distinction between the sacred and the utilitarian is, Durkheim argued, the profoundest that can be made by the human mind.   All other classificatory distinctions are derivative or minor by comparison. Even the distinction between good and evil or right and wrong is less profound, for this is a distinction that falls squarely within the category of the sacred.   The sacred, it should be emphasized, is by no means confined to things men cherish and love.   Evil things—black witches, demons, devils, hostile spirits, "bad" or "wrong" influences, and so on—fall within the realm of the sacred just as surely as do good or right things.   No greater mistake could be made than to suppose that the sacred, from any sociological point of view, is always the desired and the worshiped.   It can as easily be the hated and the feared.   The essence of the sacred, good or evil, lies in its being considered beyond the criteria of mere utility, human reason, or power.

Things and beings can, of course, pass directly from the realm of the sacred to the utilitarian, and vice versa.   The manner of this passage, however, highlights the separateness of the two realms.   Purifying rites, as in initiation, baptismal, eucharistic, and other ceremonies, are required for a thing or person to pass from the utilitarian to the sacred realm.   Cohabitation by man and woman is at best utilitarian, a matter of desire or reason, until it becomes sacred through the initiatory or purifying rites of marriage.   By contrast, the passage of things from sacred to utilitarian is more often a matter of erosion of values once sacred and of dislocation of deities and other entities of sacred regard.   Such erosion and dislocation result either from the entry of new sacred norms or else of rationalistic skepticism.   Religions vary, of course, in what is deemed to be sacred and what utilitarian. When, in the sixteenth century, Luther declared marriage to be a civil rather than an ecclesiastical ceremony, he inevitably took some of the sacred character away from the Christian conception of marriage.   Still, the great majority of Protestants would even today declare marriage a sacred rather than merely utilitarian relationship.

What is central to any religion, however, is its distinction between the sacred and the utilitarian.   A religion may or may not contain belief in a god.   It may or may not hold doctrines of immortality, heaven and hell, or grace deriving from the supernatural.   Variation in belief and rite is endless in the world's religions.   But always in religion there is the pronouncement of some things as sacred—as being beyond the mere test of utility or human rationality—and some things as utilitarian or, in Durkheim's word, profane.

One does not have to go all the way with Durkheim's analysis to agree that between religion and the social bond there is the closest of relationships. Religion sanctifies certain relationships. It is in this sense that we find religion integrative, no matter how unacceptable, even offensive, its beliefs may be to any given observer. By declaring sacred the fundamental bonds of society—those between parent and child, husband and wife, chief and followers, and others—we plainly endow them with a degree of importance and duration that would not be the case if each were regarded as being as utilitarian as the relation between seller and buyer. Religion arises out of the processes through which these bonds become suprautilitarian. And in turn, religion, as it gradually acquires its own rationale through supporting beliefs, gives profound emphasis to the bonds. Without exception the major religions of mankind, from most primitive times onward, have tended to feature and to build their fundamental doctrines and rites around those most elemental aspects of human experience: birth, marriage, and death. And in consecrating the idea of community, in giving rise gradually to the notion of the invisible and eternal community, religions helped to lessen man's fear of death and of the unknown in general. Without the continuing ties of kinship, ethnicity, and community, early man quite literally would have perished as a species before a more complex civilization could develop. These ties were a major means of protection, from infancy to old age. Hence the close relation between these ties and sacred norms everywhere.

Durkheim, it is interesting to note, did not stop with the *socially* integrative functions of religion. He entered the complex domain of man's personality and even the structure of man's mind. As sacred norms are vital in strengthening the social bond, so are they vital in strengthening man's sense of identity and his belief in self and his own virtues and endowments. The essence of religion, viewed in the believer himself, is not what religion says about things external or internal, but what it does toward making action possible and life endurable. "The believer who has communicated with his god is not merely a man who sees new truths, of which the the unbeliever is ignorant; *he is a man who is stronger.*"[2] If one believes that he has, through ritual or worship, taken on ome of the strength of the very god he is supposedly descended from, he is very apt to have a confidence, a sense of well being, even of added strength and

courage. Before one can value himself, or the human individual as
such, Durkheim tells us, there must first have been a belief in the value
of the sacred entity—be this totem or god—that alone transmits sacredness and value to humankind. Hence the fundamental importance of
the *cult*, that tight community of worshipers, of fellow participants in
the grace that is given by totem or by god. The church was eventually
derived from the cult. The church is the primitive cult in substance but
enlarged, diversified, and organized. And it is directly from the cult
that all of those states of mind we associate with religion take their
departure. Anyone who has ever

> *really practised a religion knows very well that it is the cult which
> gives rise to those impressions of joy, of interior peace, of serenity,
> of enthusiasm, which are, for the believer, an experimental proof of
> his beliefs. The cult is not simply a system of signs by which the
> faith is outwardly translated; it is a collection of the means by which
> this is created and recreated periodically.*[3]

Durkheim went beyond the integrative relation between personality
and the sacred into the relation of the latter to the very structure of
the human mind. Although his conclusions here cannot be said to have
the authority in contemporary sociology that his others do with respect to the nature of religion, they are worth brief statement. How,
it may be asked, does the human mind acquire its capacity to organize
raw experience into propositions involving the notions of causality, time,
force, mass, extent, hierarchy, and others? Some philosophers such as
David Hume have answered this question in terms of individual experience with its associations of perception and idea; others, such
as Immanuel Kant, have answered it in terms of "categories" of causality, time, space, and so on, held to be innate in the human mind and
thus anterior to experience.

Durkheim's answer—and it is at best speculative—follows directly
from his analysis of religion and his stress upon the uniquely commanding role of religion in the life of primitive man. Earliest man lived
in a world dominated by sacred norms and relationships, Durkheim
declared. Through his participation in these he gradually acquired a
sense of causality, time, space, and the other categories of thought.
From the primitive sense of the omnipotence of the tribe, of the social
bond, a distinguishable, abstract sense of power in the form of *cause*
came in the course of ages. From his experience with the ceaseless
cycle of sacred ceremonies and rites came the notion of generalized

experience divided into units of *time*, of periodicity. And from recurrent observation of the ways in which the community arranged itself to meet different challenges there came, in time, a conception of *space* and also of *order* and of *hierarchy*. Thus, Durkheim writes, the Australian aborigine's conception of space—universal space—is drawn directly from his perceptions of the arrangement of huts and groupings in his tribe. The latter are concentrically arranged, so the envisagement of space in general is concentrically oriented.

Again let it be emphasized that such conclusions regarding the origins of abstract thought are speculative and, certainly in the form in which Durkheim presented them, would produce much controversy among philosophers and sociologists today. But although the question of ultimate origins may be forever beyond reach, there is no doubt whatever that the *type* of sociological analysis of knowledge that Durkheim gives us is highly useful. The work of Marcel Granet on the symbols of Chinese culture and thought, Jean Piaget on the origins of conceptions of causality and time and space in children's minds, and of many of Durkheim's own students on similar problems (for example, Marcel Mauss on systems of primitive classification and Maurice Halbwachs on suicide and beliefs) is evidence enough of the fecundity of Durkheim's ideas on the sociology of knowledge and of the relation between sacred norms and processes of thought which extend beyond religion alone. Quite apart from primordial origins, there is no question but that our abstract ideas reflect the culture within which we live.

Let us return to the social role of sacred norms. I suggested above that, following Durkheim's perspective, we may see sacred norms as possessing integrative functions for both the social order and the individual personality. These functions help us to understand why even the nonbelieving Durkheim could declare religion—in *some* form—an eternal part of the human experience.

Consider, first, the *uncertainties of life*. Try as we may, we will never be able to reduce all aspects of life, every moment in time, to the rational, calculated, processes of preventive action. True, the nature of the uncertainties changes often in history. We no longer have to fear the predatory tiger or lion in the dark, but only a fool would say that these have not been replaced by other, equally death-dealing, entities and situations. We may build our automobiles to meet even the specifications of a Ralph Nader and our highways to the specifications of every safety engineer. Obviously, however, there are still possibilities of death or disability, no matter how carefully one chooses to drive himself. The possibilities of death or disaster for persons and societies can be reduced but never obviated totally. Hence the apprehension in most minds of the uncertainties of life, of the possibilities of bad luck, of malign circumstance. And hence, too, the reliance by a vast number of persons upon those sacred norms—and their associated mechanisms of prayer, ritual, medallion, or crossing of one's fingers—which, for want of anything better and demonstrably more efficacious, are thought to be talismanic.

Consider, second, the *alienation* that the human mind is heir to. As Hegel and Feuerbach stressed in the nineteenth century, the very capacity of the human mind for dissociating itself into subject and object is bound to produce, on occasion at least, the sense of being divided within oneself, of lacking the unity that is more comfortable for most minds. There is the kind of alienation that Karl Marx wrote of, the sense of being estranged from the work one is doing, of feeling it to be an alien strait jacket rather than a natural projection of one's own desires and needs. And there is, finally, the kind of alienation that ensues from the sense of being cut off from others, from love, friendship, membership in a group or social order. We shall come back to alienation in the next chapter. Here I call attention to it as a more or less universal and timeless state of the human condition and suggest that of all the functions of religion, surcease from alienation is one of the oldest and most widespread. Not, obviously, for all persons. Plainly, one may feel deeply alienated and succeed only in feeling more alienated by turning to religion, at least religion in the conventional sense. But students of religious behavior who take account of what religious persons have to say about religious experience consistently stress the functional role religion plays with respect to human alienation.

Consider, third, the sense of *dependence* that is found in all human beings—albeit in varying degree—as the inevitable consequence of being a social animal. Our lives are bound from infancy onward by patterns of interaction, roles, statuses, authorities; all alike are socially inherited, all alike are inseparable from human behavior. Freud thought that the sense of dependence, first acquired by the infant's relation to parent, is the origin of the religious experience. Dependence is by no means the only explanation of reliance upon the charismatic figures and the sacred norms which form religions, but it is clearly a very important one. As Durkheim noted, we do better to go to the religious, to those who have or have had genuinely religious experiences, for explanation of what is functionally vital than to the rationalistic theories of those who have known no such experience.   And, Durkheim concluded, when we do so, we find repeatedly the sense of dependence upon others greatly heightened and made more luminous and lasting through the norms of the sacred community—that is, of *sacred dependence*.   Freud saw belief in god as a magnification of what is originally a belief in the father, the child's belief in the omnipotence of the parent.   Durkheim saw belief in god as a supernatural rendering of what is, in the history of mankind, first a belief in the power of the community.

In both Freud and Durkheim, however, there is the clear contention of the role of religion in meeting the sense of need for dependence upon something larger and more inclusive than one's own being.   Freud thought, or seems to have thought, that the need for religion will disappear in time, as man becomes progressively aware—through psychoanalytic insights—of the sufficiency of his own reason.   Durkheim, whose view I believe to be the more profound, thought that the need for religion would never disappear as mankind is presently constructed physiologically and psychologically, because of the ineradicable tendency of man to distinguish between the sacred and the utilitarian.

Religions will come and go, Durkheim wrote; their sphere of control will narrow with man's expansion of knowledge of cosmos, society, and self.   But the eternality of religion is rooted in the eternality of the sacred in human consciousness.   On the evidence, it is difficult to dispute Durkheim's contention.   Note the ease with which those who abandon traditionally sacred norms or beliefs convert other norms—political, economic, scientific—from merely empirical or utilitarian significance to significance not the less sacred because no deities or supernatural spirits are involved.   All who have read William Golding's novel *Lord of the Flies* will know how easy it is under conditions of temporary stress and privation for norms to arise which are not merely sacred but supernatural—and in rather horrifying form. Such norms can arise in even the most secular-minded of groups.

There is the further fact that despite optimistic predictions by the rationalistic and secular-minded in the nineteenth century, the appeal of religion would not appear to have greatly lessened in twentieth-century industrial societies.   Marx wrote that religion was no more than "the sigh of the oppressed creature, the heart of a heartless world . . . the opium of the people," and he predicted that with the end of economic exploitation religion would pass from human experience.   Others, by no means socialist or communist in social philosophy, thought that religion could not possibly survive in the face of the spread of education and the gradual replacement of superstition by science and technology. What the future holds in such matters is only speculation. But the present situation in this country and elsewhere indicates that vast numbers of people can be educated, relatively affluent, and under no visible exploitation and still incline strongly toward religious memberships and activities. In his important study of the Detroit population, Gerhard Lenski found that religion placed very high indeed—as high as social class—as an influence on social behavior.

But whatever may be the true significance of religion at the present time or in the distant future, no one can dispute the power of its norms on human consciousness in the past. Durkheim and Weber did not err in finding in religion—in the sacred and in charismatic roles and relationships—the source of much in human culture, human social organization, and also in the varied processes of social change that history reveals. The earliest and for a very long time the only forms of art, music, drama, literature, and sculpture were sacred. Gods, goddesses, and other beings of the supernatural were the commonest subjects of these forms. Philosophy, as we know, began in ancient Greek society on the basis of themes transmitted directly from myth and religious metaphor. The power of the prophet and the magician, as we have already noted, was very great in the formative period of social organization. Even patriarchal and matriarchal roles, not to give undue emphasis to others such as kings and scholars, were strongly tinged with the element of sacredness.

Although religion and the sacred are most often thought of in connection with tradition and stability, it would be absurd to overlook their immense influence on social change and revolutionary social movements and actions. After all, the advent of Christianity effected vast changes first in Roman society and then in many other societies of the ancient world. In one of his greatest sociological works, Max Weber demonstrated the importance of the norms of Protestantism, or what he called the Protestant ethic, to the rise of capitalism in the West. Until approximately the late eighteenth century in Western Europe many social movements—from the revolutionary social movement that was Christianity as a whole during its first century or two down to the Levellers, the Society of Friends, and the Wesleyan Methodists in later centuries—took their impetus from ideas that were religious. Even at the present time, as the recent history of the Negro civil rights movement in the United States makes clear, the power of sacred norms can be great. One need only think of the charismatic influence of the late Martin Luther King. And for all the undisputed sway of technical and utilitarian norms in contemporary society, it is the persistence of sacred norms regarding human fertility that lies behind the massive problem of unchecked birthrates in a world of finite food resources. We shall return to this problem shortly—there is no better way of acquiring insight into the sheer power of norms in social behavior.

UTILITARIAN NORMS (TECHNOLOGY)

Let us not, however, exaggerate the power of the sacred in human consciousness. There are, as I have noted, other types of norms that are carried from generation to generation, that are justified and win acceptance by virtue of their instrumental, their technical, or their utilitarian value. As Malinowski emphasized, even the most primitive of peoples are well aware of the difference between the realm of the sacred and the realm of the utilitarian. Primitive man may have felt it necessary (even as many of us do) to invoke sacred blessing when he went forth on the hunt or when he cooked his food or built his hut. After all, it is good to stay on the favorable side of whatever deities may exist in sacred consciousness, and how better do this than by asking their protection and offering thanks for past protections? But primitive man, as Malinowski notes, did not make the mistake of supposing that supplication or incantation would bring down the animal, would actually cook it, or would take the place of the labor of constructing the hut.

The *interaction* of sacred and utilitarian norms provides most of the clues to the analysis and classification of cultures. Rare is the sacred norm that is not in some way supported by technical norms. The sacred altar has to be built by technical, not supplicatory, processes. But rare too is the utilitarian norm that is not attended in some degree by the sacred norm. No ancient people outdid the Romans in construction genius. But until relatively late in Roman society it was common to kill a slave and bury his body with the cornerstone of a public structure. In time the Romans abandoned this practice and, after Christianization, asked for the protection of the Christian deity or saints. And the practice of soliciting sacred reinforcement to technical processes continues today. Cornerstone ceremonies for public buildings as well as churches are still well known, and deities are invoked by presidents and warring nations.

Yet a conspicuous and enormously important trend in the history of civilization is that of *secularization*. By this, I mean the overall tendency of acts, thoughts, and beliefs which were indistinguishable in the beginning from sacred ends to become more and more secular or utilitarian in their significance, to become separated from their sacred roots in time, to become accepted for their own importance. Whereas all forms of social organization (law, learning, art, and culture generally) were once strongly suffused with religious connotations, each of these—and many other aspects of social behavior—has been freed of the sacred and conceived as an end important in and for itself. Simmel had much of this process in mind when he used the word "autonomization" to describe it. Processes previously dependent upon the sacred become liberated in time, so to speak, and achieve autonomy. One need but look at the history of art and drama to realize the degree to which activities that once were primarily manifestations of religious ritual can become important in themselves. In the history of civilization we repeatedly find vital periods of change in the condition of a given people when the process of secularization of norms is dominant. One thinks again of the fifth century B.C. in Athens or of the Renaissance in modern Europe. These were ages not merely of the ascendance of new forms of organization, new roles and statuses, but also —and inseparable from these—of new norms that depended upon reason or utility rather than sacred belief. This type of transition is one of the most vital to be found anywhere in the study of human civilization.

It is likely that no age in all history compares with our own in the respect that is accorded utilitarian or rationalist norms and in the sheer number of these as contrasted with sacred norms. It would be a mistake to suppose that sacred norms have disappeared altogether. Old ones, in one form or other, remain, and new ones make their appearance. Man's capacity for endowing his ends and means with at least some degree of sacredness is seemingly endless. But this said, it is clear that Western society today is more heavily laden with strictly utilitarian norms than any society in human history. The triumph of technology and science has effected this. Ours is truly an age of technology, often referred to as "the technological society," and the greatest single impact that the West has made upon other societies and cultures on the earth in the last century proceeds directly from the ascendancy within the West of technological norms.

Technology may be described as the institutionalization of utilitarian norms. It is the largest category within which all the norms of utility, convenience, efficiency, organization, and human reason may be placed. It would be a major error to limit technology to mere machinery and to material culture as such. Technology is no less present in rationalized, efficiency-oriented structures of organization in education, entertainment, and government than it is in the churches of our day, and even in family life. We may be most impressed by technology in the form of man's ascent to the moon through projectiles of nearly incredible physical complexity. But in its most decisive forms, as far as human conduct is concerned, technology is to be seen in the more prosaic channels of organization and ordinary learning.

What is central to technology, and what has made it the dominant force in contemporary Western society, is the application of rational principles to the control or reordering of space, matter, *and human beings*. It is not tradition, divinity, or any other sacred entity that is the controlling objective in technology. What is controlling always is the criterion of reason—of the rational utilization of materials and persons—as this may emerge from the living generation. Although science and technology may properly be distinguished, they are, in our age, plainly interlocked. The objective of each is power—power of the human mind, brought to its highest possible level of acuity and learning—over both the physical and social environments.

This, basically, is what Max Weber referred to in his central concept of *rationalization*, which we have previously encountered in this volume. Weber, citing from the poet Schiller, once referred to "the disenchantment of the world." He did not mean, as he is often mistakenly held to have meant, disillusionment. He meant the removal of sacred enchantment from more and more areas of man's experience through the application of principles drawn from human reason and empirical observation. He meant that whereas man in Western Europe had lived in a world dominated by belief in spiritual entities, gods, goddesses, spirits, and sacred taboos down to about the nineteenth century, modern man increasingly finds himself in a world in which more and more of these forms of "enchantment" have been driven out by the principles of reason and science. Technology replaces enchantment. Never wholly, of course. And, as is evident, it is possible for many persons to become enchanted, in a manner of speaking, by the principles of technology. But for most persons there is a profound gulf between the sacred and the technological.

True, there always has been a gulf. It is the very essence of the sacred that this gulf exist. Technology and technological norms founded upon simple utility and pragmatic reason existed from the beginning. But whereas in early ages of mankind—and even today in large areas of the globe—utilitarian and technological norms lay within sacred contexts (which were the dominant ones and served ends which were ultimately sacred in man's consciousness), technological norms today have nearly complete autonomy. A product of technology—whether a can opener, a mission to the moon, or such a bureaucracy as the Pentagon—becomes, increasingly, its own reason for existence.

For a long time technological norms were not autonomous. Even after the decline of the sacred had begun in Western society, after the advent of critical rationalism and empiricism in the seventeenth century, and along with this the birth of modern science, technology continued to serve ends other than its own. It served, and found its essential support in, the contexts of politics—the needs of kings and governments for technological devices that would expand power and influence in the world. In the eighteenth century technology began to serve the needs of industry on a scale never before known. Out of this came the modern industrial system. But it is a prime characteristic of what is today widely called "the postindustrial" age that the imperatives of technology require no other justification but themselves. And, as I have stressed, technology is as much present in the desires of parents to rear their children according to "the book" as it is in the electronic computer.

In more and more sectors of our own society and in more and more areas of the world the sacred mores tend to be replaced by what the sociologist Howard Odum called "technicways." We see this replacement in the whole area of agriculture. Scientific principles of genetics, fertilization, and crop production generally are driving out ways of cultivation which for countless generations have rested upon tradition and, frequently, upon invocation of the sacred against the ever-present uncertainties of life: plagues, pestilences, droughts, and so on. But the rationalization of agriculture is only one of the many spheres of human life which have become, in Weber's term, "disenchanted." There is, moreover, a high degree of interrelationship of these spheres in many instances. Thus, the advent of the agricultural technologist with his manifestly superior norms and techniques for crop cultivation cannot help but dislocate various social roles and social statuses which were organized traditionally around a different set of norms. These were norms which the tribal chief, the caste or kindred elder, the household father himself, directly represented in an authority relationship. New spheres of authority—and with them spheres of prestige and wealth—follow from the introduction of technicways and the under-

mining of traditional folkways. Such conflict of norms is widely evident
in the non-Western areas of the world today which have come under the
Western forms of technology within the past half-century and more.
The old norms persist in attenuated form, and the new, technological
norms have not yet attained full dominance. The result is often the
kind of *anomie* (normlessness) which we shall deal with in the next
chapter.

The conflict of traditional folkways and new technicways is, of
course, a clear feature of our own society. The past lives on with us
too. Some of the problems of the modern conjugal family are the
result of the disenchantment which Weber applied to European culture as a whole. For the family too has been quite extensively rationalized, and in ways that differ little from those in which industry,
government, professions, school, and church have been rationalized.
The impress of science and technology upon the several roles forming
the family is evident in the ever-greater individualization of these roles,
and the ever-greater autonomy each role possesses as the result of such
technological intrusions as scientific baby and child rearing, the automobile, radio, and television, forms of birth control, labor-saving
devices around the home, dependence increasingly upon specialists
for crucial advice in family matters, and so on. It is impossible for
the traditional structure of the family to maintain itself wholly, or for
the traditional authority of the parent to assert itself, when through all
of these and associated technicways, the *traditional functional value*
of the family and of the parent has diminished. Who needs it? A
great deal of contemporary adolescent judgment on the family might be
so expressed.

Inevitably there is in our age a revolt against technology. I say
"inevitably" because along with the functional dominance of technological norms the historic Western emphasis upon the individual has
continued, as (from the eighteenth century on) has the emphasis upon
individual rights, liberties, and equities. The spread of technology is
vividly evidenced by the incessant multiplication of the roles and
statuses which go with its norms. Whose eminence and authority are
greater today in Western culture than the scientist's and the engineer's?
All ages have their culture heroes. Our age, very plainly, gives less
honor and influence to businessmen, artists, household fathers, military
figures, and ordinary governmental officials than it does to the heroes
of technology—the Einsteins, Salks, Tellers, and Kinseys. The status
system of science and technology and the elite formed by those working in the higher reaches of these areas are formidable. Presidents and

congressional committees as well as businessmen have learned this. The prestige that in another age went to the clergyman, the businessman, or the political figure tends to go today to the scientist. In this respect at least, the prophecy of Auguste Comte in the early nineteenth century has proved correct. Comte declared that in the rationally ordered society of the future the scientist would replace the priest. He has very nearly done this.

But, given the continuing emphasis in our society upon the individual and his rights, there is, on an ever-widening front, a revolt against technology and, with it, those who are its exemplars and its teachers. Not strangely, this revolt takes many and sometimes odd forms. We see it in the rise of what has been known as hippie culture, in the spread of drug culture, in the deliberate cultivation of the bizarre, in novel manifestations of religious cults, in veneration of new and occasionally strident forms of sacred consciousness, even within youth groups which have grown up in almost wholly secular environments. Folk masses, black masses, drug masses—these, surely, would not have been considered religious in generations past. But there is abundant precedent in the history of mankind for the present affinity between revolt and the rediscovery of the sacred, in whatever form.

How fundamental and lasting the revolt against technology really is in contemporary Western culture, we cannot be sure. Certainly this revolt has been a cardinal element of much of the art, music, and literature of the past half-century. Art usually precedes social history in this respect. The secularization of Western Europe began in the paintings, sculptures, poems, and dramas of Renaissance creative intellectuals. Plainly, there is much in common today between youth revolts and the literature of disenchantment with technology that began in the nineteenth century. That literature of disenchantment began in the writings of a few romantics and conservatives and more than a few literary figures before the age of technology was well under way.

Given the sheer mass and, in present historical terms, the momentum of technology today, it would be rash to predict its downfall as the consequence of the contemporary revolt of certain intellectuals and militants from the political left. On the other hand, few structures could have seemed more massive than the Christian Church in the Middle Ages. The ideas, values, and culture that emanated from the Church filled almost every crevice and corner in Western society. Only a very rash soul in, say, the thirteenth century would have predicted the day when the Christian Church would be pushed into a relatively small area of the totality of Western culture and its power reduced to but a fraction of its former strength.   On the evidence of history, there is nothing fanciful about the thought of a future age in which technological incentives, styles, frameworks, hierarchies, and imperatives will have retreated to the same background of relative obscurity that other structures, equally imposing in their day, have suffered through the ages.

But that age, if it ever comes, is fairly far distant, it is clear.   In our day technology has no rivals among patterns of norms.   Plainly, we live today in "postindustrial" society.   The essence of the post-industrial scene is the ascendancy of technological imperatives in almost all areas of life, from the scientific rearing of infants to moon flights which excite the imagination of twentieth-century man in somewhat the same manner that the intrepid navigators of England, Spain, and Portugal excited men four centuries ago.   There is no more wonder in the fact that technology can assume priority in the human mind for a long period—irrespective of its costs in economic and spiritual terms—than there is in the fact that religion can assume such priority in other periods and other places.   We find ourselves marveling today at what medieval man would endure in the way of physical discomforts and social inequities—largely because of a belief that what happened on this earth was of infinitely less consequence than what will become of a man in the next world.   From our point of view Christian theology covered a vast number of matters which were in fact economic, political, and social.   Today the technologist is riding in as roughshod a way over the once cherished economic categories of profit, rent, and balanced budgets as the classical economists of the nineteenth century rode over the earlier cherished categories of original sin, grace, and the Godhead.

CONFLICT OF NORMS (POPULATION)

Norms, by their own nature and by the nature of social interaction, frequently conflict within a social order.   There is, plainly, conflict between the norm expressed by the commandment "Thou shalt not kill" and the norm that legitimizes killing in war or when one is a policeman.   Most such conflicts are more latent than manifest, rarely becoming the stuff of human drama or crisis.   As we saw with respect to roles and role conflicts, potentialities of conflict, abstractly viewed, generally resolve themselves in the behavior of most of us through a whole variety of mechanisms for evasion, redefinition, or rationalization.   Not often does either an individual or a social order come squarely before a conflict that can be resolved only by clear abandonment of one of the norms. When such a conflict does occur we are in the presence of one of the crises which periodically seize the life of an individual or the history of a community or nation.

One of the major normative crises confronting mankind as a whole today is that of population increase. There are many who declare frankly that the problem of population increase looms much larger in its possible effects upon civilization than does the threat of nuclear or biological warfare. The latter, by virtue of the almost instantaneous horror it evokes in human imagination, is at least a reasonably simple problem in *ethical* terms. Consensus regarding nuclear war and its threat to human existence is probably as wide as any that can be imagined.

It is different with the problem of population. No one, to be sure, wants the earth to become so laden with human bodies that chronic, mass starvation must be the lot of everyone. But at the same time a large number of people want to avoid violations of the norms they cherish regarding marriage, sexual relationships, freedom to decide the number of children wanted, and family life generally. The norm contained in the familiar Biblical adjuration "be fruitful and multiply" *need not*, and for tens of thousands of years *did not*, conflict with the norm of the good life, the norm of protection of those requiring it, the norm of seeking by all possible means to preserve rather than to destroy life. It is not new for a society to have at one and the same time an ethic that seeks to increase the number of human beings in the community and an ethic that enjoins respect for the preservation of life. What is new is the conflict, the deadly conflict, between these two ethics.

At the present time more than 3.5 billion people are alive. This figure compares with an estimated ½ billion persons in the world in 1650, with approximately 1 billion in 1800, and with but 2 billion in the world as recently as 1930. Obviously the rate of growth of the world's population is rising rapidly. Whereas this rate of increase was 0.44 percent in 1800, 0.64 percent in 1900, and only 0.75 percent as recently as 1930, the rate of population increase at the present time is around 2.25 percent. And this rate of growth is climbing constantly. Even where the actual birth rate shows signs of decreasing, such is the sheer number of persons now alive on earth, and procreating, the rate of increase for the population continues to go up.

At present rates, the world is adding 70 million persons each year, a number equal to the present combined populations of Canada and

Mexico. If present rates of increase were to continue, the world would double in population every 33 years from now on. In a mere two centuries the world would reach a population of 230 billion persons, which is nearly 70 times the total of people now on earth. Continuing the extrapolation to the point of the absurd—but nonetheless grimly eloquent—the sheer physical weight of the earth's population would be greater in another 1,750 years than the earth itself.

Such extrapolations will not become actual. And no one believes they will. Their importance lies solely in illustrating dramatically the nature of present rates of population increase. From the point of view of policy the vital matter is simply *how* the astronomical totals will be averted. Will it be by mass famine, chronic starvation for huge multitudes in the not too distant future, or by nuclear war with its capacity for exterminating immense sections of the population? Or will it be by rational, world-wide policy whereby through deliberate encouragement of intensive birth control in all countries, and especially those where the gulf between population increase and prospective food supply is widest, the horrors of the future are averted with minimum distress?

If the problem concerned only those in future decades, there would perhaps be little to encourage us in the matter, for people are notoriously unmindful of the future. The problem however, is, immediate. For it is precisely in countries where food supply is least and most precarious at the present time that many of the highest rates of population increase are found. Not in the distant future but at this very moment an immense number of children are being born for whom there will be no alternatives (given present policies) to lives of chronic hunger and starvation.

The economics of the present, not the future, illustrate the seriousness of the population problem. The gross national product is the total value of goods produced and services rendered in a given nation. By dividing a nation's GNP by the number of persons living in the nation we arrive at what is called the gross national product per capita (GNP/C). Only 2 nations in the world at this time, the United States and Kuwait (rich in oil deposits), have a GNP/C of more than $3,000. Only 3 nations are above $2,000: Sweden, Switzerland, and Canada. Now let us drop down to the grim lower levels in this ranking of nations. No less than 92 nations in the world—representing an aggregate population of just under 2½ billion, a majority of the peoples on earth—have a per capita gross national product of less than $500.[4]

Further statistics are unnecessary to point up the extraordinary seriousness—some would say the by now hopeless seriousness—of the population problem confronting the world.   The political tensions arising from the kind of imbalance we have just looked at are bound to be great.   The "have-not" nations of the world are in many instances represented by aggressive governments, governments which in the long run are not likely to settle for less than what they consider a greater share of the food and affluence now found in a few nations. The line between "have" nations and "have-not" nations may well be the single most important line that can be drawn today, more important by far than mere ideological lines.

It may well be asked, why not enlarge the food supplies of the impoverished nations through dissemination of agricultural technology from nations like the United States, where this technology has been so successful?   The answer is that this is now being done for many nations in the world.   And food supply is increasing annually in those nations— India being a classic case in point.   The difficulty, however, is that population continues to increase even more rapidly.   For, along with diffusion of agricultural technology to these impoverished countries, there has also been diffusion of public health technology in the forms of sanitary, pesticidal, and disease-preventing techniques that have dramatically lowered the death rates in many of these countries.   Given the modern technology of public health, it is relatively easy to lower death rates in even the most backward countries of the world.   But lowered death rates, when not accompanied by sharply lowered birth rates, can lead to huge increases in population, and in very short periods of time.

At the beginning of the nineteenth century, Thomas Malthus, in one of the most important books ever written in the moral sciences, *An Essay on The Principle of Population*, pointed out the grim balance that must exist between birth rates and death rates.   The "normal" or "natural" tendency of every biological species, man included, Malthus wrote, is to breed to the level of available food supply.   Such is the *potential* fertility of the species that the population of the species will always, unless checked, increase geometrically: 2, 4, 8, 16, 32, and so on.   On the other hand, food supply, by its nature, can increase only in arithmetical terms: 1, 2, 3, 4, and so on.   The inevitable result, Malthus concluded, will always be an incessant pressure of population on food supply that would be mitigated only by "checks"—in the forms of war, catastrophes, disease, for instance—which would keep the death rate high enough to balance what Malthus thought was man's basically unconquerable desire to procreate.

To leave it at this would not be quite fair to Malthus. He was, among other things, a devout Christian clergyman and a first-rate economist. Moreover, he was keenly interested in the welfare of his fellow Englishmen. He was emphatically not, as he is occasionally charged with being, a pawn of capitalist interests, a defender of economic feudalism, and a man without interest in humanitarian legislation. But as a ˉChristian of his time, Malthus did not approve the use of artificial checks on births—that is, contraceptives—and as an economist he was profoundly interested in keeping the relation close between the family and the economic system, which he thought would not remain prosperous for long without the incentives to work and gain which are nurtured in the family.

It was in this light, therefore, that Malthus suggested another kind of check on the birth rate—that which he summarized under the words "continence" and "prudence." *If* through a strong morality men remained continent before marriage, and *if* marriage were postponed by every man until he had reached an age where his job would support a family, there was considerable likelihood, Malthus thought (especially in later editions of his *Essay*), that the grim struggle between birth rates and death rates could be averted. Mankind would not forever have to depend solely upon the negative checks of war, catastrophe, and disease for maintenance of the balance between births and deaths. But, it must be emphasized, at no point in his life did Malthus ever condone the use of artificial birth controls. As an Anglican moralist, he believed (as does the official Roman Catholic Church today) that use of contraceptives would debase the function of marriage and be an invitation to gross sexual immorality outside the bonds of marriage. (It is ironic to realize that for many years Malthusianism or neo-Malthusianism was to become the name of those movements that sought to spread information on use of contraceptives.)

The fact that birth rates began to decline sharply in the nineteenth century in Western European countries and that population growth rates for a considerable time suggested actual *decline* in size of European populations in the long run, persuaded many that Malthus was not merely dismal but foolish in his conclusions. But he was not. Taking his theory *as he presented it*, a theory of the "normal" or "natural" growth of population, it is close to unchallengeable. "Normally," no doubt, populations would indeed breed geometrically, with misery the only possible check upon them. Let it be remembered that Malthus was not the only social philosopher or scientist of his day interested in the normal. Many studies in economics, political science, and anthropology were founded upon the view that the task of science is the uncovering of man's allegedly normal or natural ways.

Where Malthus—and many other economists—went wrong was in failure to realize the power of *social and cultural norms*. Man does not live simply as a biological being in a physical environment. He is, as we have seen, a social being living in a social environment, an environment in which norms can be so powerful as to not only offset man's biological nature—or his potentialities—but also affect the way in which the physical environment is perceived and, hence, lived in.

Humanitarian legislation, improvements in amount and kind of food, and control of disease all lowered the death rates substantially in Western countries in the nineteenth century. But accompanying this reduction of death rates was a sharp decrease in birth rates as the desire to live a reasonably comfortable and civilized life moderated the desire to have children. A changed economic structure gradually made a large number of children unnecessary as the means of maintaining family livelihood and providing security for parents in their old age. New interests, diversions, ambitions, all normatively expressed, vied with the ancient norm of family fertility and, through birth control, a reasonable equilibrium of births and deaths in Western European populations was maintained.

That apparent equilibrium was not to last, unhappily, as we have learned, in Western countries. For man's scientific control of environment has been such that death rates have gone steadily downward. Even though the long-run tendency of birth rates in the West (and other countries in the world too) has also been downward, their decline has not been as sharp as that of death rates. In Western countries, for the most part, the increase in size of populations has been containable, *at least on the average*, through constantly expanding capacity for food production. (But no one should be blind to sizable pockets of poverty in the United States and the West generally that are directly related to high birth rates coupled with low economic productivity.) There are, to be sure, other problems caused by present and anticipated size of population. These include pollution of land, water, and air, which we have thus far shown no ability to handle. Our problems stemming from size of population are minor, however, by comparison with those of that large percentage of countries referred to above. In these countries, not merely social and cultural degradation but sheer hunger, malnutrition, and physical distress are an increasingly common condition, which their governments cannot cope with at present. And, as is only too evident, these are problems which can be translated into political-military expressions capable of affecting the entire world.

Let us return to what I called the normative basis of the population problem in the contemporary world. The population explosion is not an iron consequence of man's reproductive capacity. It is not correct to say, as Malthus implied, that there *must* be incessant pressure of population on food supply. The cause of the population explosion is basically *a conflict between two central and sacred norms in man's life*: the norm which enjoins us to propagate our kind and the norm which enjoins us to save life at all costs. Both are ancient norms. Only in our age, however, has the advance of knowledge and of control of physical environment led to dire conflict between them.

From the beginning of mankind it may fairly be assumed that concern with balance of births and deaths was present. It required no great knowledge or insight to see the almost immediately dire consequences of too many mouths for the supply of food that could be anticipated. When necessary, there were ways of reducing the number of these mouths. These included infanticide; exposure of the sick, infirm, or crippled to die; and abandonment of the very aged. Such practices were among the ways open to man from earliest times. But these deliberate means of elimination were not usually necessary. For such was the normal toll of death from natural causes that the problem was often one of making sure there were *enough* people. Until the present century the vast majority of human beings born died at, or shortly after, birth. Those who survived infancy faced, as we know, a variety of potentially fatal diseases, not to mention disasters of all kinds.

Hence the *normative basis* of the high birth rates that for thousands and thousands of years were absolutely necessary to ordinary human survival. Because of the precariousness of life, the death at infancy of the great majority of persons born, and the incessant exposure to the possibility of death, it was inevitable that a very heavy premium would be placed on procreation. There is no society known, past or present, in which a high degree of approval, through ritual and other forms of thanksgiving, is not found in connection with human birth, particularly the birth of sons. For in the son lay the possibility not merely of continuing the all-important name and identity of the family but of being both warrior and provider to his community. In one form or another the Old Testament adjuration to "be fruitful and multiply" is found everywhere among primitive and ancient peoples. To the present moment the announcement of the birth of a child is the common occasion of rejoicing, congratulation, and thanksgiving. Today, if we look at the matter statistically, the news of the birth of yet another child might better be the occasion of sorrow—or at the very least the reading of a pamphlet on the population crisis in the world and on the subject of birth control. But because of early man's absolute need for as many children to be born as possible—a need continuing in all societies on earth until but a century ago—the birth of a child became symbolized by one of the most powerful and sacred norms to be found anywhere in human society.

The sacred-normative character of birth transferred itself, of course, to all relationships and acts in any way related. From earliest times the normative position of the parent, especially the father, was very high. The status of the patriarch with the most children—and grandchildren and great grandchildren—was particularly high. Such was the sense of primitive man's indebtedness to the mother who bore the child (an indebtedness often heightened by ignorance of the father's role in conception) that, as noted above, there is some reason for supposing that matriarchal and matrilineal systems are older than patriarchal and patrilineal systems. In any event, many of the world's religions have given a featured place to the female, to the Great Mother. And the symbolic prestige of the father and mother—arising in the first place from their fertility—was conveyed to all manner of other relationships and associations in society, as for example, in churches where the terms "father" and "mother" are widely used.

Marriage was also made a sacred norm of society from earliest times. So important was procreation that the union of man and wife had to be effected in ways that would do reverence to the gods. The very purpose of marriage was held to be procreation, not, surely, mere companionship or sexual enjoyment. Marriages that went childless were widely referred to as "unblessed." And these are conceptions of marriage that prevail in many parts of the world and in many religious circles within our own society down to the present. A whole mythology has been built around the relation of marriage to motherhood and fatherhood, one that extends itself into much psychology and family counseling. The sacredness of marriage arose from its relation to mankind's survival need of high birth rates, and it became strengthened, of course, by the key position the family unit held to so many activities and institutions in society. As a result, marriage became a major element in most of the world's religions. Hence the ancient and still widespread abhorrence of divorce. In times and places where human communities badly needed children for the adults they would become, a broken marriage had implications only too obvious. This is not to suggest, of course, that divorce was unknown in ancient societies or is unknown among primitive peoples today. Divorce rates among the latter can be very high. But so are the rates of remarriage or remating. And among the ancient peoples of the West divorce was not easily come by, for among pagan as well as Christian communities the belief was strong that marriage was sacred and too important to be subject to the wills of the participant individuals.

There is no need to expand further on the normative basis of the population problem. The essential point is that whereas, through extraordinary reduction in death rates during the past century, large numbers of people remain alive who once would have died in infancy, there is still a profound tendency for birth norms to remain ascendant. The norms which continue to encourage births and the norms which, on the basis of combined technology and humanitarianism, lead to sharp reduction of the death rate are in conflict. Even in the relatively prosperous United States there is a very substantial problem created by this conflict in norms. The birth rate in the United States has been declining ever since 1800 (with the single exception of the two decades immediately following World War II, but death rates have been declining *more* rapidly.

This situation continues to be the case, with consequences measured in terms of giant cities which we have not yet learned how to govern adequately; of ever more dangerous congestion of people on highways and in airlanes; in industrial pollution of air, water, and landscape; and countless other conditions ranging from the physical to the cultural and psychological. By comparison with countries in Asia and Latin America, our population problem is minor, for it affects standard of living rather than subsistence itself. But given the commitment of contemporary Americans and their political governments to this standard of living—its incessant increase indeed—it would be dangerous to underestimate the problem. What is called the "revolution of rising expectations" is nowhere more vivid than in the United States. High as is the average standard of living, there are notable differences in standard of living. *Relative* poverty in a generally affluent population can be more galling and more likely to engender revolution than the absolute poverty found in so many parts of Asia, Africa, and Latin America. Continued imbalance between death rates and birth rates in the United States can only aggravate our political as well as technological problems of control. Whether the norm of sanctity of human life as we have known it for some centuries in the West can survive the sheer piling up of human beings now taking place in many American cities and suburbs remains as yet undetermined. On the evidence of history, life is nowhere held so cheaply as in areas of high population density. The norms of freedom, equity, compassion, and reason in the West came into being at a time when population survival alone dictated a high regard for human life. Whether these and related norms can long remain ascendant when the problem before governments is one of reducing the amount of human life on earth is highly questionable.

What the future holds with respect to population increase is not easily foreseeable. It is easy enough to extrapolate present rates—as we did in the first pages of this section—and, as I noted, this is not a bad idea since it has the effect of dramatizing *present* problems. There are those among population experts—and they are probably slightly in the majority—who see the population crisis continuing into the twenty-first century and beyond, with ever more appalling consequences. There are others, however, who take much comfort from evidence of changes now taking place in the norms supporting high birth rates. The latter experts are impressed by growing preference in almost all countries for small families, by the widening acceptance by national governments of the necessity of firm policy in this respect, by constantly improved means of easy and cheap birth control, by the spread of technology and industry to other parts of the world (and with this spread the inculcation of middle-class and professional norms regarding family size), and, finally, by the possibility of a leveling-off of our capacity to reduce death rates.

Whether the twenty-first century will witness a population crisis beyond present capacity to imagine it or whether instead this crisis will be looked back on as an essentially twentieth-century affair is impossible to foresee. Our marvels of computer technology can advance us in space but not in time. All we can do is extrapolate rates in terms of present intensity and presently imaginable likelihood. It is enough if we limit ourselves to the immense damage already done by birth rates that have so vastly exceeded death rates in the present century. Irrespective of what the twenty-first century holds, this damage can only become greater and greater within our own century. There are already enough people and enough instances of mass hunger and degradation to make that virtually certain for some time.

Notes

1. Kingsley Davis, *Human Society* (New York: Macmillan, 1948), p. 53.
2. Emile Durkheim, *The Elementary Forms of Religious Life* (London: G. Allen & Unwin, 1915), p. 416.
3. *Ibid.*, p. 417.
4. These figures are drawn from the 1969 World Population Data Sheet published each year by the Population Reference Bureau, Washington, D.C.

10

Social Entropy

ENTROPY AND SOCIAL BEHAVIOR

In this chapter we shall explore certain forms of behavior—found in every society to some degree—known variously as *alienation, anomie,* and *deviance.* The three forms, as will be emphasized, are different from one another and must be kept conceptually distinct. All alike, however, refer to types of behavior that fail, for reasons still only partially understood in modern sociology, to meet the ordinary prescriptions that we find in the systems of authority and the roles, statuses, and norms which together form a social order and which most of us tend to follow most of the time.

From the point of view of an abstract sociological model, the "perfect" society would be one in which all social behavior was a mirror image of the norms, roles, and statuses which we pinpoint when we are concerned with describing a given social order. We need not emphasize the point that such a perfect society is never found in the annals of human history. Behavior patterns of divergence from these elements are always discerned. Usually the divergence is minor and intermittent, tending to be offset by the larger and more continuous patterns of conformity. At times, however, during critical periods of history, the divergences in a given sphere outweigh the conformities. Change is the consequence. We shall defer explicit consideration of social change until the next chapter, for it necessarily involves factors other than those which can be summarized under the headings of alienation, anomie, and deviance. True, these modes of behavior are inevitably more profuse in periods of change. But the important point here is that, *first*, by themselves they are not sufficient to generate change in a social order and, *second*, the behavior divergences we call alienation, anomie, and deviance are found in all forms of society, at all times, even though their intensity fluctuates rather widely. However stable and uniform a social order may appear to the casual glance—and this applies to primitive as well as more complex societies—careful observation will always reveal these divergences.

We shall deal with these modes of behavior as manifestations of *entropy*. I have borrowed the word from physics, where it denotes the amount of energy that is, so to speak, unavailable for work during a given natural process. The third law of thermodynamics states that every substance has a definite entropy (availability of energy to do work) that approaches zero as the temperature approaches absolute zero. As the energy becomes unavailable the entropy is said to increase. The gifted philosopher-historian Brooks Adams applied the concept of entropy to human affairs. For Adams, however, the concept was used to describe a tendency he thought he could see in the history of whole nations or civilizations, a tendency characterized by elements of decay, of a running-down of human energy, of a diminishing capacity for meeting the problems set by that nation or civilization. It was in this sense that Brooks Adams (and also his brother Henry) used the concept of entropy—not precisely perhaps, but suggestively.

Our own concern here is not with what may or may not be discerned in the histories of nations and civilizations. We are interested in concrete forms of behavior as these are to be found in any society during any age of its history in one degree or another. These are the types we call, as I have suggested, alienation, anomie, and deviance. All three can be seen as withholdings or cross uses or deviant manifestations of the human energies that normally go into support or fulfillment of the norms, roles, and statuses that make up a social order. In the aggregate, these manifestations form the social entropy that is an aspect of every form of human behavior.

There is no lack of other words to describe the forms of behavior I have in mind. "Immoral" is one of the oldest and still most common. Closely related are "bad," "evil," and "wicked" and other terms of sacred connotation. All refer to behavior that diverges in some way from what is deemed proper in a social organization. Such terms have their value, but it is not sociological or scientific value. The reasons are obvious.

There are also many secular words to describe these forms of behavior. One of the oldest is "unnatural." As we noted in the preceding chapter, ever since the Greek philosophers, there has been an effort to identify those norms and ways of behavior which are "natural" rather than "artificial," those embedded in man's nature rather than deriving simply from the social and cultural order he happens to have been born in. Corresponding to this effort has been the pronouncement of certain modes of behavior that conflict with one's conception of the natural as being unnatural. The social philosophy of the eighteenth century was rich in references to institutions and practices as being unnatural and therefore in need of extinction or reform. The word "unnatural" has even today a currency in many statutes, chiefly those pertaining to sexual behavior. But from the point of view of an objective social science, it is no more possible to declare some practices natural and some unnatural than to declare some moral and some immoral.

In the field of sociology two other words are found which, until very recently, were widely used. The first is "pathological," the second "disorganized." The first comes directly from biology or physiology where it has clear and uncontested utility. Long experience with and close observation of organic types leaves little room for doubt as to which are "normal" and which are "pathological." Such is our acquaintance with the lung or heart as it normally is constituted and normally functions that even a beginning student of physiology can easily tell whether one of these organs is normal or pathological. The world of institutions, social groups, and norms, however, is very different. What is normal? What is pathological? Before some social act is declared pathological, it is always necessary to declare, implicitly in any event, what social acts are normal to human beings. And this, as the preceding chapter made evident, is quite impossible once we lift our eyes from the time and culture in which we live to other times and other cultures. As the late C. Wright Mills pointed out in an influential essay a generation ago, the word "pathological" was once applied widely by social workers in this country to ways of behavior in ethnic and religious minorities—Catholic, Jewish, Italian, Polish, Negro, or working-class groups, for instance—on the sole ground of the difference in these ways of behavior from the norms of middle-class, Protestant, white America. The main reason, however, for eschewing the word "pathological" is that we have no way of declaring any given form of behavior categorically "physiological" or normal. There is too much diversity and change in human society.

The word "disorganization" is really no better. This too is a word widely used for describing behavior that runs counter to a majority-approved set of norms. Sociologists used to declare delinquency, crime, prostitution, narcotics addiction, alcoholism, and other social problems of American society to be manifestations of social disorganization. The prevailing assumption was that only through the breakdown of groups such as family, neighborhood, and local community could forms of behavior such as these come into existence. Or because of some directive idea or dream in an individual observer's mind of an ideal social order, an entire society or age of history could be declared "disorganized." But the word "disorganization" is at once too wide and too narrow for what is actually involved in social problems. It is too wide because disorganization, in at least some sense of the word, is what much of human history— and also human betterment—is about. Behind the appearance of the structurally new in history—the nation-state, for example, or democracy, or the labor union—may well lie the disorganization and eventual disappearance of a preceding form of organization. But the word is also too narrow as applied to most social problems, because far more than disorganization is usually involved. There may indeed be no disorganization at all, in any empirical sense of the term, behind the rise of delinquent, criminal, or other problem behavior. The essence of the problem may, and often does, lie in *organization* rather than disorganization— organization so rigid and encompassing that the individual may be driven to some more attractive group or community of interest. There is the further fact that a great deal of so-called disorganization in society is anything but that. Consider only the vast number of crimes in this country. One would be hard put to find more expertly formed organizations than those which contain the numbers racket, off-track betting, the peddling of narcotics, prostitution, and the like.

There is, finally, the word "sick." No qualified social scientist would use this word with respect to a given type of society, social system, or form of social behavior—not in scientific discourse at least. But one need only pick up the latest newspaper, magazine, or best-selling book, whether novel or social tract, to see the immense appeal the word has for large elements of the public at the present time. Whether from the political left or right, the word "sick" together with terms of a similar nature—"tumor," "cancer," and so on—mark a good many appraisals of the contemporary scene. Of these words, however, we can say what was said just above with respect to "pathological." Such words are purely metaphoric. To be sure, metaphor has its rightful place in human knowledge and understanding, but it cannot substitute for empirical analysis. Despite the undoubted polemical value of such a phrase as "sick society," there is in fact no entity to correspond to it—

anymore than there is to be found a "virtuous" spleen or a "wicked" appendix in the human body.

Having rejected a few timeworn phrases, let us now turn to the forms of behavior which underlie the phrases. Of the reality of the forms of behavior there is no doubt whatever. One does not have to be committed to a single pattern of social values to be made aware of behavior that fails to meet the specifications that lie implicit in all roles and statuses in society and are inseparable from the norms in social behavior. We have seen that no concrete form of human behavior ever meets the specifications of norms, roles, and statuses exactly. There is always some degree of divergence, however slight it may be. But recognizing this we are forced to recognize also the existence of forms of behavior which diverge significantly enough from role, status, and norm specifications to be noted not only by others but by the individuals directly involved. There are, as we have said, three main types of this divergence —alienation, anomie, and deviance.

ALIENATION

Alienated behavior is characterized by *withdrawal*. It is a mistake to confuse it with behavior that is antagonistic and that expresses itself through social protest and action. This is unfortunately a very common confusion in sociological writing. Failure to make the clear distinction between alienation and social protest does much disservice to each. Social protest, resulting in social reform and revolution, forms one of the richest and most creative chapters in the history of civilization. It reflects a mobilization and channeling of energies toward specific ideals and goals, in the process of which acts destructive of the existing order are frequently required. "Alienated" is hardly the word to describe the leaders of the English, American and French Revolutions in the seventeenth and eighteenth centuries, or the Bolsheviks who took over the Russian government in 1917, or for any of the long line of reformers to be found in Western history from Solon to Franklin D. Roosevelt. Social protest, revolt, activism, or revolution is conspicuously *committed* behavior, as committed in its way as the behavior of those who choose to defend rather than attack a social order.

Most conspicuous in alienated behavior is precisely its lack of commitment to norms and roles—*any* norms and roles. Alienated behavior is a form of withdrawal of energy from social ends and purposes. It occurs when individuals believe themselves powerless to influence their own lives or the lives of others or when the ends of a social order, or its forms of relationship, seem hopelessly remote, alien, or meaningless. It is not only the generally accepted and "official" ends in the social order that take on this appearance to the alienated. Even those ends and objectives that are found in protest, reform, or revolutionary movements seem impossible to achieve and meaningless to the genuinely alienated.

Alienated behavior is found in all institutional spheres: in family, church, neighborhood and school, as well as in the economic, technological, and political sectors. There are alienated children and parents within the kinship system: individuals whose behavior reveals substantial and continuing withdrawal from the patterns of family life. We see this withdrawal in children whose alienation is often confused with mental retardation and in mothers whose passivity and indifference reach the proportions of nearly total withdrawal from ordinary role responsibilities. There are similarly alienated students in school and college. These, let it be noted again, are not the ones vigorously concerned, active, and committed to reform. They are the ones—among them some chronic drug users and members of bizarre cults—who have, as they say, "copped out," become "turned off," that is, who have withdrawn into highly privatized spheres as the result of finding conventional education alien and meaningless. There is no institutional area without its manifestations of alienation.

Sometimes alienated behavior is specific; it is limited to a single institutional area in the individual's life. Sometimes, however, it is generalized. In this case the individual who is alienated in family, or in school or college, is alienated in other spheres of life as well. All norms, all roles, including those involved in reformist or revolutionary action, then come to seem futile, meaningless, or beyond one's power. Here a generalized, endemic, or "free-floating," alienation is to be found. Most alienation is probably of the more specific type. Sometimes the alienation of behavior in one sphere is the condition of one's turning altogether from that sphere to another, seeking compensatory fulfillment in the latter. The history of religion is marked by instances in which those who have become alienated from their social order, including efforts to change it, become profoundly absorbed by the ends of religion. The lives of mystics and saints are frequently founded on this type of alienation. Politics as well as religion, however, can provide a refuge for those alienated in other spheres of life. What Eric Hoffer calls the "true believer" in politics is a person for whom politics and political action have less to do with actual political ends than with relief from the pains of estrangement from community or self. The not uncommon phenomenon in history of individuals passing suddenly from an authoritarian politics to an authoritarian religion—or vice versa—reveals something about a tendency toward alienation in such individuals. It is important, however, not to make the mistake of placing all religious or political behavior, however intense and committed it may be, in this category. The fact that the political career of Adolf Hitler fairly clearly had behind it a rather generalized alienation from family, community, and the social order in general, with politics a form of personal, even messianic fulfillment, does not mean that this situation necessarily holds for other and equally explosive political figures in history.

Much has been written about the alienation of the artist and the intellectual, but most of this is nonsense. A study of the lives of the greatest painters, musical composers, dramatists, and philosophers does not bear out the view of some kind of inspiriting alienation behind their works. The profoundly *non*alienated lives of Michelangelo, Johann Sebastian Bach, Shakespeare, Goethe, Beethoven, and Immanuel Kant —not to mention the lives of the greatest scientists—would suggest that alienation need not be involved in creativity even at the highest reaches. And yet it is probably true that more alienation tends to exist within the broad category we call "intellectuals" than, for example, within the categories of automobile mechanics, carpenters, or even lawyers and physicians. Shakespeare's words "sicklied o'er with the pale cast of thought" may suggest a part of the reason.

Some degree of alienation will be found no doubt within every sphere of social activity at all times. It is hard to imagine the kinship system, the economy, or the political order, anywhere at any time, in which at least a few persons could not be found manifesting that kind of withdrawal of energy we call alienation. But, quite clearly, ages of history and societies vary considerably in the amounts of alienated behavior found within them. If this were not the case, much of what we have found to be true above with respect to the nature of roles, statuses, social aggregates, and systems of authority would be pointless. For, as was emphasized, each of these aspects of behavior is subject to change in time, to dislocation that is occasionally catastrophic. Then processes of social interaction do not go along as smoothly as at other times; roles and statuses do not lend themselves to as easy and unquestioned mastery by individuals as at other times. There is little doubt that there are ages of profound social change in human history in which, along with high amounts of human creativity, high amounts of alienation, whether specific or generalized, are also found. We live, as has been frequently emphasized in this book, through our

ordinary capacity to effect a "definition of the situation." Such "definition" can be extremely difficult during periods of convulsive change and
seeming disorder. Withdrawal, estrangement, or alienation, whatever
we call it, is the common result.

Such an age, manifestly, is our own. From the beginning of the
nineteenth century, when the two great revolutions (industrial and
democratic) began to reorder social roles, statuses, and social norms
and to challenge traditional systems of authority and community,
alienation has doubtless been a more common experience in the West
than it had been earlier. To say this is to make a comparison. But
it is not to suggest that earlier ages, even the medieval age, were lacking in alienated behavior. Failure to make distinctions here, however,
would be as absurd as failure to make them with respect to the varying degrees of order and change we find in history.

When we recognize the high rates of change and dislcoation, and
with these the higher rates of alienation, it is hardly strange that alienation should have become a major perspective of social, as well as
humanistic, thought during the nineteenth century. Such was the
impact of the two revolutions—and much that went with them culturally and psychologically—on the minds of such writers as Jacob
Burckhardt, Tocqueville, and Nietzsche that we find a more or less
generalized alienation in their assessments of the distinctive qualities
of modern civilization in the West and also in their prophecies of the
future of the West. Some of this generalized alienation is to be found
in the first modern sociologists: Weber, Durkheim, and Simmel. In
all of them there is a sense, or premonition, of the alienative effects of
modern large-scale democracy, of industrialism, technology, and bureaucracy upon human personality. In his early writings, Karl Marx
had declared capitalism, with its foundation in private property and
profit, to be responsible for man's alienation from himself and from the
social order. Marx thought that the abolition of private property and
profit would lead to the abolition of alienation. However, most intellectuals today would not agree with Marx. They argue that it is
technology and bureaucracy, and not the specific form of ownership of
property, that leads modern man to feel that society is remote and inac-
cessible with the individual estranged and helpless. In this, contemporary intellectuals are closer to the writings of Tocqueville, Weber,
and Simmel than to those of Marx.

Sociology's interest in alienation at the present time draws from
the perspectives of these major figures, including Marx; but today sociology is more selective and empirical. The role of the industrial

worker has been studied extensively in an attempt to discover the degree to which alienation is a part of the factory and office today.   In
a pioneering study of the effects of the assembly line and continuous-
process technology on workers, Elton Mayo and his colleagues came to
the conclusion nearly forty years ago that this type of production is
inherently alienative to workers because it eliminates contexts of
social interaction.   Only when production is combined with interaction,
Mayo and his colleagues concluded, will the toll of the assembly line
and of what is today called continuous-process technology be significantly reduced.

It is important to bear in mind that only a small percentage of
American workers are actually involved in assembly lines and continuous-process technology.   In the great majority of jobs, blue-collar
included, there is in the very nature of the work more human interaction than can be the case in the sort of work Mayo studied in the
Hawthorne plant of General Electric in the 1920s and 1930s.   Moreover, many adjustments of a human-relations kind have been made even
in the factories organized around the assembly line—adjustments in
which employees, to some extent at least, work in small interactive
groups rather than as isolated individuals.

The conclusion, often formulated in Marxian terms, that either
capitalism as such or industrialism generally *must* lead to worker
alienation would be erroneous.   Robert Blauner, who has made perhaps the most comprehensive study of the matter in contemporary industry, finds great variations among workers by industry and by nature
of the job done within an industry.   In few if any industries can a
majority of workers be found whose sense of powerlessness over themselves in their work or feeling of isolation from others reaches the level
of what we could justifiably call alienation.   And yet there remains,
as Blauner has emphasized,[1] a sizable number of American workers
whose reactions to their jobs certainly come close to alienation in the
strict sense of the word.   These workers see little opportunity to rise
in their craft, have little sense of controlling the conditions under which
they work, take little or no pleasure in their work, feel alien to its
significance, and, admittedly, would not work if economic necessity did
not compel them to do so.

Blauner observes that the reactions of workers to their jobs vary
substantially from industry to industry today.   Thus, on the basis of a
1947 Roper survey for *Fortune*, Blauner finds that 79 percent of the
workers in the chemical industry believe their work leads to recognition
through promotion.   The percentage in this respect is above 50 in other

industries such as oil refining, furniture, transportation equipment, and paper. At the bottom, however, were workers in the leather industry, only 28 percent of whom seemingly felt that their work was of a character that could lead to promotion. Other industries that fell below the 50 percent line in this respect were automobiles, textiles, iron and steel, and apparel.

Industrial alienation is by no means, then, the common state of workers at the present time. Much variation exists from industry to industry and, one may fairly conclude, from plant to plant within a given industry. A great deal depends upon the social context of work, upon the degree to which significant social interaction takes place among workers and between workers and management. There are few if any forms of industrial work so intrinsically onerous, so alienative, that the *social* context is not the decisive element. Only when a process has been converted to a rigorous assembly-line type of job, with the worker made almost literally an appendage to the machine, are attitudes of withdrawal, of apathetic resignation, likely to be much more common than in industries where technology has not taken the form of the assembly line.

One must be cautious therefore in declaring technology as such the cause of worker alienation. The same holds true of automation, which is but a more advanced form of technology. Automation will almost certainly increase the amount of alienation among workers *if* it reduces the work process to a mere assembly-line system. But, as the evidence of the present certifies, automation in industry *need not* lead to the assembly line, with the worker reduced to coglike status and cut off from interaction with other workers, as well as from a sense of control in what he does. The chemical industry is highly automated, but the evidence suggests little worker alienation.

There are intellectuals in our time who believe that technology as such is alienative in its impact. They argue that because the very nature of the machine is to absorb strength, skill, and even thinking processes which lie normally in man, the effect of technology is to degrade man, to alienate him from human fellowship and from his own nature. Hence, as we saw in the final section of the preceding chapter, the revolt against technology in our day. Careful thought would suggest, however, that there are bound to be as many situations in which technology—including the computer—enhances man's sense of power over environment and of achievement by his own standards as there are situations of reverse kind. The flight of Apollo 12 to the moon has recently been concluded successfully. A vast number of individuals, at all degrees of skill, are involved in making the Apollo flights successful. Although there are no studies to rely on, any sociologist would be justified in predicting extremely low rates of alienation throughout the huge enterprise responsible for the flights. And nowhere in the economic world today is technology more ascendant than here. Despite the laments and lucubrations of some intellectuals, there would not appear to be anything inherently alienative in the machine as such. What matters are the social contexts in which we find the machine.

Let us pass to political alienation, which is also likely to be more prevalent today than at certain other times in history. I am referring to the sense of remoteness or inaccessibility of the authorities by which one's life is governed, the degree of effective meaning one finds in these authorities, and the sense of powerlessness and lack of participation one may feel with respect to these authorities. Bear in mind that in politics, as in all other spheres of interactive behavior, the "actual" situation may be much less important than how the situation is defined by the individual. Democratic values create *expectations*, an important reason why they are always potentially revolutionary in character. When there is a gulf between actuality as it is perceived and the values one has somehow acquired, the likelihood of frustration, of protest and revolt, or of political alienation is greatly increased. It is the *relative*, not the absolute, deprivations that are important. Very probably little in the way of political alienation existed among subjects of the divine-right monarchies of the seventeenth century in Europe. A whole network of traditions and intermediate authorities contained individual lives, and there was, obviously, nothing in the idea of divine-right monarchy to encourage expectations of political rights and participation by the subjects of the monarchies. *Absolute* deprivation, by our standards, was great. *Relative* deprivation, however, is the kind that is most likely to generate protest—or lead to alienation. We shall return to this point in the next section of the chapter, for it is at the heart of the condition we call anomie.

Again it is important to stress the distinction between protest or revolt on the one hand and what is properly called political alienation. The former is characterized by commitment and mobilization of human energies. The latter is characterized by withdrawal, estrangement, and by the seeming dissipation of energies. In our time we can see both states vividly in the whole spectrum of Negro behavior, which ranges from articulate and powerful protest at one extreme to sheer hopelessness and passivity at the other. Despite a common stereotype which sees all Negroes as potentially revolt-minded, the evidence of repeated study suggests that a considerable number—the exact percentage is inevitably difficult to reach—are so far sunk in a condition of alienation, of hopelessness and feelings of powerlessness, as to make political action of any kind highly unlikely. With the genuinely politically alienated, not only does it seem impossible that the "establishment" can be made responsive to needs, but that no political action of any kind can be effective.

There seems to be a high correlation between the incidence of political alienation and the depth and extent of what we have already referred to as mass society. The mass, as will be recalled, is the aggregate that is largely lacking in internal or intermediate social bonds, that is amenable only, as Simmel pointed out, to ideas and impulses of the simplest kind and that therefore contains a good deal of relative anonymity. The mass as such, let it be remembered, is neither good nor bad. Neither is mass society as a whole. There is, after all, something to be said for the kind of individual autonomy and freedom which are found in greater degree in mass society than in, for example, folk society. And the evidence suggests that many of the more extreme kinds of prejudice and bigotry are less evident in mass society than in those types of social order where deep prejudices and bigotries are cemented into a culture by the very strength of the small social units within which they are found. As we have had frequent occasion to be reminded, there is nothing inherently good or bad in either small or large groups. The small, communal, deeply committed, and cohesive group that is based upon roles and statuses clearly understood and readily accessible, and values easily assimilated, may be a force for either good or evil, as we define human purposes. It may be a mutual aid group dedicated to pacifism and the uplift of the fallen in society; or it may be a conspiratorial, criminal, or terroristic organization.

Political alienation among some individuals is an inescapable element of mass society. All that gives individuals generally feelings of separateness, relative autonomy, social freedom, and anonymity is bound to give at least a few individuals the further feelings of isolation, of boredom, of being cut off from participation, or of the remoteness and meaninglessness of the political order. There is a sense in which personal freedom and personal alienation are simply two sides of the same coin. It would be strange indeed if mass society with its large number of huge, impersonal, highly rationalized organizations, its prevailing tendencies toward what we called "segmented" role behavior, and its only intermittent or scattered groups that combine smallness with genuine cultural significance should not be rather high in political alienation. Everything we have found to be true of the dependence of personality upon social interaction would make this conclusion a necessary one. It is, of course, wrong to infer that in mass society all individuals, or heavy majorities, are alienated politically. Some writers have drawn this inference, but there is little empirical evidence to support it. As Durkheim made lastingly clear, alienation, in the sociological sense of the word, exists only where certain conditions are present and where these conditions are concrete and capable of reasonably precise statement. We are justified in saying—in *predicting*—that a higher incidence of alienated political behavior is to be found in mass societies than in, for example, the kind of society that contained the old New England town meeting. But we are no more justified in predicting or declaring that all individuals are likely to be found alienated in mass society than we would be in predicting suicide for all individuals. The behavior of a very large number of politically committed Democrats and Republicans—and also Socialists, Prohibitionists, and quasi-totalitarian party members—suggests that alienation is hardly the word for their labors.

As noted above, alienated behavior is to be found in every institutional area. It may be as common—though much less studied thus far —in churches as in economies and polities. Nor, apparently, is any age altogether spared alienation. The records of medieval monasteries and convents leave no doubt that alienation (it was then termed *acedia*) befell more than a few of their members. Hard and unremitting prayer was the medieval prescription for ending alienation in a person. No doubt amid the clusters of superstitions and beliefs that formed the peasantry's intellectual relation to the church through the parish and parish priest, there were manifestations of alienation. But it would be absurd to suppose that as much alienation existed within churches then as undoubtedly exists today. Alienation in churches today is caused by the fact that the churches themselves have frequently become large, impersonal and rationalized in structure, sometimes rivaling the economic corporation in this respect, and that church doctrines are frequently formalized and rigid. Also, modern believers in the West are more likely by far than medieval peasant believers to be sufficiently educated to know the experience of *conflicts* of norms and roles. This takes us close to the nature of *anomie*, which we shall come to shortly. Anomie and alienation are not the same thing. But they are sufficiently alike for anomic circumstances to be closely related to those in which high rates of alienation are to be found.

What about the much discussed—and often self-proclaimed—alienation of students, especially in universities and colleges? Abundant studies of this form of alienated behavior exist, since students form easily accessible bodies of research subjects. What we find is not different conceptually from what we find with respect to industrial, political, and religious alienation. Alienation varies in incidence from one part of academic society to another and in intensity from one segment of a campus to another. It is more likely to be found among students in the humanities and social sciences than among students in the physical and biological sciences and in professional schools. The reasons for this are several, each of them no doubt subject to at least some debate. Students in the humanities and social sciences contain a larger number of the already alienated; there are more faculty members in these areas who are themselves alienated and who cannot help transmitting their state of mind to students. Moreover, the very subject matter of much literature in the humanities and social sciences today is alienation in one or another of its philosophical forms (alienation can be *learned*); and, finally, there appears to be a less clear sense of *mission*, of intellectual commitment to goals, among large numbers of students in these areas than is the case in other parts of the academic scene. These appear to be the major reasons why alienation is more common among students in the humanities and the social sciences. Impersonality, bureaucracy, and large lectures are, after all, as much a part of the university scene for physical scientists or members of professional schools as they are for humanists and social scientists.

One need only go back a generation or two in American academic life to be reassured that there is nothing inherently alienative in the university (not even in the humanities and the more philosophical areas of the social sciences). There were large universities, large lecture courses, large numbers of students with, apparently, little sense of community during the first three decades of this century in the United States. But little exists to suggest alienation, either faculty or student, as a consequence. Even today, as every study indicates, the overwhelming majority of college students are *not* alienated.

ANOMIE

In etymological terms, anomie is "normlessness." But, as we observed in the preceding chapter, there is no social behavior that is, or can be, normless. All human behavior above the level of extreme mental deficiency is normative in at least some degree. However vicious or wanting in ordinary decency and rationality some behavior may seem to us, it is related to norms—evil norms, if we like, but norms nonetheless.

From the sociological point of view, anomic behavior, then, cannot be lacking in norms. But such behavior reveals a distinct confusion or *conflict* of norms, as when an individual is vainly striving to accomplish normative goals which are not merely different but in fundamental opposition to one another. The student, for example, who may be in zealous pursuit of an education in contemporary biology but who, by reason of rearing, cannot bring himself to forsake fundamentalist-religious norms regarding the origins of the planet and of life is almost certain to experience what we call anomie. The mother who is deeply responsive to the norms of motherhood in the upbringing of her children but who is also profoundly committed to the norms of being wife, hostess, club member, career woman, or political activist also knows the experience of anomie.

Anomie is, in short, behavior characterized by tensions and distresses that arise from the effort of an individual to meet the obligations of two or more irreconcilable norms. That is, they are irreconcilable *within the framework of response of the individual concerned.* The last is a vital point. If, in the two illustrations just given of student and of mother, the conflicts described are not *perceived* as conflicts, if somehow the gulfs are bridged by mechanisms of reconciliation of the contrasting norms involved—however insufficient these mechanisms may seem to others—then there is little or no anomic behavior. We may think a man insane who has no difficulty in believing himself to be emperor while at the same time begging coins on the street. But his behavior would be anomic, in the sociological sense, only if it revealed severe stress as the consequence of trying to reconcile both identities to his own satisfaction.

Much of what we observed of alienation can be said also of anomie. It is to be found in all social aggregates, in all forms of social behavior. Doubtless no human being has ever lived who has not at least at times experienced the pangs of anomie, of tension arising from perceived conflict of normative ends. But, as with alienation, historical and comparative observation reveals different intensities of anomie from age to age, from society to society, and from culture to culture. When we view the wide range of norms in our society today—norms of success, for example, with all their diverse shapes and colors—it would be strange if we did not find the amount of anomie greater by far than in some folk village in Latin America or tribe in the hill country of India. So too with all the roles that compose our own society. The sheer number of contrasting norms which today confront the role of the woman in our society, or the role of the child, or of the father, or any of the other major roles in the social order, itself encourages a relatively high incidence of anomie.

Some sociologists have suggested abandoning the distinction between alienation and anomie. Admittedly, there is a certain amount in common between the two. There is some anomie in almost all forms of alienation and, clearly, some degree of alienation in the manifestations of anomie. But there is, basically, no more reason for failing to distinguish between alienation and anomie than there is for failing to distinguish between norms and social roles. We have dealt with alienation as a form of *withdrawal* of energy, and this largely means withdrawal from social roles, statuses, and social groups. But, as we have just seen, anomie is not, fundamentally, withdrawal from norms or roles in a given social aggregate. Anomie is a condition or behavior resulting from *perceived conflicts* of norms. The tension deriving from seemingly irreconcilable norms or desires within a single situation accounts for nearly all anomie.

Alienation is not primarily conflict-ridden behavior—although previous, irreconcilable conflicts within one's personality may lead eventually to alienation. Instead, alienation produces behavior that is withdrawn, passive, or apathetic. An alienated individual is beyond even the stimulus of anomic conflict. The difference between alienation and anomie is real and worth emphasizing, even if there is very often a functional relation between the two.

Durkheim is responsible for the first systematic treatment of anomie in modern sociology. He holds the commanding position in contemporary theoretical analyses of not only anomie as such but other forms of behavior, such as deviance, which have demonstrable relation to anomie.

Anomie, Durkheim pointed out, lies behind the incidence of one of the main types of suicide. Anomic suicide proceeds from normative conflicts which become insupportable for the individual. Durkheim was struck by the aggravating effect of economic crises upon suicide rates. He discovered that (according to the records available to him) with every major financial crisis a substantial increase occurs in the number of suicides in the population. At first thought these might seem the inevitable result of sudden increase in poverty for significant numbers of the people affected by the economic crisis. But, as Durkheim emphasized, it is not the fact of poverty that is crucial; it is, rather, the fact of the *suddenness of change* in circumstances, the sharp, disruptive effect upon a personality of being transposed from one normative sphere to another, from affluence to poverty. His demonstration of this was twofold. First he pointed to the fact that the number of suicides in a population increases with the affluence and material comfort of that population. That is, the suicide rate is by no means limited in its increases to those short periods of severe crisis when economic distress is temporarily felt. Second, Durkheim noted, poverty itself, far from inducing individuals to commit suicide, is correlated with extremely low rates of suicide. Whatever the ills and degradations of poverty, high propensity to suicide is not one of them. Why is this so? Durkheim's explanation is the avenue to his more general theory of anomie.

Poverty, he writes, protects against suicide because it is a restraint in itself. With poverty—that is, genuine, hard-core, continuing poverty, the kind that underlies a subculture and produces its own norms—there is a minimum of desires and expectations. This fact may at first sight appear paradoxical, but it is not. In order for expectations to be stimulated and to become motivational to the individual, there has to be at least some degree of possession of material comforts and at least some degree of perceived relation between desire and fulfillment. That is, one must have experienced, or seen at close hand, desire for something followed by its acquisition and, perhaps most importantly, desire further intensified, further broadened in scope, by the very fact of having seen an initial desire satisfied.

But it is characteristic of the genuinely impoverished sectors of the population that desires are minimal and expectations almost wholly lacking. We may note parenthetically that from the point of view of social change or reform the most difficult step is precisely that of *somehow rousing these desires and expectations*. The attitudes of resignation must be converted to those of achievement in which resentment at the condition of poverty succeeds apathy and inertia, and the norms of reform and activism replace, in some degree, the norms of passive acceptance. This, however, is another story. My concern (as it was Durkheim's) is that of indicating the relation of norms to economic circumstance and, from that relation, the nature of anomic behavior. It is enough, therefore, to stress that among the genuinely impoverished, within the culture of poverty, neither resentment nor ambition is commonly found any more than is the basis of revolutionary behavior. Revolutions are most likely to be found among those who are already in the process of improving economic circumstance and whose desires for the better life have already been stimulated. Hence there is nothing remarkable in the fact that revolutionary ages are also anomic ages and also, as Durkheim observed, ages of relatively high incidence of suicide in the populations affected. In our own time it is a striking fact, and an important conclusion to be aware of from every point of view, that political activism among Negroes, Puerto Ricans, and Mexican-Americans is greatest *not* among those whose economic condition is the worst but those in whose lives some degree of improvement has already taken place. We are more likely to find alienation among the genuinely

impoverished—an alienation springing from hopelessness and apathy—
than anomie. Anomie is more likely to be found (though by no means
necessarily and unvaryingly) among the Negroes, Puerto Ricans, and
Mexican-Americans who are suspended, as it were, between the culture
they have departed and the culture not yet reached.

Unhappiness, Durkheim noted (as did Sigmund Freud, though
from a different point of view, in his *Civilization and Its Discontents*),
is a frequent accompaniment of anomie. This does not mean that there is
any absolute relation between affluence and unhappiness, as some religious figures in history have suggested. It means only that because
affluence is widely associated in modern populations with the rather
recent achievement of wealth, a change occurs in the individual's norms,
in his relationships to surrounding culture, roles, and statuses. And this
sudden change, whether from higher position to lower, or from lower
to higher, can be difficult to assimilate in life styles, in definitions of
situations encountered, *and in balance of desires and possessions.* "No
living being can be happy," wrote Durkheim, "or even exist unless his
needs are sufficiently proportioned to his means. In other words, if his
needs require more than can be granted, or even merely something of a
different sort, they will be under continual friction and can only function
painfully."[2]

But needs, as we have had frequent reason to stress, are themselves
deeply conditioned by the norms of one's culture. True, there are basic
biological needs such as the needs for food, rest, and sexual gratification.
But even these are strongly conditioned by the norms of one's culture in
ways that can sometimes intensify them far out of proportion to biological requirements. Thus the sheer biological need for food bears little
relation to the needs—the normatively acquired needs—for food of certain types and quality at the specified times which the lives of most
people manifest. Assessed in rigorously biological terms of required
nutrition, human beings could live (and do now live in vast areas) on a
small fraction of what most of us think we need to remain comfortable
and moderately healthy. The same consideration holds of course for
housing and also for sexual gratification: sheer biological need for each
requires but a fraction of what, under the spur of *norms* of culture, we
are likely to declare that we need—or insist that we want.

Here, of course, lie the conditions of anomic behavior. For a great
many of us, there is frequently a contrast between what we are led to
desire by the norms of culture and what we are in fact able to acquire.
Hence "the revolution of rising expectations." In a real sense, anomie is
the spring of this kind of revolution. For, as Durkheim emphasized, the

mere act of getting is likely to intensify the desire for more, and a condition of tension arising from unfulfilled expectations ensues. The man without fame and no hope of it is likely to be comfortable in his lack of wide visibility; the man of small and growing fame is likely to be driven constantly by desires for ever greater fame. So too with social status. To be hopelessly in a lower class without apparent possibility of rising, or securely born in a high class with almost no likelihood of slipping from it, is very apt to be protection against anomie. The very act of rising in the status scale of a social order is enough, however, to quicken desire for more status, to be galled by feelings of insufficient status, and, not infrequently, to be made miserable in the possession of an actual status that many persons would envy. In his *Democracy in America*, Tocqueville stressed this point. People living in a democracy, Tocqueville concluded, are, of all peoples, the most subject to both a chronic envy of higher status and an insatiable desire for more status, no matter how high in the social scale they may climb. Hence, Tocqueville observed (in advance of Durkheim), the higher rates of suicide and mental breakdown found in nations characterized by middle-class standards and by democratic norms.

One point should be stressed here even at the risk of being obvious. There is nothing "right" or "wrong" in anomic behavior. Such behavior *may* be associated with the deviant behavior we shall discuss next; it *may* be associated with misery; it *may* be associated with desires leading eventually to suicide or personality ills. But let us not forget that anomic behavior may also be associated with strenuous and largely fulfilled desires to improve one's position in life, or to improve, through political activism, the positions of others. Anomic behavior may also be associated with extraordinary accomplishments in the arts, sciences, and other areas of culture. The old wives' tale relating to the inevitable eccentricity, even madness, of genius has at least this modicum of truth in it: those of superlative mental ability and achievement are more likely than most of us to be abnormally obsessed by a gulf between what they have actually achieved and what, given their high endowments, they think they might have achieved. For, as Durkheim concluded about anomic behavior, it is, whether self-destructive or creative in long-run effect, formed out of the disproportion between what one has and what one is led, through normative expectations, to believe he should have. It is often a conflict between ends and available means. But it is also, in the most fundamental sense, a conflict between two sets of norms, those within which one lives and those at a higher, or lower, level.

There is a very close relation between anomie and what is often called *marginality.* A marginal person, in the sociological sense, is one poised, so to speak, between two cultures or sets of norms (it could be more than two, of course), unable to become identified with either in any close and continuing way. "Inability" may arise from his being forbidden to *enter* one culture—forbidden perhaps for racial, ethnic, or political reasons—and, whether overtly or by implication, feeling *rejected* by the other. The most obvious examples of marginal individuals are those such as the half-castes in India or, in an earlier day of American history, the so-called half-breeds of the West. The first were products of Anglo-Indian sexual union, the second of American-Indian union. The position in which the half-caste or half-breed was placed can only be described as tragic. Drawing intellectually and culturally, as well as genetically, from both strains, the half-caste and half-breed were despised by both cultures, and often, as in India, denied certain basic attributes of legal identity. Another example is the child of Negro-Caucasian parentage, especially in the United States where racial lines have been drawn so closely. In this case, too, a poignant literature testifies to the difficulties encountered by those marginal from birth to two segregated races.

But marginality exists much oftener in ways less visible and dramatic than these. There is the example of the Negro from a largely uneducated ghetto who becomes successful as a writer, scientist, or professional man but who then learns that just as there is no place for him in white society where he can find his intellectual equals, there is no place for him either in the uneducated black community from which he came. This was the theme of much of the brilliant writing of the late Negro novelist, Richard Wright. The same theme enters into much of the distinguished work of other Negro writers such as Ralph Ellison, James Baldwin, and Claude Brown. Here race is, of course, the basis of the marginality, but the substance is cultural and, specifically, normative. The Negro concerned is marginal to two sets of cultural norms. He is, so to speak, *in* both, but *of* neither. Experiences of Catholic-Protestant, Jewish-Gentile, and, in the ancient world, Greek-barbarian and Roman-freedman furnish many examples of the same kind of marginality. It is as old as the mixture of peoples and cultures and, in some degree at least, will exist as long as distinct cultures and subcultures come in contact with one another, no matter how free and equal in political and legal terms peoples may become. Marginality is an experience often known by students for whom college is an introduction to a world of norms they had perhaps not dreamed of at home and who, without feeling themselves wholly an intellectual part of the new world, come to feel separated from their former world of values. Marginality is no doubt as embedded in the human condition as are alienation and anomie. But the fact of time-lessness in these terms should not blind us to the innumerable examples of marginality, alienation, and anomie which, in their extreme and highly visible manifestations, should no more be regarded as timeless and in-evitable than unemployment or poverty.

There is a close relation between marginality and intellectual achieve-ment. By the nature of his work, the artist, scientist, intellectual, and scholar must each be the recipient of impulses sent out from a variety of fields.[3] Anyone whose business it is to reflect, analyze, and draw mean-ings from experience is bound to live somewhat nearer the periphery of his own community than do most of the rest of the world. Some degree of sensitivity to, and hence involvement in, other communities is the essence of the role of the creator and the interpreter. Therefore, the seeds of unease and distress can admittedly lie in marginality. But in mar-ginality can lie also the seeds of creativity. In fact, the two types of response to marginality have a close relation to one another. There is very little in the way of creativity, in any sphere, that is not associated with unease, even agony, at times.

Throughout history the way of the creative mind has always been a difficult one. There is just enough likeness between the impact of the creative mind upon a community and the impact of the morally deviant person to bring at times the same kind of censure down upon the head of each.

DEVIANCE

The third form of social entropy we shall consider is *deviance*. In the most literal meaning of this word, all social behavior is deviant much of the time. That is, it deviates, how-ever slightly, from social norms (which are necessarily abstract) and from the ideal type of any given role, status, or custom. The process of socialization is never "perfect"—fortunately—in its consequences. No one performs a role, occupies a status, or follows a socially prescribed way of behavior exactly as he is taught. The history of any language is in considerable part a history of modifications of usage which come from deviations in speech by one generation from the preceding. All the great prophets, statesmen, philosophers, and inventors may be said to be deviant in this literal and strict sense of the word. Although it is in-correct to attribute all social change to deviance in this sense, no one can doubt that a considerable amount of social change in time is the result of deviation by one generation from the rules, codes, and norms it has been taught by the preceding generation.

In sociology, however, the word "deviance" has a somewhat different (though related) denotation. Deviant behavior, as viewed by most sociologists (and as conceived in this section henceforth) is behavior that is in *violation* of norms, particularly the norms of morality. Albert K. Cohen has the following to say about deviant behavior:

> *Deviant behavior is behavior that violates the normative rules, under-standings, or expectations of social systems.... Crime is the prototype of deviance in this sense, and theory and research have been concerned overwhelmingly with crime. However, normative rules are inherent in the nature of social systems, whether they be friendship groups, engaged couples, families, work teams, factories, or national societies. Legal norms are then but one type of norm whose violation constitutes deviant behavior.*[4]

The essence of deviant behavior, sociologically, is, then, its *violation* of norms rather than, as in the older and more literal sense, its mere variation from, or mild modification of, norms. Moreover, in sociological usage, the word "deviant" has become largely associated with behavior that falls within moral or ethical contexts. Theft, narcotics traffic, embezzlement, and homosexuality are all "deviant" in the sociological sense. Variation by the child or immigrant in use of a language being learned, or modification of one philosopher's theory by another philosopher would not qualify in sociological usage at the present time as "deviant" even though there are indeed processes common to the two types. In any event, it is deviant behavior as defined above by Cohen that will form the subject of this section.

As there is a relativity of norms and social codes in human history and society, so is there a relativity of deviance. It could not well be otherwise. Behavior punished in one society as immoral may be applauded in another. Cannibalism and incest in our social order are assuredly modes of deviant behavior. But in a society in which cannibalism is regularly and normatively practiced, *refusal* to eat human flesh would no doubt be regarded as immoral, as deviant. And, as we have seen, incest within the ruling families of ancient Egypt and of pre-Western Hawaii was fully sanctioned, even prescribed.

Are there any forms of behavior which have in all places at all times been regarded as deviant? The question is as difficult to answer as any other question pertaining to universals in human behavior. To say that "murder," "incest," and "robbery" are everywhere regarded as morally wrong hardly answers the question, for each of these words is, so to speak, loaded with moral disapproval. We can rephrase the question to ask: Is the killing of one human being by another—even within the same kinship group or local community—invariably dealt with as a crime? The answer must be in the negative. The killing of a child by its father might seem a clear enough instance of murder anywhere and everywhere, but in ancient Greece and Rome (and in many other societies) it was the normative duty of a father to put to death a child so infirm as to become a liability to the community or so delinquent as to constitute a threat to the normative order of the community. And, although "patricide" is indeed a term of horror in much of the world's literature, it too is a morally loaded word and does not take into account those peoples among whom the putting to death of the very elderly and useless in the kinship group was an obligation of the young. We would think it callous in the extreme today for capital punishment to be exercised by the guilty person's own family. We think it more humane (assuming we favor capital punishment at all) for an impersonal officer of the state to put the condemned person to death, with the family excluded altogether. But in ancient Rome, until the third century B.C., individuals, even when found guilty of a crime against the state, as in treason, were turned over to their families for execution or sentence of exile. This practice was thought to be more humane.

Today only killing that is done on order of the state and by the state's officers is regarded by most Americans as sanctionable killing. For one family to seek through vendetta to kill one or more persons in another family is to seek murder in our eyes, no matter how justified the revenge might seem. But among thousands of peoples in human history, this form of killing has been regarded as proper. What required justification among such peoples was the instituting of a political system whereby the state alone could kill in the name of retribution.

No matter what normative departures come to mind—killing, theft, incest, homosexuality, sexual relations outside marriage, and so on —we find each so hedged by definitions and by circumstances regarded as extenuating from one society to another that absolute pronouncements on deviant behavior are extremely difficult to make. In scores of religions the killing of human beings for sacrificial purposes has been regarded as not only good but necessary and sacred. Plato tells us that the ancient Spartans even approved theft within the community when it was done by a boy or young man, such theft being regarded as practice of a skill of great value against Sparta's enemies. Presumably theft in ancient Sparta by girls and women was not morally acceptable.

The above discussion suggests the immense importance of *definition* of deviance. The marriage of first cousins in our society today is not regarded as incestuous. There have been and are societies, however, in which such marriages do constitute incest. In the same way that history may be seen as a process of selection among roles, statuses, and norms, so may it be regarded as a selective process with respect to deviance.

When the British began to govern India, they found among the high castes an ancient custom called *suttee*. This practice required a man's widow, however young she might be, to cremate herself on her husband's funeral pyre. The British regarded the custom as barbaric and forbade it. Suddenly an old and sacred form of behavior became a crime—a mode of deviant behavior. But from the continuing point of view of the Hindu castes themselves, *suttee* was anything but immoral, however illegal it might have been declared by the British. The custom persisted for a long time after it was made illegal. Why? Because the sanctions applied by the Hindus to the widow who had, in their view, desecrated the memory of her husband by choosing to remain alive were for a long time more feared than anything that might be done by the British. A life spent under total ostracism—the common punishment for the widow who refused to cremate herself—was hardly attractive even though, in theory, refusal to kill herself was, in official terms, the moral as well as legal thing to do.

The conflict of institutionalized norms often brings with it widespread deviance. Especially is this true when one set of norms has a sacred place in the indigenous population and when another and contrary set of norms is imposed through political means upon that population by an alien or outside political authority. The Mormons, as we know, began the practice of polygyny some years after their religion was founded in the early nineteenth century in the United States. Whatever the initial misgivings about the practice among many Mormons, the custom of plural marriage was well established in the Mormon community when the custom was declared illegal by the United States government. In the eyes of the federal government, polygyny was a crime. In the eyes of a great many Mormons it was sanctioned by a law higher and more sacred than that of the United States. Whether polygyny is in fact deviant behavior depends, of course, solely upon reference to a set of norms. It would be regarded today as deviant behavior even among the overwhelming number of Mormons in the world, for their own norms came to terms, so to speak, with the norms of the rest of American society around the beginning of the twentieth century.

None of the above discussion should lead the reader to suppose that *objective* study and analysis of deviance is therefore impossible. Granted the great diversity of norms of right and wrong in the world throughout history, the test of deviance from the sociological point of view is always particular and concrete. The sociologist may personally incline toward norms very different from those he is studying in a social order or subculture within the social order—for example, those prescribing physically brutal female circumcision. He may choose to regard the norms themselves as deviant from his own sense of what is right and humane. It does not matter. Deviant behavior, in any useful and empirical sense, is behavior that violates the norms of the group or community within which the behavior occurs. The test of deviance in the sociological sense is its correspondence to the *particular* definition of right and wrong among a majority—or determining number—of the persons who form that group or community. That prostitution is a form of deviant behavior in American society at the present time is clear enough. It violates the norms of most Americans with respect to the proper circumstances of sexual relations. That one may himself hold a different view of the function or value of prostitution is as much beside the point as that one may draw endlessly from world history to support the view that there always have been, and perhaps always will be, prostitutes. So also with pre- or extramartial sex. Few need to be reminded that in contemporary American society a great deal of sexual intercourse takes place outside the bonds of marriage. It is nonetheless deviant behavior in the sociological sense of the term. For the majority of Americans—including most of those who themselves engage in pre- or extramarital sexual behavior—continue to support the position that sex is moral only when it takes place within marriage. Almost every study made of the attitudes of those who are or have been involved in such sexual behavior reveals that they themselves are very apt to define their behavior as immoral, although the prevalence of this view varies from group to group and may indeed be undergoing modification.

This example suggests another aspect of what I have called the definitional context of deviant behavior. We have different ways of assessing—and punishing—violations of norms. There is nothing uncommon in the phenomenon of a people overwhelmingly in support—verbal support, at least—of a given norm who nevertheless give indulgence to certain types of violations of the norm. No one would claim that premarital sexual intercourse is today regarded by most Americans as unambiguously as it was by many, perhaps most, of our fore-fathers. It is still deplored and warned against by many parents and counselors. But when it occurs it is far more likely to be forgiven if not forgotten. And in American life today a community in which a girl's respectability was forever ruined by wide knowledge that she was pregnant at the time of marriage would be rather exceptional. Perhaps it would have been a rare community even a century or two ago. We frequently exaggerate the orthodoxy of our forebears in these matters and the emancipation of ourselves.

The central point here is that most norms, however sacred they may be, have escape clauses, as it were, that may temper the manner in which an offense is regarded and punished. What was said early in the book about symbolic interaction should not be overlooked when we con-sider deviance. It is always not the offense as such but the way the offense is defined, perceived, and responded to in contexts of interaction that matters. One thinks of the tolerance of white Southerners for Negro derelictions in matters of sex, marriage, and desertion. Because most Southern whites conceived all Negroes as basically irresponsible, child-like, and inferior in moral as well as intellectual matters, the battery of norms pertaining to sex and marriage by which they judged other whites was virtually dismissed from consideration when judging Negroes. In fact some whites encouraged Negroes in such deviant behavior, for it provided fulfillment of their own convictions and prophecies regarding Negro character and conduct.

Murder is by no means the same offense from one occurrence to an-other. In ancient Germanic society a *wergild* system existed whereby unequal value was deliberately placed upon human lives. The slaying of a commoner was hardly the same offense as the slaying of a warrior-chief. This system also held true in the Middle Ages. The killing of a serf by a nobleman was relatively minor. All manner of extenuating circumstances could be found. The opposite, however, was one of the most heinous of crimes. When a serf was found guilty of killing a noble-man, he was quite literally put to death by inches in extreme torture. His body was flayed and then left for days and weeks on a public gallows for all to see and be reminded of the crime involved.

It is one of the marks of the relative equalitarianism of the modern legal state that this kind of class-defined punishment does not occur—at least in theory. Under the law, all men are equal, and all murders are equal. But what we find in fact when we survey the sentences given over a ten-year period is a striking disproportion by ethnic and social class. More Negroes and Mexican-Americans, for example, receive the death sentence than do middle-class whites. It is easier for the middle-class, educated white to win early parole or commutation of sentence than it is for those of lower status, class, and ethnic groups. Quite apart from sentence, we tend to *perceive* murders differently for the reason that we view each in context. The murder of a wife's husband by her lover is certainly perceived differently by most Americans than the murder of the lover by the jealous husband. Not very many years ago it was largely impossible to get a conviction from juries in this country when the murder was of the second type.

There is, then, nothing inflexible or absolute about social norms. For we perceive their violations only in the act of defining them. And in defining them we find ourselves almost automatically judging degree of guilt by what we know of the circumstances. Often norms will persist for long periods of time in a population, with no manifest desire to change the norm in abstract terms but with a coexisting desire on the part of large elements of the population to see *circumventions* take place under proper circumstances. American experience with prohibition is a case in point. True, there was a substantial number of Americans, perhaps a majority, that did not concur with the aim of the Eighteenth Amendment from the time of its adoption. But even among those who did favor it— as did much of the white population of the South and Midwest—there was a widespread view that violations of the law against sale of liquors should be treated lightly and moreover that liquor should be available through whatever means—bootlegging or concoctions at home. In short, a norm can be accepted widely while at the same time a kind of institutionalized evasion of the norm is also accepted.

Despite the fact that we think of law as the embodiment and means of enforcement of norms, it can also be, in a literal sense, *the creation of deviance*. British law made *suttee* a type of deviant behavior in India. Specific legal enactments made the taking of opium and marijuana deviant in this country. Until the end of the nineteenth century there were few laws and little popular concern affecting narcotics in the United States. So many veterans of the Civil War had acquired the opium habit from the use of the drug in Civil War hospitals as a painkiller that it was rather widely and tolerantly known as the "soldiers' delight" in this country. Physicians were rarely checked by public authorities in their prescriptions of drugs. Drugstores were generally left alone in their sales of narcotics under the guise of "patent medicines." Then, early in the present century, new laws were passed by Congress, enforcement became quite suddenly relatively severe, much publicity went out from the federal agency responsible for enforcement, and, almost overnight, narcotics became a matter of horror to many Americans and the central element of a whole new illicit industry. (How little "horror" there had been in narcotics earlier, despite the number of those addicted in many communities, can be inferred from the respect accorded Thomas de Quincey's classic *Confessions of an English Opium Eater.*)

At the present time the smoking of marijuana is illegal; it has been so for several decades. The use of marijuana enters the same realm of deviant and criminal behavior in which other offenses, such as robbery, rape, and murder, fall. That it produces an effect upon the smoker is clear enough. What is not so clear in informed judgment is whether marijuana and its effects come nearer the "hard" narcotics (opium, heroin, and others) in their consequences or to the drinking of hard liquors. That the latter can produce baneful effects is clear from the heavy toll of alcoholism on Americans. The drinking of alcohol is not a crime, however, or even defined as deviant behavior. Does marijuana tend to be a route to the hard drugs? No doubt it does at times. But, as the evidence suggests, there are other routes. It is not part of my intent to seek to judge the true significance of marijuana in its effects upon individuals and the community. We know that experts differ at the present time. My only intent is to stress the fact that if, as is entirely possible within the next decade, judicial reassessment should wipe out the present illegality of marijuana, an entire area of present deviance would disappear at once. It would have been defined away. *Behavior* would not necessarily change (although it is predictable that much of the present thrill and fun of smoking marijuana would disappear among young people once it was ruled legal and, in consequence, much of its use in this sector of society would disappear). It would simply be no longer defined as deviant.

How changes in law and moral opinion affect the incidence of deviance is nowhere better illustrated than with respect to the smoking of tobacco in this country. Within the memory of many of us, the smoking of cigarettes by students and by women generally was either forbidden or seriously frowned upon. Rules on nearly all college campuses were unyielding for many years with respect to student—and often faculty—smoking. In some middle-class American communities, until perhaps a half-century ago, a woman who smoked cigarettes was regarded as being a prostitute in all probability. However, a good many women—respectable women—did begin to smoke cigarettes, especially after World War I. Gradually the sense of deviant behavior was lessened. Gradually rules against smoking by college students were modified or eliminated. We may say here that a whole area of deviance was wiped out of American life *not* by banishing cigarettes but by redefining cigarette smoking in such a way as to virtually eliminate the moral or normative element. Today, however, because of the widely publicized results of medical studies on smoking and the campaign by governmental agencies and private crusades alike to ban or reduce advertising of cigarettes, we may well be at the start of a new cycle of the whole matter.

Abortion is a good example of deviant behavior that may well be eliminated within the next decade or two in this country—as it has already been eliminated in Japan and Sweden, among other countries—through laws which sanction medically authorized abortions for those desiring them. At the present time, the health of the mother must be in jeopardy for an abortion to be allowed. The most recent opinion survey available reports that a majority of the American people favor continuation of laws against voluntary abortion even when performed with medical approval and within properly licensed circumstances. But the size of the majority appears to be diminishing constantly. Equally important is the apparent fact that more and more Americans are inclined to view with rising tolerance those instances in which a physician is found to be, or thought to be, performing abortions when they are justified in his judgment. Already one may see the beginnings of sanctioned evasions of the norm— while generalized support of the norm forbidding voluntary abortions continues among a large number of Americans.

Our discussion thus far should indicate that there is much more to deviant behavior than the simple act and more to its elimination than mere identification of an act with appropriate punishment. To emphasize that deviant behavior is behavior *defined* both by the actor himself and by those in the surrounding social order is no denial of the existence of deviant behavior. Deviance is in no way comparable to a tumor in an otherwise healthy body, requiring only its excision for cure. This is an all too common image, in the popular mind, of deviant behavior and of social problems generally. But the image is false, and it is worth emphasizing again that analogies between the social order and the biological organism are dangerous—never more so than when forms of social behavior are described in terms drawn from medical pathology. The essential point is not merely the fact that deviant behavior draws strongly from processes that it shares with the behavior we regard as proper or right in society. The essential point is that a vast amount of deviant behavior in history is the consequence of the ways in which human behavior is defined in its relation to the norms of any social order.

This last statement brings us once again to the ideas of Durkheim, this time to a profound discussion of crime in his *The Rules of Socio-*

logical Method. There is, Durkheim explained, a normality to crime in the social order that arises from its relation to the ways by which human beings define norms and the different approximations of the norms found in the behavior of individuals. As long as there are moral values, in short, and as long as there is a differential approximation to these values on the part of individuals in society, there is bound to be a certain amount of deviant behavior. It could not be otherwise. Whenever any norm or ideal type exists—whether of beauty, courage, academic brilliance, moral goodness, rectitude, or any other—the actual behavior of human beings with reference to each of these norms will inevitably vary. Some persons will be more courageous, brilliant, or good than others. On a purely behavioral base, Durkheim concluded, the morally objectionable (deviant) behavior of some is as inescapable as is the morally acceptable or virtuous behavior of others. When we consider the existence of variability in human behavior, that is, of individual differences, and the existence also of those ideal types in the normative sphere we call values, there is bound to be a whole range of approximations by human beings to these ideal types. If sexual propriety—however its ideal type in a culture is defined abstractly—is at issue, there cannot help but be some whose behavior will correspond more closely to the ideal type than that of others. We may wish to pronounce a certain, perhaps imaginary, saint as the most moral of all human beings in this respect on the ground that, according to belief, not even a thought of "lust" ever crossed his mind. And at the opposite extreme we may put someone such as the Marquis de Sade, most of whose adult life was apparently spent in devising ever more ingenious modes of sexual gratification. The extremes are easily identified. But what of the vast number of human beings whose sexual behavior falls between these extremes? Some are saintly, but not as saintly as our first example. Some are libertine, but not as libertine as the Marquis de Sade. At what point in the wide range do we draw a line? Where do we say: "On this side of the line lies behavior ranging from the indelicate to the grossly immoral; on the other side lies behavior ranging from the acceptable to the virtuous"? No categorical, abstract answer can ever be given to that question in the sphere of morality—not without the most careful scrutiny of the group or culture concerned in concrete place and time. We find that all groups and cultures in history keep moving the line first one way, then the other. One of the commonest of experiences, at least among peoples who have left us records, is the alternation of relatively "moral" and "immoral" periods. In England the very strait-laced Elizabeth I banished courtiers on the mere rumor of scandal; then, the free and easy era of the Stuarts arrived, followed by the grim and severe period of Puritan ascendancy. After the Puritans, there was once again a relatively relaxed period during the eighteenth century, which produced Fielding's *Tom Jones*. The celebrated Age of Victoria followed through most of the nineteenth century. And then, almost predictably, there was a reversal during the reign of her successor, Edward VII. Plainly, what occurs in this alternation is not so much change in behavior as change in ways of defining the acceptable and the forbidden.

Durkheim used the striking example of a society of saints to demonstrate the omnipresence of immorality, the functional necessity of crime in any social order.

> *Imagine a society of saints, a perfect cloister of exemplary individuals. Crimes, properly so called, will there be unknown; but faults which appear venial to the layman will create there the same scandal that the ordinary offense does in ordinary consciousness. If, then, this society has the power to judge and punish, it will define these acts as criminal and will treat them as such.*[5]

The relation between variable behavior and human definition of this behavior is much the same in the context of morality as in that of academic intelligence. If we were to skim off the top one percent of students in the half-dozen outstanding academic institutions and gather them in a single place (with faculty to match), we should have a concentration of the very bright by all ordinary standards. Not a dullard in the lot! But once processes of interaction commenced in this supercommunity of intellect, once the inevitable process of defining superior and inferior achievement within that community began, some would be found brilliant and some would be thought dull.

Durkheim's thesis regarding the omnipresence of crime and immorality in human society should not be misinterpreted. It should not be regarded as a demonstration of the inevitability of any particular type of crime, or any particular rate of crime, or of the permanence of a particular level of morality. Crime may be necessary, in the sociological sense, in any social order. But it does not follow that headhunting, cannibalism, lynching, or extreme manifestations of racial discrimination are necessary. And the point should not be missed that it is the human capacity to keep raising the standard by which conduct is judged that offers the greatest hope of obliteration of the grossest evils.

There is still another sense in which Durkheim referred to the necessity of crime in the social order. Crime is a major means by which our all-important moral values can be periodically reaffirmed and thus kept strong as elements of social solidarity. Human society cannot exist, Durkheim declared, except on the basis of moral consensus. But there is always the danger that this consensus will become weak and tenuous through the erosion of time. The community will suffer. Hence the importance of those offenses which from time to time remind community members of the importance of the norms that the offenses violated. In the sense of horror or repugnance awakened by the offense itself in the surrounding community lies the possibility of the reaffirming of values that every group or community requires from time to time in the interest of preservation of its moral consensus.

There is a similar relation between an act of deviance and moral consensus in the community that we have seen to exist between an act of conflict and social cohesion in the community. The deviant act does indeed violate the normative order, and a sufficient number of deviant acts within a short period can subject the normative order to great strain. Acts of conflict have much the same effect upon the bonds of cohesion among individuals. And these, too, when sufficient in number, can seriously damage a social structure. But in both cases—deviance and conflict—the effects most of the time remind members of the community of the values and ties concerned and lead to a strengthening of each.

From the Durkheimian propositions regarding the normality, even necessity, of deviant behavior, the conclusion has been drawn by some writers that the *amount* of deviance tends to remain about the same from one age to another in a society. New forms of deviance do indeed arise occasionally, but a place is created for them, so to speak, by removing some of the old ones through the processes of redefinition of deviance. As public opinion puts the stamp of deviance on new forms of behavior, it removes the stamp of deviance from some of the old.

The sociologist Kai T. Erikson, in his recent book *Wayward Puritans*, has shown fairly conclusively that this constancy of volume of deviance existed even among the sin-sensitive Puritans of seventeenth-century New England. From the time the Puritans arrived in the new land, acts of deviant behavior occurred—adultery, fornication, profanity, assault, theft, and others—and were accordingly punished by Puritan councils. In time new forms of deviance, veritable "crime waves," made their appearance in the forms of the hated and feared antinomianism, Quaker doctrines, and witchcraft. The moral conscience of the devout Puritans was as outraged by these as the consciences of some Americans have been by doctrines of anarchism or new life-style practices of some young people. The guilty were caught when possible and

severely punished. But, Erikson notes, the records do not show that the
amount of deviance changed appreciably, that is, the amount of defined
and recorded deviance. For, with the agitation provoked by antinomianism or witchcraft, there was a lessening of regard for the prior types of
deviance. Boundaries were redrawn, and an offense—loose behavior,
vituperative language, or assault—that would have been characterized
and punished as deviant a decade earlier was, under the new circumstances, virtually ignored.

The American college campus during the present century shows
much the same tendency with respect to constancy of volume. One need
but ask any college graduate now in his fifties or sixties if there was
deviance on the college campus in his day. There was indeed—cigarette
smoking, drinking and purchase or concoction of liquor, petting, marriage without permission of the college authorities, the wearing by girls
of short skirts and lipstick to class, riots generated by athletic fever, and
many other acts which made their way to the records of deans' offices.
Students were disciplined and some expelled, for any of the offenses cited
above. The so-called roaring twenties had their full manifestation on
college campuses in the United States.

Suppose for a moment that all of the above modes of deviance still
existed. After all, there was not one that the college authorities succeeded in banning or otherwise eliminating from campuses. Add to
these the new ones which have made their appearance within the past
decade or two: the use of pot, LSD, and other drugs, open possession of
contraceptives by the unmarried, bizarre types of dress, long hair on
boys, sit-ins for political or academic objectives, and so on. If the old
continued to exist along with the new, the volume of deviance would
indeed be greater than that of the 1920s. But the old forms of deviance
are gone. Petting, drinking, marriage while still in undergraduate
status, short skirts, and cigarette smoking, which are in abundant existence today on the campus, are not instances of deviance. They have
been defined for the most part as morally neutral. Deviance, in sum, is
not something inherent and lasting in any particular type of behavior; it
is a property *conferred* by social definition upon behavior.

One of the reasons why the true incidence of a specific form of deviance—theft, assault, statutory rape, for instance—is almost impossible
to determine in our society is the selective way it is perceived by persons,
including the police and other official record keepers. Much of this behavior was simply ignored for a long time when it existed within ethnic
enclaves—especially among Negroes, Mexican-Americans, and Puerto
Ricans. What the average white meant by crime was crime that affected

him or his neighborhood.   And this was chiefly the type that was recorded until very recently.

We can reverse the illustration.   Studies show that much behavior
among middle- and upper-class white adolescents that is delinquent by
ordinary standards goes not only unpunished but even unrecognized and
unidentified by whites generally and by police officials.   The same behavior in working-class areas or among certain ethnic groups is immediately identified and pronounced delinquent—that is, deviant.   The middle
class in this instance is inclined to be more indulgent toward the delinquencies of its own than toward those of other class and ethnic elements of the community.   Behavior regarded as delinquent in one sector
is regarded as merely mischievous in another.   Time and place also
affect the matter.   Youthful depredations upon fruit orchards a century
ago, chronic truancy from school, the upsetting of outhouses on farms,
and so on, may have aroused appropriate responses, but they were not
often dealt with in official records as manifestations of criminal or delinquent behavior.   One does not need to underline the observation that
counterparts of these forms of behavior today are generally dealt with
as deviant and delinquent.

One other important aspect of the definition of deviant behavior
must be mentioned—the relation it has to the amount of machinery of
law enforcement at any given time.   In the same way that the incidence
of officially defined mental retardation or mental illness would almost
certainly double if there were to be a doubling of our capacity to care
for mental disabilities, so, in all probability, would the amount of officially
defined deviance rise were there a substantial rise in the number of law-
enforcement officers.

To make this point is not to adopt a cynical attitude toward crime
and its apprehension.   We are only recognizing once again the fact
of the relation between incidence of deviance and our social capacities to
perceive deviance.   In the long run, communities and their officials tend
to recognize, define, and deal with the types and amounts of deviance
which fall within their powers of doing something about them.   It is a
fair guess that when and if present laws on the use of marijuana are
repealed, and marijuana is relegated to the domain of the morally neutral,
the major reason will be the incapacity of law-enforcement agencies
to deal with this act under present laws *and at the same time deal with
other forms of deviance* whose growth in volume may appear more press-
ing than the use of pot.   It is *then*, on the historical evidence, that marijuana will be "found" mild in its effects on the human system.   So, as
we observed, was it with the great majority of acts of deviance on college

campuses which took place a half-century ago. They continue, but they have been given the status of either proper behavior or else are regarded as morally neutral.

The final point I wish to make about deviant behavior takes us back once again to what has been repeatedly observed in this book about behavior generally—its symbolic, interactive, and role- and norm-based quality. We shall never understand deviance if we persist in regarding it solely from the point of view of its moral undesirability. This is not to say that many of the acts presently regarded as deviant—theft, murder, rape, chronic use of, and traffic in, harmful drugs, arson, assault, and others—are not socially and morally undesirable. They are indeed. We have every right to pronounce them evil, just as we have every right to pronounce acts of ethnic or religious discrimination evil. But such pronouncements do not help in the understanding of the acts. And there can be little or no control apart from objective understanding.

Unhappily, our understanding of the causes of deviant behavior is still meager. For too many centuries deviance was dealt with in the philosophical and theological literature in the unadorned terms of such concepts as original sin or free will. Evil occurs, it was said, because man is in part evil by nature or because individuals choose to be evil. This long period of characterization of deviance was followed, in the nineteenth and twentieth centuries most notably, by theories of determinism. Instead of doctrines of original sin and free will, there were (and are) doctrines declaring deviance to be induced in individuals by impersonal environmental factors over which they have no control. In the nineteenth century theories of climatic, biological, racial, and economic determinism were used to explain deviance. The Italian physician-criminologist Cesare Lombroso held crime to be the result of biologically based "criminal types," without power of restraint from their acts. Others found, or thought they found, clear correlations between types of crime and types of climatic or geographic locale. Still others, among them Marxists down to the present moment in the communist countries of the world, declared crime and other forms of deviance the inevitable result of exploitative economic systems. They declared that only with the abolition of private property as a value in the human mind would crime be abolished.

There are also theories of social determinism, many of these still ascendant in popular consciousness. It is said that poverty causes crime or induces modes of behavior that are deviant. Since, on the surface, this is a plausible explanation, we shall observe that among the genuinely impoverished, that is, within the hard-core cultures of poverty, there is less crime than there is among the relatively affluent on earth, and particularly the middle class. Poverty's degradation of human personality is reason enough for its abolition. It is not necessary to fasten rates of crime onto it any more than it is to attribute rates of suicide, anxiety neurosis, or anomic behavior to poverty.

Still other theories hold that deviance is caused by lower-class or working-class norms, that certain offenses such as assault and theft are perceived differently by lower-class youth and that their acts are sanctioned as means of acquiring wordly goods which they feel separated from. Or it is said that crime is the consequence of exposure to middle-class values or success goals when, at one and the same time, either from ethnic or social-class causes, the individuals involved are excluded from the socially sanctioned channels of achievement of these values or goals. Or, in still another version of the matter, crime is held to be the consequence of formation of subcultures by those who, unable to participate in the ordinary processes of upward mobility in society, find organized ways of flouting these processes. One of the oldest doctrines of social determinism in American sociology is that which sees deviant behavior as the inevitable consequence of "social disorganization," of loss of primary-group controls in metropolitan centers.

It would be absurd to suggest that no elements of value lie in some of these theories, especially the last ones mentioned. But it has to be admitted that they have taken us very little of the way to an understanding of the larger problem of deviant behavior in the social order, the problem that may be put in the form of the question: Why, within the same or similar environmental circumstances, do some individuals commit acts of deviance where others do not?

Several criticisms, of varying importance, can be leveled at the doctrines and theories mentioned. In the first place, entirely too much of the so-called *theory* of deviance rests upon what is but a highly specialized and limited form of deviance—juvenile delinquency. The range of deviance is a broad one, as we have seen. It includes a great many forms of violation of norms which can neither be identified with nor rooted in juvenile behavior. To set forth what purports to be a theory of deviance on the basis of materials drawn from youth behavior alone is a little like formulating a theory of the causes of international warfare on the basis of materials drawn from domestic squabbles or street gangs. There may be *some* transfer value, but not much. If youth behavior were not so easily studied, so available, we might well be further along in our understanding of the larger problem of deviance.

But of much greater importance is the criticism that can be directed

against any and all forms of *determinism*. Basically, it is as wrong—
and useless—to declare that one's lower-class position "drives" or "induces" or "constrains" him to the commission of deviant acts as to declare
that the cause lies in the climate, or in one's glandular or hormonic
nature, or in capitalism or in technology. The same observation may
be directed against much of what is called "subculture" in the study of
deviant behavior. Even when we are in fact dealing with a subculture
worthy of the name, it is as hazardous to make subculture a determining
cause as it is to make social class or religion or society at large a determining cause.

What Robert M. MacIver emphasizes so powerfully in his *Social
Causation* for the study of social phenomena generally is nowhere more
applicable than to many theories of the cause of social deviance. We
cannot properly deal with social causation in deterministic terms. We
cannot expunge from consideration the purposive, choice-making individual, and the interactive character of human behavior. Human
beings are never particles of metal in a magnetic field. Always, the
choice-making, situation-defining mind of the human being is at work.
It is at work within specifiable conditions, to be sure, including social,
cultural, and biographical conditions of past, present, and expected
future which the mind manages to bind into a context of motivation.
But conditions accepted, social action is always purposive and definitional. It is not *merely* the consequence of environmental determination.

In a brilliant recent work on deviant behavior (above any other
study in my view), David Matza has pointed out the difficulties of the
contemporary study of deviance—difficulties which, as he suggests,
proceed from the inability of too many sociologists to forego the kind
of hard determinism which must forever be declaring juvenile deviance
induced or constrained by environment circumstances over which the
youthful deviant has, by definition, no power of resistance, no aptitude
for calculated choice of a given pursuit. Matza writes:

> *Given the assumptions of constraint and differentiation, the fre-
> quency with which delinquents more or less reform is most perplexing.
> . . . Anywhere from 60 to 85 percent of delinquents do not apparently
> become adult violators. Moreover, this reform seems to occur irre-
> spective of correctional agencies and irrespective of correctional service.*
>
> *Most theories of delinquency take no account of maturational re-
> form; those that do often do so at the expense of violating their own
> assumptions regarding the constrained delinquent. Why and by what
> process do youngsters once compelled or committed to delinquency*

cease being constrained? Why and by what process is the easy con-
tinuity from juvenile delinquency to adult crime implicit in almost all
theories of delinquency not apparent in the world of real events?[6]

Hence the unwisdom I cited above of using juvenile deviance or
delinquency as a model for generalizations on "the deviant act" or "the
deviant community" or "the deviant role." Hence, too, the even greater
unwisdom of subscribing to the premises of determinism in the study of
deviant (or any other) behavior, even when this determinism is considerably subtler and more sophisticated than the types we ordinarily associate with determinism. And hence, finally, the extreme unwisdom of
deleting from sociological consideration those elements which most of the
great sociologists, from Weber to MacIver, have declared fundamental
—the elements of intentionality, of definition of situation, of purpose, and
of symbolic interaction.

Nothing in the above discussion is intended to suggest that deviant
behavior, any more than the behavior of the conformist, is beyond sociological generalization or scientific understanding. Deviance, like alienation and anomie, is a constant feature of all societies and cultures we
know anything about. Each exists in some degree in all ages. No one
of them can be declared the fixed consequence of any particular form of
economic, political, or social system. Neither deviant, nor alienated,
nor anomic behavior is simply constrained or induced in the individual
by impersonal circumstances. No instance easily comes to mind of
anyone's being *driven* to any one of these three forms of social entropy.
All alike are manifestations of what we have described as interactive,
role, status, and normative behavior, subject to essentially the same kinds
of explanation given to other forms of behavior.

Notes

1. Robert Blauner, *Alienation and Freedom* (Chicago: University of Chicago Press, 1964), especially p. 206.
2. Emile Durkheim, *Suicide* (New York: The Free Press, 1951), p. 246.
3. Charles Page has suggested, in an important insight, that intellectual disciplines can be marginal, in the sense used in this chapter. He points out
that much of the positive contribution of sociology, for instance, comes from
the marginal position it had for years among the social sciences. See
his "Sociology as a Teaching Enterprise" in Robert K. Merton *et al.*
(eds.), *Sociology Today* (New York: Harper Torchbooks).

4. Albert K. Cohen, "Deviant Behavior," in *International Encyclopedia of the Social Sciences* (New York: Macmillan, 1968), Vol. 4, p. 148.

5. Emile Durkheim, *The Rules of Sociological Method* (New York: The Free Press, 1950), pp. 68–69.

6. David Matza, *Delinquency and Drift* (New York: Wiley, 1964), p. 22. This book could well become one of the most important single works in the history of American sociology.

III

SOCIAL CHANGE

11

The Problem
of Social Change

THE CONCEPT OF CHANGE

Our discussion of the social bond has thus far been confined to the elements and processes which provide structure, which supply stability and persistence in social relationships. The words "stability" and "persistence" are, of course, relative. As has been made abundantly evident in these pages, conflicts, disharmonies, tensions, and strains are almost constantly involved in social behavior. No matter how stationary or placid a given social structure may appear to be, no matter how old it may be, everything we know about the processes of social behavior suggests the presence in this structure of role strains, status conflicts, and normative contradictions, in at least a mild degree. Elements of at least incipient deviance, alienation, and anomie are always present in social behavior.

But these, for all their dynamic quality, are not change. They may be associated with change. They are very likely indeed to be accelerated by change. But precisely the same strains, conflicts, and tensions can also be associated for very long periods of time with *persistence.* This is a vital consideration in the study of social behavior that is all too often overlooked. It is assumed that because internal strains and conflicts almost constantly exist in a social organization or group, change must be taking place. But this is very far from the truth.

There are countless peoples in the history of mankind for whom change has been minimal and infrequent.   It would be plainly absurd to suppose that there were no conflicts of role, of status, or of interest within these peoples and cultures.   The institution of caste in India, the patriarchal family system in China, the village community through- out Asia and much of the rest of the world as well—all of these, as we know, existed for very long periods.   To believe that these institutions were without persistent conflicts of role, status, and norm, without evi- dences of deviance, anomie, and alienation, would be to believe nonsense. But change is something else.

Change is a succession of differences in time in a persisting identity. Each of the elements of the definition is crucial: "succession of differ- ences," "in time," and "persisting identity."   Let us start with the last. Until we have in view some persisting identity—whether it be a tree, a human being, a state, a kinship system, a social role, or a norm—we have nothing on which to pronounce change.   The mere existence of *differences* is not enough.   To arrange a dozen different things in front of one is to exhibit differences but not change.   We encounter change only when we perceive a succession of differences in some con- tinuing entity, differences which manifest themselves in time.

The Christian church has had continuous identity since the late first century A.D.   (We know too little about the period immediately after the life of Jesus to speak with any confidence of it.)   There is no diffi- culty in describing Christianity in such a way as to connect—historically and sociologically—the church of the late first century in Rome and that diverse assemblage of beliefs, sects, and churches which is Christianity in the twentieth century.   It is not necessary to believe in the dogma of apostolic succession for one to be aware of a persisting organizational identity that we call the Christian church.   Manifestly, however, Chris- tianity has changed over a period of nineteen centuries.   How else could we describe the succession of differences of condition which its history reveals?   We see both persistence and change.

Or consider the English language—more specifically, the language spoken by the inhabitants of the British Isles.   To compare the written or spoken language of this area in the twentieth century with that spoken and written in Chaucer's time, for example, is to be aware of a succession of differences in syntax, in vocabulary, in spelling, and in various other respects.   But the differences of condition are nonetheless differences within a persisting identity.   It would be something else entirely to array before us, for instance, the differences between English, Chinese, and Swahili.   For change to exist there must be successive differences, and they must be in time and within a continuing entity.

There is no need to multiply illustrations. What is important is to stress the fact that differences as such, differences or variations from some arbitrary, statistical norm or differences of behavior within some purely classificatory type, whether kinship or religion or language, do not in themselves constitute change. Lest this fact seem too obvious to have been mentioned, it will suffice to refer to the very large number of works, most of them to be found in the now very old literature of "social evolution," in which logically classified differences of some social type —religion, social stratification, kinship, or whatever—*are* regarded by their authors as synonymous with social change. But if there is any indication of change in these classifications, it is of logical type, not change in the substantive, empirical sense we are interested in here.

Let us now proceed to another important point regarding the problem of change: I have just stressed, first, that change cannot be made synonymous in our thinking with mere action or interaction and, second, that it cannot be made synonymous with a mere array of differences. Let us now proceed to this vital proposition, one that will be central in all the discussion of change that follows in this chapter: *Change cannot be deduced or empirically derived from the elements of social structure.*

The belief that change can be so derived or deduced is one of the oldest in Western thought. We find the belief in existence as far back as Aristotle's *Politics*. And even today the same belief lies at the heart of much sociological theory, particularly that to be found in structural functionalism and systems theory. No one will dispute the fact that it is an attractive belief. For the whole complex problem of change in time is marvelously simplified by the assumption that the crucial elements of change lie *within* the structure or pattern of social behavior we happen to be concerned with at any given moment. But attractiveness and simplification do not necessarily indicate correctness. And, for reasons that will be detailed and made clear in succeeding sections, we are obliged to refer to belief in structurally induced change as a major sociological fallacy.

At the beginning of Chapter 3 I spoke of the fallacy of all efforts to deduce or derive the elements of social behavior from the elements of biological behavior: instincts, reflexes, drives, and needs, all embedded in man's biological nature. Such efforts, as we saw, are fruitless because of the nearly limitless potentialities of social behavior which man's brain and capacity for speech give him and, second, because of the whole distinctive area we know in the study of social behavior as *symbolic interaction*.

To seek to derive change—its sources, mechanisms, continuities or discontinuities, and alleged directions—from the elements of social structure—role, status, norm, and so on—is as fallacious and self-defeating as it is to seek to derive the elements of social structure from man's native biological endowment. Deviance, as we have seen, may be so derived from social structure; for deviance is an inescapable aspect, in some degree, of all social behavior. But deviance is not change, though it may on occasion be related to change. Conflict, tension, or strain may also be deduced or derived from social structure, for it is hardly conceivable that such processes should not be present, role, status, and norm behavior being what they are.

When we pass, however, from deviance—or the varied processes of conflict and strain to be found in any social structure—to social change, we pass to a realm that is no more reducible to the elements of social structure than these are to the elements of biology. For we are in the realm of history—of event, time, place, and circumstance.

PERSISTENCE AND CHANGE

We begin, not with change, but with persistence and fixity. There is nothing paradoxical in this. Despite the abundance of phrases in both popular and learned thought attesting to the omnipresence, the constancy, the timelessness of change, all empirical evidence suggests that in the history of any specific mode of behavior, persistence occupies a formidable place. True, many conflicts, tensions, and ingrained hostilities may lie beneath the surface. Quite obviously this is the case in caste, slavery, and other relationships in which power and exploitation figure prominently. No mode of social interaction, as we have noted, is without at least occasional manifestation of conflict within. But despite a very old and still widespread conception in social thought, internal conflicts and tensions do not necessarily generate actual changes of structure. We might wish this were the case, for it could wonderfully simplify understanding of change.

But if we limit ourselves to what we can observe, whether macroscopically or microscopically, we do not find this self-engendered change in any social structure. What we do find—and in vast abundance—are persistence and fixity. Each of these is reconcilable with internal conflicts of role, status, and norm, which can indeed bulk large.

The university as we find it in Western society since the twelfth century is a prime illustration. There is no doubt that changes have taken place in its structure. To compare the University of South Dakota, Harvard, or Ohio State with the university as we find it in the abundant records for the thirteenth century at Bologna, Paris, or Oxford is to see substantial differences. But there are also substantial similarities. Or, better, compare the present reality of the University of Bologna in Italy with its character in the thirteenth century. There are differences and there are similarities. The first indicate changes which have taken place at various times; the second indicate striking elements of persistence of type.

Although *what* is taught today is very different from what was taught eight hundred years ago, we cannot, as sociologists, overlook the persistences of the *ways* things are taught. Now, as then, we find the university organized in terms of colleges, faculties, institutes; we find its work parceled out in the forms of curricula, courses, and lectures. Today, as then, the prime protagonists are groups called faculty and students. And as surely today as eight hundred years ago, the permission of the faculty is required before a student may receive what was then and is now called a degree or license. The norms of academic consensus remain much the same, as do the criteria of advancement, whether faculty or student advancement.

Even the conflicts reveal a striking similarity. Records make clear that students in Bologna in the thirteenth century fought for, even if they rarely got, rights to participate in the structure of authority in the university. Violations by students of the civil (and canonical) order were commonplace, frequently violent, met by attacks in the form of reprisal by outraged townspeople and, occasionally, by censure or excommunication by the chancellor or bishop. One may securely assume that role conflicts and value contradictions, for faculty and students alike, were rife then as now. No one familiar with any concrete sector of medieval society will believe that it was not subject to conflicts of all kinds, frequently violent ones. Religion may have been unified; the social order was not.

I deliberately chose the example of an institution whose central function, which is the pursuit of the intellectually new, might evidence an unusual and even continuing amount of change from century to century—change of structure as well as of content of teaching. Surely, if internal conflicts, or even conflicts between university and immediate environs, had very much to do with change, we should not expect to find the present-day structure of the university as strikingly like its thirteenth-century prototype as we do in fact find it. And, forgetting all precepts from conventional sociological theory about the ubiquity and constancy of change, we have to admit that the university and its ways manifest remarkable conservatism from generation to generation, no matter what the varying political attitudes of its members. If such conservatism or fixity of type is apparent in an institution dedicated to the search for the new in knowledge, it is easy to understand these same conditions in institutions such as the church, family, caste, and village community. For in these the preservation of the old takes on calculated, even ritualistic, status.

Why should we boggle at the idea of persistence and fixity in social behavior? Chiefly, I believe, because we confuse change with mere social interaction, or mobility, or physical movement from place to place, job to job, and so on. If one wishes to define these as change, all well and good. But if what we are searching for are the causes of change of type or structure in a social order, we are plainly concerned with something else. Social interaction is incessant, as are the innumerable modes of deviance and anomie and alienation. But all alike are reconcilable with persistence and fixity in social types. Consider only the number of undoubted role tensions, not to say domestic squabbles and hatreds, in the history of the family in the West during the past two thousand years. But the number of changes of structure of the family and changes of dominant roles in the family have been few. Most are directly related to events outside the family, in other spheres of society, which proved to have substantial impact upon the family. Deviations from the norm of monogamous marriage have always been present in the form of evasions—some of which have been sanctioned evasions, some not. But the norm of monogamy, like the structure of monogamy with its roles and statuses, goes on century after century. Periodically religious and secular reformers appear and point to a different, more rational, more effective way of meeting the set of problems— socialization of the young, among others—that the family, as we know it, meets. Innumerable "proofs" are fashioned of the "bankruptcy" of marriage, of its all too evident lack of relation to the sexual needs of male and female, and of instabilities made manifest by desertion and divorce rates. But monogamous marriage, like Ol' Man River, keeps rolling along.

There are literally hundreds, even thousands, of examples of the patently inefficient and irrational elements in our culture that continue generation after generation, century after century. The calendar is an excellent example. As a long line of would-be reformers have pointed out, the calendar we use, and have used with but minor modifications for thousands of years, is not merely built upon the names of now-forgotten pagan religious figures, but far worse, it is built upon conceptions of time that are as needless today as they are obsolete. Hence, our unequally long months and other varied and absurd devices, which make calendar time equate more or less with solar time. The veriest novice at calendar reform (there is, or was until recently, an association for calendar reform) could present us today with a calendar far superior to the one we have. But all efforts at such reform have failed (that of the French Revolution lasted only the length of the Revolution itself) since Pope Gregory, in 1582, quite literally suppressed ten days of that year and ordained that thereafter the years ending in hundreds should not be leap years unless they are divisible by 400. This procedure was a rather clumsy but at least effective way of meeting the problems which the centuries-old Julian calendar presented. And the reason for Gregory's reform, it should be noted here for future reference, was a *crisis*, a religious crisis having to do with the all-important location of the vernal equinox. Despite the manifest superiority of the Gregorian over the Julian calendar, arising from its closer relation to the actual solar year, only Roman Catholic countries accepted the reform in the beginning. Protestant nations took to it grudgingly and suspiciously, and the Eastern Church did not accept it until the twentieth century. Rarely is change desired.

What is clear in the relatively unimportant (after all, we *do* get by) instance of the calendar, or in instances of systems of weights and measures, of coinage, of styles in dress, of automobile design, of speech patterns, syntax, and so on is even more strikingly true in those areas of life today which threaten to become crucial to man's existence on earth. Witness such crucial areas as population norms, pollution of air, water, and sound, and hopelessly obsolete forms of government in cities and states. Persistence and fixity are very powerful realities. It would be simple if we could find a valid scapegoat for each of these. But we cannot, unless we point to ourselves and our ordinary ways of living. Habit, custom, adaptation even to the absurd and potentially lethal, use and wont, and sheer inertia—these are, as we have been able to see in our examination of the elements of the social bond, strongly built into the socialization process. Truly, change is for most of us an ordeal, an agony, something to be resisted at all costs.

If change were a constant and internally embedded feature of social life, we would surely see it most plainly today in that area of human culture that is by its very nature the most committed by its norms to incessant change. I refer particularly to science, but also generally to human knowledge and its pursuit. And it is true that if we fix our attention upon the whole of science over all centuries in all places, we find a striking amount of change. But to argue from this that change

is therefore constant in science is to belie the facts utterly. Despite the
itch to know that is popularly held to be the very essence of philosophy
and science, actual studies of both within finite time and concrete place
reveal quite extraordinary resistances to change. Thomas Kuhn in his
brilliant *The Structure of Scientific Revolutions* has documented this
resistance in key areas of the physical sciences during the past several
centuries. And what Robert K. Merton has shown in his sociological
studies of the nature of scientific behavior (this in contrast to vague
constructions of science as a "social system") is that the fierce competi-
tiveness of scientists in all areas has not only to do with hunger for
priorities in discovery but also with what can only be described as a
hoarding—with all the familiar defenses of one's hoard—of what one
has. Science, as Kuhn makes evident in his treatment of several centuries and as Merton makes clear in sociological terms, can suffer from
the kind of conventionalization of the old and hostility to the new that
we are more accustomed to thinking of in areas of politics, religion, or
life styles.

A generation ago the literary historian John Livingston Lowes
demonstrated conclusively in his *Convention and Revolt in Poetry* that
even in the supposed haven of the incessantly creative and, hence,
change-inducing mind, routinization, conventionalization, and downright conservatism of type are very common, with genuine change rare.
In literature and in science, as in religion, fixity is real.

There is nothing really surprising in any of the preceding discussion, not in light of what we have already found to be true of the mechanisms of social interaction, including socialization, and of the nature
of roles and norms. Only as the result of certain *assumptions* regarding
change, assumptions that may be likened to Francis Bacon's "idols of the
mind," does so much of sociological theory continue in manifest contradiction with what empirical studies of social behavior reveal about
change. These assumptions, as I have suggested, were originally drawn
from the analogy between society or culture or an institution and the
biological organism. And I believe it worth emphasizing that it is in
those theories today most strongly characterized by biological premises
—theories of social systems and social functions—that the image of
social change as growth is most powerful. These are the theories in
which we are most likely to find labored and largely useless comparisons
of social change with "differentiation," "immanent development," "functional realization," and elaborate sequences of "stages of growth" for
institutions that admittedly bear no relation to the actual history of any
specific geographical area or any finite time period.

It is frequently claimed, in justification of these functionalist and growth theories, that they represent the application of the insights of modern biological evolutionary theory to the study of society. They do not. There is not the slightest substantive relation between the conclusions, much less the methods, of the theory of evolution in contemporary biology and the conclusions regarding the nature of change reached by those sociologists who work with abstract universals such as social systems. The latter come directly from a view of developmentalism that is very old in Western society, that goes back indeed to Greek preoccupation with the life cycle of the organism as the key to the understanding of all change in the universe. The contemporary biological theory of evolution, on the other hand, rises directly from the highly empirical studies of post-Darwinian biologists, particularly those in the field of genetics. One does not find here reliance upon any model of self-contained growth, upon assumed patterns of differentiation, or upon hoary concepts of stages, immanence, and cumulative variation.

CHANGE AS PROCESS

If the first step in the understanding of social change is the understanding of the phenomena of persistence and fixity, the second is a clear distinction between two very different types of social change. In making this distinction I follow the late A. R. Radcliffe-Brown. What he writes on change is of crucial importance.

> The word "change" (and more particularly "process") is ambiguous in relation to society. I want to differentiate two totally different kinds. One goes to a primitive society, witnesses the preliminaries to a marriage ceremony, the ceremony itself, and its consequences: two individuals, formerly unrelated or in a special relationship, are now in another, that of husband and wife; a new group has been organized, which develops into a family. Obviously, you have here something which you can call social "change" or "process." There is change within the structure. But it does not affect the structural form of the society.... They are analogous to the changes which the physiologist can study in an organism—the changes of metabolism, for instance. The other type of change occurs when a society, as the result of disturbances induced either by internal developments or impact from without, changes its structual form.

These two types of change it is absolutely necessary to distinguish and to study separately. *I would suggest that we call the first kind "readjustment." Fundamentally, it is a readjustment of the equilibrium of a social structure. The second I would prefer to call "change of type." However slight the latter may be, it is a change such that when there is sufficient of it, the society passes from one type of social structure to another.*[1] *(Emphasis added.)*

Here, then, in Radcliffe-Brown's succinct phrasing, is the distinction we need if we are to proceed to an empirical study of change in any identifiable form of social behavior. It is a distinction between the kinds of "readjustment" of behavior—the ordinary forms of interaction, movement, and mobility and the adaptations from day to day which are to be found more or less constantly within any type of institutionalized behavior—and *those changes of type, or form, or pattern of behavior* which are so much rarer and far more significant in the history of human institutions. The first kind of changes is clearly compatible with *persistence of type.* The second, obviously, is not.

The principal point of Radcliffe-Brown's paragraphs is the fundamental importance of keeping the two kinds of change separate. It is essential, he tells us, to distinguish between them and to study them separately. But, unfortunately, much of Western social thought from Aristotle to contemporary sociological functionalists has failed to make this distinction. For, it is tempting to suppose that the *second* kind of change, change of structure or type, is the cumulative result of the *first* kind of changes, those day-to-day readjustments of behavior, those constant conflicts of role, status, and norm which are to be found in greater or lesser degree all the time. Hence the fascination of the model or image of growth in the single organism. In growth is to be found most vividly that fusion of the two types of change—with the first becoming incrementally and cumulatively the second.

But however tempting it may be to apply the model of growth and its properties, it is useless—worse, highly deceptive—when our subject is the historically verifiable, concrete, and empirical changes which the study of social behavior reveals. Again let it be emphasized that if we are contemplating the whole of civilization, past, present, and future, something akin to the growth of the organism may doubtless be premised. But this premise is metaphoric. Or if we are dealing with constructed social systems, abstract and timeless systems, instead of actual social behavior in time and place, the model of growth may have relevance. But its relevance is limited to the constructed social system.

The model of growth cannot lend itself to an understanding of those actual, historical structures of behavior whose changes are, or should be, the real object of the sociological study of change.

Consider again the university in the West over eight centuries, or black-white relationships in the United States over three centuries, or the mode of social behavior in India we call caste over more than two thousand years. In each of these, both types of change are to be found. Beyond question those readjustments of behavior Radcliffe-Brown mentioned are, and have always been, operating in each. And, if we look carefully at the *historical* record—the record of what actually happened in time and place for each of these relationships—we do indeed find clear evidences of change of the second, or structural, type. We do not, however, find many of these latter. In all three of the relationships, processes of persistence have been tenacious. Until a few years ago in this country, most white attitudes toward the Negro were not very different from those of the eighteenth and nineteenth centuries. Until perhaps a half-century ago, the basic caste structure in India was not different from what it had been thousands of years earlier. The records on both of these examples are clear. Still, changes of structure do take place now and then. And these are the changes, obviously, of greatest interest to sociology, because the understanding of them is of great importance to society and government.

How, under what circumstances, in what ways, and with what effects do changes of social structure take place? This is clearly the vital question. It is one that can be answered only in terms of, first, the demonstrable characteristics of social behavior and, second, those data which the historical record or which direct observation reveals. Assumptions regarding growth and differentiation, models of social systems, and models drawn from either biology or physics are all useless unless they can explain the kinds of actual changes which observation shows to have taken place in the history of an institution or organization —not change in the timeless realm of the abstract.

TIME, PLACE, AND CIRCUMSTANCE

I shall begin with the observation that the importance of time, place, and circumstance to the study of change will be obvious to all who have not yet been seduced by the allure of timeless, placeless, and abstract social systems.

From Aristotle through Leibniz, Comte, Marx, and Spencer down to contemporary theorists of social systems, a single, glittering ideal has existed in the study of social change. This ideal involves propositions concerning change that are so abstract and so general as to reduce to nullity references of a specific sort to time and place and circumstance. There is nothing wrong with the ideal of generality or of abstractness as such. All knowledge, especially scientific knowledge, aims at generality. The central point, however, is how, on what basis, the generality is attained. If it is the consequence of sound, empirically oriented study of social behavior generality is valuable. If, however, the generality is the consequence of utilization of analogies, as in the analogy of organic function and growth, we have something very different. The latter is hardly the aim of any science that seeks to discover and to explain.

It would be convenient, of course, if we could overlook the particularity of social behavior—and of history and geography. But, plainly, we cannot. For all social behavior takes place in time, in setting, and under historically formed circumstances. Whatever generalizations regarding change we arrive at must be formed on the basis of particularity, even though to go beyond particularity is a proper goal of social science. For this reason, we can learn the most from those studies of change which have been done by *historians*—historians of institutions, organizations, communities, ideas, art forms, and so on—and by those sociologists and other social scientists whose work demonstrates *a high degree of concern with historical actuality.*

Unfortunately their number is not large. For, apart from historians, social scientists have overwhelmingly tended to follow the lead of those whose so-called evolutionary theories of the nineteenth and twentieth centuries have aimed, even as did those of Plato, Aristotle, and Lucretius in the ancient world, at a generality that proceeded not from particularity but from abstraction—abstraction *from* particularity; abstraction in the form of some analogically derived model of *the* social system, or some timeless, placeless conception of kinship, property, capitalism, religion, or other institution.

True, theorists of the last-cited kind can employ with great ingenuity the particularity of time, place, and circumstance to illustrate supposed "natural" developments or cycles or trajectories of some generalized, abstract institution. Many of the social evolutionists of the eighteenth and nineteenth centuries did this. Many scholars do so today. Manifestations of a given institution—religion, for example—are drawn copiously from areas and periods throughout the world and time. These are arranged in some more or less arbitrary and logical order, ranging from the simple to the complex. (A whole host of value assumptions are, of course, present in any such ordering; for who is to say what is "simple" and what is "complex" in matters of religion, property, political government, and the like? We shall overlook these, dubious as they are, for they do not affect the essence of the matter.) The essential difficulty or distortion of this approach lies in the supposition that in this logical, classificatory arrangement anything exists that can be properly said to be relevant to *change*. Change is the succession of differences in time in a persisting identity. We have added to this the vital attributes of place and circumstance. But unless one is willing to grant empirical reality to "religion"—irrespective of *what* religion, *where*, and *when*—or to any other abstract institutional universal, there is nothing that can be said to have changed, or to be changing, when we are offered these classificatory presentations of "data" drawn from all places and all times to fit some preconceived notion of what *the* development of religion has been. To describe totemism in Australia, then pantheism in East Africa, and ancestor worship, polytheism, and monotheism, each with a manifestation drawn from a different place and time, is without question an interesting enterprise. So is the effort, through structural, cultural, or some other type of analysis, to decide which is the "less developed" and which is the "more developed" type.

But we are told nothing about *change* in such an enterprise. There is variation, if we like, but it is variation of logical type. It is not variation in the sense of change, as when we say that a change took place in Christianity in the sixteenth century in Western Europe, or that a change is taking place at the present time in Hinduism as the result of dislocation of caste in many areas, or that a change took place in American Protestantism when blacks began to be allowed a decade or two ago to attend white church services. In such instances we have something more than statistical variation; we have variation in the sense of *modification of a way of behavior that is specifiable in historical and geographical terms*. However, what can one do with "religion" conceived as a universal—except classify its manifestations?

We can learn a great deal about the processes of change by taking a single religion in a specified area over a period of time: Christianity in Western Europe or, if we prefer, in France, or in Paris, or in some small village in France. Properly approached, a work such as Kenneth Scott Latourette's study of the history and expansion of Christianity tells us much about the processes of change in religion.

A great number of studies of change exists in the historical and social sciences. These are found in longitudinal investigations of actual communities, cities, nations, social classes, kinship systems, specific social values or ideas; in the whole rich literature of "applied" anthropology with its studies of the contacts of peoples in different parts of the world, especially the British anthropological studies of South and East Africa; in the field of so-called comparative history; and in the burgeoning study of what is widely, if inaccurately, called the "development" of the new nations. These last, with their numerous and frequently sharp breaks with tradition, and with the very considerable number of social scientists ready and able to observe the changes involved, furnish an especially rich source of materials.

The scholars responsible for the kind of studies I have in mind are too numerous for full mention. I shall simply cite the work of a few individuals of notable stature: Max Weber's studies of religious and economic change, Frederick J. Teggart's investigations of Rome and the changes leading to its political decline, Robert K. Merton's treatment of the rise of science in the seventeenth century, Seymour Lipset's analysis of agrarian socialism in Canada, Asa Briggs' studies of urban change in England, Malinowski's and Radcliffe-Brown's studies of social and cultural change in primitive areas occupied by European invaders, Thomas Kuhn's investigations in the history of the sciences, Lynn White's study of technology and social change in medieval Europe, Marc Bloch's study of European feudalism, Rushton Coulborn's comparative studies of feudalism, Kingsley Davis' works on society and population, especially of Latin America and India, George Homans' studies of social organization in the British Isles, Cyril Black's treatment of change in the new nations today, Reinhard Bendix's investigations of industrialization in several countries.

Instead of beginning with a self-defeating assumption of the omnipresence and constancy of change in a given mode of social behavior or social organization, the best *empirical* studies of change first ask in effect some vital questions. How and under what circumstances does change take place? What forces have been required to shake people free of established and often obsolete ways of behavior? What forces are involved in the periodic replacement of old social roles, statuses, and norms by new ones? What is the relation, if any, between minor changes *within* a given pattern of social behavior and the more substantial but rare changes *of* such a pattern? How do the events and changes of one major sphere of society impinge upon those of another? What, in sum, are the sources, causes, and nature of change?

When these questions are not asked, we learn far less about the nature of change, about the immensely important problem of bringing needed change about in the world, than we should. At a time when an increasingly enlightened social policy seeks proper ways of inducing badly needed change—change, for example, in the norms which attend high birth rates, in the inherited roles and statuses which make genuine civil equality difficult to achieve, and in traditions that continue to hold large numbers of people to lives of poverty and submission—we are all too often lacking in the kind of knowledge necessary to the problem.

Note

1. A. R. Radcliffe-Brown, *A Natural Science of Society* (New York: Free Press, 1957), p. 87. Wilbert E. Moore, in his *Social Change* (Englewood Cliffs, N.J.: Prentice-Hall, 1963), makes substantially this distinction. I regard Moore's book as the best done by any living sociologist on the systematic study of change.

12

The Nature and Source of Social Change

CHANGE AND CRISIS

The first point to be made about change is that wherever it exists in substantial degree, it is associated with some form of crisis. Under the spell of so many of the developmental notions of change—change as growth, change as slow, gradual, and continuous increment, change as progress, and so on—too many writers have neglected the crisis element in change. But if we wish to consider change, in contrast to mere action and interaction, or minor adaptation, we dare not omit the element of crisis.

As W. I. Thomas stressed in his own distinguished studies of social change, crisis is a relationship between human being and environment precipitated by the inability of the human being (or social group or organization) to continue any longer in some accustomed way of behavior. Crisis is a form of attention, of conscious, heightened attention, that is wrung from us in moments of emergency when breakdown is manifest in our ordinary ways of behavior. Individuals, groups, whole nations periodically experience crises.

Most of us do everything we can, of course, to shore up the old ways. Such is the shock of enforced social change that most people will often employ what the nineteenth-century English philosopher Jeremy Bentham called "fictions." No matter how extreme the need for change in our old ways, we adopt, in effect, verbal, legal, religious, or other fictions through which we convince ourselves that change of behavior is *not* needed, that the old and cherished, if properly understood, can continue despite all overt evidence of its unsuitability.   Much of the world's literature consists, basically, of justifications and rationalizations of practices that have become obsolete and even injurious.   One thinks, for example, of Aristotle, one of the wisest and most humane of all the ancient philosophers, who sought to justify slavery in the ancient city-state rather than yield to the entreaties of those radicals of his day who believed slavery inhumane and inefficient.   Few of us are altogether immune to the practice of creating fictions, by which we so often prop up what should be dismantled.

There is, as we reflect on it, nothing astonishing about this character of the human mind.   Social behavior, after all, is *learned* behavior; the most vital aspects of this behavior have been learned within the first five or ten years of life.   Language, accent, attitudes toward others, conception of self, career images, emotional disposition toward social values, and mode of dress, of eating, of sleeping are all consequences of the socialization process and manifestations of the individual's control over his environment and himself.

As Thomas emphasized, *control* is the conscious or unconscious aim of all human behavior.   Every element of culture is a reflection of a society's control over environment.   Equally true is the fact that every element of the individual socialization process is a means of acquiring control, with language undoubtedly the major means of control in individual life.   With personal or collective achievement of control, Thomas wrote, *attention* can wane, can be allowed to become dormant. Control has been reduced to habit in the individual, to custom or institution in the larger social order.

But periodically control is threatened by novel elements in the environment or by some incapacity on the part of the subject.   An accustomed way of behavior no longer works properly.   Generally, human beings make every effort to avoid confrontation with this breakdown of a behavior pattern.   The power of habit and custom are great because they are reflections of adaptation or control which make the hard work of thought, of *attention*, unnecessary.   Thought, in the full and proper sense of the word—a sense that does *not* include mere reverie, reminiscence, association, or ordinary stream of consciousness—is, for most of us, agonizing.   And the older one becomes, the more agonizing it is.   Hence the tendency of most of us to spend most of our lives, after a certain age, in repeating what we know, in finding mere extensions or adaptations of what we learned through the hard process of thought at some earlier time in life. With rare exception, artists, scientists, statesmen, and technologists do this; there is little wonder, then, in the fact that others do.

The historian Elting E. Morison, writing on the subject of technological change and the appalling difficulty of bringing it about, especially in large organizations, tells the following story.

During World War II in Britain when armaments were becoming scarce and use of manpower critical, time and motion studies were made of gun crews in the artillery. It was hoped that the speed of operation of each gun could be increased. In one such study of a gun crew numbering five men, a peculiar act was noted. At a certain point, just before the firing of the gun, two of the men simply stood at attention for three seconds, then resumed the work necessary to the next firing. This was puzzling. The men themselves could not explain it; it was a part of the technique they had learned in gunnery school. Neither the officers nor the instructors at gunnery school could explain it either. All anyone knew was that the three-second standing at attention was a "necessary" part of the process of firing the highly mechanized piece of artillery. One day an old, long-retired artillery colonel was shown the time and motion pictures. He too was puzzled at first. He asked to see the pictures again. Then his face cleared. "Ah," he said when the performance was over. "I have it. The two men are holding the horses."[1]

Not for close to half a century had horses drawn artillery, but they once had—holding the horses while the gun fired was necessary. The horses disappeared from the artillery, but the way of behavior went on. We laugh, and say the story is one more illustration of military inertia and add to it the familiar stories of military opposition to the introduction of tanks in World War I, to the introduction of aircraft ("it will frighten the horses"), and so on. But the history of the academic, legal, medical, and engineering professions is not different, except in details. Nor is the rest of society different. Once "control" is gained through some kind of habit or institutionalization of behavior, no effort ordinarily will seem too great to protect that form of control, to avert the possibility of its being dropped or significantly changed. The appeal of habit is the possibility it affords *to suspend conscious thought*, to transfer thought elsewhere to spheres not yet reduced, or easily reduced, to habit. The consequence is that few of us can be said to welcome change—at least in those primary spheres where we feel most deeply identified—family, work, religion, and others.

Still, despite our best efforts sometimes, despite firmly fixed habits, despite what Walter Bagehot called the "cake of custom," change does take place. A way of behavior or thinking, either in the individual or in the social order, becomes so patently ineffective, or so downright injurious, that human beings from time to time feel compelled to change. Or sudden exposure to new ideas and new ways of behavior—the result of mixture of peoples through trade, migration, wars, or other means —may lead to loss of satisfaction in the old.

As W. I. Thomas describes the process of change, the sense of *loss of control* of the situation is followed by an awakening of *attention*.

> *Attention is the mental attitude which takes note of the outside world and manipulates it; it is the organ of accommodation. But attention does not operate alone; it is associated with habit on the one hand and with crisis on the other. When the habits are running smoothly, the attention is relaxed; it is not at work. But when something happens to disturb the run of habit, the attention is called into play and devises a new mode of behavior which will meet the crisis.*[2]

The history of any people will reveal crises from time to time. Among primitive peoples the exhaustion of game, intrusion of outsiders, floods, drought, pestilence, famine, and defeat in battle are among the oldest causes of crisis in human history. Few if any peoples have not suffered all of them at one time or other. For a great many peoples even today they remain powerful causes of crisis. But, especially in contemporary civilization, there are countless other causes of crisis. Few Americans who are today in their fifties will forget the crisis in this country that *visibly* began with the stock market crash of 1929 and that had become, by 1931, an economic depression more severe than any known in national history. Many millions were thrown out of work, hunger was widespread, prices and wages fell, and a mood of panic had seized the country by March 1933 when Franklin D. Roosevelt took office as President. Panic and related states of mind were caused by the inability of old ways to meet the problems they were supposed to meet. *Control*, in the sense used above by Thomas, was lost, at least temporarily. *Attention* was awakened in the circumstances of crisis, and change—very considerable change by the standards of that day—took place. Even so, few who experienced the Great Depression will forget the formidable opposition to change of any kind on the part of a substantial minority in this country numbering many millions. One need only go to the newspaper files to find a record of the many for whom change was too great an ordeal even when old ways had plainly become inadequate and new ways of meeting such problems as employment, relief, social security, and price stabilization were clearly called for.

But the crisis element in change, with large numbers of persons nonetheless holding tenaciously to old ways, often permits innovation-minded individuals or elites to come to the top. The sporadic, the intermittent, as well as the crisis-born nature of change is well illustrated by the contrast between the many who, for the most part, suffer the inconvenience or even the disaster of the old, and the few, usually a very few, persons who see crisis as the sole opportunity for needed change and who possess the personal powers of accomplishing it. Crisis lay behind the remarkable reforms of Cleisthenes in ancient Attica, reforms which, as we have seen, ushered in the great fifth century B.C. Crisis lay behind the assumption of power by Augustus in Rome at the end of the first century B.C. and then the momentous conversion of the Republic into the Empire. If we consider any of the major changes in history—changes which involve whole legal orders, social organizations, religions, and which extend into all areas of a society for centuries following—we almost always find some one individual, or a relatively small elite, at work. Hence the momentous significance of Charles the Great, Martin Luther, Oliver Cromwell, Napoleon, Lenin, Hitler, Franklin D. Roosevelt, and Martin Luther King. Crisis in conjunction with some individual of superior powers, in each instance, led to extraordinary changes. The "great man" theory of history by itself is insufficient. The following words from W. I. Thomas make evident nonetheless the crisis role of the superior individual.

> *Whatever importance we may attach to group-mind and mass-suggestion, the power of the attention to meet a crisis is primarily an individual matter, or at least the initiative lies with the individual. The group, therefore, which possesses men of extraordinary mental ability is at an advantage. . . . The relation of the "great man" to crisis is indeed one of the most important points in the problem of progress. Such men as Moses, Mohammed, Confucius, Christ, have stamped the whole character of a civilization.*[3]

It is sometimes thought that a sociological theory of change is, almost by definition, one that dispenses with such seemingly random and conceptually unassimilable beings as great men. If so, so much the worse for any sociological theory of change. For major changes are incomprehensible save in terms of superlatively endowed individuals, or effectively marshaled elites, working *within social circumstances*, usually those of crisis. The life of Winston Churchill makes sufficiently evident how, apart from circumstances of crisis, a gifted individual can live much of his life unmarked by any of the stigmata of greatness— until a crisis such as that which struck an unprepared England in the late 1930s, in the face of the rising might of Nazi Germany, comes into existence. Only then does the great man, Winston Churchill, appear. Prior to that he had been simply Churchill, known to have been responsible for the fiasco of Dardanelles in World War I. Some thought him clever; others thought him to be a turncoat, clever at best, but hardly possessed of the stuff of greatness. Closely similar characterizations were made of Franklin D. Roosevelt until his election to the Presidency in 1932.

To suppose that a sociological theory of change can dispense with either the existence of the individual or the setting of historically formed social crises and can base itself solely upon the supposed dynamisms of impersonal role and status interactions within "the social system" is absurd. The greatest of sociologists, including Max Weber, have never thought any such supposition to be feasible. So far was Weber's approach from being one neatly encapsulated by any concept of social growth that he tended, in much of his work, to make change the consequence of charismatic individuals. In the force of charisma, Weber thought, as this is to be witnessed in many spheres of social life— religious, political, military, intellectual—lies the mainspring of substantial change. Hence Weber's fascination with the problem of whether significant change can be expected in a social order in which large-scale and impersonal organization, especially bureaucracy, takes command and threatens to choke off the emergence of highly gifted or charismatic individuals. The appearance of an Adolf Hitler in the highest seat of German power only a few years after Weber's death may have made application of Weber's view premature. However Hitler's appearance in no way nullified Weber's theory of change.

But again let us emphasize that the crucial point is not the emergence of the individual, good or evil, least of all *which* individual. The crucial point is that of envisaging social change in a way that allows us to distinguish clearly between mere adaptations or minor modifications on the one hand and, on the other, those profound mutations of structure or role or status which always involve crisis.

CHANGE AND EVENTS

The notion of crisis in change leads us directly to consideration of the relation of change to *events*. An event is not a change, though it may be closely related to change. An event is a *happening*, an *occurrence*; it takes place in time and, of course, in setting. From one point of view the human past is a long succession of events which we like to imagine are linked genetically, as human lives are linked genealogically. An invasion is an event; so is a migration, a war, a revolution, an insurrection, the founding of a nation or association, a treaty, a plague, a landing on the moon. There are great events and there are trivial ones. No one can go through a single day without experiencing events in the form of encounters with others, with immediate environment, or, vicariously, through word of mouth or the news media. A single event may, by virtue of its crucial impact, alter one's whole career or life. A major event can also alter the character of an entire nation or culture. The Norman invasion of England in 1066 was an event that profoundly affected the social organization, culture, language, and system of political authority and social stratification of England. The now celebrated Supreme Court decision in this country in 1954, declaring "separate but equal" educational facilities unconstitutional, was an event. It is hardly necessary to expand upon the consequences of this event in many areas of American life.

Theoretically, every event is datable since it cannot be abstracted from time and place. There is an adventitious, even random, character to most events. This does not mean they are without relation to circumstances, to social and cultural conditions. But the precise character of this relation, above all, the actual incidence of the event, can never be deduced from the conditions. The assassination of Archduke Ferdinand on a July day in 1914 in Sarajevo, which touched off World War I, certainly did not occur in a vacuum. Had it not been for conditions of chronic nationalist unrest and hatred in the Balkan area the event, in all probability, would not have occurred. But irrespective of this, no one examining these conditions at the time, however meticulously, would have been able to deduce from them, to predict, an assassination on that day in that place. Such a student of the time and place might have concluded in advance that there was "high probability" of an assassination—but, as a scholar or scientist, he would have been forced to add "someplace, sometime; it is not certain when or where." Or, we might add here, even *whether*. For an assassination is but one of a vast number of possibilities, even when we are given the social and political conditions that existed in the Balkans in 1914.

The study of social change cannot be separated from the study of events, much as some social philosophers and sociological theorists would like to separate them. From Aristotle on, there has been a marked unwillingness in the history of social thought to deal with the problem of social change *in terms of events.* There are two main reasons for this unwillingness. First, events are by their nature unpredictable, fortuitous, and more or less random. They cannot be dealt with in the ordered ways dear to philosophers and scientists. Second, as we have already observed in this chapter, the very conception of change in society tended to rule out consideration of events. From Aristotle's *Politics* down to the works of contemporary functionalists and theorists of social systems, the prime objective of the study of change has been study of the processes of change that are declared to be *natural* to the social entity being considered. To deduce or derive change from structure has been and is the dominant approach. Hence the systematic neglect of events. An event is external and does not grow out of the structure. It is an occurrence or happening that springs from a very different, even unrelated, area of life. But, wish as we might, we cannot understand social change apart from consideration of events—even if our consideration must always be retrospective and historical rather than analytical or systematic.

From the point of view of the structure of caste in India the invasion of the British in the eighteenth century was purely random and fortuitous—in short, an event. But it was, as we know, crucial to the future of caste and many other Indian institutions in the long run. How else can we understand the changes in caste which very clearly *are* taking place in India today, apart from the impact of a whole set of economic, moral, legal, and intellectual forces which, on the record, are inseparable from the British occupation of India?

The patriarchal family in China is several thousand years old. Despite its undoubted internal conflicts and role tensions, it persisted as a social type in China until the nineteenth century. Then, under the impact of Western influences—forming an event which by no stretch of imagination could have been deduced from the structure of the patriarchal kinship organization—certain notable changes of type took place. These were followed by others—military, industrial, technological. And today, under the impact of communism, of a set of principles of social reconstruction which emanate from Marx, Engels, Lenin, and Stalin, the structure of kinship is being even more drastically changed.

The relation between changes in the structure of the Chinese family system and the instrusion of Western values is clear enough. The record shows that changes in the Chinese family followed almost directly the impact of Western values of individualism, contractualism, and disengagement of the small conjugal family from the wider structure of traditional kinship. Such, however, is the influence of the theoretical perspective I have been describing that we find sociologists such as Marion Levy declaring, despite a testimony of history they know very well, that "the *motivation* for change in China lay *primarily* in the stresses and strains created by, but contained *within* the 'traditional' structure."[4] But if this were so, there would not be, surely, the chronologically intimate relation between changes in the Chinese family system and the impact of events caused by the West.

Were internal stresses and strains, when sufficiently prolonged in time, the cause of social changes, we should expect to see such changes in those institutions and cultures which are characterized by geographical or social *isolation*. But in fact, as every anthropologist and historian knows, isolated cultures and institutions evidence, above all others, not change but fixity and persistence of type—and, on the record, over very long periods of time. It is all very well to suggest, in accord with a conventional wisdom that insists upon locating the sources of change *within* the type, that beneath the apparent fixity substantial changes of a cumulative character are building up. The fact remains, however, that we have no evidence of these, or at least of any which do in fact culminate in profound structural changes. Again it is useful to stress that inner conflicts and deviances are not in themselves at all inconsistent with perseverance of structure in the history of an institution or organization.

Hence the high correlation, so often noted by historians and by social scientists, between periods of pronounced change in an area and the impacts of such events as invasions, migrations, new trade routes, wars, explorations—in short, conditions of crisis precipitated by intrusions of circumstance. The twentieth century is very probably the greatest single century of social change in all human history—certainly in the scope of this change and in its diversity. There is scarcely an area today of any size or prominence on earth that is not the setting for manifold change. Along with these far-flung changes in social organizations in the world there are, and have been for a century or two, an enormous number of those impacts and intrusions we call events. Apart from these events from which modern economic, political, and social history is formed, no understanding of the structural changes so obvious today in the social organizations of peoples on all continents would be possible.

From one point of view all of the above discussion is obvious. No one acquainted with the data of history, or with any concrete mode of social behavior over a substantial period of time in an area, could fail to find it obvious. It becomes less obvious, however, when one turns from the historical record to those theories of change, as prominent today as in earlier centuries, which in effect dispense with the historical record in their preoccupation with what is called "natural change" or "normal change." This is the kind of change which, it is said, inheres *in* the form of social behavior and which will manifest itself in time if not interfered with. To which, returning once again to the empirical, we can only say: there is no change, none, at least, beyond those small, frequently self-canceling, adjustments and readjustments which go on ceaselessly within any form of social structure, however fixed or stable it may be. Again let us make the vital distinction between the relatively minor changes, variations, or deviations from the norm found everywhere at all times when human beings interact and those profounder changes of structure and type which the record shows to be relatively infrequent and almost always characterized by distinct crisis. Failure to make this distinction, or to keep it in mind while engaged in the study of change, lies behind the conclusions of so much sociological theory—conclusions which seek to derive the second type of changes from the first and which, in the process, neglect the vital role of events.

It would be a profound error to assume that events are solely of the dramatic kind suggested by invasions, migrations, and wars. From the point of view of one structure of social behavior, the impact of some major change in another structure is an event in the full sense of the word. Consider, for instance, the momentous study of change that is to be found in Max Weber's *The Protestant Ethic and the Spirit of Capitalism.* Weber is one of that rather small group of modern sociologists very sensitive indeed to the necessity of studying social change historically rather than as an extension of a largely metaphoric view of social growth in which causes of change are assumed to lie in the structure.

We may properly and usefully see Weber's study as a reaction to Marxism. Marx and Engels, declaring the priority of economic forces in the study of all change, had explained the rise of capitalism by reference to sources of change *within* the feudal economy. Out of the gradually accumulated contradictions within the feudal economy, Marx and Engels wrote, came in due time the change of structure represented by the appearance of capitalism, first in England, then in other countries. Each of these countries, Marx wrote in the Preface of his major work, *Capital*, would reveal the same tendencies, "working with iron necessity toward inevitable result," that England had. "That is the reason," Marx explained, "why England is used as the chief illustration in the development of my theoretical ideas." Even, Marx went on, "when a society has got on the right track for the discovery of the natural laws of its movement—and it is the ultimate aim of this work to lay bare the economic law of motion of modern society—it can neither clear by bold leaps nor remove by legal enactments the obstacles offered by the successive phases of its normal development."

No one will deny the immense prophetic, the quasi-religious, utility of such a theory as this. Applied to capitalism itself, as all Marxists then and since have applied it, the theory could hold up the millennial promise that capitalism would destroy itself through the same internal, self-resident forces which had brought it into being. The theory also could foresee a new form, socialism, emerging from the "womb" of capitalism just as capitalism had, in Marx's growth-modeled terms, emerged from the "womb" of the feudal economy. Such a theory can give hope of ultimate liberation from evil, just as do many religions. It is, however, inadequate as science.

The great merit of Max Weber's study of the rise of capitalism is that it proceeds directly from Weber's own repudiation of what he called "emanationism"—the growth-modeled view of change emanating from structure—and from his frank acceptance of the necessity of studying economic change historically, that is, empirically. And when Weber turned to the actual circumstances, in time and place, of the rise of capitalism, he found certain prior, *noneconomic* changes vital to an understanding of this momentous economic change. These changes were external to the economic order itself and, from the point of view of the study of the economic order, can only be thought of as *events*. These prior, external, noneconomic changes were certain profound modifications of men's evaluation of work and wealth—changes which, Weber demonstrated, were inseparable from Protestantism, and particularly Puritanism.

It would be erroneous to imply here that every element of Weber's argument has been found to be correct by subsequent historians and other scholars concerned with economic change. Nor, as close reading of *The Protestant Ethic and the Spirit of Capitalism* makes very plain, did Weber ever argue that the conditions of this great economic change were solely religious. Scores of works have demonstrated since Weber's classic study that the rise of capitalism cannot always be associated with the prior appearance of the Protestant ethic or, for that matter, with dominantly religious values at all.   But such demonstrations are of less consequence than the fact that they have *not* succeeded in upsetting the larger Weberian theory that social change can only be understood by reference to what have here been called time, place, and circumstance. Weber's argument is as valid today as in his time: apart from crises created by events in their impact upon social behavior, social change of major or structural types cannot be understood.   Change *cannot be deduced or derived from the structure itself*—whether this structure be economic, kinship, religious, or political.   This is surely clear to everyone except those who dispense with events on the ground that events, being by definition unpredictable, can therefore have no place in a *scientific* study of social change.   But recognition of events is crucial to understanding.   That the study of social change and also our capacity for effecting needed changes in society have improved so little throughout the centuries is testimony to one more example (and a powerful one) of persistence and fixity—in this case, fixity of the idea of growthlike, internal, self-generating, and cumulative change.

Let us, before dropping the concept of event and the necessity of consideration of events in the analysis of change, briefly consider one more of the problems posed—the present condition of black power in the United States.   One can understand how some of the protagonists in this movement would adopt a view of its rise set largely in the terms of black power itself—of its growth among Negroes through the centuries of American (and also African) history, the product of bitter conflicts between white and black, of the accumulation in time of tensions and motivations toward revolt which had to result sometime in the explosive behavior we today associate with the blacks in their relation to a largely white-dominated civilization.   A whole mystique of negritude has appeared, just as a mystique of Manifest Destiny appeared earlier in American thought with respect to the nation, to the white race, and to each of numberless other single aspects of human behavior through the ages.   No one should doubt the power, perhaps even the necessity, of such a dogma of social action when a social movement is forming.   Again we can remind ourselves of what the mystique of the *nation* effected in Western Europe in the decades immediately after the French Revolution, for good or bad, and what the mystique of the proletariat, in Marxist hands, has effected in so many parts of the world in this century.

But if our concern is not the formation of a certain kind of collective self-consciousness but is instead an understanding of the empirical realities behind the rise of black power in the mid-twentieth century, we shall of course have to abandon mystique. We shall also abandon any notion that this great movement today is the product of internal forces alone, or of forces alone bounded by black-white interaction. We shall be obliged to turn to events, not just the events, sometimes violent and dramatic, within the several centuries of black-white relationship in the United States but the events in spheres as distant from this relationship conceptually as the rise of the Protestant ethic was from the beginnings of capitalism in England. I refer again to such events as the rise and spread of the factory system, the moral consciousness among Americans first produced in New England in Unitarian and other religious circumstances, the spurt of technology and its spread to all areas, the effects of mass education, those of the two World Wars and their stimulus to internal migration in the United States, and those of constitutional, political, and administrative actions which, although not in the first instance precipitated by black-white issues, nonetheless came in time, in various circumstances, to have impact upon the whole condition of black-white relationships. To suppose, in short, that the conditions which objective analysis reveals to have been crucial in establishment of the black-white relationship as we find it in the mid-twentieth century are conditions deducible from anything that could possibly have been found *in this relationship* at any point in its history is to believe in dogma, not the value of historical analysis in the understanding of social change.

One final point with respect to events and change needs to be made. I have said that on the record no substantial change in a social group or organization, or in the structure of any form of social behavior, takes place except under the impact of events that cause crises. It does not follow, of course, that all events necessarily lead to substantial social changes. This, plainly, could never be substantiated in any proposition. Events occur or happen all the time in the life of the individual or in the history of a social organization. Usually events can be assimilated without much difficulty in the life organizations of individuals and by the codes and customs of societies. Many an invasion has taken place, or war broken out, or migration, famine, drought, or flood occurred, without the major elements of a social organization being more than transitorily affected. We should not forget what we have found to be true of any social organization or pattern of social behavior—its tendency to persist, to hold tenaciously to old ways as long as possible through deeply embedded processes of socialization and through adherence to norms, accustomed roles, statuses, and systems of authority.

To predict change merely on the basis of the impact of some event, large or small, is hazardous. The conflict between the social bond and the crisis which may be precipitated by some major event appears to be as often resolved in favor of persistence of the old as in acceptance of the new.

CONTINUITY AND DISCONTINUITY

Few conceptions are more widespread in Western thought than that of the continuity of change. The concept of continuity is also a product of the view of change that derives from the metaphor of growth. Like other derivations from this metaphor, the idea of the continuity of change takes on more meaning, or at least utility, in the large or the abstract than it does in the small and concrete.

To say that the development of mankind has been a continuous one, passing from the very simple in culture through successively more complex manifestations to the panoply of ideas, values, and things which comprise Western civilization at the present time is intelligible enough. Each successive condition or stage, we say, has emerged from its predecessor. Change throughout, we also are prone to say, is continuous, with no gaps to be found, assuming all data are made available. Consider, for example, the "art of war," an abstraction as stated, but one with meaning to all of us. If we were to arrange in functional and logical order every known manifestation of the weapons of war, from the simplest club or spear to current biological or nuclear horrors, we could surely see the principle of continuity illustrated. But it is *classificatory* continuity—continuity of change *only* if one grants empirical or substantive reality to "the art of war" with its examples drawn from every corner of the earth. It is easy enough to talk about continuity in this sense, and it is acceptable so long as one holds in mind what he is doing. When an ethnologist such as the late Robert H. Lowie writes on the political state with the declared intent of "vindicating the principle of continuity," he can do this, just as Lowie did, by arranging progressively more complex instances of political association from the most primitive tribe to the Roman Empire in a continuous series. His examples of political association are drawn from areas as far apart as the Plains Indians and the Romans. This system tells us much about gradations of differences and about classificatory continuity. But it tells us nothing about *change*, that is, actual, empirical change.

What the examination of changes in any finite area and period of time reveals is not the continuity of change but its *discontinuity*. The discontinuity of change proceeds from the same circumstances that make the concepts of crisis and event necessary to the study of change. We could speak validly of the continuity of the changes in some concrete area or institution only if we could show that each successive change emerges from its predecessor in the series. If the well-attested facts of intrusion from one area or sphere to another (in reference to events as described above) could be ignored and if there were no impacts or interferences to be discerned in the historical record of whatever is being studied, we might be able to speak with confidence of the "continuity of change." Only, however, in the realm of abstract social systems or in that of the great wholes and universals of such evolutionists as Herbert Spencer can these circumstances of intrusion, impact, and interference be ignored. They are, as we have observed, inseparable from the actual, historical record.

There is one sense of the word "continuity" that is incontestable. That is its literal meaning of things continuing in time. The earth continues, though with modifications from time to time. Mankind continues, though with even more dramatic modifications through ages of civilization. We may even speak of the continuity of time, though this presents certain difficulties. Continuity in the sense of persistence is hardly to be doubted. This, as we have seen, is abundantly manifest in the record of any area or form of behavior.

Much of what is in fact involved when we speak of continuity comes from the element of persistence. One speaks of the continuity of English history. There has been for many centuries, since the Norman Conquest at least, a single persisting identity that we properly call the English people or English civilization. Many events have occurred, many changes have taken place during those centuries in the British Isles, but we are nonetheless justified in speaking of the continuity of English history. And we are justified in so speaking even though, as every textbook on the subject makes plain, the inhabitants of England were exposed through all those centuries to an intermittent barrage of intrusions or impacts from the outside—sufficiently evident in the history of English thought, technology, industry, and polity. But if it were not for the fact that certain basic institutions and life styles have continued from age to age, have persisted, despite the modifications and alterations which have taken place in these institutions and life styles, we should have a very difficult time in demonstrating continuity. Certainly *the changes as such in English history* manifest no continuity from one to the other. How could they, given the often random, the intermittent, and the externally derived sources of these changes?

To argue that *change* is continuous is to argue not merely that change goes on constantly but that it reveals in its successive manifestations some kind of *genetic linkage* of these successive manifestations. It is to argue that each discrete change that we identify in the record literally emerges from a preceding change in a series of changes, that one change engenders another by virtue of some potentiality it has for "giving birth" to another change. And to argue that change is continuous is to argue, finally, that in this genetic linkage of changes something akin to organic growth is present from the start, with each later stage drawn cumulatively from prior stages, as so plainly occurs in the succession of changes any organism reveals in its growth.

But in the study of social behavior over time, in an identifiable area, with full attention given to what actually happens (in contrast to what might be drawn from some abstract model or constructed social system), we find none of these arguments capable of demonstration. For in fact change is *not* continuous, and the successive changes which are manifest in the record do *not* emerge genetically one from the other. Nor is there any evidence of the continuous accumulation of small or micro-changes into the larger or macrochanges that is so evident in organic growth or that might properly be inferred from some process over which a single intelligence presides from start to finish—as when one "develops" an idea into a larger idea or policy.

Durkheim wrote tellingly on the subject of the discontinuity of change in his *The Rules of Sociological Method*. In the study of change, Durkheim wrote, we begin with the *social milieu*. The social milieu is formed at any given time by the assembled circumstances and conditions of whatever change it is we are seeking to account for. The social milieu is our point of departure and it remains our effective context of investigation. All the data necessary to account for the change are to be found quite literally within this milieu, even though we may choose to divide the milieu into the data of "past" and of "present." If it is granted that this milieu is itself a product of history—of varied processes of persistence and fixity and stabilization, as well as of the events, changes, and impacts of past and present—it is nonetheless the context of the study of any given change. Properly conceived, that is, in terms of *all* the data relevant to our problem, this milieu is all we need for our study of the change in question.

What we *cannot* do, Durkheim emphasized, is to seek to derive our change genetically from some prior change, with this change in turn derived from some change still prior.   I italicize Durkheim's important words on the matter: *"The antecedent state does not produce the subsequent one, for the relation between them is exclusively chronological."*⁵ The fundamental point in this statement from Durkheim is not the one he himself immediately draws in his discussion, that "all scientific prevision is impossible." This point to be sure is important enough if only as a prophylaxis against all those efforts, so widespread at the present moment, to "read the future" by the alleged study of changes which supposedly contain within them all necessary changes of the future.   But the larger importance of Durkheim's statement and the full surrounding discussion is analytical.   What Durkheim is saying is that while time or chronology is indeed continuous, we are never justified in imposing this continuity of time upon the events and changes which take place in time in any area.   In short, genetic continuity does not exist from change to change or event to event.   We cannot validly assume that small events or changes grow up into large events or changes, interact in some manner, and produce little events or changes, ad infinitum.

Discontinuity, not continuity, is the principal identifying characteristic of social change.   How could it be otherwise?   We do not live in tightly closed, insulated social systems, each endowed, like an organism, with its own autonomous pattern of growth or change. As I have emphasized throughout this book, the study of society is in substance, in empirical reality, the study of the varied *ways of social behavior*, which we encounter in the forms of institutions, organizations, social roles, statuses, and norms.   When Weber abandoned the Marxian model of capitalism, considered as a self-contained social system with its supposedly internal laws of development, and turned instead to man's socialized ways of economic behavior, to social actions, and to social norms, he discovered that there is no possible way in which economic change can be analyzed in and by itself. What the "rise of capitalism" turned out to be, as Weber studied the matter, was not a process understandable in the terms of continuity—that is, the continuous, organismic growth of one economic system out of an antecedent one.   On the contrary, as Weber came to realize, a profound discontinuity was involved; one formed by the impact upon traditional economic ways of certain changes that had taken place in a *noneconomic* sphere of social behavior, that is, in the sphere of religion.   The immense superiority of Weber's envisagement of social change to the Marxian model of growth flows directly from Weber's realization that autonomous, self-generating systems do not exist in the social world; that continuity of change does not, cannot, exist; that what we are given is a highly complex and *discontinuous* set of events and changes.

Does the lack of continuity of change mean that a *science* of change is an impossibility? Does it mean that therefore the all-important idea of *cause* must be ruled out of analysis. Not by any means. There is no more warrant for making continuity of change a premise of its scientific study than there would be in making the reality of emergent growth a premise. And, as we saw in the opening chapter of this book, when the scientist, physical or social, seeks *causal* explanations, he is seeking explanations grounded in empirical conditions in which a high degree of *probability*, not necessity, is the aim. To look for the causes of that change we call the rise of the political state, or the rise of industrialism, in any area does not assuredly carry with it any obligation to find these causes in some prepotent condition in the form of social organization which immediately precedes it. If such were the case, we could jettison all the sources of change we have found to lie in events and circumstances which by no stretch of the imagination can be located in the preceding form of social organization.

IS CHANGE NECESSARY?

Change is "necessary" in at least two senses. It is necessary in the sense that few if any forms of social behavior are likely to go unchanged over any considerable period of time no matter how isolated and seemingly stagnant a people or culture may appear to be. True, there are enough recorded instances of peoples—preliterate, folk, or peasant, and religious communities existing in guarded enclaves, as well as others—to make clear that it is possible for a people to go for very long periods with but infinitesimal changes evident in behavior. But even among these, given time, some change is likely to take place. In still another sense change is necessary. One does not have to be either a reformist or an idealist to grant that change is usually necessary in almost any imaginable social condition. That is, change is necessary (though by no means inevitable) from the point of view of the ideal or norm against which the condition is assessed. Few if any would doubt that change in our tax structure is overwhelmingly necessary at the present time.

But neither of these senses is implied in most sociological statements which declare change to be necessary. What is implied is the view that change is made necessary by the very nature of social behavior. Because human beings are in continuous interaction, it is said, and because movement, activity, and purposive endeavor are the very stuff of the social bond, change is "necessary." It is "necessary" in the sense that it must take place, and take place constantly, or at least most of the time.

This sense of the words "necessary" and "necessity" as applied to change must, of course, be rejected. There is no need to repeat what has already been said in this chapter. It will suffice merely to observe that, on the record of history, not change but *persistence* would appear to be "necessary." In fact, however, except in the broadest and loosest of senses, neither change nor persistence is necessary. Each may or may not be found at any given time.

There is still another use of "necessary" and "necessity" which after thousands of years continues to enjoy wide currency in prophetic or dogmatic thinking about civilization. When the great religious philosopher St. Augustine declared that mankind's history, from Adam to the eventual ending of the world in holocaust, was a *necessary* history, he meant that it had been made so by the will of God, a will that God himself chose to see realize itself slowly, gradually, and continuously over a period of several thousands of years. We cannot dispute this use of "necessary," not empirically at least. For veiled as it is by St. Augustine's momentous concepts of "the city of God" and "the city of Man" and undergirded by premises of suprarational, supernatural divine omnipotence, this sense of "necessity" is in a realm outside that of critical philosophy or science.

Unhappily, this Augustinian sense became secularized as the centuries passed in Western intellectual history. We find the concept, *without* the divine undergirding Augustine had given it, in the writings of many social philosophers of the eighteenth and nineteenth centuries. Progress, development, growth, and change were all held to be as necessary in some pattern or other as each had been held to be necessary by Augustine in the light of God's direction of human affairs. But now, in these secularized, social philosophies, it is not divine direction that is premised, except in a few very remote instances. What is suggested is that some form of direction lies within mankind—or civilization, or culture, or some single institution such as property, family, or religion.

It is *necessary*, wrote Marx and Engels, that mankind everywhere evolve from primitive communism to slavery to feudalism to capitalism. And it is *necessary* that this same succession culminate eventually in universal communism. It is *necessary*, wrote Comte, that human knowledge pass everywhere from a condition characterized by religious belief alone to one based upon metaphysics and, in due time, to a final condition reflecting the triumph of positive science. It is *necessary*, wrote the anthropologist Lewis Morgan (whose work was used by Engels), that the family, property, and the state each develop through a series of stages that can be authoritatively described.

There are many millions, perhaps hundreds of millions, of people today who believe in the necessity of change in the sense I have just mentioned. Some are Christian, some Moslem, some Marxist; others draw their belief from some other world view. For all these people, the necessity of change arises from the nature of the entity they are concerned with—the city of God, civilization, knowledge, "history," the economic system, or whatever it may be. Change was necessary for most of the social evolutionists of the nineteenth century—necessary in that it arose from allegedly endemic processes, from the very nature of man in his interaction with others. Nothing could have been more certain in the minds of such thinkers as Condorcet, Comte, Marx, and Spencer than that civilization would reach a certain point in time, a point of fulfillment of man's purpose on earth, precisely as every organism must, unless it is interfered with, reach its fulfillment in maturity through the necessary processes of growth.

Necessity in this sense is plainly an act of faith, a dogma, a means of living with present uncertainties and deprivations. It is not even certain that human beings, for the most part at least, could live without such dogmas, religious or secular. In them are to be found the sinews of hope and purpose. We should not depreciate them. But, whatever their value and our need for them religiously or metaphysically, they have nothing to do with the scientific or critical understanding of change in social behavior—that is, finite, empirical social behavior in time and place. Here no necessity is to be found, no irreversibility, no iron determinism.

Few social scientists worthy of the name believe today in these determinisms and necessary patterns involving past, present, and future. But the idea of necessity in change may be found nonetheless, stated in modified and more limited ways. We find economists writing—though not nearly as often as they once did—of the business cycle and its necessary fluctuations, moving from deflation to inflation with various intervening stages describable. It is notable, however, that what was accepted as nearly axiomatic along this line even a scant generation ago has much less following today. Planned efforts by government and business have, in effect, taken a good deal of necessity out of the so-called

business cycle. Certain historians and sociologists have thought themselves in possession of a similar cycle applied to revolutions, suggesting
that once a revolution begins, it moves as a general rule through certain
stages until it completes itself. We find, similarly, occasional references
to "crime cycles."

The *cycle*, in fact, has been a persuasive model of necessary change
in human affairs ever since the Greeks. Why not? In the organic
world the cycle of life is before us all the time. Physicians and epidemi-
ologists write of the cycle of a disease, and sometimes, seemingly
engrossed with their metaphor, they lose sight of sick people. So with
the social scientist. The cycle is doubtless as good an image as any if
one feels obliged to "explain" through analogy. And like any analogy
the idea of the cycle may even succeed in turning attention to some useful
part of the data involved, data which might otherwise have been omitted
from consideration. But, whatever the occasional heuristic value
of the model of the cycle, we should not make the mistake of believing
that social behavior changes in accord with any pattern of necessity,
cyclical or other.

UNIFORMITARIANISM

I use a word here that comes
directly out of eighteenth- and nineteenth-century efforts to account for
change through some assumed uniform process. The doctrine of
uniformity, under whatever name it may go by today, is as widespread in
social theory as it ever was in earlier centuries. And this doctrine has
the same difficulties and ambiguities today that it had in earlier periods.
These arise from the effort to make an assumed constant serve as the
means of explanation for extremely variable and diverse social behavior.

Like most of the other conventional assumptions regarding the nature of social change, the notion of uniform processes operating to cause
change stems in large degree from the analogy of organic growth.
Plainly, any biological organism grows through metabolic and other
biochemical processes present in the organism from the very start.
Elements of the atmosphere, food, rest, and others affect these processes,
stimulate or retard them. But in growth, where it can be properly said
to exist, the fundamental causal processes are in the organism and are
as uniform as the structure of the organism.

In the late eighteenth century, when the science of modern geology was coming into existence, there were many philosophers who declared that the whole history of the earth could be understood in terms of fixed, uniform processes—such as erosion—as operative and determining in the remote past as in the present. It was in geology that uniformitarianism first achieved the status of being a scientific theory. But that status did not last for long. Even in the eighteenth century there were those who recognized the impossibility of accounting for the present shape and structure of the earth merely through processes said to be operating uniformly at all times. These critical minds were then disparaged under the label "catastrophists." Their views were said by the apostles of uniformitarianism to make any genuine science of geology impossible since the "catastrophes" they predicated were unique events of the past, unrecoverable in their details and not to be assessed in studies of the present. Needless to emphasize, no geologist today holds uncompromisingly to any uniformitarian theory. That uniform processes do operate, and have operated throughout past time in the history of the earth, is incontestable. Erosion is but one of them. But no geologist supposes for a moment that the Sierra Nevada Mountains, or the Alps, or any of a whole host of other major features of the earth can be accounted for in terms of these uniform processes, can be understood, that is, through study of what is to be seen today on the surface of, or within, the earth. The science of geology must recognize, in short, the operation of events and changes in the past which have been decisive and which are not a part of the scene at the present time.

There are spheres of social science today, however, in which the search for uniform process continues unabated. Uniformitarianism was a cardinal part of eighteenth- and nineteenth-century theories of social change, development, and progress. Thus, Immanuel Kant thought that the development of human society could be explained by the ceaseless operation of that process he called "unsocial sociability"—man's simultaneous need for and revolt against relationships with others. Comte found the motivation for social change in the human psyche— more specifically, in an instinct which drives man to incessant improvement of his own faculties. Given the human craving for knowledge, power, and status, Comte concluded, no other cause of the change of society over time need be sought. This craving has always existed, it does now exist, and it always will. Marx, to use one more example drawn from the past, also had a uniform process with which to account for social change—class struggle. All history, Marx and Engels wrote, is a history of class struggle; and in this continuing struggle lies the source of the changes which society has manifested over many centuries and millennia.   According to Marx, what we can observe of class struggle today is our guide to the understanding of past changes.

No doubt all these views would be rejected today by most social scientists.   But the belief in uniform processes of change through which the manifold diversities of change can be "scientifically" explained continues in the social sciences.   The uniform process cited may be the conflict of roles that goes on incessantly within all social aggregates, or it may be the human faculty for perceiving discrepancy between the actual and the ideal, thus impelling men to constant drive toward change, or it may be any one of the other processes which we have seen in preceding chapters to be inseparable from social interaction.   There is no question, of course, of the existence of processes of *interaction* which are relatively uniform from age to age, from people to people, in human society.

But what do these processes have to do with the myriad diversities of change that the actual history of a given area or institution reveals to us? They have *something* to do with change; there is no doubt of that.   Conflicts, purposive strivings, tensions, hunger for knowledge, food, power, and status do indeed go on constantly.   And they will almost always be present in conjunction with social change.   The difficulty lies, of course, in the fact that these same processes are fully compatible over very long periods of time with the opposite of change—that is persistence, fixity, and structural maintenance.

To say, for example, that the present-day dislocation of caste in many areas of India is the consequence of struggle that has been going on for millennia is of little help as an explanation when we remember that for a very long period of time this struggle was containable within the structure of castes in India.   It is all well and good to note that the progress of science or of knowledge generally is the result of man's itch to know, of his insatiable craving for further information and enlightenment.   But how does this constant help us with the problem of accounting for those relatively brief periods in which knowledge can be seen to spurt markedly and those much longer periods of conventionalization or routinization. Of the fixed and deeply embedded existence of conflict between black and white in the United States, commencing with the introduction of slaves brought from Africa, there is surely no question.   But how does this constant enlighten us when we seek to explain the manifest differences in time which the struggle between black and white reveals.

Consider the vital institution *language*.   Philologists have no difficulty in demonstrating the existence within any language of constant processes of modification and alteration in speech, vocabulary, and syntax. Ordinary use of language in an area from generation to generation shows the existence of these processes. They tell us much about the difference between the language used by Americans today and that used in the time of Lincoln, or of Washington, or of the Pilgrims. At least some of these not very considerable changes can be explained in terms of processes of linguistic use which were present from the time of the landing at Plymouth Rock. Others, however, can be explained only by the impact of events upon the language, events such as the successive immigrations of peoples from Europe, the substantial influence on American speech of Negro culture, the leveling of social classes through the power of administrations such as those of Jackson and Lincoln, and the advent of television and radio with the resulting blurring of once distinct cultural regions with their native accents, linguistic styles, and dialects.

Consider again the illustration used in another connection—the Norman Conquest in England in 1066. Among other major changes which took place in English society was the change in the language spoken. We distinguish the Anglo-Saxon or Old English that preceded the Norman Conquest, the Middle English that followed it, and then the modern English that was fairly well established by the sixteenth century. No great effort needs to be made here to make clear that whatever uniform processes may have been operating in the language in England in, for example, the year 1000—and still operating—they will hardly help us to account for that major difference in the language that was a consequence of the Norman Conquest with its introduction of French and its several other effects. Nor will these same uniform processes help much in any account of the changes in the language which took place sporadically thereafter, with long periods of quiescence between changes. Changes resulted from such *non*uniform "forces" as the Reformation, the industrial and democratic revolutions, great writers, and a whole succession of other impacts and events, none of which could conceivably have been derived as a uniform process in the language at the start.

Uniform processes do indeed exist in language and in each of the other spheres of culture and society. These uniform processes are bound to be involved in or associated with change. The danger of the concept of uniform process in the understanding of social change lies, however, in the fact that what explains everything often explains nothing. Were social behavior a monolith, were it devoid of the changes and diversities which in fact characterize the condition of any social aggregate over a sufficiently long period of time, we could happily take rest in some such explanatory proposition as "class conflict," "role strain," "the quest for power," "man's itch to know," or the perceived discrepancy between the actual and the ideal at any point in the history of a people. All these are real; all are constant; they may be said to be uniform from place to place and time to time—at least, if defined with sufficient generality— and they are indeed aspects of social change.

But, like other attributes of social change which have been conceptually derived from the model of organic growth, the attribute of uniformity exists when there is *no* change. The same criticisms which were directed previously against the concepts of internal source, continuity, and necessity apply equally to the cherished doctrine of uniformity.

SOCIAL STRUCTURE AND AND SOCIAL CHANGE

It is time now to go back to the elements of the social bond, of social structure. I have possibly left the impression in the sections immediately preceding that these elements of structure have nothing to do with an understanding of social change. If so, this would be unfortunate. What I have repeatedly said is: *social change cannot be conceptually deduced, directly derived from, or fully understood in terms of the structural elements of the social bond.* We cannot, by study of patterns of interaction within the family, or the school, or the industrial group, or even the nation, account for the changes which in fact take place in such social aggregates. We are obliged to take into consideration the crises and discontinuities precipitated by the historical relationships of these aggregates to other forces in society.

But knowledge of social structure or of what I have called the elements of the social bond is not irrelevant to an understanding of social change. Not by any means. Change is, after all, *change of something*. And if we are to analyze change we are obliged to know the nature of what it is that changes. The character of a change, as well as its intensity, will always be affected by the character of the entity that changes. A given event may well be virtually catastrophic for one type of social structure but have only the slightest effect on another type.

There are innumerable instances of groups and ways of behavior in an area which are unaffected by the impact of events on them. Other ways of behavior in the same area may show marked change as the result of the same impact of events. We cannot, in sum, generalize in advance with respect to the possible dislocative or transforming character of events and crises. All that we have learned about the nature of social aggregates, systems of social authority, roles, statuses, and norms makes clear that by virtue of their highly adaptive character, their powerful tendency to persist—or, rather, the powerful tendency of human beings to retain accustomed ways—substantial change will not take place easily, not without crisis of some degree. We do not, most of us, routinize our behavior with the simultaneous intent of changing it at the first opportunity. It is the very character of the most fundamental forms of social behavior—to be found in kinship, religion, nationalism, political commitment, for instance—that those following them seek to maintain them until maintenance becomes impossible.

Hence the necessity of understanding the nature of the social bond. The necessity arises not from the fact that the social bond in itself generates change. It arises from the fact that until we understand the nature of the social bond we shall be unable to distinguish usefully among social structures which *are* changed or modified in a situation of stress or crisis and those which, in the same or similar situation, are *not* changed. It is a matter of record that in any disaster, for example, natural or man-made, the reactions of groups as well as individuals vary widely. Some are destroyed or reduced to nullity as social structures. Others reveal striking persistence of structure, of roles, statuses, and norms. The impact of Hitler and the immense power of National Socialism upon the social structures of German life produced, as is well known, remarkably diverse responses. Some social structures were profoundly altered under this impact; others were not. In India at the present time, under the heavy impact of technological and political pressures, some castes show clear signs of dissolving, whereas others appear as strong as ever in the allegiances they inspire from their members.

We cannot generalize in advance about the capacity of a given type of event or crisis to effect change in social behavior. In ethnology and history there are innumerable examples of tribes, communities, cultures, and whole peoples who, although exposed for long periods to traits or ideas coming from the outside, reveal little if any acceptance of these. The same traits or ideas may yield pronounced change within very short periods of time when brought in contact with still other peoples or cultures.

Analysis of a social structure cannot tell us when or under what circumstances a change of the structure will take place or even, as we have seen, whether a change is likely. The reason for this lies in the fact that the sources of substantial changes of structure rarely if ever lie within the structure itself.   There is always the relationship between the structure and each of numerous other spheres of society, a relationship that will be as often determined or affected by what lies in the *other* spheres as in the structure under our consideration.   But although this is so, it is equally true that what we can learn from analysis of any given social structure will tell us much about the *ways* in which change will be manifest in that structure once change commences.   For *social* change is, basically, change of roles, statuses, and norms in any social aggregate, and what we know about these cannot help but be clarifying.

The anthropologist George Murdock rightly notes that a social structure acts as a *filter* for environmental disturbances.   Whether the disturbance is an earthquake, a war, an invasion, the introduction of new forms of technology or social values, or a political decree or a constitutional decision, the matter of *how* (and even whether) any one of these disturbances will affect a given social structure cannot be divorced from what we know about the structure and the roles and statuses which form it.   In the physical world the way a crystal will shatter is predetermined by the structure of the crystal; structure here acts both as a mode of resistance to impact and as the means of transmission of the impact.

Nothing comparable to a crystal exists in social behavior.   Still, it is clear enough from studies of the actual occurrence of a social change that the *specific type* of structure will have a substantial effect upon the ways in which the change is manifest and also in the degree to which the change is more or less probable under a given impact.

The foregoing comments can best be illustrated by a brief statement of what it is we look for when we study social change.   There are four crucial aspects of any such study.   There is, first, the matter of the *source* of the change.   We cannot predetermine this—not, certainly, from study of the entity itself, unless it is organic and living.   Second, we must be concerned with the *means of transmission* of the precipitating factor or factors to whatever it is we are studying: group, role, status, or norm.   These means are both external to the structure and internal. The external means are intermediary to the structure and the source of the change; the internal means are the channels within the structure itself through which the precipitating factor—disaster, intrusion, command, or whatever—is transmitted.   How easily and in what concrete ways the transmission will take place are best learned, of course, from the components of the structure itself.   Third in our assessment of change are the actual *alterations of the structure itself*—alterations of organization, authority, roles, and statuses.   Necessarily, to understand the nature of change a considerable period of time must be involved, for these alterations do not usually take place overnight. Fourth, there are all the complex and subtle absorptions of the alterations within the life styles, personalities, and characters of the human beings whose behavior constitutes the structure. These are the *psychological modifications*. New harmonies and disharmonies cannot help but be the product of the alterations. Strains, tensions, and conflicts in some degree will almost surely be found in response to these alterations. And, almost as surely, they will continue for very long periods of time without, however, necessarily affecting structure or life style.

Notes

1. Elting E. Morison, "A Case Study of Innovation," *The California Institute of Technology Quarterly* (Spring 1960). Most of this fascinating article deals with another and far more important problem of technological change—the introduction of continuous-aim firing in the United States navy early in the present century.
2. The quotation and much of my own discussion here are drawn from the Introduction which Thomas wrote for his *Source Book of Social Origins* (University of Chicago Press, 1909). His theory of crisis underlies much of his later work, including *The Polish Peasant*.
3. Thomas, *op.cit.*
4. Marion Levy, *The Family Revolution in Modern China* (Cambridge: Harvard University Press, 1949), p. 86. Italics added.
5. Emile Durkheim, *The Rules of Sociological Method* (New York: The Free Press, 1950), p. 116 ff.

13

History and

Social Change[1]

The most hopeful sign of advance in our knowledge of the nature of social change is the substantial narrowing in recent years of the gulf that for too long lay between the disciplines of sociology and history—especially in the United States. Whatever the reasons for this gulf, they appear to have been largely overcome in each of the two disciplines. Historians are making more and more use of such fundamental sociological concepts as community, role, authority, and anomie in the interpretation of their data. Indeed some of the best sociology of the past decade or two has made its appearance in the works of historians—Richard Hofstadter, Stanley Elkins, Oscar Handlin, Kenneth Stampp, to name but a few. In the works of all of these historians one finds fertile use of both the concepts and the conclusions of sociologists.

Equally impressive is the increased use by sociologists of the data of history. If there is a single tendency apparent at the present time in American sociology (and I believe this is even more apparent in Europe) it is the widening reliance upon the data of history rather than, as was for long the case, the data of ethnology, for purposes of comparison. Comparison, as we have had frequent occasion to emphasize, is the very framework of detached inquiry. One may compare structures, processes, and events in space—that is, from one contemporary society to another—

or one may compare them in time through utilization of the multitudinous data left by past generations. Each approach serves its purpose; each is necessary in degree. But until recently the kind of comparison in time that the study of history makes possible was sadly neglected in American sociology.

For the sociologist, the greatest single value that can come from the study of historical materials lies in the understanding of change. In the preceding chapter I stressed repeatedly the point that we cannot hope to understand the dynamics of change on the basis of studies of social interaction and social structure alone. An understanding of the processes and causes of change requires the kind of longitudinal view that is afforded by temporal distance—by being able, through the records kept by generations, to see what happened to a given form of behavior, to a social movement, organization, community, or role over a substantial period of time.

Time is indeed the essence of the study of change. How else save through utilization of fairly long periods of time can we be certain of what is actually change—substantial change—in contrast to mere modification or even ordinary mobility and social action? Apart from the recognition of time in the experiences of peoples for whom time, circumstance, and personage have been important enough to record (and there are many such peoples) there is no clear or valid way of identifying change. This fact must be the point of departure.

HISTORY AND DIRECTIONALITY

Is there a direction of change in historical time. Most of us assume there is even when we feel constrained to withhold judgment of what precisely the direction is. Since at least the time of the ancient Greeks the belief has been widespread among Western philosophers and social scientists that history and time have a trend, a direction, much like the flow of a river. This is the subject we must first concern ourselves with in this chapter—the problem of directionality of change in time.

There are two major patterns of direction suggested by the study of the past, both old in Western thought, both found widely in present-day writing—the *cycle* and *trajectory*. The Greeks and Romans were profoundly convinced of the *cyclical* character of change; and we are largely indebted to such philosophers as Plato, Aristotle, Polybius, and Seneca —all of whom dealt extensively with the subject in their studies of human society—for a view of the directionality of change that is nearly as wide-spread today as it was then.   Shortly I shall touch upon the theories of Spengler, Toynbee, and Sorokin.   It is enough now to emphasize that in the writings of all three of these twentieth-century philosophers of history the element of the cycle is strong.

But the cycle is not the only possibility when we are considering the direction of historical change.   There is also the familiar pattern of direction known as the *trajectory*.   Theoretically, the course of civilization—either civilization as a whole or any individual civilization or, for that matter, any institution or social aggregate—can be described in this perspective rather than that of the cycle.   From the time of St. Augustine, at least in the Western intellectual tradition, the Greek-born idea of multiple, recurrent cycles of change has been under challenge by a view of history which sees it as a unitary process, with a beginning, a middle, and an end or ultimate purpose.   Actually, St. Augustine envisaged human history as cyclical but as cast in the form of but *one* cycle—a cycle that had begun with Adam, that had reached maturity in the appearance of Christ, and that would at some not very distant time terminate in the destruction of this world and passage of the blessed to heaven and the damned to hell, each of which states was declared by St. Augustine to be unchanging and eternal.

What we see following St. Augustine in Western thought, especially after philosophers from the Renaissance on began to doubt the necessity and even the imminence of the world's destruction, is at once a secularization of the Augustinian vision and a bending of the line of the cycle into a trajectory.   Mankind, this new vision declared, had its beginning at some point in the past, but, unlike the life cycle of the organism, there will be no decline or destruction.   Mankind, civilization, culture—these will go on forever.

The modern idea of progress was formulated in these terms.   Beginning with the French philosophers Pascal, Fontenelle, and Perrault in the seventeenth century, a view of civilization made its appearance in which not only the straight-line view of human history was taken but the further view that the direction of the line would always be upward. Mankind, having progressed from primitive origins in the remote past, would continue to progress on into the indefinite future through precisely the same forces which had brought man to his present point of eminence.

Progress is not, of course, the only possible conclusion to be drawn from the assumption of a trajectory in human history.   Degeneration or deterioration is an equally logical conclusion, depending upon the premises of one's thought regarding excellence.   In fact, a large number of Western philosophers—including the Greeks and Romans—have had a rather mixed view of progress and degeneration. Even within the confines of the classical cycle, and certainly within the conception of the trajectory, it was possible to see some aspects of civilization becoming better and others worse over time.

One of the most persistent views along this line is that which sees the progress of knowledge inextricably related to the degeneration of human happiness. There were many Greeks (though by no means all) who held the view that Hesiod set forth in the seventh century B.C. In the beginning was a golden race of mortals, infinitely happy but spared, Hesiod tells us, of all knowledge. The golden race was followed by a silver race and then by a bronze and, finally, by an iron race of men. Each, Hesiod declares, knew more and had greater control of environment, but each was less happy than its predecessor, more given to strife, hatred, and misery. Hesiod, holding as did most Greeks to the idea of an endless succession of identical cycles of human history, believed the time not far off (he saw himself as living in the Iron Age) when the cycle would reach its completion; society would disappear and once again a Golden Age would make its appearance, with men ignorant of the arts but blissful in their trust and love of one another.

This view of the mixed direction of history is, as I say, a persistent one in Western thought. We find it in St. Augustine's writings, cast of course in Christian cosmology and anthropology. Hesiod's Golden Age becomes in the writings of Christians the Garden of Eden from which Adam and Eve were driven and condemned to incessant toil and hardship as the consequence of their violating God's command not to partake of the fruit of knowledge. Salvation for Christian philosophy lay not in any new Golden Age on earth but in that final transcendence through which the good would pass to heaven and the evil to hell. In the eighteenth century Rousseau set forth a secularized version of this view in his *Discourse on the Arts and Sciences* and his *Discourse on the Origin of Inequality*. Mankind has progressed, Rousseau wrote, in terms of his command of nature, his knowledge of the arts and sciences. But mankind has deteriorated, has fallen away from its original condition of relative equality, justice, compassion, and happiness. Given the institutions of property and social class, all human knowledge has been but an added means of reducing man's happiness and decency. Where Hesiod saw salvation in the turn of the cycle, where St. Augustine and Christian thought saw salvation in man's deliverance from earth and eternal rest in heaven, Rousseau (and most of his contemporaries in the eighteenth century) tended to see salvation in terms of a remaking of social institutions on earth.   In Rousseau's writing the first really clear view of the redemptive power of secular revolution is evident.

But progress, degeneration, and other states of moral being are not by any means the only manifestations of belief in historical direction. It is possible to see direction in history that is not related at all to judgments of good and bad or happiness and unhappiness.   One may abandon the latter and emphasize direction conceived entirely in the movement of society from one state to another, with each stage identified in cultural, social, or political terms rather than the terms of moral evaluation.   When Aristotle, in his *Politics*, said that the course of political development is from kinship to federations of clans to community and, ultimately, to the polis, he was tracing direction in change.   More, he was declaring directionality to be a fixed character of change irrespective of how we may assess this directionality in moral terms.

Here, as with respect to judgments of progress and degeneration, the appeal of the idea of directionality in history has been a powerful one. Many Greeks and Romans, as well as many philosophers of the period from the Renaissance on in modern Europe, characterized the direction or directions of change in terms of successive conditions of culture and thought.   An interest in primitive origins was inevitably an aspect of this concern with direction.   It was important to know original conditions if one was to rigorously derive from them the series of stages which followed, a series culminating in the present or a future that could be sketched by the more imaginative.   Lucretius, a first-century B.C. Roman philosopher, described in great detail in his *On the Nature of Things* the lineal stages of culture through which mankind had passed, as far as he was able to reconstruct them from what he knew of contemporaneous simpler peoples or from a learned and lively imagination. Four centuries later, St. Augustine, although deeply committed to the view of history that stemmed from the Old Testament, presented, in *The City of God*, a view of mankind's passage from primitive cultural origins through ever more complex stages down to the wonders of the world that St. Augustine saw around him.   A Christian convinced of the imminent ending of the world, St. Augustine was nevertheless classical in his appreciation of history as directional movement.

But ancient and medieval interest in the direction of change in time was small by comparison with that to be found in European writings from about the sixteenth century on.   The desire to discover the direction of history became widespread in the eighteenth century and very nearly universal in the nineteenth century.   This does not mean that the philosophers concerned were without interest in themselves effecting changes in the social order. Far from it. It was indeed as a kind of undergirding of reformist or revolutionary aspirations that many writers sought to discover the trend or movement of society in time. Given knowledge or belief that society was *tending* toward some goal—equality, justice, democracy, socialism, or other—that would be realized in the future, efforts in the present could be comforted, and also guided, accordingly. In both the eighteenth and nineteenth centuries there was a kind of subtle interplay between what was desired in the way of a good society and what seemingly could be deduced from study of past and present trends.

Much of the social science of the nineteenth century was greatly concerned with establishing the nature of the direction of human history or evolution. Comte, Marx, Spencer, Sir Henry Maine, Edward Tylor, Henry T. Buckle, and Lester H. Ward are but a few of the more important social philosophers and scientists whose works were strongly oriented toward finding, describing, and assessing the direction that human society seemed to be taking in time from past through present to future. Nor was human society as a whole the only consideration. Frequently interest was focused on a single institution or value—property, kinship, democracy, or capitalism. Each, it was thought, could be shown to have its direction of change in time, with at least the general outline of the future to be discerned through extrapolation of the direction that linked past to present. Some of the social philosophers were conservative in political orientation. For them this discovery of the direction of human history was tantamount to a warning to refrain from meddling through government legislation with what was happening on its own. Others, however, were radical, even revolutionary. Marx was one of these. For the revolutionists the great value of ascertaining the direction of human history lay, as I suggested previously, in thus being able to guide realistically one's present revolutionary tactics. From whatever point of view—scientific or activist, radical, liberal, or conservative—interest in the assumed direction of history was paramount in the nineteenth century.

Nor has interest disappeared in our own day. Where are we heading? What does the future hold? These questions are as profuse in contemporary writing as in the writing of any period of the past. And the answers, in general shape at least, are not very different from those which may be found at one time or another during the past twenty-five hundred years. Ideas of progress, degeneration, and cyclical fluctuations exist alongside visions of a Golden Age in the past, in the present, and in the remote future. Predicting the shape of things to come, the direction or trend of the future, is more likely to be the work of institutes today than of single philosophers and historians. For the native ingenuity of a Lucretius, a Condorcet, a Marx have been substituted banks of computers which, it is hoped, will hurl us across time and into the future just as computers send missiles across space to the moon.

Despite computers and despite the immense structure of modern scientific knowledge and of all the techniques of investigation which were unknown even a century ago, the fundamental premise of these inquiries into directionality of change, of these forays into the future, remains the same as in times past. And this premise is that there *is* directionality of history and change, that the potentialities of the future lie in the present just as those of the present lay in the past. "The present," wrote the eighteenth-century philosopher Leibniz, "is big with the future." We believe this is true today, and so, no doubt, will our descendants, assuming that man has a future in which reflective consciousness remains possible and as vital as it has for the past several thousand years. I shall come back shortly to the important premise that changes and events are linked in time directionally. It is a premise that requires critical consideration in social science as contrasted with millennialist faith.

First, however, we shall briefly consider a few of the major philosophers of historical change in our own day—Oswald Spengler, Arnold J. Toynbee, and Pitirim Sorokin—whose contributions, written with great learning and profound imagination, are fit successors to the works which stretch from the ancient Greeks down through the nineteenth century. The first point to be made about all three is that, along with impressive differences of conclusion, there are some significant likenesses among them. And the most important of these likenesses is the common acceptance of the Greek-born idea of the cycle in which to arrange the data of human civilizations in time. I do not mean that any of the three uses the model of the cycle for civilization as a single whole, thus implying the gradual running-down of culture and society everywhere, with the implication of total collapse at some future time. In the works of all of them, history is regarded as *plural*. There is no one history in which all human experiences of past and present may be confined in linear fashion. All three writers see the past and present instead as forming a plurality of histories of discrete civilizations, with relationships among these civilizations largely incidental. For Spengler, Toynbee, and Sorokin the first important task is to arrange the experiences of mankind into significant wholes, that is, specific civilizations such as the Egyptian, classical, Chinese, and Indian civilizations and others, includ-

ing that of the Western Europe which followed the disappearance of the
Roman Empire. The second task is to interpret each of these discrete
civilizations through a perspective of historical change.

It was Spengler, whose *The Decline of the West* was largely written
before World War I and published shortly after, who first captivated
twentieth-century readers with the idea of civilizations going through
more or less inexorable rhythms of cyclical change. Spengler seems to
have thought the idea of historical cycles was a creation largely of his
own mind, proceeding only from a few insights of his fellow Germans
Goethe and Nietzsche. So lacking in correct knowledge of Greek and
Roman ideas of change was Spengler that he even declared the Greeks
and Romans ignorant of ideas of change, history, and development.

The human past, Spengler writes, may be divided into some eight
major civilizations or cultures. All these are held to be "of the same
build, the same development, and the same duration." Naturally, the
details of the eight major cycles of civilizations differ. Spengler does
not suggest that each and every event repeats itself from one cycle to
another, from that of, say, Egyptian or Chinese to classical, Arabic, or
European. No more does he espouse any thought of cyclical reincarna-
tion of specific historical figures. It is the *structure* of history and change
that interests Spengler, the main stages and transitions, the origins, re-
alizations, and completions of the cycle in each. And these, he tells us,
are the same from one culture to another. Each goes through largely
identical origins, stages of maturation, of senescence, and each in time is
destined, like any biological organism, to wither and die out—then to
be succeeded by some other cycle of cultural development and decay.
Spengler goes so far as to work out what he calls a theory of "con-
temporaneity" for his eight major cultures. Cultures are contemporary
in terms of some equivalent stage of growth and decay. Thus, Spengler
wrote, present-day Western society is "contemporary" with Roman civilization, for example, during the latter's final centuries of decline. Styles
of thought, art, philosophy, science, even mathematics, as well as archi-
tecture, government, family life, and religion, have reached about the
same ripe stage, and this clearly augurs, Spengler concludes—in the very
title of his two-volume work—the decline of the West, with its termina-
tion to be expected in some not very distant century. Spengler writes:

> *A culture is born in the moment when a great soul awakens out
> of protospirituality of ever-childish humanity and detaches itself, a
> form from the formless, a bounded and mortal thing from the bound-
> less and enduring. It blooms on the soil of an exactly definable land-*

scape, to which, plant-wise, it remains bound. It dies when this soul has actualized the full sum of its possibilities in the shape of peoples, languages, dogmas, arts, states, sciences, and reverts to the proto-soul. . . . Every culture passes through the age-phases of the individual man. Each has its childhood, youth, manhood, and old age.[2]

Despite a very considerable learning and concrete insights into his-torical periods which frequently illuminate them brilliantly, Spengler was anything but a sound historian. Fascinating to many as a philos-opher of decadence, he has never been considered seriously by the vast majority of historians and sociologists as a scholar, much less a scientist of historical change. To seek to divide the human past into eight (or, for that matter, ten or twenty) discrete cultures or civilizations, each con-ceived as an organism going through an appointed life cycle of growth and decay, each duplicating the others' lines of development in thought, law, government, economy, religion, and the arts, is a task likely to be of more interest to mystics and searchers for dogma than to serious his-torians and social scientists.

Of far greater importance and scholarly value are the works of Toynbee. His *A Study of History* is the product of one of the great scholars of the present century. There is no retreat to mysticism in Toynbee's massive work (in finished form it contains some fourteen volumes); there are no appeals to protosouls, no lapses into sheer unin-formed intuition and fabrication such as we find in Spengler. This does not mean *A Study of History* is without errors and serious mis-conceptions. A great many historians and sociologists have pointed these out. But the book is a genuine effort at a comparative history of civilizations. Toynbee finds not eight but twenty-one major civilizations of past and present: not merely the obvious ones dealt with by Spengler but also those of Sumer, the Andes, ancient Mexico, ancient Russia, and others. Toynbee in nowise aims chiefly to content himself with setting forth a fixed cycle of genesis and decay through which all civilizations move inexorably. There is, to be sure, some of this in his overview of the twenty-one civilizations. But of far greater concern to Toynbee, and to all who are interested in the possibilities of the comparative study of historical change, is *the arrangement of his inquiry into specific ques-tions.* It is this fact that gives Toynbee's remarkable volumes such a large potential of usefulness to sociologists and other social scientists. He may be, and frequently is, wrong or subject to modification in his answers. But at least we are provided with questions and answers of a more or less empirical kind.   Bona fide historians and social scientists can work from those.

Toynbee's volumes ask four main questions, each with numerous subquestions.   The first concerns the genesis of civilization: What are the conditions which allow or stimulate the rise of civilizations—the conversion of what had been preliterate, simple, more or less lethargic peoples into the kinds of civilization of which the classical, the Indian, the Chinese, and the Mayan are notable types?   Second, what are the factors involved in the expansion and development, in what Toynbee calls the "growths" of these civilizations?   Third, what accounts for the breakdowns of civilizations, that is, the conversion of what had been for centuries a highly dynamic, innovative, intrepid, and enterprising people into one characterized by mere routinization and repetition of the old?   Fourth, what leads to the disintegration of historical civilizations, the passing into nothingness or atavistic primitivism of civilizations? Unlike Spengler, Toynbee does not declare decline and disintegration to be inevitable for Western civilization.   But no one can be blind to Toynbee's belief in the high possibility of there happening to the present civilization what took place for so many other civilizations in the past. Of far greater importance, however, are the specific theories and insights which Toynbee utilizes in comparative histories.   One such theory, for example, is that of challenge and response, whereby the specific works and achievements which culminate in civilizations are seen as responses to specific environmental challenges, physical and social alike.   According to his theory of proletariats, internal and external, the power of a civilization to resist the second, the external, is contingent upon its ability to prevent formation of the first within it.   Another theory deals with the rise of creative individuals, of "geniuses," in terms of common processes among cultures and communities.   In sum, Toynbee's monumental work is filled not merely with the kinds of material but with the insights historical sociologists can properly use.

Much the same can be said of the work of the late Pitirim Sorokin. Toynbee may be said to be the historian pushed by the nature of his materials into becoming the sociologist.   With Sorokin the reverse is true.   His desire to see in macrocosmic terms what earlier researches into the nature of social behavior had taught him in smaller compass best explains his four-volume *Social and Cultural Dynamics*.   Like Toynbee's work, Sorokin's is, whatever its errors or failings, written in the spirit of scholarship and science—written with specific questions in mind about the behavior of peoples in large aggregates over long periods of time.

Sorokin confines himself for the most part to the classical and Western cultures, both of them considered within common framework and subject to the same kinds of questions, but each held more or less separate from the other. There are only brief excursions into other cultures such as Chinese, Indian, and Sumerian. Each of Sorokin's two great cultures, classical and Western, is found to be an integrated whole, functionally and in terms of what Sorokin calls logico-meaningful relationships. The major changes of each culture are seen by Sorokin to be immanent, to proceed in short from structural and functional conditions within the discrete civilization. These major changes are, for Sorokin, of a quasi-cyclical (or pendular) kind. He finds that not merely idea systems, forms of art, literature, and philosophy, but modes of social behavior generally, including family systems, laws, governments, and economies, evolve over long periods of time fluctuating from the *ideational* to the *sensate* with an intervening, mixed *idealistic* stage. The ideational stage is essentially the sacred-communal society of the kind found in earliest Greece and Rome and, later, in Western medieval society. Here the emphasis is on corporate solidarity of groups and the binding character of norms. Sensate society, in contrast, is characterized by a high degree of individualism, utilitarianism, skepticism, and a strong tendency to convert sacred values into secular ones. The intervening period has elements of both types of society in fruitful union. During this idealistic stage, by virtue of the short-lived union of corporate and individualistic structures and of sacred and secular values, a society is given the kind of impetus that is found in such rare but consequential periods as the fifth century B.C. in Attica, the first century A.D. in Rome, and the Renaissance in modern Europe.

It is directionality of change, then, that is featured in Sorokin's ideational-idealistic-sensate cyclical alternation. Moreover, directionality is held to arise from the very nature of civilization—any civilization given a long enough time. Like Spengler and Toynbee, Sorokin holds that what is essential and determinative in the history of any civilization or sociocultural system proceeds *from* that civilization or system, not from the milieu or external forces. The latter, he tells us, may accelerate or retard, just as external circumstance may affect the rate of growth of the organism. But the fundamental causes of direction are to be found in the entity itself.

Bearing the seeds of its change in itself, any sociocultural system bears also in itself the power of molding its own destiny or life career. Beginning with the moment of emergence, each sociocultural system is the main factor of its own destiny. This destiny, or the system's subsequent life career, represents mainly an unfolding of the immanent potentialities of the system in the course of its existence.[3]

Although Sorokin restricts his attention mostly to only two civilizations—classical and Western—he leaves no doubt in the reader's mind that he regards his three-phase cycle of historical direction as applicable to all civilizations. It is the nature of a civilization to commence, he explains, in the sacred-communal context of the ideational. Thought, action, art, government, family, and other aspects of the social and cultural order are in the beginning suffused by belief in the sacredness of things. All man does has for its ultimate purpose the veneration of the gods. This was true in the earliest times of classical civilization, and it was true again during the early Middle Ages of Europe or, Sorokin describes the period, the *beginning* age of Western civilization. But in time the sacred-communal becomes transfused with alien values: individualism, secularism, utilitarianism, and others. The ideational passes gradually into the idealistic, as was the case in the middle period of Greco-Roman civilization and in the Renaissance of Western European. Now there is a mixture of sacred and secular values, with development of the human being the highest goal. For a brief period civilization is at the very height of its creative powers in the realm of art and philosophy. Gradually, however, the ideational or sacred element recedes or dissipates itself under the impact of individualism and secularism. And the idealistic period is then succeeded slowly but inexorably by the sensate period. In this period virtually nothing remains of the sacred. All has become utilitarian, hedonistic, with all aspects of man's knowledge held to be justified solely by the material comfort or pleasure they bring to the living. Decadence, cultural morbidity, immorality, cynicism, despair, the incessant search for pleasure, political corruption, increased factionalism within and wars externally—all these, as Sorokin writes, characterize the sensate period, especially in its late phases. Out of the prolongation of this sensate period must come in time the disappearance of the civilization itself, to be followed, on the evidence of the pluralism of history, by some other civilization, perhaps this time a civilization in Asia or Africa, one even now entering its first great period of existence, the ideational. This civilization too will know in the fullness of time the fruits of the seeds of change which it contains within itself— fruits first manifest in an idealistic then in a sensate period. Such, for Sorokin, is the origin and the destiny of each civilization, the direction of its history.

A CRITIQUE OF
DIRECTIONALITY

What are we to say about the search for directionality in history, of which the works of Spengler, Toynbee, and Sorokin are only among the more notable examples? First, this search is undoubtedly an imperishable part of human consciousness by now, at least in the West. To ask the question, Where is civilization going? seems to most of us as natural as to ask, Where has it come from in the past? Both questions, and a host of others closely related, are so deeply embedded in the major philosophical, theological, and historical works of the West that they enter our consciousness at even the most elementary levels of education. Whatever the validity of directionality as a scientific concept, then, we may take for granted its lasting character as a dogma, as an article of prophetic faith. The belief that mankind or civilization is moving in some direction—most would say forward, some might say backward—is probably as nearly ineradicable a belief within the Western tradition of historical consciousness as any to be found.

But this belief is, from any analytical or scientific point of view, thoroughly imprecise and subjective as well as inseparable from analogy and metaphor. Only by conceiving the vast totality of all human beings who have ever lived on earth as forming some kind of entity, something comparable to a being or organism, is it possible to think in terms of directionality for civilization generally. Only by likening a specific civilization such as ancient Rome to some similar entity, conceived as autonomous and possessed of its own inherent powers of growth and decay, decline, and death is it possible to deal with directionality in its history.

What does it mean in terms of fact to say that Roman civilization—or any other—went through processes of genesis, growth, maturation, decay, decline, and death? By what measures and criteria do we pronounce the culture and ideas of one period in Roman history as development or maturity and the culture and ideas of a later period as decay or decline? In the organic world we are clear enough about the attributes of senescence, decay, and death. Everyone knows an aged or infirm human being from a young and vigorous one. But how, except by subjective and metaphoric judgments, do we similarly pronounce societies and civilizations as being in decline or dying?

What do we actually see in history from the records given us? I mean history in the concrete sense of the events and changes undergone by a people living in some denotable area, such as the Italian peninsula and adjacent regions? We see generation after generation of people living in the area, from very early times down to the present moment. The numbers of people in the area have fluctuated, to be sure. Many changes have taken place. On the other hand, many things have continued unchanged or have been only slightly modified during the two and a half millennia for which we have record. We see, through the records, human beings born, mating, rearing children, working, worshiping, playing, educating, writing, and, after a certain point, philosophizing, speculating, and governing. We see generation succeeding generation, each new one accepting, modifying, rejecting, occasionally effecting major changes in the works of preceding generations. We see, depending upon our moral or esthetic disposition, good and evil, greatness and meanness, tragedy, comedy, bathos, nobility, baseness, success, and failure. We see, quite objectively, men's energies turned to war, peace, trade, industry, arts, letters, religion, and all the other spheres of culture.

But, in spite of the ideas of Spengler and Toynbee and many others, we do *not* see cycles of genesis and decay. We do not see direction at all, *except for the directions we impose upon the data from our own vantage points.* We shall come back to this matter of directionality and its assumed reality in a moment. For now let us stay with the supposition—a very attractive one, as I have said—that a civilization, such as Rome, can be said to have undergone cyclical development in time. To have a cycle of change or history there must, obviously, be some entity or thing that undergoes the cycle, that can objectively be said to have manifested growth and decay and death. Where is it? People have lived continuously for at least twenty-five hundred years in the geographical area we call Rome. There have been many changes, many infusions of new peoples, many reverses or successes (by whatever standards, the Romans' or ours), and so on. But to convert the empirical, objective picture of human beings in a concrete area into an entity that is declared to have a pattern of change resulting from forces internal to itself, as I have said, calls for analogy or metaphor in highest degree.

In the first place, any assumption of the autonomy, the discreteness of Roman life is false. The Romans, and all who have continued to live in that area, have been in incessant contact with other peoples. The evidence is clear that, through commerce, exploration, and war, the peoples living in the Italian peninsula were continuously and decisively in contact with other peoples—Greeks, Celts, Teutons, Slavs, even the peoples of the Middle East and of the Far East, including the

Chinese. Intermixture was incessant. Who *were* the Romans? Were they the original horde of Latins who entered the peninsula, replacing the Etruscans? Or were they the mass of interfused peoples we find living in Roman Europe in the third century A.D.? We identify any entity by its boundaries. Of the physical separateness of individual human beings there is no question. But how, in fact, do we identify separate civilizations except by strong use of analogy or metaphor? What were the boundaries of Roman civilization? They were in constant flux politically. But the more important point is simply that in any genuine social, cultural, and political sense there were no boundaries at all. Whatever pride Romans may have taken in being Romans, they and their ways extended over large sections of the earth, and in the process of extending themselves the Romans became inevitably caught up in the ways of other peoples.

We write easily about the decline of Roman civilization, just as certain intellectuals write of the decline of American civilization. But no matter what century we take as the supposed dividing line for "decline and fall" *there were people who continued living in the area.* True, there may have been fewer persons in a given part of Roman territory than there had been earlier, but no one acquainted with the potential horrors of overpopulation today will take *that* as a sign of decline. Physical, biological, and mental powers were as great as in any earlier time. Even though by some standards the culture of, for example, the seventh or eighth or ninth century was perhaps less profuse, less interesting than what had existed earlier in Rome, by other standards—those of Christian ethics, for instance—the culture could be regarded as superior.

In sum, we cannot speak of genesis, development, maturation, decline, and fall when we deal scientifically or objectively with human history, as we assuredly can when the object is a plant or another organism in nature. When we consider human history, all we can objectively ascertain are the facts of continuation of peoples marked by persistence, changes, and events. There were, in the Italian peninsula, people known as Etruscans (and perhaps others before them), followed by Romans, and then many others in all degrees of intermixture. They lived, produced children, died; they maintained ways of behavior; they changed ways of behavior. That is all. The rest is interpretation.

Let us turn now to a second major difficulty with the assumption of directionality. I refer to its presumed genetic or genealogical character. Theoretically, once we possess necessary genealogical data, we can trace our ancestry as human beings back to the very first emergence of *Homo sapiens* in the evolutionary process. Obviously there are no breaks in the chain of human generations that is formed by the well-understood processes of biological reproduction.   There could not possibly be any breaks unless one believed in successive acts of creation.

But whereas a genealogy of human beings is obvious enough, a genealogy of the events, changes, and actions of mankind's social and cultural existence on earth is anything but obvious.   To assume that events are genetically linked, with each event the product of some preceding event and the necessary source of some succeeding event, requires a good deal of imagination.   Moreover, it requires a suspension of ordinary empirical processes of thought, and the use of analogy and metaphor.   A simple illustration will clarify what I am suggesting here.   I sit in my study for several hours.   During that period a considerable number of events (however trivial) occur: books are opened, letters answered, the typewriter used, the telephone answered, coffee brewed and drunk, a manuscript examined and rewritten here and there, a visitor received for a brief conversation, and so on.   These events are given a certain degree of unity by virtue of the fact that all of them involve me. (I am deliberately omitting the events also occurring in the study over which I have no control, such as a bee buzzing at the window, a fly settling here and there in the room, a branch rustling in the tree outside, the air conditioner going on and off, or a small cloud of dust entering from the construction work outside.)

Can we possibly declare these events to be *genetically* related to one another, with one event the product of a preceding one and producing still another?   It is almost instinctive for those of us living in the Western intellectual tradition to answer this question affirmatively.   But very little second thought is required to make us aware of the fact that the events, in their totality, *cannot* be shown to be genetically related.   Not as events.   Considering all that has happened in the study over a period of several hours, it would be very difficult indeed to establish genetic sequence, much less directionality, of events.   And if it is difficult or impossible within so modest a time span and locale, with a single identifiable person giving at least some degree of unity to what happens, how infinitely more difficult, how precarious, are the alleged genetic sequences and directionalities which are found for whole civilizations or for nations or even communities.

We cannot deny, of course, the objective *differentness* of conditions in time.   That the size of Paris is different today from what it was in the thirteenth century admits of no doubt.   If we wish to say, in simple summary, "Paris is vast today; it was small in the thirteenth century," we are of course saying, in effect, that the direction has been from the small to the large.   Or if we wish to declare (and we would have good ground to do so) that relative to the number of *Gemeinschaft* types of social aggregates there is a much higher number of *Gesellschaft* aggregates in Western Europe today than there was in the thirteenth century, we would, in a sense, be casting the differentness in terms of a direction.

But the direction is in the mind of the beholder.   The sheer number and diversity of directions which have been propounded by historians, philosophers, and social scientists over the past few centuries are sufficient indication of the highly subjective and speculative nature of the enterprise.   Comte, Marx, Tocqueville, Spencer, Buckle, Durkheim, and, in our own day, Toynbee and Sorokin may be properly held to be learned men, conscientiously and profoundly interested in the direction of history, in "the way things are moving," in the "march of events and changes in time."   But the differences of conclusion from one to another are sufficient to persuade us perhaps that directionality, for all its undoubted appeal to the human mind, even its dogmatic necessity for the human mind, dies not lie in events and changes and persistences themselves.   Directionality lies in the mind of the beholder.   It is, and can only be, a conclusion made possible by metaphor and by a series of arbitrary assumptions regarding genetic relationships, homogeneity of subject, and ascriptive causality set forth genealogically.

One must view skeptically, therefore, those reconstructions of the past in the forms of cycles or trajectories.   By arbitrarily accepting some data and excluding much other data, some kind of cycle can no doubt be discerned in the history of, for example, the Roman people.   Or, if one insists upon conceiving civilization as a single great whole, one can deal with it in terms of some assumed direction in time.   Civilization, we say, has moved from the homogeneous to the heterogeneous, or from the communal to the individualistic, or from handicraft to computer technology, or from the original goodness of the Golden Age to present corruption and misery.   We can say any of these things, and we do.   The question is, do we mean anything when we say them?   I repeat, in any concrete, empirical, substantive sense, "civilization" or "mankind" can only be taken to mean the vast, nearly incommensurable totality of ways of living of all the peoples who have ever existed on earth.   How does one make an entity out of this far-flung and diversified conglomerate of peoples and acts?   The answer is, we cannot.   What we do is define "civilization" (usually with great advantage to ourselves) as a cluster of certain traits, material and immaterial, and trace this imaginary cluster from the simple aborigines of Australia or Tierra del Fuego to the complexities and splendor of, for example, Harvard University.   Thus, we conclude triumphantly, civilization has progressed, or civilization has developed constantly through ever greater differentiation.

The word "differentiation" deserves extra explanation, for it is one of the most overworked words in sociological theory at the present time. It is a matter of indisputable fact that Western culture today is far more differentiated socially, politically, economically, and technologically than, for example, Western culture in the thirteenth century. This contrast must be explained by some process with directional character, and it is common to invoke the notion of "differentiation." We are more differentiated, more specialized, today than yesterday: very well, let us call the process responsible for this condition "differentiation." Further, let us declare that all large-scale, historical change proceeds by differentiation. The reader will recognize readily the rather tautological quality of this process of reasoning. It is a little like "explaining" the action of LSD on the human mind by reference to its "trip-inducing" biochemistry.

But whether our claimed process for explaining a given, assumed direction is differentiation, class struggle, the historical dialectic, divine providence, or whatever, the important point here concerns directionality itself. I have suggested that despite the popular prophetic appeal of the idea of directionality and its undoubtedly salutary effects upon consensus in the social order and upon resoluteness in the human mind, directionality is not something that can be substantiated in fact.

At the present time a large number of persons and institutes are occupied with what is declared to be scientific forecasting of the future. Much of this is chiliastic. The approach of the year 2000 awakens much the same kind of spell in the Western mind that the year 1000 did. But whereas that date evoked largely religious responses, the year 2000 evokes responses of allegedly *scientific* forecasting of what lies ahead, with the help, of course, of computers. Just as computer technology has made possible man's leap through space to the moon, so, it is thought by many persons, will the right kind or the right number of computers make possible the leap of man's mind through time to the twenty-first century, or even to a point beyond that. The computer, it is declared, can predict the direction of history.

But it cannot. All that computers can do for us is to marshal, classify, arrange and rearrange, quantitatively, what is fed to them. This will always be true of computers, no matter how refined and useful they become. They can only do what they are told to do, and although they can do this in ways far beyond the capacity of human beings, their fundamental limit remains.

Computers will be able to forecast the future only to the extent that man's mind can forecast it. And man's mind can forecast it only to the extent that there is a direction of change clearly to be found in the present—a direction that is itself related to a past direction culminating in the present. All one can say is that no clear, agreed-upon, and scientifically verifiable "direction" has yet been found.

This does not mean that a future point in time, the year 2000, for instance, cannot become the subject of highly informed guesses. What was said in the preceding chapter about the phenomenon of persistence, of fixity, can profitably be recalled here. Much of what we have will continue, subject to only minor modifications. There are good sociological reasons to predict that in the year 2000 there will be schools, universities, mass media, high-rise buildings, perhaps visits to the moon on a daily schedule, and so on. But all of this exists now and we need only project it. The same is true of quantitative rates—number of automobiles produced and babies born, air-miles flown, campers in public parks and forests, miles of freeway, and so on and on. By extrapolation, we can project present or even accelerated rates of increase.

Beyond this type of forecasting is that of certain gifted, intuitive individuals who have a greater measure of success in prophesying the new than do most of us. It is a matter of record that the science fiction writer, Arthur Clarke, a decade ago prophesied that men would be put on the moon in 1969. But this prophecy has little or no relation to directionality in American history. Rather, we see here a gifted mind's appraisal of resources, assessment of political and technological feasibility, and—as Arthur Clarke would be the first to concede—a certain degree of luck. A depression, a war, the election of a national administration convinced that "moondoggling" must be scotched, and a host of other possibilities might well have intervened to upset the prophecy. Human prophets and forecasters do exist, have always existed, and presumably will always exist. Although we usually have a better record of their announced successes than of their failures, their accomplishments —like those of necromancers, haruspices, and Bible diviners—should not be overlooked. Such men are generally shrewd and observant and have intuitive minds. And, like many successful poker players, they have a certain measure of luck denied the rest of us.

But forecasts of the year 2000 should not be confused with the scientific use of historical materials. For all their banks of computers at the present time, institutes for forecasting what lies ahead do not on the record do any better than what a very considerable number of individuals have done in the past. There are few who cannot say with

Tennyson, "I dipt into the future, far as human eye could see, Saw the Vision of the world, and all the wonder that would be." Some do it well, others badly; none can do it scientifically.

SOME SOCIOLOGICAL
USES OF HISTORY

By "history" I mean the data of human behavior as revealed in time and in place, in the past and in the present. I do not mean the *narrative* form of presentation of the record that has been, for at least twenty-five hundred years, the single most popular method of dealing with the data of human behavior in time. I stress this distinction, for the narrative mode of history writing, which we may properly call historiography, has been with us so long and is so deeply embedded in our intellectual culture that it is far too easy to think of the past in its relation to the present as being inseparable from a narrative framework.

There is nothing inherently wrong with the narrative method of historiography. For certain purposes there is no alternative to it. If we want to know what happened in a certain area between two successive dates in time, there is no clear substitute for the narrative method. The relation between the words "history" and "story" is more than merely etymological. What we think of as history, in the sense of historiography, began a very long time ago with the stories told by wise men and bards about their own peoples. Usually the stories were in a sacred context, as in the history we find in the Old Testament with its long series of persons and events issuing genealogically from Adam and Eve and their expulsion from the Garden of Eden. Among the early Greeks, Homer, in his way, was a historian. He told magnificent and still-enchanting stories of what befell Odysseus and his brave companions in their voyages, exploits, privations, and wars. Hesiod, with his story of the origin of the world through successive acts of the gods and his story of the succession of races of men (golden, silver, bronze, heroes, and iron), was also as much a historian as a storyteller. In both Homer and Hesiod, as in the books of the Old Testament, there is much that we would today call hard fact. But there is also much that we would call mythical, allegorical, and, for us at least, historically false.

Differentiation between the historian as such and the bard or storyteller became both real and important by the time of the rationalist period of ancient Greek thought. The greatest of the Greek historians was Thucydides, of the fifth century B.C., whose remarkable history of the war between Athens and Sparta is admired even today for its high degree of objectivity and its dispassionate view of individuals and events. The histories of Thucydides represent historiography at its best. His works give an account of exactly what happened—when, where, and how—with no appeal to causal forces other than those found in human beings and events themselves. Allowing only for greatly improved techniques for recovering data and verifying authenticity, there is no substantial difference between the works of Thucydides and those of leading historians of our own day. The objective, whatever the period or subject, is still to tell exactly what happened in time, person by person, event by event, as a means of explaining how the present has come to be as it is.

I repeat, there is nothing inherently wrong with narrative historiography, and there are times when it is indispensable. But it is a great mistake to suppose that history—in the sense of human behavior in time and place—must be limited to this narrative framework. It is not only a mistake; positive harm can come of this supposition, for there are certain liabilities built into the narrative method as we find it most commonly.[4]

First and foremost is the confinement of the true multiplicity of history to the unitary design that is inseparable from historical narrative. There is not one history for any area, or any people, but a plurality of histories—economic, political, moral, technological, religious, cultural, social. At any given moment a large number of events are taking place, people behaving in diverse ways, actions of all kinds impinging upon one another. But when the historian elects the narrative form of presentation, he is required by the very nature of the form to convert this actual multiplicity into a unity that may be pleasing to the reader and a tribute to the selective and organizational skills of the historian. But the unity nonetheless distorts the materials themselves.

There is a close relation between the unitary narrative, as a method of dealing with historical materials, and the assumption we examined in the preceding two sections, that of the directionality of history. Few historians (at least few whom we ordinarily think of as historians, in contrast to philosophers of history) would concede that their purpose is to find historical "direction," as have Spengler and Toynbee and before them Condorcet, Marx, and Comte. Most historians would probably agree with the late H. A. L. Fisher in whose monumental *History of Europe* we find explicit renunciation of any effort to find in history plot, rhythm, or "predetermined pattern." There is nothing, Fisher writes, but "the play of the contingent and the unforeseen."

And yet the fact that Fisher's *History of Europe* is narrative in structure tells us that for him there is something more than the play of the contingent and the unforeseen. The actual number of persons, events, and situations which fill the past in that arbitrarily chosen area we call Europe is astronomical—beyond recovery or even count. In the mere act of selecting those persons, events, and situations which Fisher's highly informed mind regarded as significant and determinative, he succeeded in fact in giving his materials at least a modicum of the plot, rhythm, and pattern he forswore in his preface. Merely by choosing the narrative method of telling what happened in Europe, by assuming that event begot event, just as person begot person, the whole structure taking on the kind of directionality that is inherent in any genealogy, Fisher did what he had said he would not do—generalize and exhibit pattern.

It is in this sense that narrative history is an art form—which is in no way to disparage it. Since the actual number of persons and events in an area over a long period of time is inconceivably vast, since there is in fact not one but a large number of histories taking place in the area (as many, in fact, as there are individuals and their biological descendants, not to mention the plethora of types of activity), and since events do not "cause" succeeding events in genetic fashion, the art of the historian is required to impose unity upon the materials. And within the narrative framework he can only impose unity by selecting arbitrarily in terms of whatever criteria of significance seem to be relevant. Granted, there is selection of data in all scholarly investigation. But there is an important difference between selection that is governed by *the nature of a question one is asking* about social behavior and selection that is bound up with a certain literary form. If we ask the question, What are the causes of revolutions? we will select data, but our selection will be guided by a search for all that is relevant to answer *this* question. If we undertake to write the history of civilization, or of the United States, or California, a very different kind of selection of data takes place—one that is thrust upon the historian by the structural requirements of a unitary narrative in the presence of unlimited multiplicity of actual "histories" within the subject.

There is another difficulty inherent in the narrative or historiographical way of dealing with the data of human experience in time. This is the asserted *uniqueness* of events and personages. Almost everything in the ordinary historical narrative points to the uniqueness of each of the persons, situations, conditions, and events which follow one another chronologically.   On the evidence, most historians do not believe in repetition or in more than the most superficial of resemblances among their various wars, revolutions, great men, and governments.

In truth, events and situations, like human beings, are unique.   Beyond question, man's mind and his capacity for willed, purposive action endow him and each of his actions with a degree of distinctiveness not likely to be found elsewhere in the universe.   But uniqueness is also a feature of everything physical and biological.   For example, no other tree exactly like the one just outside my study window has ever before grown or ever will.

But uniqueness does not mean that things, actions, events, and persons do not have, within their several classes, much in common, much that cannot be made the subject of comparative investigation and the basis of comparative generalization.   There are assuredly elements of the French Revolution unique to it.   The same is true of the Russian Revolution.   But each revolution involved overthrow of a certain type of government; each became manifest in a succession of events, personages, roles, statuses, elites, and structures of authority that permit a considerable measure of likeness to be found.   Max Weber did not doubt that Buddha, Jesus, Martin Luther, and Oliver Cromwell were highly individual beings, but neither did he doubt that all were charismatic, not merely in social type but in relation to surrounding milieu. This fact was made the basis of comparative study and generalization. One must proceed carefully in such enterprises.   An important reason many historians were for a long time skeptical and even disdainful of sociological uses of history was that not all sociologists followed the same kind of scrupulous care in the handling of materials as did Weber. In the quest for uniformities, classes of events and changes, and patterns of resemblance, the sociologist-historian all too often carelessly or superficially casts the radically unlike into like frameworks.   But individual delinquencies of this sort have not prevented the sociological study of history from becoming an important area of modern social science and, at its best, as much admired by the historian as by the social scientist.

Since Weber's fertile sociological studies of history there have been a few sociologists interested in the uses of history for throwing light upon problems and concepts of sociology.   At the present moment there is high promise of a substantial increase in quantity and diversity of sociological work in this area.   One thinks of Robert Merton's studies of the history of science, of Reinhard Bendix on processes of industrialization and bureaucratization in earlier centuries, of Barrington Moore's investigations of the social origins of dictatorship and democracy, of Seymour Lipset's work on social class and politics, of Alvin Gouldner on ancient Athens and its cultural changes, of Charles Tilly on social movements in Western Europe, of Kai T. Erikson's studies of seventeenth-century Puritanism in New England. There are other studies, one of the most distinguished being the investigation George Homans made some thirty years ago of English villagers in medieval times. Only a very few historical studies by American sociologists equal this one in its exemplary use of historical documents and its focusing of attention upon sociological problems and processes without ever, however, sacrificing the particularity of subject matter. Some of this work is more comparative in framework than the rest, and this will probably be the main line of sociological use of history. Which is as it should be. But comparative or not, a rising amount of first-line sociological work in the United States and Europe is being conceived in historical terms.

Sociological use of historical materials is by no means limited to sociologists. For at least a century there have been historians in Europe and America who display interest in social history—institutions, social groups and movement, and patterns of social interaction. Some of the more notable of these historians prior to the present generation were Fustel de Coulanges, Otto von Gierke, F. W. Maitland, Frederick Jackson Turner, Charles Beard, and Marc Bloch. In the writings of these men one can find much astute use of what are in fact today's central sociological concepts. At the present time there are hundreds of historians in Western countries for whom the old conventional narrative framework has become outworn and whose researches into the past differ little at all from those of social scientists into the present. Concepts of social role, social status, elite, norm, community, anomie, deviance, and the like are often used in these works. A concept, as has been repeatedly stressed in this book, is a means of throwing light on what observation reveals. Whether the scene is strife-torn Paris in the year 1789 or Mayor Daley's riot-torn Chicago in 1968, there is no reason why the same concepts should not be of great value in our understanding, provided, of course, such concepts are used discriminatingly and with a strong sense of their relevance to the data involved.

The sociological use of history does not mean, in sum, the search for clear-cut directions in history, the quest for social meaning in history, or the imposition of some one or a few patterns of interaction upon the vast diversity of history. Nor does it mean wanton disregard of the particularity of history—any more than sound sociology involves disregard of the particularity of experience around us. Nor, finally, does the sociological use of historical material carry with it the inevitable disregard of time, place, and circumstance. Far from it.

What the sociological use of history does require, however, is abandonment of the narrative format as the exclusive means of presenting the materials of the past. It involves also abandonment of any notion of time as a single, homogeneous flow, irreversible, onrushing, like the flow of a river, from a point infinitely remote in the past to a point infinitely remote in the future. As there are many societies, many cultures, many histories, so are there, in fact, many *times*. And, finally, the sociological use of history requires abandonment of the notion of each person, each role, status, or norm, or each event and action as unalterably unique and incapable of utilization in a comparative framework.

History, in the sense of the particularity of social behavior in the past as well as the present, for the social scientist is an enlargement of field, of laboratory, if we like. Although on many matters there is much less evidence to be had among the documents, archives, and other means of access to the past than there is within the immediate present, this is hardly the crux of what is involved. Sheer volume of data is of less importance always than type and sufficiency of data and its relevance to important problems. Plainly, the sociological study of the historical past, like the study of contemporary peoples other than our own, has certain advantages of perspective. The greatest of these is detachment, the ability to see things more or less unfreighted by the stereotypes we carry in our minds with respect to our own—and other—cultures. Almost equally important is the long view—the view that can only be had from examination of what actually happened to a way of behavior, role, status, social aggregate, or norm over a considerable period of time.

Nowhere is the long view more important than in the study of social change. As we saw in the preceding chapters, it is only too easy to mistake mere motion or interaction for change. In the short view it is hard to distinguish the conflicts, deviances, and modifications *within* a structure of social behavior from the changes which, less frequently, occur in the structure itself.

This is in no way to derogate the importance of the present. The sociologist begins with the present—its problems, themes, and patterns of behavior. He takes these, properly conceptualized, in the form of questions and hypotheses to the past. The past is not conceived as a unitary, linear flow of time and event (there are, as we have noted, as many "pasts" as there are peoples and areas), but rather as a vast and diversified realm of human experiences, subject to comparative investigation. The central questions of sociology relating to the nature of the social bond and its changes can as well—if not always as easily—be directed to the experiences of the ancient Greeks, Romans, Indians, or Chinese as to those of contemporary middle-class Americans. The latter are, by now, fairly thoroughly researched. What is crucial, at bottom, are not the categories of "past" and "present," but the envisagement of social behavior in comparative terms, whether those of time or space.

Notes

1. This chapter draws heavily from my *Social Change and History: Aspects of the Western Idea of Development* (New York: Oxford University Press, 1969), especiallys Chaps. 7 and 8.
2. Oswald Spengler, *The Decline of the West*, I, trans. by Charles F. Atkinson (New York: Knopf, 1926), 104f.
3. Pitirim Sorokin, *Social and Cultural Dynamics* (Boston: Porter Sargent, 1957), p. 646.
4. This discussion is based in large part upon that in Frederick J. Teggart, *Theory of History* (New Haven, Conn.: Yale University Press, 1925), Chaps. 1–6.

14

Major Processes
of Social Change

In this final chapter I shall consider four major processes of change which have been recurrently involved in human history. All four are of intrinsic importance in human history and each in its own way is a vivid example of the relation between social structure and social change.

The first major process of change is *individualization*, by which I mean the release of individuals from the constraining ties of long-fixed, traditional social codes or authorities. The second is *innovation*—the circumstances involved in cultural efflorescence of high or distinctive order. Third is the process of *politicization* in which the assertion of power, whether individual or collective, succeeds the ordinary processes of custom and tradition. The fourth is *secularization*—the passage of sacred norms into secular, the replacement of a social order largely governed by religious values by one in which utilitarian or secular values are dominant. These four processes are obviously not the only important ones involved in social change, but they are assuredly among the most important, as our experience with the present makes clear enough.

Several points must be emphasized before we consider each of these processes separately. There is a sense in which all of them are permanent aspects of social behavior, embedded in the very character of social interaction. But this, while true, fails to account for the extraordinary diversity of intensity which these processes reveal when comparatively viewed in history. It is true that something in the nature of individualization or innovation is always going on. The study of the past, however, suggests clearly that at certain times, in specifiable places, these processes are to be seen in heightened intensity which produces results that have unusual and long-lasting significance.

The second point to emphasize follows directly from the first: it is the unevenness of the processes in time and place. This point is, of course, only a special instance of what we have found to be generally true of social change. Social change, in its major, significant forms, is intermittent, discontinuous, and uneven. Nowhere are these attributes more evident than with respect to the four processes I am concerned with in this section.

Third, it is important to stress the recurrence of the processes. Individualization, innovation, politicization, and secularization, even in their forms of heightened intensity, have manifested themselves repeatedly in human history. All may be seen, at different times, in the histories of such ancient and far-flung peoples as the Chinese, the Persians, the Indians, the Greeks, and the Romans, among others. All may be seen operating in different places, in varying intensities, in the present. The process of individualization associated with the emergence of the citizen-individual from the ties of the kinship community in sixth-century B.C. Athens has much in common for the sociologist with the process of individualization to be seen today in the new nations and also, let it be emphasized, in the emergence of blacks and Mexican-Americans in this country from the ties of the ghetto community. To be sure, no instance of the operation of the process is exactly like any other instance. But such uniqueness does not mean that important similiarities *for purposes of investigation* do not exist. It is in this sense that I speak of the recurrence in history of the processes.

In sum, to say that each of these processes is a permanent feature in the history of human behavior is true in some very general sense, but this idea detracts substantially and critically from the *inconstancy* and *unevenness* of the actual historical manifestation of each in time and place. Similarly, to say that each such manifestation is unique is to detract from the clear fact of the *recurrence* of each, considered as a process, in time and the wide distribution each has had geographically.

INDIVIDUALIZATION

By "individualization" I mean the complex set of elements involved when we speak of the release of the individual from the ties and constraints of community. Admittedly there is a certain degree of exaggeration involved in the world "release." It is not necessary to repeat in detail what was emphasized in the earlier chapters on authority, roles, and statuses. There is no behavior in social context that is not bound in some degree to social authority, role, and status. Therefore we have to consider release in somewhat relative terms. But however we consider it, the phenomenon of sudden individualization, of release of considerable numbers of individuals from the ties—suddenly perceived as restraints—of old, deeply fixed social codes and communities is a real one in the history of human society. If the word "individualism" had not taken on (as it has in the United States) extraneous ideological connotations, we could summarize the process in one phrase, "rise of individualism."

However we describe it, what is central is the process or processes whereby human beings come to feel conscious of themselves *as individuals* rather than primarily as members of a group. The history and comparative analysis of social organizations make clear the rarity of those bursts of change in which individualization is predominant. Far more common is the phenomenon of human beings so deeply committed to a given idea system, so strongly rooted in community and moral code, that the sense of individuality, of the "I am I" feeling, is a muted one. It is by now a well-known fact that Rousseau's state of nature—if by this is meant the way human beings lived in primitive times—was not what he thought it to be: eminently individualistic, spontaneous, and free. The study of ethnology teaches that the more primitive in type the social organization, the greater the likelihood of the submergence of the individual. And study of the most ancient texts, codes of law, and religious writing reinforces the judgment that for long ages in the history of mankind sheer desire for survival dictated a high degree of conformity and subordination to the social group.

No mistake could be greater than that of supposing the sense of individuality most of us in contemporary Western culture feel from infancy on, set as it is amid powerful norms which in effect urge us to be ourselves, realize ourselves, be true to ourselves, and so on, is a universal sense in time and space. There are large numbers of people even today, despite the penetration of Western values to so many parts of the earth, for whom individuality is by no means a recognized concept. And in the past, before man's political control of his fellows and technological control of environment reached anything like present levels, the sense of individuality must have been very weak indeed. In Durkheim's extreme phrase, the individual in earliest times was "lost in the depths of the social mass."

It is true that Durkheim's phrase carries the matter somewhat beyond what we have learned from ethnologists more recently about the at least minimal degree of individuality in the primitive levels of culture. But it is also true that the more primitive the type of society, the greater the degree of individual commitment to tribe, clan, village, and household. And it is precisely in ages when these units, through alien contacts become weakened in their control of the individual that release of the individual and the beginnings of individual self-awareness and responsibility, whether creatively or self-destructively, are found. As F. J. Teggart wrote a half-century ago, we find such beginnings historically in times of the social dislocation and normative conflicts which so often follow upon contact with alien peoples. Then there is release of personal initiative, the creation of personal responsibility, and the recognition of personal worth and individuality.[1]

Again it is important to realize that, when considered as a major social change in human history, this "release of personal initiative," this dawning of consciousness of self, this assertion of individuality has taken place not once but many times. Wherever we find the mixture of cultures, with alien idea systems in fruitful contact, with new roles created by the pressure of circumstance, and with indigenous moral authorities challenged, we are likely to find this momentous type of change in the history of a people.

Power—that is, the intrusion of personal power—is a common manifestation of the beginnings of such change. Durkheim perceptively writes, in *The Division of Labor*:

> *Rather than dating the effacement of the individual from the institution of a despotic authority, we must, on the contrary, see in this institution the first step towards individualism. Chiefs are, in fact, the first personalities who emerge from the social mass. Their exceptional situation, putting them beyond the level of others, gives them a distinct physiognomy and accordingly confers individuality upon them. In dominating society, they are no longer forced to follow all its movements. . . . A source of initiative is thus opened which had not existed before. There is, hereafter, someone who can produce*

*new things and even in certain measure, deny collective usages.
Equilibrium has been broken.*[2]

Durkheim's words throw much light upon an oft-noted affinity in
the history of peoples—the affinity between the first stirrings of marked
individualization and the emergence of single individuals of great personal power.   We shall come back to this important point when we
consider the process of politicization.   It is enough here to say that,
paradoxical as it may at first seem, there is no necessary contradiction
between political power, especially in its larger individual manifestations,
and the profusion of individualism in a people.   Quite apart from what
the histories of ancient peoples reveals in this respect, it is impossible to
miss the linkage in our own time between the suddenly intensified individualization of blacks and Mexican-Americans in American culture
and the appearance of highly endowed leaders whose own assertion of
individuality is inseparable from the assertion of their individual powers
against the authorities, internal and external, which maintain ghettoes
and other cultural enclaves.   To cite a quite different example, it is
worth noting that in the history of American universities, the spurt forward that takes place at a given time in the history of some universities
is almost invariably associated with the commanding presence of a
powerful president of marked individuality.   The individuality of the
leader—whether in Durkheim's primitive social mass, among the He-
brews at the time of Moses, in the Greek tribal system from which, first
Solon, then Cleisthenes emerged, or with respect to the black and Mexican-American ghettoes of our own time—appears to be a powerful stimulus to the proliferation of intensified individualization among others.

Again it should be emphasized that individualization considered as
an abstract, generalized social process goes on in at least mild degree
all of the time.   Individualization is an aspect of the socialization process.
In even the most custom-bound, tradition-ribbed folk or preliterate peoples, there is bound to be some stirring of individualization at any given
time.

From the point of view of the problem of major social change, however, this endemic, routine process is insufficient for purposes of explanation.   If we are to account for those momentous ages of individualization
which are found recurrently (but never constantly or uniformly), we
are obliged to seek data from what Durkheim called the social milieu.
This means we must give attention to such events as are to be seen in
the myriad conflicts of cultures, the clashes of idea systems, and the
emergence, through whatever kind of historical crisis, of dominant per-

sonalities. The study of individualization, considered as a process of change, is, then, sociological, but it can never be divorced from the study of historical events. This was true in the age of Cleisthenes; it is true in the age of Mohandas Gandhi, Martin Luther King, and Cesar Chavez.

INNOVATION

All change has, of course, an element of innovation. Our interest in this section, however, is cultural innovation—the kind that is found so brilliantly in the so-called culture explosions of human history: in the Assyrian ninth and eighth centuries B.C., in the Greece of the sixth and fifth centuries B.C., in the China of the third century B.C., Rome in the first century A.D., India in the fourth and fifth centuries A.D., in the Western thirteenth century, and in such ages as those of Shakespeare in England, Molière in France, and Calderón in Spain. In our own day, there are the culture explosions of the Jews and, more recently, that of Negro artists, musicians, intellectuals, and creative writers. These are but a few; there are many others. They vary, of course, in the sheer brilliance of their contributions. Few ages of cultural innovation have been, or are likely to be, greater than that of Greece from the sixth to fourth centuries B.C. This age included Heraclitus, Herodotus, Thucydides, Aeschylus, Sophocles, Euripides, Phidias, Praxiteles, Socrates, Plato, Aristotle, and many many others, all of whom had, within that very brief period, so profound an influence in creating what we know today as Western culture.

But though there is an impressive number of such periods taking all peoples and all recorded time into consideration, the far more important point is the relative rarity of such periods when compared with the total number of centuries in the history of any people. For every fifth century B.C. of Greece, there are dozens of centuries of relative sterility, of mere conventionalization or routinization.

As Teggart has pointed out, a single century can contain cultural figures as far-flung, eminent, and lasting in influence as Zoroaster in Persia, Lao-tse and Confucius in China, Mahavira (founder of Jainism), Gautama Buddha in India, the prophets Ezekiel and Isaiah, Thales in Ionia, and Pythagoras in southern Italy. All these disparate, widely separated figures, each destined to be of great and persisting importance not only in his own but in world culture, lived in the sixth century B.C. As Teggart emphasizes, their appearance within so limited a period of time constitutes "a class of events." Teggart continues:

Yet though the correspondence of these events has frequently been observed, no serious effort has ever been made, so far as I have been able to discover, to treat the appearance of these great teachers— within a brief compass of time—as a problem which called for systematic investigation. But without this knowledge, how are we to envisage or comprehend the workings of the human spirit? The history of human achievement, indeed, displays extraordinary variations of advance and subsidence. How are the outstanding advances of men at different times and places to be accounted for?[3]

One way they have been accounted for, and still are, is through the word "genius." We are prone to say that genius is unaccountable, unpredictable, and undiscoverable. Men are great by reason of superlative biological and mental endowments, they achieve great things, and they leave their works behind them. In the nineteenth century, the English eugenicist Sir Francis Galton tried to show in his book *Hereditary Genius* the ineradicable basis of individual cultural creativity in biological ancestry, in demographic type, even in family line. Why were the Aristotles, Senecas, Augustines, Michelangelos, Newtons, and Molières of the past great? Because of what Galton called genius. These men, he said, were of highly superior biological type: hence their highly superior cultural achievements. The explanation, in short, is presented in terms of biologically innate qualities.

The great difficulty with this kind of explanation is that it fails to account for the *social and historical manifestations* of the creative excellence we are concerned with here. Granted that the biologically transmitted qualities are necessary, they are not *sufficient*. They do not, and cannot, give an explanation of the peculiar social selectiveness of the phenomenon we are dealing with. For example, these innate qualities cannot explain why a certain people or ethnic strain attains marked distinction at one time but perhaps not again for hundreds, even thousands of years. They do not explain why certain other peoples or ethnic strains suddenly manifest large numbers of creative individuals when, to the best of our recorded knowledge, they never have before in history. What we know about the biology of populations suggests that the *proportions of innate excellence* are about the same from people to people and from age to age. What varies, and greatly in history, are the *proportions of manifest, socially and culturally expressed excellence.*

It is the sporadic, thus far unpredictable, character of these ages that is of the greatest interest to the historical sociologist. A single people, the Chinese or the Greeks, for instance, may for centuries live and work in the same area and be subject to a variety of influences without manifesting any notable tendencies toward creative distinction. Then, within a single short age, as in the fifth century B.C. in Greece and the third century B.C. in China, an immense burst of cultural innovation takes place, with relatively large numbers of individuals engaged in works that shape thought and behavior for centuries, even millennia, afterward.

Or we may look at the matter in terms of single disciplines rather than of peoples. Consider the histories of science, painting, sculpture, literature, and philosophy. In each of these areas the record reveals the uneven, the wavelike, character of inovaiton. Merely glance at a good history of any one of these areas, and it becomes apparent that for every century of substantial creative efflorescence there are a dozen of relative sterility, of mere conventionalization of what has been done before. We can hardly claim that biology is responsible. It is unlikely, to say the least, that the genetic production of superior individuals is greater at any given time. And to take refuge in "environment," that is, the direct impact upon individuals of what is to be found in cultural environment at any given time, is equally useless as far as explanation of the sporadic character of cultural innovation is concerned.

Recognition of this clustering of innovation in time and space is very old. Nearly two thousand years ago the Roman Velleius Paterculus commented on it, noting the relatively short periods of greatness in the several fields of the arts and philosophy and the relatively long periods of mere imitation or even dearth. He wrote:

> *Though I frequently search for the reasons why men of similar talents occur exclusively in certain epochs and not only flock to one pursuit but also attain like success, I can never find any of whose truth I am certain, though I do find some which perhaps seem likely, and particularly the following. Genius is fostered by emulation, and it is now envy, now admiration, which kindles imitation, and, in the nature of things, that which is cultivated with the highest zeal advances to the highest perfection; but it is difficult to continue at the point of perfection, and naturally that which cannot advance must recede.*[4]

From Velleius through Turgot and Hume down to such scholars as Teggart and Kroeber in the twentieth century, this clustering of genius has been commented upon, wondered at, made the subject of fascinating conjecture. But, as the anthropologist-historian Kroeber wrote in 1944, "the cause or causes . . . remain unknown, and constitute a great problem of inquiry."[5] Neither Velleius' musings on "emulation" nor speculations on the effects of social and cultural factors such as those we find in Turgot and Hume carry us very far, although they are much to be preferred to those of Galton, which rested solely on the concept of biologically based genius.

Explanations of these periodicities in innovation when found in satisfactory form will be in social and cultural terms. They could hardly be other. The problem lies in the configurations, the patternings of these social and cultural terms of explanation. We are obliged to pursue a cautious course, trying to avoid the use of elements and forces which, while admittedly and clearly present in the ages of high innovation, are also found in ages of opposite character.

It is clear that the problem of innovation in time is closely related to that of individualization. What else indeed is innovation but the directing in intellectual and cultural directions of those powers we described as marking very high individuality? In the release of the individual we note qualities which are to be found whether this release is manifest in the emergence of the political leader or of the great artist or philosopher. In each instance individualization of high order is apparent. But that is only the beginning. We have not, through some concept such as "individualization" met our problem, which is that of accounting for the specific and widely separated periods of individualization and innovation.

It is equally clear that broad cultural themes in a social order are involved. A society, such as that of Western Europe in the thirteenth century, primarily interested intellectually in questions of grace, the Godhead, and man's soul is more likely to have great theologians such as Abelard, Anselm, and Aquinas than physical scientists and more likely to see its architectural energies expended in design of a Chartres Cathedral, or a Notre Dame or Canterbury, than in commercial or governmental buildings. In the histories of cultures, the presence of broad themes (whether military, religious, artistic, scientific, or philosophical), within which individual works are found and assessed and to which the energies of creators are directed, is apparent. But we still have to account for the appearance and then the disappearance of the themes.

Plainly, economic affluence is a major factor. A considerable degree of "surplus wealth" is required for a society to be able to afford the existences of the Aristotles, Mozarts, Shakespeares, and Einsteins of history who might otherwise be compelled to devote their talents to farming or hunting. The great ages of cultural achievement have been, without exception, ages of wealth or aristocracies or elites of wealth, or both. Such elites need not be private elites. We know, for example, that for many years the political government of ancient Attica offered substantial financial prizes to dramatists for the writing of the plays, which were widely attended in the fifth century B.C. by Athenians and others. Wealth, whether distributed by government, aristocracy, individual, or foundation, is assuredly a factor in the kind of age we are considering. But before jumping to a quick conclusion, let it be remembered that there have been far more ages of economic abundance (relatively speaking) in history than there have been ages of outstanding cultural creativity. Again, we must distinguish between the merely necessary and the sufficient.

Cultural (including technological) *level* is important. No matter what the coincidence of gifted individuals and historical factors, achievements in any given area are bound to be dependent in some degree upon what has already been done, that is, upon the cultural base afforded creative talents. Making due allowance for the individual achievements of Aristotle, what he did is hardly comprehensible apart from the philosophical foundations laid by Plato, Socrates and, well before them, the great philosophers of Ionia. Technological level can be vital even in the areas of the purest arts. What Bach and Beethoven composed would not have been possible had it not been for the technological base represented by the instruments of the orchestra each composed for.

There is also the *city* and its special social character. It is difficult to think of much cultural innovation in the history of civilization that has not taken place in cities, or at the hands of individuals whose formative periods of development were spent in cities. When we think of great ages of cultural innovation we think of Athens, Rome, Florence, London, Paris, Vienna, New York, and their immediate environs. The medieval phrase "the city makes free" may be interpreted in many ways. There is no need to repeat here what was said in earlier chapters about the distinctive social characteristics of urban aggregates. It is enough to bear in mind the relative anonymity, the social and psychological open spaces, the higher degree of social density and also diversity and differentiation of interaction, the social and physical mobility, of the urban setting. All of these conditions are bound to provide setting for that special kind of individualization that is cultural innovation.

Closely related is the phenomenon of social dislocation, loosening of social codes and mores, the relaxing of traditions and inherited intellectual or moral systems. Great cultural ages are invariably ages of social ferment, though here as with the other elements it would be hazardous to argue from the existence of social ferment to necessary cultural brilliance.

Still, the kind of loosening of ties that exists within periods of social ferment appears to be necessary, along with very considerable social change, social dislocation, anomie—and, it must be emphasized, *deviance*.

In the strict sense, Buddha, Lao-tse, Jesus, and Mohammed were deviants who were not at all interested in deviance for its own sake. For them, as for all of the genuinely creative in the history of religion and morals, deviance from the accepted is but a step to revelation of what they have believed to be a higher or better norm. The same is true of such intellectual deviants as Socrates, Lucretius, Roger Bacon, Galileo, Pasteur, Freud, and Picasso. Some have paid with their lives, their freedom, or civilized comfort for their deviance. Most have at one time or other been the objects of hate, ridicule, scorn. So often indeed has this last been true that one can almost assess the truly creative, the genuinely innovative, by the degree of dislike and rejection they so commonly receive from contemporaries. How can one be a truly radical thinker, composer, or artist and be accepted and loved by his contemporaries? I would not wish to carry that statement to the level of an absolute. There are exceptions. There is every reason to believe that Aristotle was admired in his own time; so was the greatest of the Bachs. But deviance, however conceived, is assuredly involved in what I have here called innovation. And it is in societies or ages of history that tend to be rather rich in generalized deviance (as in history's bohemias, Left Banks, Greenwich Villages, and university campuses) that we are perhaps most likely to find those more creative forms which are the stuff of cultural innovation.

One final word on political context. It would be agreeable to our general values at the present time if we could point to democracy, equality, and humanitarianism as involved in the great ages, in the resplendent clusters of genius I have been discussing. Unfortunately, we cannot. This is not to say, of course, that such ages and clusters are incompatible with democracy, equality, and humanitarianism. But, on the evidence of history, there have been some spectacular outbursts of intellectual creativity, in the arts, sciences, philosophy, and religion, in ages and areas which were anything but democratic, equal, and humanitarian.

Some degree of *freedom* appears vital. The great works of culture have not been created, for the most part, in secret cellars, garrets, or caves. They have been produced in ages and places where a considerable measure of personal autonomy existed, although some degree of political despotism may have flourished, and men were *not* thought to be equal, and the privations of the masses were frequently a matter of indifference to the privileged. Despotisms of the past have been either unwilling or unable to choke off such autonomy as have twentieth-century totalitarianisms, in which personal autonomy, individual eccentricity or deviance, and cultural diversity have been regarded with loathing and dread. True, Socrates was compelled to drink the lethal hemlock (and in the greatest democracy of the ancient world!). But Western philosophy would not be what it is had he not enjoyed for many years a very considerable autonomy of personal movement and intellectual freedom. Galileo was required to abjure, at least for the public record, belief in movement of the earth. But there is little if any evidence to suggest that his inherent creativity was much impaired by the despotisms of his time, ecclesiastical or political. There are many instances of men living in creative ages, such as the French Enlightenment and the Russian cultural renaissance of the nineteenth century, being forced sometimes to flee for safety (as was Voltaire) or occasionally imprisoned (as was Dostoevsky). But these people nonetheless seem to have had sufficient freedom to produce a vast amount of distinguished work. In short, achievement has varied contexts in history.

On the evidence there is a rather high degree of creative achievement possible within the kinds of political despotism we associate with the so-called absolute monarchies of history. This does not mean that political despotism is a cause of such achievement. It may mean only that both conditions—achievement and despotism—are associated with the relaxation of other restraints in society which are far more prejudicial to the free mind: restraints of custom, tradition, and sacred norms. The assertion of personal power that may be associated with the release of the individual from the impersonal kind of constraint found in social codes and customs may also be associated with the outburst of creative imagination, the release of individual cultural innovation.

POLITICIZATION

The concept of politicization brings us to another of the major processes of change in history. Politicization too is recurrent in time and widely distributed in space. As with each of the other processes, its significance to historical sociology lies in the fact that there has been no single encompassing process of politicization for mankind but a great multiplicity of manifestations of the process. These manifestations can be compared in time as well as space.

By politicization I refer to the process whereby power, or the assertion of power, or the struggle for power, or the extension of power becomes a dominant consideration in a social order, with strongly modifying effects. It may be that the political order first comes into existence in an area when, as the result of some crisis, the special authority of the political order supersedes or strongly represses the authorities of other, more or less competing associations. Or the political order may come when essentially nonpolitical associations such as church, labor union, or university become internally dominated not by issues arising from their own purposes but by those drawn from the political order. In all of these situations we may fairly say that the process of politicization is operative.

Politicization in the first of the senses just cited is to be seen nowhere more brilliantly and also fatefully than in the celebrated reforms (revolution is the apter word) of Cleisthenes at the end of the sixth century B.C. in Attica. By his liquidation or marked subordination of the ancient personal authorities of tribe, clan, and household, and by his establishment of the territorial unit, the city-state with subunits resembling townships called demes, and by his transfer of Attican rights, duties, and key memberships from kinship to territorial society, Cleisthenes inaugurated the political order for Attica. There have been many such inaugurations in history.

We can turn to either Western Europe of the sixteenth century or to any one of the new nations in Africa, Asia, or the Middle East for abundant illustration of politicization in the second of the senses mentioned above. In each of these, the structure of the political order had for some time been in existence, but the claims of other associations in the larger social order were powerful, leading to frequent challenge to the authority of the state and to overall political enfeeblement. What politicization meant in the sixteenth century in Europe, and continued to mean thereafter (as, for example, in the contemporary new nations) is the forcible subjugation of such organizations as kindred, church, village community, autonomous town, and others. Many of their functions and authorities were transferred to the political order.

Politicization in the third of the senses cited above is to be seen in those periods when the intrinsic values and ways of behavior of essentially nonpolitical organizations such as church, labor union, guild, or university become in large measure supplanted by the issues, power struggles, and means of action ordinarily confined to the political order. In our own day universities and many professional and learned societies illustrate politicization in this sense. They have done so not only in the United States but, for a considerably longer period of time, in other countries, Western and non-Western. Issues drawn from national politics such as civil rights, integration, defense policy, foreign relations, and international war frequently have greater and more decisive significance on university campuses or in learned and professional associations today than do some of the older, more indigenous issues of these organizations.

Much the same kind of politicization can be seen at other times in the histories of peoples—in the Christian Church after Constantine made Christianity official in ancient Rome; in the sixteenth century, the age of the Reformation; in the merchant and craft guilds of Europe, especially in the seventeenth century; in the aristocracy, feudal-born, in France after the rise of the absolute monarchs; in labor unions, especially in Western Europe in the early twentieth century. In all these instances we observe the rather sudden replacement of issues and values indigenous to the organizations mentioned by issues and values taken directly from the political order.

There are, in short, a number of important forms of the process of politicization. There are also a number of kinds of consequence, usually assessed in terms of good and bad, favorable or unfavorable. To adopt the view that politicization is in itself either good or bad would be very poor sociological reasoning. Few would quarrel with the effects of the Cleisthenean reforms which ushered in both the cultural creativity and the political democracy of the fifth century B.C. in ancient Attica. Politicization here was a vital means of the release of individuals from forms of social authority which had become as tyrannous as they were ineffectual in meeting Attican military and economic problems.

The point referred to above, in the discussions of both individualization and of innovation, should be borne in mind here. The political order, strictly defined, has often in history been the means of providing a medium within which individuals could live and not be under the total influence of either kinship or religion or village community. Paradoxical as it may seem, the political state has been the means, at many junctures in history, of *creating* individualism—through its distinctive concept of citizenship and through the powerful ideas of rights and freedoms directly granted by the state.

On the other hand, we clearly do not associate the kind of politicization involved in the rise of the totalitarian orders of the twentieth century, or of the quasi-totalitarian social order of the Roman Empire from the first century A.D. on, or of many other forms of political despotism in the past and present, with the values of liberation or freedom. The politicization of the churches, labor unions, universities, professional associations, and almost all other forms of association in Germany during the period 1933–1945 left little that was socially viable in the years immediately following Nazi Germany's defeat in World War II. There were few autonomies, individual or group, during the high point of Nazi totalitarianism. All, or nearly all, had been politicized, had been made differential aspects of the state.

Let us turn briefly to the problem of the rise of the political state in different areas at different times. As we noted in Chapter 6, following Max Weber's treatment of the matter, the political state is the only association founded on force alone. I do not mean, nor does Weber, that other forms of association do not on occasion employ force or that the state invariably uses it. Rather, Weber is saying that force is a means *specific to the state*. In the political order alone, force is given legitimacy. Other forms of association—family, church, guild, business enterprise, labor union, profession, cultural society, and so on—take on their distinctiveness by reason of the special *end* that belongs to each. The state, however, is different. "Ultimately," writes Weber, "one can define the modern state sociologically only in terms of the specific *means* peculiar to it, as to every political association, namely the use of physical force."[6] In every form of association known to man force is an occasional—or sometimes frequent—possibility. Labor unions, churches, and families, as well as criminal syndicates, are known to employ force. But the state, as Weber writes, is the only form of association in which the actual or potential use of force is legitimate and an inextricable element of the very nature of the association.

What are the circumstances under which the state as a specific type of association arises in history? Invariably the circumstances of war, strife, conflict of some kind—circumstances beyond the capacity of existing institutions to contain them. Marx did not err in describing the state as an institutional device for repressing conflict; he erred only in giving exclusive attention to one type of conflict—class conflict. Between the political state and war, whether external or internal, there is as close a relation as there is between the family and socialization of the young, between the church and devotion to the sacred, or between the school and instruction. Again I should emphasize that I am referring here to the *circumstances of the rise of the state* in an area, to the conditions of the process of politicization, not to the total character of a state that has long been in existence. Over a long period of time the state may take on a large number of functions, many of them taken or accepted from other institutions, many of them humane, civilizing in consequence, and indispensable to whatever kind of economic and social order has become associated with it.

The political state has arisen not once but many times in human history. The precise conditions of its rise vary, of course, from time to time. But there are nonetheless certain clear elements in common among these multiple appearances. I have said that the first and perhaps most distinctive is the element of force or war. The state arises when, as the result of conflicts no longer capable of being contained by existing institutions, a new form of authority comes into being whose express purpose is repression of these conflicts and the maintenance of public order. But following these precipitating causes or conditions, other elements distinctive to the state appear almost immediately. One is the *territorialization of authority.* Unlike other associations whose authorities are linked to the functions they perform—economic, religious, or familial—the authority of the political state is almost from the beginning an adjunct of bounded territory. The second major element of the process of politicization is its *individualization of preexisting social aggregates* in the area through the directness of tie that is established between the political government and the individuals who are members of the preexisting social aggregates. We noted above, in the discussion of the process of individualization, the close link between this process and the assertion of political power by some individual or individuals. There is a close, even necessary, relation between the processes of individualization and politicization. Only through the state's penetration of traditional social authorities to the individuals who live under them can its own authority be said to be manifest. The third major element is the *centralization* of authority in the area that falls under the newly established political state. Unlike the authorities of other associations, which tend to be multiple, concentric, and with considerable degree of autonomy of the clans, kindreds, parishes, castes and subcastes involved, the authority of the political state is focused in its single government, and the authority extends itself through agencies of its own creation, each directly responsible to the government.

None of the above discussion is intended to suggest that the qualities I mention as essential to the process of politicization spring into existence fully shaped. Centuries may pass before these dominant structural characteristics of the political order become fully diffused through a population or become fully known by those governing or those governed. Almost always there is a persistence of the social elements of the old order which enter into often complex relationships with the social elements of the political order. Old habits and beliefs regarding the *personal* nature of authority are usually so deeply ingrained that newly formed political orders often borrow from them. A good deal of time was required in the late Middle Ages for the King of the Franks to become widely thought of as the King of France. The imperial government of China was a conglomerate of techniques of political administration, of political consciousness, and, at the same time, of persisting authorities of clan, village, and guild (which were often governments in themselves). In Communist China at the present time we can observe the process of politicization occurring in striking degree, just as it took place in Soviet Russia during the late 1920s and the 1930s under Stalin, who must rank with the most powerful of political figures in all history.

Roman history gives us a fascinating insight into the techniques of politicization in the age of Augustus, first and greatest of the line of Roman emperors that was to last more than a thousand years. Within the brief period bounded by the dates 18 B.C. and 30 A.D. some of the most important changes in the entire history of Rome took place. Politicization was the dominant context of these changes, a politicization that reduced the powerful structure of Roman kinship society to little more than an assemblage of weak household groups. The once mighty kindreds and clans and other groups based upon kinship descent became hardly more than a memory. When Augustus decreed that each individual male was entitled to keep for himself, rather than to turn over to his family, the gains of living, he dealt a major blow to the economic structure of traditional kinship. And when he ordered all Roman households to place a small statue of himself alongside the ancient and sacred *lares* and *penates*—gods of the hearth—he struck forcefully at the spiritual structure of the kinship system. The age of Augustus is one of the most vivid and concentrated ages of politicization known to us. It is also, as we know, one of the great ages of cultural production—in philosophy, the arts, and in science and technology. What was from one point of view an age of political power was from another point of view an age of intense social individualism, of large numbers of individuals liberated, so to speak, from old and confining memberships and roles. And, from still a third point of view, it was a period of extraordinary cultural creativity.

Again it is important to guard against the easy conclusion that the personal political power of the ruler, or rather the sudden thrust of power, was the cause of it all. We cannot be sure what the causes are of either ages of extreme social individualism or high cultural creativity and innovation. It is enough to conclude that, on the evidence, politicization, in high intensity, invariably seems to be present.

One other historical manifestation of politicization should be mentioned. This took place in the area known today as China, in the third century B.C. Into this area, then unnamed and without political unity or identity, came the people from the northwest known to themselves as the Ch'in. Within three generations, one of them, Prince Cheng, founder of the Ch'in dynasty which was to give its name to the entire land mass and its inhabitants, had brought political organization into being in every bit as full a sense as did Cleisthenes in Greece and Augustus in Rome. Cheng centralized administration over the entire area, laying the foundation for the civil service that was to become without equal in the world for many centuries. He developed a network of roads and canals, bringing immense areas of land into fertile cultivation. He also abolished the feudal authorities that had been in existence for many centuries and removed the great clans from formal participation in government. Cheng began and largely finished the Great Wall which was to be the most famous military fortification in the world. This Great Wall repelled a group of Central Asian attackers, forcing them to shift their migrations to the west, thus affecting decisively the history of Rome and the later West as well. The records make clear that here, as elsewhere, the upsurge of political power, as well as the spread of politicization as a process of change in the area, was closely associated with a high degree of individualism. And, finally, the age is one of the most famous in China's history for its scholarship and literature. Indeed, the closest adviser to Prince Cheng was Li Ssu, the most eminent scholar of his day.

In sum, politicization as a process is frequently associated with periods of extraordinary achievement when its effect is the breaking of old and sterile codes and the eradication or subjugation of groups in the population which have become obsolete or corrupt. For in such instances a genuine release of individuals is effected by power. But, with the experience of totalitarianism fresh in mind, one would not wish to declare politicization to be uniformly and universally a creative process.

SECULARIZATION

The last of the four major processes of change in history is that in which the dominance of religious or sacred values in a population is terminated, however briefly, among however small a minority of the population, by values drawn directly from human reason. I have chosen the word "secularization" to describe this process. Almost equally appropriate for our purposes would be

Max Weber's word "rationalization." For what is central in the change
is the ascendancy of rationality over the merely traditional or the religiously authoritative. The chief difficulty in using Weber's term—and
the fault is not his—comes from the present wide association of it with
political and organizational norms alone. I have in mind here the kind
of change that is associated with the rise of critical rationalism, as in
ancient Greece and again in the Western Renaissance, and also the
rise of systematic science, as in the seventeenth century in England and
France.

As with the other three processes, secularization, from one point
of view, is a constant in human behavior. We may say that *something*
is always being secularized in our lives. But although this is true, it
is outweighed in significance by the fact that there are certain ages in
which secularization reaches a high point of intensity, elicits the creative attention of minds of highest quality, and leads to an unwonted
emphasis on individual reason rather than mere obedience to tradition.
The process of secularization results in the novel respect for values of
utility rather than of sacredness alone, control of environment rather
than passive submission to it, and, in some ways most importantly, concern with man's present welfare on this earth rather than his supposed
immortal relation to the gods.

The secularization process has occurred many times in human history.
If the most famous and seemingly most consequential case was that
which began in the islands off Greece approximately at the end of the
eighth century B.C., reaching its climax in the works of Aristotle some
three hundred years later, this may be only because we are Westerners,
long accustomed to veneration of the Greek heritage. Similar ages have
occurred, sometimes of shorter, sometimes of longer, duration, in Asia,
Southeast Asia, and Africa.

Secularization, or rationalization, is a vivid process of change today in those areas where Western idea systems (derived from the
rationalist ideal begun by the Greeks) are in conflict with the traditional-
sacred norms of caste, kinship, village, and the immense variety of
supernatural beliefs long dominant in the minds of native peoples.
Secularization is also a vivid process in the successive experiences of
minority groups in the United States. We are as justified, I believe,
in referring to the remarkable experience of the Jews (not only, of
course, in the United States and not only in the twentieth century) as being as much a process of secularization or rationalization as we are in referring to this experience as one of individualization or cultural innovation. A similar situation, in some ways, holds for the blacks—here and

also in other countries. The shaking-off of old norms of submission, of valuation of heaven over earth, of the religious-familial context in which most blacks lived their lives for so long, and the replacement of these by the norms of enhanced respect for individual reason, of welfare, individual and collective, and by norms of material wealth, success, and social status is secularization in action.

If we are prone to give greatest interest and respect to the secularization process in ancient Greece it is because the Greek heritage is largely what Western secular culture is all about. The sheer diffusion of this Western secular culture during the last century or two in the world justifies our close attention to this case.

We know that the early spiritual world of the Greeks was dominated by religious myth, sacred norms extending back many centuries or even millennia, and belief in fate, chance, and inexorable destiny. This extraordinary people began settling in the Aegean peninsula and the adjacent islands of the Aegean Sea, as well as the shore of what is today western Turkey, sometime before 1000 B.C. The sacred norms that governed their thinking and their culture were set down in detail, first by Homer, then by others, who documented them in later centuries, but before the rise of Greek rationalism. These sacred norms were distinctive and unique indeed, but comparative observation places them nonetheless in the category of the sacred-mythical, which contains the experiences of countless other peoples. Nothing could happen that was not the will of the gods. Everything in man's existence, his relation to physical and social environment alike, lay in the hands of the gods. Submission and obeisance were the honored responses of the human mind. Ritual was the cast of thought, with its incessant emphasis on the perpetuation of what had been.

A fundamental change began in the Greek mind, as I have noted, somewhere toward the end of the eighth century B.C. By the late seventh century B.C. this change was in full momentum, reaching its high point so far as *physical* thought was concerned in the successive works of such extraordinary minds as Thales, Empedocles, and, above all, Heraclitus. Now, in both writing and in lectures, explanations of things were cast not in the rhetoric of myth and ritual but in the language, astonishingly modern, of *natural* causation, process, and event. Ideas of the origin of the universe, of the earth, of man himself along with all other forms of organic life began to appear. These ideas represent the beginnings of the Western theory of physical and biological evolution. Instead of appeal to the gods and to arcane spirits, we find theories of origins in terms of such familiar and natural things as fire, water, and organic growth.   Studies began to be made of different parts of the earth and sea.   Records were kept, classifications of organisms made, and expeditions formed to remote parts of the known world for purposes of comparison—the kind of expeditions of which the recent landing on the moon is a lineal succession.   In however dim and tentative a sense, the sciences of geology, botany, biology, and human physiology had begun.

It was but a step, a momentous one to be sure, to direct this same spirit of rationalist inquiry to man himself, as a thinking being, and to his institutions.   The same speculations which had been made by an Empedocles or Anaximander about man's physical habitat were now directed —by the Sophists, Socrates, Plato, Aristotle, and many others—to man's social setting.   For Aristotle the same fundamental principles which gave unity to his meteorological and geological systems of thought and to his physics and chemistry also gave unity to his studies of political constitutions and of the relations of cultures and societies and institutions to one another.

It would be absurd to suppose that *all* the Greeks underwent this kind of secularizing metamorphosis. Have all the Western Europeans since undergone it?   Indeed not!   Nor can we argue that in the seventh century B.C. all mythical reasoning was suddenly laid aside even by a Heraclitus or, three centuries later, by an Aristotle.   Usually, even in ages of the most critical of rationalisms, elements based upon myth and metaphor persist in some degree.

Nor can we assume that once formed in the minds of such great rationalists as the succession beginning with the physical philosophers of Ionia, the spirit of rationalistic inquiry and control of environment persisted through all subsequent centuries.   It certainly did not in Greece itself.   By the late fourth century B.C. we are in the presence of a whole variety of ideas of fate, chance, and the helplessness of man before the gods—a variety of ideas that Sir Gilbert Murray epitomized in his phrase "the failure of nerve." The spirit of rationalism, plainly, is not indestructible.   It is as intermittent and as fleeting in man's history as any of the manifestations of the other processes we have been concerned with.

True, rationalism did not undergo total extinction.   Many texts remained and were discovered and rediscovered by other peoples in later centuries.   The Romans made these Greek ideas the basis of their own great age of secularism in the first century B.C. and for a century or two following—an age that was soon to be submerged by the non- or antirationalist doctrines of the mystery religions from the East which flooded Rome by the late first century A.D. Among these religions was Christianity, which was to succeed in virtually eliminating secular rationalism from the European continent for more than a thousand years. Then, in the Western Renaissance and still later in the Age of Reason, ideas formed in the image of those which had first risen among the Greeks two thousand years earlier became dominant in thought. These ideas produced the philosophies we associate with modern rationalism, the belief in control of environment, and first the physical and then the social sciences.

We have lived for several centuries now in an age of secularization, of rationalization. To argue permanence for this age would be, on the testimony of history, absurd. Nonsecular, nonrationalist systems and theories have very evidently not disappeared. The conflict between sacred and secular norms, as we observed in Chapter 9, is, a continuing one. Religion remains a powerful influence on the human mind. The sacred, in some form, is, as Durkheim has told us, ineradicable from human consciousness. There are convictions of the rule of fate, destiny, chance; beliefs in astrology and other mystic or supernatural systems of thought; attitudes of submission to the weight of circumstance and environment. All of these are found (even among college students) in substantial degree in the United States today, where economic affluence, political democracy, and the spirit of individual reason have a considerable following and where secular-rationalist values have, for the moment at least, high ascendancy. But the relative ease (in historical terms at least) with which the values of critical rationalism and science may be superseded by those of myth and unexamined dogma is all too well illustrated by the rise and ascendancy of Nazism in Germany, a country regarded by most of the world through the 1920s as in the vanguard of rationalism.

What are the causes of these recurrent, widely separated manifestations of the process of secularization? As with the causes of the other processes, we can speak with some certainty in general terms even if the specific and sufficient causes may continue to elude us.

Abundant studies of the burst of Greek rationalism referred to above point to the decisive effects of *mobility* in its varied forms. Mobility by itself may possess no element of change. But when mobility brings people, as the migrations of Greeks brought them, into contact with many other peoples and their diverse customs, beliefs, and values, it can create at least the setting of intensified reflection regarding one's own culture. The all-important role of the *stranger* is involved too. In most peoples throughout history the stranger is feared. The original Latin word for stranger and enemy was the same. But when, through whatever means—trade, exploration, even war—a people become at least willing to permit strangers in their midst, an opening is formed for critical view of themselves. For the mere presence of the stranger is a reminder of difference—however much this difference may be feared at first.

Cultural contact is closely related, and deserves especial emphasis. To suppose that the secular rationalism I speak of here arose *indigenously* among the Greeks, without contribution by others, would be nonsense. The Greek age of rationalism was preceded by that of the Egyptians and the Babylonians in each of whom, though perhaps not in as great degree, the same upthrust of secular reason had occurred. The Greeks were acquainted with these cultures through their own travels and through the reception of traders and explorers from the Middle East and North African mainland.

This fact also suggests the vital role of *geographic location* not merely in this process but in the other three we have considered. Geographical determinism is to be distrusted in our thinking. Historical geography —that is, place envisaged in terms of history—is indispensable. Repeatedly, sea coasts with natural harbors, river valleys, and, areas adjacent to mountain passes have been the sites of outbursts of individualization, innovation, secularization, and also of the strong assertion of political power. Once we investigate the fact of human migration (which has been going on since the earliest bands of human beings foraged for food), it is clear that certain parts of the earth's surface are more likely than others to be the natural locations of human contacts and, thence, of the stimulus of ideas and values thrown together, however briefly. Before seapower made fruitful navigation of the seas possible, areas of the earth such as river valleys into which people after people poured seeking secure habitation and those near passes of the great mountain chains provided the major geographic opportunities. With the achievement of seapower, however, this situation changed. Then sites such as Athens and Rome, with their close-by ports, were to dominate. And as such masterful historical geographers as Alfred Mahan and Halford McKinder have made clear, much of the history of the world can be written in terms of seapower. The coming of mechanized transportation—rail, automobile, and plane—has of course changed this. But the role of historical geography has not been diminished, only modified.

Toynbee, among others, has pointed to the causal influence of *environmental challenge*. Not the environments in which ease of life has been dominant but, rather, those in which, in addition to other elements such as access, fertility of soil, and generally clement climate, some recurrent feature of the environment has constituted a challenge—these appear to be the environments in which some degree of secular rationalism made its earliest appearance. That the recurrent problem of the Nile's flooding should have evoked schemes of engineering control, themselves connected with necessary techniques of mathematical measurement and assessment, is a reasonable surmise. But it is reasonable only if we are dealing with a people for whom rational response to the challenge—rather than flight—appeared the proper solution. The same is true of so many of the other challenges and responses Toynbee has set forth in *A Study of History*. Whether among Greeks, Romans, Aztecs, Chinese in the age of Prince Cheng, when the Great Wall was the response to military challenge, or the European settlers of New England, environment may indeed set the challenge. But response, including the *will* to response, is not something that radiates from either terrain, military danger, or opportunity for continued settlement in an area.

A great deal of understanding of the conditions of rationalization, especially with respect to political organization, but hardly less in the spheres of music, art, and philosophy, has come from Max Weber's comparative studies. To take rationalization as only a unilinear process in all time, as some kind of inexorable principle of development through which all peoples or institutions must pass, does great harm to Weber's studies. Although it is true that in his emphasis on rationalization in the modern West, Weber himself made the process seem sometimes like such a principle, we get a very different sense of the matter from his comparative studies. There we find the process set forth as one recurrent in time, separated widely in space among civilizations, and the subject of systematic investigation that has not been improved upon thus far in historical sociology. Weber's great feat was to be able to show the connection between what I have here called secularization or rationalization and such dissimilar forms of behavior and thought as the structure of the modern state, the entrepreneurial system in economy, the rise of the European style of military organization, and modern science, as well as certain distinctive forms of art, philosophy, and music. But however much Weber may have been influenced by the Western experience, and indeed given to brooding over it, the process of rationalization is, in his works, a diverse and repeated manifestation in human history.

I have argued that *individualization, innovation, politicization,* and *secularization* are among the major processes of change in human history.

There are others, but none, I think, of greater influence and effect. To take any one, or for that matter all of them, and convert them into "tendencies," "evolutionary" or "developmental" laws of mankind, or into large-scale universals of human directionality, would be to defeat not only my own central purpose in their brief examination in this chapter but also their scientific sociological study. For the latter proceeds by comparison and contrast, by recognition of the plurality and, in substantial outline, the recurrence of major human experiences.

The four processes of change are found in the experiences, at one time or other, of the Chinese, Indians, Persians, Greeks, Romans, and innumerable other peoples, including, as I have repeatedly emphasized, the contemporary peoples of the new nations of Asia and Africa and also of ethnic strains within the American population at the present time. Whether in the experience of the Jews or the blacks in this century, especially in the United States, we are given superb opportunity for the detailed, microcosmic study of processes such as those I have mentioned. But to lift such studies out of time and circumstance, out of the larger category of manifestations that includes countless other peoples, past and present, would be to foreclose on the rich opportunities for scientific study of change that lie in historical sociology.

Notes

1. Frederick J. Teggart, *The Processes of History* (New Haven: Yale University Press, 1918), pp. 86–87.
2. Emile Durkheim, *The Division of Labor in Society* (New York: Macmillan, 1933), p. 195.
3. Frederick J. Teggart, *Rome and China: A Study of Correlations in Historical Events* (Berkeley: University of California Press, 1939), pp. xi–xii.
4. Velleius Paterculus, *Roman History*, Bk. I, 16–18. Cited by A. L. Krober in his *Configurations of Culture Growth* (Berkeley: University of California Press, 1944), p. 18.
5. Kroeber, *Configurations of Culture Growth, op. cit.*, p. 16.
6. Max Weber, "Politics as Vocation," in C. Wright Mills (ed.), *From Max Weber: Essays in Sociology*, trans. by H. H. Gerth (New York: Oxford University Press, 1946), pp. 78–79.

Epilogue: Sociology, Social Policy, Social Action

An epilogue is properly a place for either retrospect or prospect. I prefer prospect. What are we to say about the relation between sociology and social policy, between sociology and social action? The only real justification of any social science is the degree to which it can creatively influence social policy and be one of the sources of constructive social action. If the concepts in this book have demonstrable relevance to the urgent issues that confront us in contemporary society, they are valuable and worthy of continued development. If they do not have such relevance, they should be scrapped.

But what do we mean by "relevance"? This is a much used and abused word at the present time. The dictionary tells us it means "bearing upon or connected with the matter at hand . . . applicable, germane, apposite." This is well and good. But our question is not yet answered. For what *is* the "matter at hand"? Are we to see it and define it solely in terms of those manifestations which can be observed by anyone, even a child, no matter what his degree of knowledge or commitment? Or are we, in more mature and informed fashion to see the matter at hand as it really tends to be—complex, closely involved in other matters, with depths which ordinary, uninformed vision cannot hope to reach?

Surely we mean the second. For knowledge that is genuinely relevant does not limit itself to the surface or the fringes of problems.

It seeks out the forces and elements which, although often hidden from easy view, are nonetheless crucial. Such knowledge takes routes to the solutions of problems which, to the impatient and purely action-minded, can often seem circuitous, even evasive. To the angry suburban house-holder demanding that "something be done immediately" about disorder in the community, or to the militant and intensely idealistic worker for civil rights, the route taken by social science to the understanding and control of problems of violence and ethnic injustice can very often seem so indirect as to be useless.

But it is not. One need but consider the history of medicine and the health sciences with respect to the succession of diseases that have plagued mankind. Had *all* human beings confined their actions to the ready and seemingly direct antidotes that once were staples for smallpox, typhoid fever, malaria, syphilis, and other diseases, we should hardly have reduced their incidence to the present relatively low point. Study of diet and of the effects of presence and absence of niacin could hardly have seemed relevant to the ravages of pellagra in this country until a few decades ago. That is, in the opinion of most persons—those who wanted relief immediately and directly. One does not like to think back on some of the nostrums and patent medicines that *did* seem relevant to the majority of persons suffering from this disease. Happily, there were a few scientists for whom relevance meant study of the causes, no matter how long this study required. And, once discovered, these causes made it possible for wise action and sound policy to be instituted with regard to food as treatment.

The same is true in the quest for social justice. It is an ancient quest. And if there are times when we feel we have gone considerably farther down its road than might have seemed likely even a generation or two ago, there are more times in our lives when we are depressed by how little seems to have been done to make a decent life possible for millions of people in our own country and for many hundreds of millions elsewhere in the world. In so many ways, the quest for the good society is more complex and hazardous than the quest for physical health or control of the physical environment generally. Not least among these complexities and hazards is the fact that often the very techniques we successfully employ to solve one set of social problems themselves create fresh problems of a degree and type that sometimes make the faint-hearted despair. There is also the problem of what has been so well called "the revolution of rising expectations." Each new gratification of need or desire raises the threshold of expectations of more gratifications. And this is exactly as it should be. For only thus has the condition of man been made better over a period of many thousands of years.

What is the relation of sociology and the social sciences to the ancient quest for social justice? Not very close, in the judgment of all too many in our time. We are surrounded by social problems, many of them of awesome proportions. We see, even in our own country, one of the most affluent in the world, conditions of poverty, degradation, exploitation, and acute misery. They are problems which plainly call for action, for the shaping of public policy in ways designed to make possible a decent life for those whose right to it is every bit as great as our own.

Often we who work in the social sciences must seem to be, in the words of the poet W. H. Auden, "lecturing on navigation while the ship is going down." Of what avail is it to lecture on the principles of social organization while vast numbers of persons in the world are suffering— are waiting, so to speak, to be liberated from tyrannous authorities, degrading roles and statuses, and from obsolete values? The question is a natural one. I have no doubt that it was asked by many in the time of Socrates. Certainly it has been asked countless times since. But there is no other way of answering the question than in the words of Socrates himself. Knowledge and knowledge alone can make us free: free *from* the irrationalities and deprivations which are everywhere to be seen and free *to* rise to ever higher levels of civilization.

We may like to think of the great figures of civilization, from Moses, Cleisthenes, and Buddha in the ancient world to Abraham Lincoln, Louis Brandeis, and Martin Luther King in the modern world, as men who *did* things, who were *doers* rather than thinkers. This is a false distinction. Doers they were indeed, but what they did was based always upon intellectual insight, upon extraordinary powers of knowledge, as well as upon the moral qualities we so often associate with them. "Knowledge is power," wrote Francis Bacon more than three hundred years ago. This has always been true and always will be. Knowledge is the single greatest advantage the civilized mind has over the brute.

I have several times in this book referred to the revolution initiated in ancient Athens by Cleisthenes. To the historian, to the social scientist, to any humane mind, the changes effected by Cleisthenes must rank among the greatest to be found anywhere in history. No one will question the moral values that lay behind his works, or the personal courage and insight. But along with these lay an acquired *knowledge*, not the less impressive for the fact that he was forced to acquire it largely through his own personal efforts and experience. And what knowledge it was!   It was a knowledge of political forms, if we like, and of techniques of political action.   But it was a knowledge also of the nature of social groups, of types of authority, of social roles, social statuses, and social norms.   To deny Cleisthenes the identity of sociologist—applied sociologist—in his remarkable works simply because the label would never have occurred to him would be like denying Shakespeare the identity of master spirit of literature because he held no academic degree or Mozart the identity of musical genius because he never attended a school of music.

Greatness of this kind is by no means limited to the past.   Far from it.   Greatness is still to be seen, though never in the amount we might wish.   In our own day we have seen Martin Luther King achieve feats of liberation and organization no less remarkable than those of Cleisthenes.   To have been as powerfully responsible as he was for quickening the aspirations, heightening the imaginations, and raising the threshold of expectations of millions of Negroes in the United States —and hence throughout the world—required courage, boldness, and willingness to act.   Of this there is no question.   But it also required profound *intellectual insight* and, above all, *knowledge*. Martin Luther King, whether he knew it or cared about it, was, like Cleisthenes, an applied sociologist.

Very few of us are, or can hope to be, endowed with the personal intellectual powers of those I have just mentioned.   It is the function of science, of scientific method, of knowledge of scientific concept and principle, to equalize, though perhaps never perfectly, the balance.   I say "the" function.   There are other functions of science and of knowledge.   But the one I have just mentioned seems to me the greatest. Lacking, as most of us do, the innate powers of insight and leadership which are to be found in a few persons, we compensate, so to speak, by what we acquire through disciplined and systematic learning.

Many of us crave social action.   And it is good that we do.   But history is strewn with the wrecks of social movements that lacked the knowledge requisite to their success.   Everyone knows the difference between the bumbling amateur and the skilled professional.   We have seen this difference in a wide variety of spheres—from prize fighting or football at one extreme to the writing of books and the composing of music at the other.   The history of revolutionary movements can be well written in terms of those whose leaders were, so to speak, professionals and those who were amateurs.   The overriding function of knowledge is to convert the amateur into the professional.

So with social action in our time.   Is sociology relevant to it?   Of course it is—in different amounts and degrees, depending upon the nature of each that is at hand. Sociology is relevant because the essential ends of all social action are inextricably related to the roles and statuses human beings occupy in society, the dislocation of roles and statuses where necessary, their fashioning anew where possible, and to the whole variety of norms, authorities, and social aggregates that are manifest in social behavior.

To argue, as some do in our day, that the goals of sociology as a science should be scrapped and replaced by the goals of action is an appalling thought. It is appalling in its flouting of human enlightenment, in its courting of irrationalism, and in the inevitable defeat which must befall social action that aspires to humanitarian ends. Let us grant that the essential goals of science do not appear at first sight to be related to the action most of us know to be necessary in society. The goals of science are, as we have seen, two: discovery and explanation. Often the results of science can seem intolerably slow in forming, and these results, even when achieved and publicized, can appear woefully remote from ends of action immediately at hand. Again I can only refer to the history of medicine, to the vast number of scientific efforts and also results which lay behind those occasional, dramatic breakthroughs, as in the discovery of penicillin and the antibiotics which have effected wonders in the physical health of man.

Fortunately, there is no need for choosing between science and action in the social world. Why should there not be *both*, as there are so plainly at the present time? No man is completely a scientist. The scientist is also cast in many other roles in society, and among these is that of *citizen*. No one familiar with the actual lives of scientists in the world today—physical as well as social—can doubt the capacity of a large number of scientists for departing the laboratory or study on occasion and taking up the responsibilities of citizenship—which include, when necessary, social protest and social action.

Albert Einstein, whom many would rank as the greatest physical scientist of the twentieth century, found no more difficulty in combining his role of physicist with that of social idealist and, at times, activist than he did with combining love of physics with love of music—and other things in life as well. Einstein was a passionate worker for peace in the world; he gave much of his strength and genius to this end. But had anyone suggested to him that the essential ends of physics be converted from discovery and explanation to those equally noble but profoundly different ends which lie in the quest for peace and social justice, he would have been horrified. Such a suggestion could only have seemed to this remarkable and gentle mind the counsel of irrationalism.

I have been referring to the relation between science and action. The latter suggests something else of profound concern at the present time—*social policy*.

It is perhaps a tribute to the very successes of the social sciences during the last few decades that today no government in the civilized world would seek to govern without the counsel of social scientists—economists, political scientists, and others. We live in a period of history when the responsibility of political government has extended to almost all spheres of society and to literally every age of the individual human being. From cradle to grave, in the areas of child development, education, housing, economic development, social welfare, and many others, the modern state makes its presence felt. The day is past when law and order are the only functions of the political state—however vital these may still remain.

When we view the nature of the modern state, how can we expect the social sciences *not* to be involved? Whether it is the management of budgets and central banks, the policies necessary in public housing and urban renewal, the establishment of an atmosphere of nonviolence in an area where violence has reigned, or any of the other activities which by now even most of our conservative citizens recognize as proper responsibilities of government, the applied role of the social scientist is unavoidable. True, not all social scientists are—or should be—applied social scientists. But whether one remains entirely immured within his basic research or spends all of his time in an advisory role to government and industry, there is no doubt that the ultimate goal of any science is that of being relevant to the social and material needs of human beings.

Here we come back to that troublesome word "relevant." In the same way that there are many idealists at the present time who demand instant relevance of all social science to immediate action, so are there, in government halls, in industry, and elsewhere, those who declare that the sole purpose of social science is to advise and counsel. In short, all social science should be *applied* science.

To these latter voices we can say essentially what was said above. Applied science calls for science capable of being applied. And this in turn calls for science that is left free to follow the imperatives of discovery and explanation. I am not making here any arbitrary and hard distinction between "pure" and "applied" science. As I noted in the

Preface, and in several places in the book, some of sociology's most valuable theoretical concepts arose in the course of what was manifestly an applied or practical venture. It was, after all, for the ostensible purpose of finding out how to curb the high rates of suicide that Durkheim was led to make his epochal study—a study from which has flowed so many of the key concepts of the science of sociology. But reducing the number of suicides was, in fact, only *one* of the purposes. And it was the ability of Durkheim to keep clear in his own mind the fundamental norms of science, the norms of discovery and explanation, that alone enabled him to throw light upon the goal of reducing the incidence of suicide in the population.

The present danger confronting sociology in its relation to social policy arises directly from its opportunity. Were sociology not clearly useful to legislators and administrators in government—useful in the setting of policy as well as its execution—the dangers that now exist would not be present. What are the dangers? Foremost that of letting the objectives, the ends, the problems, the researches of sociology be set by practical and applied goals alone. Following from this are the risks which are always attendant upon the autonomy, the intellectual freedom, and the motivations of the scientist who is diverted from intrinsic interests to those which are handed to him.

There is a degree of freedom apart from which science even in its rudest forms is impossible. I am not referring here to those cruder forms of interference with freedom which have existed for many centuries—the interferences of malign or ignorant rulers, whether of state, church, school, or economy. At least they are readily recognizable.

The newer threat to scientific freedom and autonomy is not always so easily recognized, or, even when recognized, so easily repulsed. For the newer threat that I have in mind stems directly from functions which so many in the social sciences prize—functions of advisory, counseling, and even directive significance in government. There is also the fact of governmental, industrial, and foundation sponsorship of much social science—and, obviously, also physical science—at the present time. True, we could hardly do without this. Social science costs a great deal of money for its effective advancement, far more money than the college or university itself can afford to grant its scientists for their work. Hence the necessity of governmental and other subventions from the outside and the rising appeal of such subventions. And, hence, all too often, the loss of that scientific autonomy that is vital to science. For, if a scientist commits his energy, time, and money to some stated objective, some practical end for which he was granted the support in the first place, it is not easy to maintain that willingness to go, intellectually, wherever one's fancy or interest directs.

In the history of science an old adage has repeatedly been illustrated: He goes farthest who knows not where he is going. Neither radar nor penicillin was discovered by individuals who were looking for either—or, for that matter, anything else very concrete. Of course those looking were anything but amateurs, anything but unprepared minds. *Chance favors the prepared mind.* Nowhere is this truth more evident than in the history of science. Nearly all the great scientific creators have referred to the element of luck, of chance, of the purely fortuitous in their major discoveries. What they do not so often refer to are the far greater elements involved: first, disciplined preparation of mind and, second, elbow room, autonomy, sheer intellectual freedom of movement with which to actually recognize the unexpected discovery and to then work with it, at no matter what expenditure of time and effort.

These, then, are the two major challenges sociology faces in its public role at the present time—the challenge of social action, which we so desperately need, and the challenge of social policy in which the social sciences are so desperately needed. Neither can be evaded; neither can be cynically ignored or flouted. So much is true. But there is another truth, one that seems to me even greater and, at the present moment at least, more compelling. This is the truth that any science will be helpful, pertinent, and relevant in the long run only to the extent that it is left alone to pursue its unique and vital objectives of discovery and explanation.

The Next Step

AN INFORMAL BIBLIOGRAPHICAL ESSAY

I can think of no better way of concluding this book than by listing a few volumes and articles which may have the effect of quickening and deepening the reader's interest in some of the matters dealt with in the preceding pages. My listing will be, I am frank in saying, very selective and somewhat unsystematic. I shall set the titles down pretty much as they occur to me in the writing. That is why I call this appendix an informal bibliographical essay rather than a bibliography. The reader who desires more had best go to the reference department of the library—which, as I think of it, is not a bad idea in any event.

What follows, then, is no bibliography: merely an earnest of some of the bibliographical riches which are to be found in sociology's house of intellect.

General

Some of the best and most stimulating writings in any field of thought are in the form of articles rather than books. Peter I. Rose, in *The Study of Society* (New York: Random House, 1967), has compiled and integrated a splendid collection of such articles, representing every major area of contemporary sociological thought. For readers interested in the specific application of sociological themes and concepts to American society, it would be difficult to improve on Robin Williams, *American Society: A Sociological Interpreta-*

tion, 3rd ed. (New York: Knopf, 1969). Those who have not already read David Riesman, *The Lonely Crowd*, new ed. (New Haven, Conn.: Yale University Press, 1969), have in store for them the finest sociological treatment of American culture since Alexis de Tocqueville's *Democracy in America*, which was published nearly a century and a half ago. Robert K. Merton and Robert A. Nisbet (eds.), *Contemporary Social Problems*, 2nd ed. (New York: Harcourt, Brace & World, 1966) shows how sociology sheds light upon major social problems in contemporary society.

Concerning Sociology as a Science

Max Weber's "Science as Vocation" is a profound, often moving, and wholly pertinent statement of the nature of social science and of the relation of science to moral values. It can be found in several anthologies, among them H. H. Gerth and C. Wright Mills (eds.), *From Max Weber: Essays in Sociology* (New York: Oxford University Press, 1946). George C. Homans, *The Nature of Social Science* (New York: Harcourt, Brace & World, 1967) is short, sprightly, and immensely readable. If I disagree with some of its content, that is all the more reason to mention it here. I find Scott Greer, *The Logic of Social Inquiry* (Chicago: Aldine, 1969) very impressive in its easy but knowledgeable command of theory and method and in the uniting of these with the data of human experience. Phillip E. Hammond (ed.), *Sociologists at Work* (New York: Basic Books, 1964) is valuable for its accounts, written by sociologists themselves, of how certain major pieces of research were done. Robert K. Merton, *Social Theory and Social Structure*, 3rd ed. (New York: The Free Press, 1969) should be read not only for its wise words in the first section on the relationship between theory and research but also for its notable sections on the sociology of science. Finally, no one should miss the experience of reading C. Wright Mills, *The Sociological Imagination* (New York: Oxford University Press, 1959). Contentious, brilliant, deeply felt, it is in itself a splendid product of the sociological imagination.

Concerning the Sources of the Sociological Imagination

Genuinely useful and readable studies along this line are few and far between, though we seem now to be, at long last, in a rather fertile period of scholarship. Of reference books, large and small, there is no end. What I have in mind, however, are works that do not bore us with who-said-what-when but deal with the major ideas, concepts, and themes of sociology in both intellectual and social contexts. A classic work, one that has profoundly affected American sociological thought, is Talcott Parsons, *The Structure of Social Action* (New York: McGraw-Hill, 1937). Its analyses of Weber, Durkheim, and Pareto, among others, have proved seminal. Raymond Aron, *Main Currents in Sociological Thought*, 2 vols. (New York: Basic Books,

1965, 1967) contains fascinating intellectual portraits of the major sociologists in Europe. H. Stuart Hughes, *Consciousness and Society* (New York: Knopf, 1958) has the great advantage of the historian's knowledge of larger processes of history within which to set his analyses of Weber, Durkheim, and others. Robert A. Nisbet, *The Sociological Tradition* (New York: Basic Books, 1967) is a thematic interpretation of modern sociology from Marx and Tocqueville to Simmel, Weber, and Durkheim, in which the central themes of sociological thought are dealt with as responses to the two great revolutions, industrial and political, in the nineteenth century. For a different assessment of much the same ideas and contexts, I recommend Irving Zeitlin, *Ideology and the Development of Sociological Theory* (Englewood Cliffs, N.J.: Prentice-Hall, 1968). Leon Bramson, *The Political Context of Sociology* (Princeton, N.J.: Princeton University Press, 1961) deals penetratingly with the rise of sociology in Europe and has the great advantage of extended treatment of American sociological thought, especially with respect to the concepts of collective behavior and mass society. Since Max Weber and Emile Durkheim are incontestably the major influences on present sociological thought, the reader would be well advised to read—in addition to one or more of the works of these titans—Reinhard Bendix, *Max Weber: An Intellectual Portrait* (New York: Doubelday, 1960), or Julien Freund, *The Sociology of Max Weber* (New York: Pantheon Books, 1968), and Harry Alpert, *Emile Durkheim and His Sociology* (New York: Russell and Russell, 1961), w:hich is the most thorough study of Durkheim, or Robert Nisbet, *Emile Durkheim* (Englewood Cliffs, N.J.: Prentice-Hall, 1965). No completely adequate history of American sociological thought exists yet, but Charles H. Page, *Class and American Sociology*, rev. ed. (New York: Schocken, 1969), throws much light on this area from the vantage point of his searching study of the theory of social stratification in the United States. As I write this, Alvin Gouldner and Lewis Coser are each completing studies of the history of sociological thought which, given the authors' stature as historians of ideas, can hardly fail to be valuable.

Concerning the Nature of the Social Bond

Since the sections that follow cover this subject in detail, I will be very brief here. A. R. Radcliffe-Brown, *A Natural Science of Society* (New York: The Free Press, 1957) is a brief, masterful treatment of the social character of the social bond—one, however, that does not lose sight of human beings, of the concreteness of social behavior. I recommend strongly Edward Shils, "Primordial, Personal, Sacred, and Civil Ties" for its unique insights into the forces that hold human beings together. It can be found in the Peter Rose anthology noted above. Denis Wrong, "The Oversocialized Conception of Man in Modern Sociology" should be read not only for its intrinsic high quality but as a kind of prophylaxis against all efforts to reify or externalize the social bond. It is contained in Ephraim M. Mizruchi (ed.), *The Substance of Sociology* (New York: Appleton-Century-Crofts, 1967), as well as other anthologies. For a different and valuable approach to the nature of the social bond, one that draws creatively and critically on the post-Freudian tradition, see Philip Rieff, *The Triumph of the Therapeutic* (New York: Harper & Row, 1966).

Concerning Social Interaction

Apart only from the seminal writings of George Herbert Mead, Charles H. Cooley, and W. I. Thomas—all referred to in the text—the most illuminating work on social interaction I can think of for general purposes is Herbert Blumer's brilliant article "Society as Symbolic Interaction," which appears, along with some other excellent pieces, in Jerome G. Manis and Bernard N. Meltzer (eds.), *Symbolic Interaction* (Boston: Allyn and Bacon, 1967). It is a pleasure to recommend, in this same volume, the essays on the subject by Guy E. Swanson, Erving Goffman, and Anselm L. Strauss. Erving Goffman, *Presentation of the Self in Everyday Life* (New York: Doubleday, 1959) is a classic and, like everything else he has written, immensely readable.   More difficult in some ways, but nonetheless intellectually accessible, is George C. Homans, *Social Behavior: Its Elementary Forms* (New York: Harcourt, Brace & World, 1961).   Homans' book is valuable for its highly empirical treatment of the several forms of social interaction that I have dealt with briefly in the text of this book.   For analyses in depth of two of the specific types of social interaction I have mentioned, I suggest, for further reading, Lewis Coser, *The Functions of Social Conflict* (New York: The Free Press, 1956) and Peter M. Blau, *Exchange and Power in Social Life* (New York: Wiley, 1964).

Concerning Social Aggregates

On the significance of size to the character of social aggregates there is nothing comparable to Georg Simmel's writings in either gracefulness of style or breadth of imagination. See Kurt H. Wolff (ed. and tr.), *The Sociology of Georg Simmel* (New York: The Free Press, 1950). I also recommend George C. Homans, *The Human Group* (New York: Harcourt, Brace & World, 1950) for its imaginative and comprehensive treatment of the several types of social aggregates. Robert Redfield, *Little Community* (Chicago: University of Chicago Press, 1955) and also his *Folk Culture of Yucatan* (Chicago: University of Chicago Press, 1941) are beautiful and profound. Lewis Mumford, *The Culture of Cities* (New York: Harcourt, Brace & World, 1938) and also his more recent, and comparatively oriented, *The City in History* (New York: Harcourt, Brace & World, 1961) are magnificent in both breadth of canvas and illuminating detail.   On the nature of formal organization I can think of no study as fine as Philip Selznick, *Leadership in Administration* (New York: Harper, 1957); the profound and influential writings of Peter Blau, particularly his *Dynamics of Bureaucracy*, 2nd rev.

ed. (Chicago: University of Chicago Press, 1963) and, with W. Richard Scott, *Formal Organizations* (San Francisco: Chandler, 1961), should also be considered. Robert A. Nisbet, *The Quest for Community* (New York: Oxford University Press, 1953) is concerned with, among other subjects, the problem of community and also of voluntary association in mass society. For a different and immensely valuable view of mass society and its relation to human personality, see Joseph Gusfield, *Symbolic Crusade* (Urbana: University of Illinois Press, 1963) and any of his more recent pieces on the subject. Gusfield reminds us of the tonic or positive aspects of mass society instead of those more commonly dealt with in the sociological tradition. Harold Wilensky, *Organizational Intelligence* (New York: Basic Books, 1967) is important for its clear-headed statement of the nature of communication in large-scale aggregates and also for its consideration of the larger social and moral issues involved. On the important subject of reference groups there is nothing that compares, in either vision or detail, with what Robert Merton has written in a long section of his *Social Theory and Social Structure*, a work that is valuable in so many of the areas dealt with in this book. Finally, as an unexcelled inquiry into how social aggregates actually form in a society, there is no better work than Marc Bloch, *Feudal Society*, 2 vols. (Chicago: University of Chicago Press, 1961). The first volume concerns "the growth of ties of dependence," and this process is described with all the historical and sociological skill for which this brilliant and brave casuality to Nazi terror is noted. The second volume of the book, which is equally valuable and readable,, deals with the several types of fully formed association in feudal Europe.

Concerning Social Authority

Robert Bierstedt, "The Problem of Authority" is superbly thought out and written and has greatly influenced the sociological study of authority and power. It can be found in the Peter Rose anthology previously referred to. See also Bierstedt, *The Social Order* (New York: McGraw-Hill, 1957). In many ways the finest *complete* study of authority since Max Weber is that of Robert M. McIver—a lifetime study manifest in several of his books of which I shall emphasize here only his classic *The Web of Government*, new ed. (New York: The Free Press, 1965). Max Weber, "Politics as Vocation" is as fresh and vital today as when he first delivered it in an address before students and faculty at Munich in 1918. It is also found in the Gerth and Mills volume of Weber's work referred to above. Bertrand de Jouvenel, *On Power* (Boston: Beacon Press, 1962) is somewhat rambling in style and diffuse in structure, but its historical insights into the nature of power are fascinating. Both Seymour Martin Lipset, *Political Man* (New York: Doubleday, 1960) and William Kornhauser, *The Politics of Mass Society* (New York: The Free Press, 1959) are immensely readable and distinguished by broad knowledge and rich insight. One of the greatest of all interpreters of totalitarian power and of revolutionary contexts of power is Hannah Arendt. See her *Origins of Totalitarianism* (New York: Harcourt, Brace & World, 1966) and also her *On Revolution* (New York: Viking, 1963). It is a pleasure to refer also to Peter Drucker's great *The End of Economic Man* (New York: John Day, 1939). Finally, I recommend the incomparable insights of Thucydides not only on the politics of Athens in the fifth century B.C. but also the politics of the twentieth century.

Concerning Social Roles

Despite the passage of several decades, *Social Relations and Social Roles* by the late Florian Znaniecki (reprinted in 1965 by Chandler Publishing Co.) seems still the best general work on the subject of social roles. To it should be added, by the same author, *The Social Role of the Man of Knowledge* (New York: Columbia University Press, 1940). It is a model of sociological and historical study of a specific role in society. No one should fail to read Erving Goffman on social roles. He has, quite literally, gone into asylums, hospitals, gambling casinos, and prisons—as well as the more ordinary institutions of society—for his brilliantly written, scientifically conceived, vignettes. See, among his other works, *Encounters* (Indianapolis: Bobbs-Merrill, 1961) and *Asylums* (New York: Doubleday Anchor, 1961). For an imaginative and scholarly work on the social role of women, I recommend Mirra Komarovsky, *Women in the Modern World* (Boston: Little, Brown, 1953). On role conflict and role tension, William Goode, "A Theory of Role Strain" is valuable and can be found in his *The Dynamics of Modern Society* (New York: Atherton Press, 1966). No better treatment of the role problems of teachers and students exists than Charles H. Page, "Sociology as a Teaching Enterprise," in Robert K. Merton *et al.* (eds.), *Sociology Today: Problems and Prospects* (New York: Basic Books, 1959). Morris Janowitz, *The Professional Soldier* (New York: The Free Press, 1960) is a splendid model of systematic role study. Finally, it would be absurd to conclude this section without reminding the reader that ever since the eighteenth century the novel has been a superb source of knowledge about social roles and also social status. From Fielding and Smollett in the eighteenth century, through Stendhal, Flaubert, Balzac, Gogol, Tolstoi, Dostoevsky, Dickens, Thackeray, and Mark Twain in the nineteenth, to Galsworthy, Aldous Huxley, Cather, Hemingway, O'Hara, Cozzens, Bellow, Roth, and Malamud in our own age, the novel has been one of the most reliable sources of insight into the roles and statuses of which human society is composed. So, obviously, has the drama from Aeschylus to Eugene O'Neill, Tennessee Williams, and Arthur Miller. But that fact surely requires no emphasis.

Concerning Social Status

The greatest work written on social status in American society is still the second volume of Alexis de Tocqueville's *Democracy in America*. There are so many editions of this classic in translation that none need be cited

here. First published in 1840, the book will be as fresh and relevant tomorrow as it is today. On the preoccupation of American sociology with the
study of social class and status—and a splendid introduction to the subject
itself—I recommend "An Introduction Thirty Years Later," in Charles H.
Page, *Class and American Sociology*, referred to above. Reinhard Bendix
and Seymour Martin Lipset (eds.), *Class, Status and Power*, 2nd ed. (New
York: The Free Press, 1966) is a justly admired anthology of some of the
best pieces written on the subject of social status. Undoubtedly, the single
most influential article on stratification written in the past quarter-century in
this country is Kingsley Davis and Wilbert Moore, "Some Principles of
Stratification." It has been reprinted in various anthologies, among them the
Peter Rose volume. E. Digby Baltzell, *Philadephia Gentleman* (New York:
The Free Press, 1958) and, by the same author, *The Protestant Establish-
ment: Aristocracy and Caste in America* (New York: Random House, 1964)
are splendid in content and gracefully written. Among other valuable and
fascinating works on the many aspects of social stratification are C. Wright
Mills, *White Collar* (New York: Oxford University Press, 1951), John
Dollard, *Caste and Class in a Southern Town*, 3rd ed. (Garden City, N.Y.:
Doubleday, 1957), Ely Chinoy, *Automobile Workers and the American
Dream* (Garden City, N.Y.: Doubleday, 1955), Gerhard Lenski, *Power
and Privilege* (New York: McGraw-Hill, 1966), Irving Louis Horowitz,
Three Worlds of Development (New York: Oxford University Press, 1966),
and Barrington Moore, *Social Origins of Dictatorship and Democracy* (Boston: Beacon Press, 1966). On the subject of the elites in society the reader
might begin with Suzanne Keller, *Beyond the Ruling Class* (New York:
Random House, 1963) and T. B. Bottomore, *Elites and Society* (New York:
Basic Books, 1965). Since I have chosen to deal with ethnicity in this book
under the heading of social status, I want to refer to at least a few of the
many excellent books today available. Gunnar Myrdal, *An American Dilemma* (New York: Harper, 1944) is the most famous study of the American
Negro and his relation to democracy. Even though much of its material is
now out of date, its profound and prophetic interpretations deserve reading.
Kenneth Clark, *Dark Ghetto* (New York: Harper & Row, 1965) is a rich
reading experience. Its perceptions are brilliant, and its style matches its
content. I recommend also Nathan Glazer and Daniel P. Moynihan, *Beyond
the Melting Pot: The Negroes, Puerto Ricans, Jews, Italians, and Irish of
New York City* (Cambridge, Mass.: M.I.T. Press) and Peter Rose, *They
and We* (New York: Random House, 1963). One of the great values of
Tamotsu Shibutani and Kian M. Kwan, *Ethnic Stratification* (New York:
Macmillan, 1965) is the genuinely comparative perspective the materials
are set in. Along the same lines and of equal excellence is Richard Scher-
merhorn, *Comparative Ethnic Relations* (New York: Random House, 1970).
The classic work on the caste system in India is still Emile Senart, *Caste
in India: The Facts and the System*. First published in 1896 in France, it
was translated and published in England (Methuen) in 1930, and is still
widely available. Gerald D. Berreman, "Caste in India and the United
States" is a splendid comparison of caste in India with the position of the
Negro in the United States. It can be found in the Peter Rose anthology.

Finally, on the subject of occupations and occupational mobility—an extremely important area of contemporary research—the authoritative work is Peter M. Blau and Otis Dudley Duncan, *The American Occupational Structure* (New York: Wiley, 1967). This is sociological research at its very finest.

Concerning Social Norms

It would be difficult to improve here on William Graham Sumner, *Folkways*, published in 1906. It exists in many printings and is readily available in most public libraries. Another masterpiece on norms, their genesis, function, and integrative role, is Elsie Clews Parsons, *Fear and Conventionality*. It was published in 1914, written by one of America's most original social scientists. Unhappily and inexplicably, it is out of print and difficult to find except in larger libraries. On a different aspect of the subject there is Edward T. Hall's original and important *The Silent Language* (Garden City, N.Y.: Doubleday, 1959), an effort, and a brave one, to uncover what might be called the substrata of our visible symbols and norms. For a fictional but wholly convincing account of how a set of norms—eventually sacred norms—of chilling cruelty can arise in a human group, I recommend William Golding's superb novel, *Lord of the Flies.*

On sacred or religious norms, the writings and sociological analyses of Durkheim and Weber are probably still the best. Let me add here, however, a few more recent works. Bronislaw Malinowski, *Magic, Science, and Religion* (New York: Doubleday Anchor, 1954) is the product of a near genius of modern anthropology. All of Peter Berger's writings on religion are excellent. Berger is a first-rate sociologist who has a fine sensitivity to religion. I will cite here only his *The Sacred Canopy* (Garden City, N.Y.: Doubleday, 1967). Elizabeth K. Nottingham, *Religion and Society*, rev. ed. (New York: Random House, 1970) is a splendid study. See Gerhard Lenski, *The Religious Factor* (New York: Doubleday Anchor, 1961) for documentation of the continuing power of religion as a source of social and political motivations in contemporary society. It is an outstanding piece of sociological research. I recommend also N. J. Demarath, III, and Phillip E. Hammond, *Religion in Social Context* (New York: Random House, 1968). Since one of the most striking developments today on the college campus is the turn to religion—often in exotic and bizarre form—it would be well to read Andrew Greeley's fascinating "There's a New-Time Religion on the Campus" (*The New York Times Magazine*, June 1, 1969). In this last connection I strongly recommend George Hedley, *Religion on the Campus* (New York: Macmillan, 1955).

On technical norms—technology—I always think of Lewis Mumford, *Technics and Civilization* (New York: Harcourt, Brace & World, 1934), a truly historic book in the study of technology. Daniel Bell, "Notes on the Post-Industrial Society," Parts I and II, *The Public Interest* (Winter 1967; Spring 1967) is a penetrating account of the impact of technical norms on the historic structure of capitalism. Victor Ferkiss, *Technological Man: Myth and Reality* (New York: George Braziller, 1969) is good in itself and deserves praise for having avoided the pitfalls that usually ensnare intellectuals when they turn to technology.   Warren G. Bennis and Philip E. Slater, *The Temporary Society* (New York: Harper & Row, 1968) is a thoughtful inquiry into the political issues raised by technology.   I like Robert Boguslaw, *The New Utopians* (Englewood Cliffs, N.J.: Prentice-Hall, 1965) for its highly informed and astringent commentary on computer technology. Robert Heilbroner, "Do Machines Make History?" *Technology and Culture*, 8 (July 1967) is excellent and also a good means of making acquaintance with this important journal.   For a comprehensive account of the social contexts of modern science, see Bernard Barber, *Science and the Social Order*, rev. ed. (New York: The Free Press, 1952).

On the greatest of all contemporary social problems, overpopulation, the best single volume from the sociologist's point of view is, without question, William Peterson, *Population*, rev. ed. (New York: Macmillan, 1961).   It deals with the subject comparatively and historically.   Ronald Freedman (ed.), *The Vital Revolution* (New York: Doubleday Anchor, 1964) is brief, authoritative, and eminently readable.   Philip M. Hauser (ed.), *The Population Dilemma* (Englewood Cliffs, N.J.: Prentice-Hall, 1963) is first rate.   Anything by Kingsley Davis on the subject is important and well written, as, for example, "The World Population Crisis" in the anthology *Contemporary Social Problems* referred to at the beginning of this essay.

Concerning Social Entropy: Alienation, Anomie, Deviance

On the idea of alienation, Lewis Feuer, "What is Alienation?: The Career of a Concept" is a splendid introduction to its historical and philosophical aspects.   It can be found in Maurice Stein and Arthur Vidich (eds.), *Sociology on Trial* (Englewood Cliffs N.J.: Prentice-Hall, 1963).   Melvin Seeman, "On the Meaning of Alienation," *The American Sociological Review*, Vol. 24 (1959) applies the idea of alienation to sociological theory and research.   For the influence of alienation on the mainstream of sociological thought, see my *The Sociological Tradition* (New York: Basic Books, 1967). Robert Blauner, *Alienation and Freedom* (Chicago: University of Chicago Press, 1964) is an expert and highly responsible use of the concept in the contexts of modern industrial life.   Kenneth Keniston, *The Uncommitted: Alienated Youth in American Society* (New York: Delta Books, 1967) is an extraordinarily fine application of the concept with respect to students and academic life.   I also emphasize Daniel Bell, *The End of Ideology: On the Exhaustion of Political Ideas in the Fifties* (New York: The Free Press, 1959) and the volume of essays Bell has edited, *The Radical Right* (New York: Doubleday Anchor, 1963) which deals in considerable degree deals with right-wing extremism in light of the perspective of alienation.

On anomie and its relation to normative conflict, in personality and the social order, there is still nothing more penetrating, it seems to me, than the famous chapter on the subject by Durkheim in *Suicide*, to which I referred in the text.   Robert Merton, "Social Structure and Anomie," which can be found in his *Social Theory and Social Structure*, as well as in many anthologies, is classic, and has had immense influence on contemporary sociology. David Riesman, *The Lonely Crowd*, to which I have referred in several connections, is a profoundly relevant work. So is the pioneering work by Everett Stonequist, *The Marginal Man*, new ed. (New York: Russel, 1962), which points out some of the consequences for creativity of anomie. Marshall Clinard, *Anomie and Deviant Behavior* (New York: The Free Press, 1964) is another first-rate work in all respects. See also Ephraim H. Mizruchi, *Success and Opportunity: A Study of Anomie* (New York: The Free Press, 1964). Finally, no one should miss reading one of the greatest novels of the age, Ralph Ellison, *The Invisible Man* (New York: Random House, 1952) for its brilliant insights into the marginal role of the Negro in American culture.

Deviance offers one of the richest areas for contemporary sociological research, but space here permits me to mention only a very few of the many available works that I have encountered. I admire, especially, Marshall Clinard, *Sociology of Deviant Behavior*, rev. ed. (New York: Holt, Rhinehart, and Winston, 1963) and David Matza, *Delinquency and Drift* (New York: Wiley, 1964). Howard S. Becker, *Outsiders: Studies in the Sociology of Deviance* (New York: The Free Press, 1963) is an excellent work in all respects, fitting representation of Becker's superb studies of deviant individuals. Kai T. Erikson, *Wayward Puritans* (New York: Wiley, 1966) is as rich in theoretical as historical insights into patterns of deviance. Albert K. Cohen, *Delinquent Boys* (New York: The Free Press, 1955) is a classic that has powerfully affected the field of study. See also Ephraim H. Mizruchi and Robert Perrucci, "Norm Qualities and Deviant Behavior," in Ephraim H. Mizruchi (ed.), *The Substance of Sociology* (New York: Appleton-Century-Crofts, 1967). And, since Durkheim is the primary theoretical influence in the study of deviance, the reader might wish to look up his now famous chapter on the subject in his *Rules of Sociological Method*, which was first published in 1895.

Concerning Social Change

As the final chapters of this book have perhaps suggested, I do not find very much of high quality in contemporary sociology on the general and theoretical aspects of the study of change. Nevertheless, I include here several luminous exceptions. Frederick J. Teggart, *Theory of History* and also his *Processes of History*, are both contained in a single volume published by the University of California Press. Kenneth E. Bock, *The Acceptance of Histories: Toward a Perspective for Social Science* (Berkeley: University of California Press, 1956) is extremely important, as are some of the articles he has contributed to various journals. Wilbert Moore, *Social Change* (Englewood Cliffs, N.J.: Prentice-Hall, 1963) is an outsanding work, brilliantly and remarkably comprehensive for so short a volume. Although I disagree with some of the book's perspectives, it is still valuable and recommended reading. Robert M. McIver, *Social Causation* (New York: Harper Torchbooks) falls into a similar category—I cannot agree with some of the author's propositions regarding the nature of change, but I continue to read them. Beyond question, Talcott Parsons, "A Functional Theory of Change," in Amitai Etzioni and Eva Etzioni (eds.), *Social Change* (New York: Basic Books, 1964) is the best single statement of the functionalist view of change. I disagree with it almost completely—which is my reason, apart from respect for almost anything Professor Parsons writes, for mentioning it here. Robert A. Nisbet, *Social Change and History: Aspects of the Western Theory of Development* (New York: Oxford University Press, 1969) examines the historical sources, some of the philosophical contexts, and a few of the faults in the prevailing theory of change in sociology.

Now to some of the excellent *empirical* studies of social change that, unlike theoretical treatments, exist in considerable abundance. What is notable about the following works—and there are many others—is that they treat change as a social problem, rather than merely an *assumed* process and, furthermore, deal with it in terms of history, that is, in terms of *the concrete particularity of social behavior*. From these works the reader should gain some sense of the attributes of *crisis, discontinuity, impact,* and *intrusion*—attributes which, as I emphasized in the text, are fundamental to social change.

Alvin Gouldner, *Enter Plato* (New York: Basic Books, 1965), deals with both intellectual and social change in ancient Athens. Reinhard Bendix, *Nation Building and Citizenship* (New York: Wiley, 1964) explores fundamental processes of political change in several countries. So does Seymour Martin Lipset in his *The First New Nation* (New York: Basic Books, 1963), a work that is comparative in thrust even though primarily concerned with the United States. Sidney Hook, *The Hero in History* (Boston: Beacon Press, 1955) throws much light on the relation between change and great men in history. Robert K. Merton, *Science, Technology, and Society in Seventeenth Century England* (Bruges, 1938) relates scientific and technological change to events and changes of the social order. Oscar Handlin, *The Uprooted* (Boston: Little, Brown, 1951) is concerned with the changes in culture resulting from the migration of people from one society into another. Crane Brinton, *The Anatomy of Revolution* (New York: Vintage, 1957) deals comparatively with four revolutions: English, American, French, and Russian. Barrington Moore, *Social Origins of Dictatorship and Democracy*, cited above, is also comparative and historically concrete. T. H. Marshall, *Class, Citizenship, and Social Development* (Garden City, N.Y.: Doubleday, 1964) is concerned primarily, though not exclusively, with English social change. Charles Tilly, *The Vendée* (Cambridge: Harvard University Press, 1964) deals sociologically with a famous counterrevolution in France in 1793 and its effects on the social order. H. G. Barnett, *Innovations: The Basis of Cultural Change* (New York: McGraw-Hill, 1953) examines contemporary Western and also primitive materials. Irving Louis Horowitz, *Three Worlds of Development*, already referred to in the section on social status, deserves mention again, in the present context. Daniel Lerner, *The Passing of Traditional Society* (New York: The Free Press, 1958) is a pioneer study on social change in the Middle East. Bronislaw Malinowski, *The Dynamics of Culture Change* (New Haven, Conn.: Yale University Press, 1945) represents one of the many excellent studies of change in native cultures as the result of European impact. C. E. Black, *The Dynamics of Modernization* (New York: Harper & Row, 1966) applies the principles of comparative history to contemporary new nations. Bryce Ryan, *Caste in Modern Ceylon* (New Brunswick, N.J.: Rutgers University Press, 1953) is concerned with the numerous elements leading to change of caste and its position. Lynn White, *Medieval Technology and Social Change* (New York: Oxford University Press, 1962) is excellent.   Elting E. Morison, "A Case Study of Innovation," *The California Institute of Technology Quarterly* (Spring 1960) is an article that contributes more to our knowledge about the actual mechanisms of social change, in technological context, than any other work of approximately the same length.   Margaret Stacey, *Tradition and Change* (Oxford: The Clarendon Press, 1960) examines the impact of a new industry on an old country town. E. Franklin Frazier, *Black Bourgeoisie* (New York: The Free Press, 1965) deals with the major processes of change that are producinng an ever more powerful black middle class.   In "Disaster," Charles F. Fritz deals with the social impacts of major catastrophes. His article can be found in *Contemporary Social Problems*, 1st ed., as cited previously.   Finally, C. K. Yang's two related works *The Chinese Family in the Communist Revolution* (1959) and *The Chinese Village in the Early Communist Transition* (1959), both published by the M.I.T. Press, provide detailed studies of social change under political centralization.

One final bibliographical observation on social change remains, namely this: the two most promising sources of future books and articles on the mechanisms of social change are all around us in the black revolution in the United States and the vast phenomenon of modernization in the world at large. From these two areas of change we will learn—we are learning—more, I think, about the dynamics of change than our social science has ever before uncovered.

Concerning Sociology and Social Policy

Here I shall be extremely brief.   Gideon Sjoberg (ed.), *Ethics, Politics, and Social Research* (Cambridge, Mass.: Schenkman, 1967) is an outstanding collection of pieces by sociologists detailing, often from personal experience, the kinds of moral and political issues that so often affect sociological research. Raymond A. Bauer and Kenneth J. Gergen (eds.), *The Study of Policy Formation* (New York: The Free Press, 1968) is valuable for its insights into the contexts of policy making in industry and government. Finally, Michael Reagan, *Science and the Federal Patron* (New York: Oxford University Press, 1969) is a clarifying analysis of the relationship between government and the physical and social sciences.

Index

Abortion, 288
Adams, Brooks, 54, 261
Adams, Henry, 54
Adaptation, 36
Age, status and, 190–1
Aggregates
  closed, 97–100, 134
  dyads, 84–6
  gemeinschaft, 32, 33, 105–7
  gesellschaft, 32, 33, 105–7
  interaction and, 111
  interrelatedness of, 111
  large-scale, 92–7
  nature of, 51, 80–3
  open, 97–100
  personal, 100–5
    politician's role and, 172
    type of authority and, 125
  primary groups, 37, 89
  reference groups, 107–11
  size factor, 84–97
    totalitarianism and, 133
    type of authority and, 119
  small groups, 88–91
  territorial, 100–5
    politician's role and, 172
    type of authority and, 125–6
  triads, 86–8
  see also Class; Small Groups
Alienation, 93, 264–73
  anomie distinguished from, 274–5
  of artists, 266
  capitalism and, 267–8
  defined, 55
  degree of deprivation and, 270
  examples of, 265
  generalized, 265–6
  industrial, 267–70
  of intellectuals, 266
  mass society and, 96–7, 271–2
  political, 270–2
  politics and, 265–6
  poverty and, 276–7

religion and, 240, 265–6, 272
social change and, 266–7
social protest distinguished from,
  264–5
sociological interest in, 267–8
specific, 265–6
withdrawal characterizes, 264–5
see also Entropy
Anarchy, 141–2
Anomie, 273–80
  affluence and, 277
  alienation distinguished from, 274–
    275
  as conflict of norms, 273–5
  defined, 55
  democracy and, 278
  marginality and, 279–80
  mass society and, 96–7
  positive effects of, 278
  "revolution of rising expectations"
    and, 277–8
  suicide and, 275–8
  technology and, 247
  unhappiness and, 277
  see also Entropy
Arensberg, Conrad, 167
Aristocracies, size factor, 90
Aristotle, 317, 323, 327, 348, 379,
  390
Artists
  alienation of, 266
  role, 175–6
Asch, Solomon, 70
Auden, Wystan Hugh, 297
Augustine, Saint, 334, 346, 348
Augustus (Roman emperor), 286
Austen, Jane, 203
Authority
  aggregate characteristics and, 119,
    125–6, 131–2, 135–6, 142
  charismatic, 33, 143–4, 168, 234,
    235, 320–1
    see also Authority, personal

415